the handbook of pluralistic counselling and psychotherapy

SAGE was founded in 1965 by Sara Miller McCune to support the dissemination of usable knowledge by publishing innovative and high-quality research and teaching content. Today, we publish over 900 journals, including those of more than 400 learned societies, more than 800 new books per year, and a growing range of library products including archives, data, case studies, reports, and video. SAGE remains majority-owned by our founder, and after Sara's lifetime will become owned by a charitable trust that secures our continued independence.

Los Angeles | London | New Delhi | Singapore | Washington DC

the handbook of pluralistic counselling and psychotherapy

Edited by
Mick Cooper and Windy Dryden

Los Angeles | London | New Delhi
Singapore | Washington DC

Los Angeles | London | New Delhi
Singapore | Washington DC

SAGE Publications Ltd
1 Oliver's Yard
55 City Road
London EC1Y 1SP

SAGE Publications Inc.
2455 Teller Road
Thousand Oaks, California 91320

SAGE Publications India Pvt Ltd
B 1/I 1 Mohan Cooperative Industrial Area
Mathura Road
New Delhi 110 044

SAGE Publications Asia-Pacific Pte Ltd
3 Church Street
#10-04 Samsung Hub
Singapore 049483

Editor: Susannah Trefgarne
Assistant editor: Laura Walmsley
Production editor: Rachel Burrows
Copyeditor: Elaine Leek
Proofreader: Danielle Ray
Indexer: Elizabeth Ball
Marketing manager: Camille Richmond
Cover design: Lisa Harper-Wells
Typeset by: C&M Digitals (P) Ltd, Chennai, India
Printed and bound by CPI Group (UK) Ltd,
Croydon, CR0 4YY

Chapter 1 © Mick Cooper and Windy Dryden 2016
Chapter 2 © John McLeod and Julia McLeod 2016
Chapter 3 © Terry Hanley, Aaron Sefi and Zehra Ersahin 2016
Chapter 4 © Mick Cooper, Windy Dryden, Kate Martin and Fani Papayianni 2016
Chapter 5 © Barry L. Duncan and Jacqueline A. Sparks 2016
Chapter 6 © Jacqueline A. Sparks and Barry L. Duncan 2016
Chapter 7 © Mick Cooper 2016
Chapter 8 © Terry Hanley, Adam Scott and Laura Anne Winter 2016
Chapter 9 © Terry Boucher 2016
Chapter 10 © Laurence Spurling 2016
Chapter 11 © Mick Cooper and Gerhard Stumm 2016
Chapter 12 © Rolf Sundet and John McLeod 2016
Chapter 13 © John McLeod and Rolf Sundet 2016
Chapter 14 © John McLeod 2016
Chapter 15 © Windy Dryden 2016
Chapter 16 © Meg John Barker 2016
Chapter 17 © Robert A. Neimeyer 2016
Chapter 18 © Thomas Mackrill and Bettina Jensen 2016
Chapter 19 © Lynsey McMillan 2016
Chapter 20 © Julia McLeod, Mhairi Thurston and Kate Smith 2016
Chapter 21 © Andrew Reeves 2016
Chapter 22 © Laura Anne Winter, Feng Guo, Katarzyna Wilk and Terry Hanley 2016
Chapter 23 © Timothy A. Carey 2016
Chapter 24 © Lynne Gabriel 2016
Chapter 25 © Mary Creaner and Ladislav Timulak 2016
Chapter 26 © Julia McLeod, Kate Smith and Mhairi Thurston 2016
Chapter 27 © Terry Hanley and Laura Anne Winter 2016

First published 2016

Apart from any fair dealing for the purposes of research or private study, or criticism or review, as permitted under the Copyright, Designs and Patents Act, 1988, this publication may be reproduced, stored or transmitted in any form, or by any means, only with the prior permission in writing of the publishers, or in the case of reprographic reproduction, in accordance with the terms of licences issued by the Copyright Licensing Agency. Enquiries concerning reproduction outside those terms should be sent to the publishers.

Library of Congress Control Number: 2015939832

British Library Cataloguing in Publication data

A catalogue record for this book is available from the British Library

ISBN 978-1-4739-0398-2
ISBN 978-1-4739-0399-9 (pbk)

At SAGE we take sustainability seriously. Most of our products are printed in the UK using FSC papers and boards. When we print overseas we ensure sustainable papers are used as measured by the PREPS grading system. We undertake an annual audit to monitor our sustainability.

Contents

About the Editors and Contributors   viii

1 Introduction to pluralistic counselling and psychotherapy   1
  Mick Cooper and Windy Dryden

Part 1   Fundamentals   13

2 Assessment and formulation in pluralistic counselling and psychotherapy   15
  John McLeod and Julia McLeod

3 From goals to tasks and methods   28
  Terry Hanley, Aaron Sefi and Zehra Ersahin

4 Metatherapeutic communication and shared decision-making   42
  Mick Cooper, Windy Dryden, Kate Martin and Fani Papayianni

5 Systematic feedback through the Partners for Change Outcome Management System (PCOMS)   55
  Barry L. Duncan and Jacqueline A. Sparks

6 Client strengths and resources: Helping clients draw on what they already do best   68
  Jacqueline A. Sparks and Barry L. Duncan

7 Core counselling methods for pluralistic practice   80
  Mick Cooper

Part 2   Therapeutic orientations   93

8 Humanistic approaches and pluralism   95
  Terry Hanley, Adam Scott and Laura Anne Winter

9 Cognitive behavioural approaches and pluralism   108
  Terry Boucher

10 Psychodynamic approaches and pluralism   122
  Laurence Spurling

11	Existential approaches and pluralism *Mick Cooper and Gerhard Stumm*	134
12	Narrative approaches and pluralism *Rolf Sundet and John McLeod*	147
13	Integrative and eclectic approaches and pluralism *John McLeod and Rolf Sundet*	158

Part 3 Issues and goals — 171

14	Helping clients address depression *John McLeod*	173
15	Helping clients address problematic anxiety *Windy Dryden*	184
16	Helping clients improve their interpersonal relationships *Meg John Barker*	198
17	Helping clients find meaning in grief and loss *Robert A. Neimeyer*	211
18	Helping clients address addictive behaviours *Thomas Mackrill and Bettina Jensen*	223
19	Helping clients address eating problems *Lynsey McMillan*	235
20	Helping clients who have health issues *Julia McLeod, Mhairi Thurston and Kate Smith*	247
21	Helping clients who are suicidal or self-injuring *Andrew Reeves*	259

Part 4 Professional issues — 273

22	Difference and diversity in pluralistic counselling and psychotherapy *Laura Anne Winter, Feng Guo, Katarzyna Wilk and Terry Hanley*	275
23	Boundaries: A pluralistic perspective and illustrative case study of the patient-led approach to appointment scheduling *Timothy A. Carey*	288
24	Ethics in pluralistic counselling and psychotherapy *Lynne Gabriel*	300

25 Supervision in pluralistic counselling and psychotherapy   314
    Mary Creaner and Ladislav Timulak

26 Training in pluralistic counselling and psychotherapy   326
    Julia McLeod, Kate Smith and Mhairi Thurston

27 Research and pluralistic counselling and psychotherapy   337
    Terry Hanley and Laura Anne Winter

Index   350

About the Editors and Contributors

Mick Cooper is a Professor of Counselling Psychology at the University of Roehampton and a chartered counselling psychologist. Mick is author and editor of a range of texts on person-centred, existential and relational approaches to therapy, including *Existential Therapies* (Sage, 2003), *Working at Relational Depth in Counselling and Psychotherapy* (Sage, 2005, with Dave Mearns) and *Pluralistic Counselling and Psychotherapy* (Sage, 2011, with John McLeod). Mick has also led a range of research studies exploring the process and outcomes of humanistic counselling with young people. Mick's latest book is *Existential Psychotherapy and Counselling: Contributions to a Pluralistic Practice* (Sage, 2015).

Windy Dryden is Emeritus Professor of Psychotherapeutic Studies at Goldsmiths University of London, and is a Fellow of the British Psychological Society. He has authored or edited more than 210 books, including the second editions of *Counselling in a Nutshell* (Sage, 2011) and *Rational Emotive Behaviour Therapy: Distinctive Features* (Routledge, 2015). In addition, he edits 20 book series in the area of counselling and psychotherapy, including the Distinctive Features in CBT series (Routledge) and the Counselling in a Nutshell series (Sage). His major interests are in rational emotive behaviour therapy and CBT; single session interventions; the interface between counselling and coaching; pluralism in counselling and psychotherapy; writing short, accessible self-help books for the general public and demonstrating therapy live in front of an audience.

Meg John Barker is a writer, academic, therapist and activist specialising in sex and relationships. Meg John is a senior lecturer in psychology at the Open University and has over a decade of experience researching and publishing on these topics, with a particular focus on sexual and relationship communities, including bisexual, polyamorous, and kink communities. Their publications include the relationship self-help book *Rewriting the Rules*, as well as books for practitioners on mindfulness and on gender and sexual diversity. Website: www.rewriting-the-rules.com. Twitter: megjohnbarker.

Terry Boucher is a Consultant Counselling Psychologist working in both the NHS and private practice as a Partner of Vivamus Psychologists. He works across a number of settings providing management, direct client work (individual and group), clinical and professional supervision, and training. He is experienced in working with a number of psychological presentations and specialises in working with those who have chronic pain. He has written two other book chapters, one considering the application of CBT in clinical settings (*Therapy and Beyond*, John Wiley & Sons, 2010) the other on issues relating to working in the field of chronic pain (*Diagnosis and Beyond*, PCCS Books, 2012).

Timothy A. Carey is a Professor and Director of the Centre for Remote Health in Alice Springs and Vice-President of the Australian Psychological Society. He is a clinician, teacher, and researcher who conducts a psychology clinic in the public mental health service in Alice Springs and is interested in the effective and efficient delivery of mental health treatments. He has over 100 publications and has presented papers and workshops at national and international conferences.

Mary Creaner is an Assistant Professor with the Doctorate in Counselling Psychology and Course Director of the MSc in Clinical Supervision, Trinity College Dublin. She is an accredited therapist/supervisor with the Irish Association for Counselling and Psychotherapy and a member of the American Psychological Association. Mary has a particular interest in supervision practice, training and research and her publications include a recent book, *Getting the Best Out of Supervision in Counselling and Psychotherapy* (Sage, 2014).

Barry L. Duncan is Director of the Heart and Soul of Change Project (heartandsoulofchange.com), CEO of Better Outcomes Now (betteroutcomesnow.com) and the developer of the clinical process of the Partners for Change Outcome Management System (pcoms.com), a SAMHSA designated evidence-based practice. Barry is a therapist, trainer, and researcher with over 17,000 hours of clinical experience. He has over 100 publications, including 17 books addressing systematic feedback, client rights and the power of relationship. Combining those topics, his latest book, *On Becoming a Better Therapist* (2nd ed., APA, 2014) describes PCOMS as a way to improve client outcomes, accelerate therapist development and help therapists re-remember why they became therapists in the first place.

Zehra Ersahin is a counselling psychologist in professional doctoral training at the University of Manchester. Zehra started her journey in the field of counselling psychology in Turkey, further specialising in online, energy line, and creative therapies. She resides in the UK currently, on a national scholarship for further training. She completed her MSc in Social Cognition at UCL, and is now in the final year of her doctoral studies. After completing her studies in the UK, she is planning on continuing her career back in Turkey, delivering teaching and training at a state university. She adopts a pluralist stance to therapy, and her current interests lie in online youth counselling, as well as trauma interventions and recovery. Through her involvement with Kooth.com as a practitioner and researcher, she has also been involved in service development, various conference contributions, and published projects.

About the editors and contributors

Lynne Gabriel is a tutor, researcher and psychotherapy practitioner at York St John University in York, UK, where she is Programme Director for the MA in Counselling and Director of the counselling clinic. Lynne is an Associate Professor and a Reader in Counselling and Ethics at York St John, a Senior Fellow of the Higher Education Academy and a Fellow of the British Association for Counselling and Psychotherapy (BACP). She is a former Chair of BACP and previous Chair of conduct and ethics committees for the professional association. Lynne is currently working with BACP on the development of counsellor education and development. Lynne has published two key texts on practice ethics, *Speaking the Unspeakable: the Ethics of Dual Relationships in Practice Counselling and Psychotherapy* and *Relational Ethics in Practice: Narratives from Counselling and Psychotherapy*. Lynne sits on the Editorial Board of the *British Journal of Guidance* and is a member of the Board of Governors for Respect, a UK organisation working with domestic violence.

Feng (Davy) Guo is a Doctorate in Counselling Psychology Trainee at The University of Manchester. His research interests lie in developing culturally responsive therapeutic approaches, specifically for the Chinese cultural content. He is also involved in developing mental health services and training programmes in China.

Terry Hanley is the Programme Director for the Doctorate in Counselling Psychology at the University of Manchester. He is a Fellow of the Higher Education Academy, an Associate Fellow of the British Psychological Society and was Editor of *Counselling Psychology Review* between the years 2009 and 2015. He has a keen interest in training therapists in research skills and is a co-author of *Introducing Counselling and Psychotherapy Research* (Sage). Additionally, his own therapeutic practice and research has primarily focused around work with young people and young adults, a topic on which he is also lead editor of the text *Adolescent Counselling Psychology* (Routledge).

Bettina Jensen is a senior lecturer in psychology at the Institute for Social Work, at Metropolitan University College in Copenhagen. Bettina teaches bachelor students and post qualifying courses on alcohol and drug abuse and psychiatry, focusing on understandings, interventions, treatment approaches and supervision. Bettina has previously worked as a clinical psychologist and supervisor at a refuge for the homeless, at an alcohol and drug treatment facility, and in psychiatry.

John McLeod is affiliated to the University of Oslo and the Institute for Integrative Counselling and Psychotherapy (Dublin). He is author of books and articles on a range of topics in counselling and psychotherapy, and is committed to the development of research-informed, flexible and collaborative approaches to the delivery of therapy.

Julia McLeod is Lecturer in Counselling at the University of Abertay and Programme Leader of the Postgraduate Diploma in Counselling. Trained in Transactional Analysis and person-centred approaches to therapy, she has many years of experience as a counselling tutor, and has research interests in the areas of counsellor training, embedded counselling, the therapeutic role of yoga, and the process and outcome of therapy for people with long-term health conditions. She is co-author of *Counselling Skills* (Open University Press, 2nd ed., 2011) and *Personal and Professional Development: A Practical Guide for Counsellors, Psychotherapists and Mental Health Practitioners* (Open University Press, 2013).

Lynsey McMillan is a pluralistic counsellor and trainer with a private practice in the North East of Scotland. She works with a range of clients and specialises in disordered eating. She has a particular interest in self-compassion and believes that cultivating self-compassion is a key task in promoting well-being and sustaining long-term behaviour change. Lynsey studied at the University of Abertay, Dundee where she researched psychotherapeutic approaches to obesity and eating disorders. She is also a facilitator of the Understanding Your Eating programme; a psycho-educational treatment for emotional eating devised by Prof. Julia Buckroyd. Lynsey is UyE's online specialist and can be found via the website: www.understandingyoureating.co.uk.

Thomas Mackrill is accredited as specialist and supervisor in psychotherapy by the Danish Psychological Association and holds a PhD from the University of Copenhagen. He is a psychology lecturer at Metropolitan University College in Copenhagen, and is involved in developing technology for youth social work practice. He has spent many years working with families with alcohol problems and has published research in this field as well as research on client agency and qualitative methods.

Kate Martin is the founder and Director of Common Room Consulting Ltd, which promotes the views and expertise of children and young people with lived experience across disability, health and mental health. Kate has over 15 years' experience of promoting children and young people centred communication, shared decision-making, collaborative practice, co-production, and of empowering young people to speak up about the social, policy and practice issues that affect their lives.

Robert A. Neimeyer, PhD, is a Professor of Psychology, University of Memphis, where he also maintains an active clinical practice. Neimeyer has published 27 books, including *Techniques of Grief Therapy: Creative Practices for Counseling the Bereaved*, and serves as Editor of the journal *Death Studies*. The author of over 400 articles and book chapters and a frequent workshop presenter, he is currently working to advance a more adequate theory of grieving as a meaning-making process.

Fani Papayianni is an HCPC Registered and BPS Chartered Counselling Psychologist. She works as an Associate Lecturer and Placement Tutor for the Doctorate in Counselling Psychology at Glasgow Caledonian University and as a self-employed practitioner. Her current interests – in the area of research, teaching and workshop design/delivery – include various features related to mental health and psychotherapeutic practice such as: self-concept, assertiveness, transitions, resilience, post-traumatic growth, meta-therapeutic communication, pluralistic practice, therapists' personal material.

About the editors and contributors

Andrew Reeves is a BACP Senior Accredited Counsellor/Psychotherapist and has over 25 years' experience working in a range of settings as a social worker and therapist, including child protection, vulnerable adults, mental health crisis intervention and education. He has written extensively about working with risk, including *Counselling Suicidal Clients* (Sage), *Challenges in Counselling: Self-harm* (Hodder Education) and *Working with Risk in Counselling and Psychotherapy* (Sage). He is past Editor of *Counselling and Psychotherapy Research* journal.

Adam Scott is a trainee counselling psychologist at the University of Manchester. He has research interests in pluralistic therapy, self-care in psychologists and counselling psychology training. He currently offers therapy to clients at an NHS Eating Disorder Service and male survivors of sexual abuse and rape at Survivors Manchester.

Aaron Sefi is a Service Development Manager and Research Lead for Xenzone, who provide KOOTH.com, an online counselling, support and advice service for young people. Aaron has conducted small-scale research projects evaluating school-based and online counselling, and goal-based outcome measures. He has been published in peer-reviewed journals such as *Pastoral Care in Education* (2011, 30: 1) and *Counselling Psychotherapy Research* (2011, 11: 4). He has also contributed chapters to *Adolescent Counselling Psychology: Theory, Research and Practice* (Hanley et al., 2013), and recently contributed training sessions to the Counselling Minded e-learning programme.

Kate Smith is a lecturer in Counselling at Abertay University, Dundee. She is a registered counsellor with the British Association for Counselling and Psychotherapy. Her doctoral studies were on the impact of narrative identity on memory for people with depression, and her other research interests include the social and emotional effects of diabetes, and ethical training issues in mental health.

Jacqueline A. Sparks is a professor in the Department of Human Development and Family Studies at the University of Rhode Island. She teaches primarily in the graduate Couple and Family Therapy Program. Her research focuses on the systematic use of client feedback to privilege client voice and improve outcomes. Her other interests include training therapists using the Partners for Change Outcome Management System, transforming mental health systems to promote socially just services, and critical analysis of pharmaceutical industry influence on research, media, and practices in psychotherapy.

Laurence Spurling is Senior Lecturer in Psychosocial Studies at Birkbeck College, University of London, and is Director of the Birkbeck pre-clinical and training courses in counselling and psychotherapy. He has worked for many years as a psychoanalytic psychotherapist in the National Health Service and in private practice. He is the author of *An Introduction to Psychodynamic Counselling* (Palgrave, 2nd ed. 2009) and *The Psychoanalytic Craft: How to Develop as a Psychoanalytic Practitioner* (Palgrave, 2015).

Gerhard Stumm, PhD, is a freelance person-centred therapist in Vienna, Austria, with a special interest for existential perspectives, a clinical and health psychologist, and trainer of the 'Forum', a training institute for person-centred therapy. Publications include co-editor of *Wörterbuch der Psychotherapie* (*Dictionary of Psychotherapy*) (2000), *Die vielen Gesichter der Personzentrierten Psychotherapie* (*The Many Faces of Person-centred Psychotherapy*) (2002), *Praxis der Personzentrierten Psychotherapie* (*Practice of Person-centred Psychotherapy*) (2014), and editor of *Psychotherapie: Schulen und Methoden* (*Psychotherapy: Schools and Methods*) (2011).

Rolf Sundet is an associate professor at the University College of Buskerud and Vestfold and a specialist in clinical psychology at the Ambulant Family Section, Department of Mental Health for Children and Adolescents, Hospital of Drammen Vestre Viken Health Trust. He is a co-author of *Self in Relationships: Perspectives on Family Therapy from Developmental Psychology* (Karnac, 2004, with Astri Johnsen & Vigdis Wie Torsteinsson). His major interests are in collaborative, narrative and dialogical practices with a special focus on routine outcome and process monitoring through service user feedback and participation within a pluralistic framework. He lives in Drammen, Norway.

Mhairi Thurston is a lecturer in Counselling at Abertay University, Dundee. She is a registered, accredited counsellor and trainer and a governor of the British Association for Counselling and Psychotherapy. Her research interest is in the social and emotional effects of acquired sight loss and she has published a range of papers in this area. Mhairi is Chair of VISION2020UK Counselling and Emotional Support Services group.

Ladislav Timulak, PhD, is Course Director of the Doctorate in Counselling Psychology at Trinity College Dublin. He is involved in the training of counselling psychologists and psychotherapists. He has written several books and over 60 peer reviewed papers and chapters. His most recent books include *Research in Psychotherapy and Counselling* (Sage, 2008), *Developing Your Counselling and Psychotherapy Skills and Practice* (Sage, 2011) and *Transforming Emotional Pain in Psychotherapy* (Routledge, 2015). He maintains a part-time private practice.

Katarzyna (Kasia) Wilk is a Doctorate in Counselling Psychology trainee at the University of Manchester. Her research and therapeutic practice interests lie in understanding how diversity impacts upon personal identity, the role of spirituality in therapy, and exploring innovative service development approaches to meet the needs of diverse clientele.

Laura Anne Winter is an HCPC Registered Counselling Psychologist and BPS Chartered Psychologist. She currently works as a Lecturer in Counselling Psychology at the University of Manchester. She continues her therapeutic practice in an NHS Complex Primary Care Psychology Service in South Manchester. Current research interests include the impact and experience of social injustice and inequality on individuals and groups, and how professionals in therapeutic professions respond to this, and training issues in counselling psychology.

1

Introduction to Pluralistic Counselling and Psychotherapy

Mick Cooper and Windy Dryden

THIS CHAPTER DISCUSSES

- The development of a pluralistic approach to counselling and psychotherapy
- The key pillars and principles of a pluralistic approach
- Research evidence on the pluralistic approach
- The aims, content and style of the handbook

DEVELOPMENT OF THE PLURALISTIC APPROACH

The origins of the pluralistic approach to therapy discussed in this book were developed by Mick Cooper and John McLeod in 2006. They stemmed from the idea that all therapeutic approaches offered useful insights into how to help people therapeutically. Cooper and McLeod's views, in particular, were a reaction to what they saw as dogmatism within the counselling and psychotherapy field, and the lines that were being drawn between different therapeutic orientations. Their goal was to create and develop an approach to therapy that was flexible and suited to the needs of each individual client.

An original paper on the pluralistic approach was published in 2007, entitled 'A pluralistic framework for counselling and psychotherapy: implications for research' (Cooper & McLeod, 2007). This article laid out the basic principles of a pluralistic approach within a research-informed context. At the same time, McLeod and Cooper developed two courses oriented around pluralistic principles: the Postgraduate Diploma in Counselling at the University of Abertay and the Doctorate in Counselling Psychology at Glasgow Caledonian University and the University of Strathclyde.

Pluralistic research clinics were also established at both Abertay and Strathclyde universities. McLeod and Cooper, together and separately, began to deliver workshops on pluralistic therapy around the UK and at training events and conferences.

In early 2011, Cooper and McLeod published *Pluralistic Counselling and Psychotherapy*, which provided a coherent and comprehensive introduction to the core principles and practices of a pluralistic approach. Since its publication, the book has had over 100 citations on Google Scholar and has become the standard text for pluralistic therapy. Later in 2011, the Universities Psychotherapy and Counselling Association, in association with the Research Centre for Therapeutic Education at Roehampton University, held an international conference on 'A pluralistic approach to practice? – Implications for the psychological therapies'. The papers for this conference were later published in a special issue of the *European Journal of Psychotherapy and Counselling* (vol. 14, issue 1) (Bowen & Cooper, 2012; Cooper & McLeod, 2012; Dryden, 2012; McLeod, 2012; Miller & Willig, 2012; Ross, 2012; Thompson & Cooper, 2012; Watson, Cooper, McArthur, & McLeod, 2012). Windy Dryden, who attended the conference and authored a commentary on the main papers for this special issue, began to develop an interest in the interface between the pluralistic approach and cognitive behaviour therapy (CBT). He started to work more closely with Cooper and McLeod on developing a pluralistic approach in Britain.

Since the publication of *Pluralistic Counselling and Psychotherapy* in 2011, a number of pluralistic trainings in counselling, psychotherapy and counselling psychology have developed in the UK (see Chapter 26, this volume). In addition, several introductions to the approach have been published in counselling and psychotherapy textbooks (McLeod & Cooper, 2012, 2015; McLeod, McLeod, Cooper, & Dryden, 2014).

In the UK, the field of counselling psychology has been particularly receptive to pluralistic ideas and practices. Applications of the approach have been discussed in the British Psychological Society's (BPS) Division of Counselling Psychology (DCoP) journal, *Counselling Psychology Review* (Scott, 2014; Scott & Hanley, 2012; Wilk, 2014); and pluralistic concepts and practices have featured extensively in two recent texts: one on counselling psychology work with adolescents (Hanley, Humphrey, & Lennie, 2012) and the other on counselling psychology's contribution to therapeutic and social issues (Milton, 2010). In addition, in 2013, the BPS DCoP provided funding for a pilot study of pluralistic therapy for depression (Cooper et al., 2015). The study, based at three research clinics in the UK – the University of the West of England, the Metanoia Institute and the University of Strathclyde – assessed the outcomes, acceptability and helpful aspects of a pluralistic therapeutic intervention for depression (see below). The pluralistic therapy for this study was delivered by trainee and qualified counselling psychologists, trained and supervised by John McLeod at the University of Abertay.

Internationally, training and talks on pluralistic practice have been delivered by McLeod and Cooper around the world, and a Master's level training in pluralistic practice has now been established in Ireland (see Chapter 26: 330, this volume). Although dissemination in the US is more sparse, the feedback-informed approach of Duncan, Miller, Sparks and colleagues (see Chapter 5, this volume) bears many similarities to the pluralistic model.

The developments outlined above convinced us that the time was right to publish a handbook on pluralistic counselling and psychotherapy, bringing together in one volume the burgeoning work that is being done in this field and acting as a foundation and catalyst for further developments.

PILLARS AND PRINCIPLES

Pluralism can be defined as the philosophical belief that 'any substantial question admits of a variety of plausible but mutually conflicting responses' (Rescher, 1993: 79). More than that, it is an ethical commitment to valuing diversity; and a wariness towards monolithic, all-consuming 'truths', because of the way that they can suppress individuality and difference. In respect to counselling and psychotherapy, a pluralistic approach implies that there are a variety of views that can be taken on a wide range of therapeutic issues, and that there is no inherent right or wrong way. This standpoint forms the grounds for three pillars that underpin a pluralistic approach to counselling and psychotherapy.

The first pillar is *pluralism across orientations*. This means that a pluralistic practitioner is open to considering a variety of different ways in which clients get distressed and, correspondingly, a variety of different ways of helping them. Taking this stance poses a direct challenge to the 'schoolism' that has been endemic in the field of counselling and psychotherapy.

The second pillar is *pluralism across clients*. This is marked by the emphasis that is placed on recognising and celebrating diversity across clients. What follows from this is that pluralistic practitioners are keen to offer each client a bespoke approach to counselling and psychotherapy rather than one that is 'off the peg'.

This relates closely to the third pillar of a pluralistic approach: *pluralism across perspectives*. A pluralistic therapeutic approach advocates that *both* participants in the therapeutic relationship – clients as well as practitioners – have much to offer when it comes to making decisions concerning therapeutic goals and the selection of therapy tasks and methods. This means that a pluralistic approach emphasises shared decision-making (see Chapter 4, this volume) and feedback (see Chapter 5, this volume) across clients and therapists.

These three pillars of the pluralistic approach can be expressed through the following principles:

- There is no one right way of conceptualising clients' problems – different understandings are useful for different clients at different points in time.
- There is no one right way of practising therapy – different clients need different things at different points in time.
- Many disputes and disagreements in the therapeutic field can be resolved by taking a 'both/and' perspective, rather than an 'either/or' one.
- It is important that counsellors and psychotherapists respect each other's work and recognise the value that it can have.

- Counsellors and psychotherapists should acknowledge and celebrate clients' diversity and uniqueness.
- Clients should be involved fully at every stage of the therapeutic process.
- Clients should be understood in terms of their strengths and resources, as well as areas of difficulty.
- Counsellors and psychotherapists should have an openness to multiple sources of knowledge on how to practise therapy: including research, personal experience and theory.
- It is important that counsellors and psychotherapists take a critical perspective on their own theory and practice: being willing to look at their own investment in a particular position and having the ability to stand back from it.

RESEARCH EVIDENCE

As a relatively new development in the field of counselling and psychotherapy, the evidence base for pluralistic counselling and psychotherapy is still at a nascent stage. Nevertheless, there are several lines of evidence in the psychotherapy research field that provide initial support for a pluralistic approach to counselling and psychotherapy.

First, clients seem to do better in therapy when it matches their preferences (Swift, Callahan, & Vollmer, 2011). More specifically, clients who receive a preferred intervention are 'between a half and a third less likely to drop out of therapy prematurely compared with clients who did not receive their preferred therapy conditions' (Swift et al., 2011: 307); and also show a small but significant increase in outcomes ($d = 0.31$). This is consistent with the research in the field of shared decision-making (see Chapter 4, this volume), which shows that patients are more satisfied with their medical treatment and less likely to drop out if they are involved in making decisions about their healthcare (Joosten et al., 2008; The Health Foundation, 2014).

Second, there is a strong relationship between client–therapist agreement on the tasks and goals of therapy, and therapeutic outcomes (Horvath, Del Re, Fluckinger, & Symonds, 2011; Tryon & Winograd, 2011). That is, clients do best in therapy when they feel that their therapists are striving for the same therapeutic goals as they are, and are in agreement about the best therapeutic methods to be used.

Third, there is research to suggest that flexible practice, tailored to the needs of individual clients, is experienced by clients as a helpful and important aspect of therapy (Cooper et al., 2015; Perren, Godfrey, & Rowland, 2009). This is supported by quantitative research suggesting that flexibly tailored practice can, in certain instances, lead to improved outcomes and greater engagement with therapy (e.g., Jacobson et al., 1989).

Fourth, randomised controlled studies indicate that the use of systematic client feedback – which is integral to the pluralistic approach (see Chapter 5, this volume) – can lead to significantly enhanced therapeutic outcomes, particularly for clients who might otherwise deteriorate in therapy (Lambert & Shimokawa, 2011). Indeed, feedback-informed treatments are now recognised as evidence-based programmes by the US government's Substance Abuse and Mental Health Services Administration (SAMHSA).

In addition, UK-based studies of a specifically pluralistic practice – both for clients with depression (Cooper et al., 2015, see above) and for a more heterogeneous sample (Cooper, 2014) – have shown that it has relatively positive outcomes, as well as good rates of engagement and retention. As indicated above, these studies have also found that most clients value the flexibility and collaborative approach that is at the core of pluralistic practice.

ABOUT THE BOOK

Aims

The Handbook of Pluralistic Counselling and Psychotherapy aims to be the definitive text for trainee counsellors, psychotherapists and psychologists wishing to think and practise in a pluralistic way. More specifically, it hopes to provide trainees and practitioners with:

- Hands-on guidance to developing their pluralistic practice: providing the tools, skills and practice frameworks
- A step-by-step understanding of how the ideas and methods of different orientations can contribute towards a pluralistic way of working
- The tools and understandings needed to work with clients to achieve the most common goals
- The tools and understandings needed to work with clients wishing to address common issues
- An understanding of a range of professional and practice issues that will be of significance to all therapists wanting to work in a pluralistic way.

For trainees on specifically pluralistic courses, this handbook should act as a core text across the duration of the programme and beyond. Other books will also be needed to help develop a more detailed comprehension of particular methods or understanding, but this handbook should act as an 'integrating hub' for trainees to draw together the different approaches into a coherent pluralistic framework. For trainees on other courses – integrative, eclectic or otherwise – this handbook also provides a coherent framework for integrating therapeutic understandings and practices; as well as a source of stimulation and guidance. Our hope is that more experienced practitioners will also find much in this handbook to stimulate them and to learn from: providing the most comprehensive guide, to date, to pluralistic theory and practice and its relationship to other approaches.

The Handbook of Pluralistic Counselling and Psychotherapy builds on Cooper and McLeod's (2011) core text, *Pluralistic Counselling and Psychotherapy*, but can be regarded as a 'stand alone' text. Hence, reading the 2011 text should be regarded as recommended, but not essential.

Structure

Following this *Introduction*, the handbook is divided into four parts: Fundamentals of a pluralistic practice, Therapeutic orientations, Issues and goals, and Professional issues.

Part 1: Fundamentals of a pluralistic practice

The chapters in Part 1 describe the core principles of a pluralistic approach to therapy, and discuss and illustrate their application in therapeutic practice. In Chapter 2, *Assessment and formulation in pluralistic counselling and psychotherapy*, McLeod and McLeod provide a framework for collaborative pluralistic assessment and case formulation, and discuss challenges and future directions. Chapter 3, by Hanley, Sefi and Ersahin, is titled *From goals to tasks and methods*. It builds upon an understanding of assessment and formulation in pluralistic therapy by looking at the collaborative development of therapeutic goals and how these can be used to inform the selection of therapeutic tasks and methods. This theme of collaborative practice is developed in Chapter 4, *Metatherapeutic communication and shared decision-making* by Cooper, Dryden, Martin and Papayianni which examines the ways in which therapists and clients can discuss the therapeutic process and make shared decisions. A structured feedback tool to aid this process is then discussed in Chapter 5, *Systematic feedback through the Partners for Change Outcome Management System (PCOMS)*, by Duncan and Sparks. In Chapter 6, these two authors then go on to discuss a key focus of pluralistic counselling and psychotherapy, *Client strengths and resources*. In the final chapter in this part of the book, *Core counselling skills for pluralistic practice*, Cooper introduces and illustrates a range of basic counselling methods that can be used as the foundations for pluralistic practice.

Part 2: Therapeutic orientations

Chapters in Part 2 of the book explore pluralistic counselling and psychotherapy in relation to the major therapeutic orientations. These chapters have two main aims: first, to consider how these approaches align with a pluralistic perspective – in terms of areas of commonality, areas of difference and ways in which the orientation can be practised from within a pluralistic framework; second, to give an overview of the understandings and methods from these orientations that can contribute towards a pluralistic way of working. In this part of the book (Chapters 8–13), we have focused on the major therapeutic orientations: humanistic approaches (Hanley, Scott and Winter), cognitive behavioural approaches (Boucher), psychodynamic approaches (Spurling), existential approaches (Cooper and Stumm), narrative approaches (Sundet and John McLeod), and integrative and eclectic approaches (John McLeod and Sundet).

Part 3: Issues and goals

Part 3 focuses on the most common issues and goals that clients bring to therapy, and presents a range of understandings and methods – from across the therapeutic orientations – that have been found to be helpful in supporting clients in this work. Authors of these chapters were encouraged to draw broadly from across the different therapeutic approaches; and to discuss how the different methods and understandings compare, contrast and can be integrated together. Case examples and excerpts of dialogue are used throughout the chapters to illustrate the different methods. The chapters in this part of the book (Chapters 14–21) look at: helping clients address depression (John McLeod), helping clients address problematic anxiety (Dryden), helping clients improve their interpersonal relationships (Barker), helping clients address grief (Neimeyer), helping clients address addictive behaviours (Mackrill and Jensen), helping clients address eating problems (McMillan), helping clients with health issues (Julia McLeod, Thurston, Smith), and helping clients who are suicidal or self-injuring (Reeves).

Part 4: Professional issues

The chapters in the final part of this handbook address a range of professional and practice issues that will be of significance to all counsellors and psychotherapists wanting to work in a pluralistic way. In Chapter 22, *Difference and diversity in pluralistic counselling and psychotherapy*, Winter, Guo, Hanley and Wilk explore the meaning of difference and diversity in relation to pluralistic therapy and its therapeutic implications and impacts. In Chapter 23, entitled *Boundaries: A pluralistic perspective and illustrative case study of the patient-led approach to appointment scheduling*, Carey then discusses and illustrates a pluralistic approach to boundaries. Gabriel goes on to explore the broader concept of ethics in pluralistic counselling and psychotherapy in Chapter 24. In Chapter 25, Creaner and Timulak discuss *Supervision in pluralistic counselling and psychotherapy*; and Chapter 26, by Julia McLeod, Smith and Thurston, examines *Training in pluralistic counselling and psychotherapy*. In the final chapter of the handbook, *Research and pluralistic counselling and psychotherapy*, Hanley and Winter discuss a range of issues with respect to research and pluralism, and outline an agenda for research in relation to this framework.

The handbook's key features

We have tried to make the content of this handbook as accessible and engaging as possible. To this end, each of the chapters is clearly structured with the following key features:

- Overview: a series of bullet points to signpost structure and coverage of the chapter
- Client examples and studies throughout the chapter to illustrate how the theory works in practice
- Use of research evidence wherever possible
- Summary at the end of the chapter of the key learning points
- Exercises/points for reflection at the end of the chapter, to facilitate discussion and student learning
- Reading suggestions for key texts, resources or websites that readers can consult if they wish to read further.

While we have suggested to authors that they use terms and concepts that have come to characterise pluralistic practice, some have preferred their own nomenclature or conceptual framework. In particular, while some authors have kept to the tripartite structure of 'goals', 'tasks' and 'methods' (see Chapter 3, this volume), others have preferred to merge the concepts of 'tasks' and 'methods'. This demonstrates another hallmark of the pluralistic development in counselling and psychotherapy: its ability to contain different views on pluralistic practice.

SUMMARY

The pluralistic approach to counselling and psychotherapy was developed in the mid-2000s by John McLeod and Mick Cooper, and since then has attracted broad interest from across the counselling, psychotherapy and counselling psychology fields. Pluralistic counselling and psychotherapy has three key pillars – pluralism across orientations, pluralism across clients, and pluralism across perspectives – and these can be expressed in a number of core principles. Pluralistic practice is supported by several lines of research evidence, with an emerging body of empirical evidence for pluralistic therapy itself. This handbook aims to be the definitive text for pluralistic trainees and practitioners and those interested in this new development. It is divided into four parts which look at: the foundations of the pluralistic approach; its relationship to key orientations; therapeutic practices that can help clients address key issues and goals; and key professional issues for pluralistic practitioners.

EXERCISES/POINTS FOR REFLECTION

1. What attracted you to this book and/or the concept of pluralistic counselling and psychotherapy?
2. What are your goals in consulting the chapters in this book?
3. What doubts, reservations and objections may you have to pluralistic counselling and psychotherapy?
4. What strengths do you have as a counsellor or psychotherapist that you might bring to pluralistic practice?

You may find it useful to note down your answers to these questions and keep them in mind as you work your way through this handbook.

We would appreciate any feedback that you have on this handbook, that might help us improve future editions (Twitter: @SusannahTSAGE).

FURTHER READING

Cooper, M., & McLeod, J. (2011). *Pluralistic counselling and psychotherapy*. London: Sage. The core text on pluralistic counselling and psychotherapy.

Dryden, W. (2012). Pluralism in counselling and psychotherapy: personal reflections on an important development. *European Journal of Psychotherapy & Counselling, 14*(1), 103–111. Critical reflections on pluralistic therapy.

McLeod, J., & Cooper, M. (2015). Pluralistic counselling and psychotherapy. In S. Palmer (Ed.), *The beginner's guide to counselling and psychotherapy* (2nd ed., pp. 322–332). London: Sage. Succinct introduction to the pluralistic approach.

McLeod, J., McLeod, J., Cooper, M., & Dryden, W. (2014). Pluralistic therapy. In W. Dryden & A. Reeves (Eds.), *Handbook of individual therapy* (6th ed., pp. 547–573). London: Sage. A more detailed overview of pluralistic counselling and psychotherapy and its implications for practice.

Ross, A. (2012). The new pluralism – a paradigm of pluralisms. *European Journal of Psychotherapy & Counselling, 14*(1), 113–119. Further critical reflections.

Resources

www.pluralistictherapy.com This URL takes you to a site where you can download, for free, many of the tools referred to in this handbook, along with other resources.

REFERENCES

Bowen, M., & Cooper, M. (2012). Development of a client feedback tool: a qualitative study of therapists' experiences of using the Therapy Personalisation Forms. *European Journal of Psychotherapy and Counselling, 14*(1), 47–62.

Cooper, M. (2014). *Strathclyde pluralistic protocol*. London: University of Roehampton.

Cooper, M., & McLeod, J. (2007). A pluralistic framework for counselling and psychotherapy: implications for research. *Counselling and Psychotherapy Research, 7*(3), 135–143.

Cooper, M., & McLeod, J. (2011). *Pluralistic counselling and psychotherapy*. London: Sage.

Cooper, M., & McLeod, J. (2012). From either/or to both/and: developing a pluralistic approach to counselling and psychotherapy. *European Journal of Psychotherapy and Counselling, 14*(1), 5–18.

Cooper, M., Wild, C., van Rijn, B., Ward, T., McLeod, J., Cassar, S., ... Sreenath, S. (2015). Pluralistic therapy for depression: acceptability, outcomes and helpful aspects in a multisite study. *Counselling Psychology Review, 30*(1), 6–20.

Dryden, W. (2012). Pluralism in counselling and psychotherapy: personal reflections on an important development. *European Journal of Psychotherapy & Counselling, 14*(1), 103–111.

Hanley, T., Humphrey, N., & Lennie, C. (Eds.). (2012). *Adolescent counselling psychology: theory, research and practice*. London: Routledge.

Horvath, A.O., Del Re, A.C., Fluckinger, C., & Symonds, D. (2011). Alliance in individual psychotherapy. In J.C. Norcross (Ed.), *Psychotherapy relationships that work: evidence-based responsiveness* (pp. 25–69). New York: Oxford University Press.

Jacobson, N.S., Schmaling, K.B., Holtzworth-Munroe, A., Katt, J.L., Wood, L.F., & Follette, V.M. (1989). Research-structured vs clinically flexible versions of social learning-based marital therapy. *Behaviour Research and Therapy, 27*(2), 173–180.

Joosten, E.A., DeFuentes-Merillas, L., De Weert, G., Sensky, T., Van Der Staak, C., & de Jong, C.A. (2008). Systematic review of the effects of shared decision-making on patient satisfaction, treatment adherence and health status. *Psychotherapy and Psychosomatics, 77*(4), 219–226.

Lambert, M.J., & Shimokawa, K. (2011). Collecting client feedback. In J.C. Norcross (Ed.), *Psychotherapy relationships that work: evidence-based responsiveness* (2nd ed., pp. 203–223). New York: Oxford University Press.

McLeod, J. (2012). What do clients want from therapy? A practice-friendly review of research into client preferences. *European Journal of Psychotherapy and Counselling, 14*(1), 19–32.

McLeod, J., & Cooper, M. (2012). Pluralistic counselling and psychotherapy. In C. Feltham & I. Horton (Eds.), *The Sage handbook of counselling and psychotherapy* (pp. 368–371). London: Sage.

McLeod, J., & Cooper, M. (2015). Pluralistic counselling and psychotherapy. In S. Palmer (Ed.), *The beginner's guide to counselling and psychotherapy* (2nd ed., pp. 322–332). London: Sage.

McLeod, J., McLeod, J., Cooper, M., & Dryden, W. (2014). Pluralistic therapy. In W. Dryden & A. Reeves (Eds.), *Handbook of individual therapy* (6th ed., pp. 547–573). London: Sage.

Miller, E., & Willig, C. (2012). Pluralistic counselling and HIV-positive clients: the importance of shared understanding. *European Journal of Psychotherapy and Counselling, 14*(1), 33–46.

Milton, M. (2010). *Therapy and beyond: counselling psychology contributions to therapeutic and social issues*. London: Wiley–Blackwell.

Perren, S., Godfrey, M., & Rowland, N. (2009). The long-term effects of counselling: the process and mechanisms that contribute to ongoing change from a user perspective. *Counselling and Psychotherapy Research, 9*(4), 241–249.

Rescher, N. (1993). *Pluralism: against the demand for consensus*. Oxford: Oxford University Press.

Ross, A. (2012). The new pluralism – a paradigm of pluralisms. *European Journal of Psychotherapy & Counselling, 14*(1), 113–119.

Scott, A.J. (2014). How to skin a cat: a case for and against the use of mindfulness-based cognitive therapy in pluralistic therapy. *Counselling Psychology Review*, *28*(1), 81–90.

Scott, A.J., & Hanley, T. (2012). On becoming a pluralistic therapist: a case study of a student's reflexive journal. *Counselling Psychology Review*, *27*(4), 29.

Swift, J.K., Callahan, J.L., & Vollmer, B.M. (2011). Preferences. In J.C. Norcross (Ed.), *Psychotherapy relationships that work* (2nd ed., pp. 301–315). New York: Oxford University Press.

The Health Foundation. (2014). *Person-centred care: from ideas to action*. London: Author.

Thompson, A., & Cooper, M. (2012). Therapists' experiences of pluralistic practice. *European Journal of Psychotherapy and Counselling*, *14*(1), 63–76.

Tryon, G.S., & Winograd, G. (2011). Goal consensus and collaboration. In J.C. Norcross (Ed.), *Psychotherapy relationships that work: evidence-based responsiveness* (2nd ed., pp. 153–167). New York: Oxford University Press.

Watson, V., Cooper, M., McArthur, K., & McLeod, J. (2012). Helpful therapeutic processes: a pluralistic analysis of client activities, therapist activities and helpful effects. *European Journal of Psychotherapy and Counselling*, *14*(1), 77–90.

Wilk, K. (2014). Using a pluralistic approach in counselling psychology and psychotherapy practice with diverse clients: explorations in cultural and religious responsiveness within a Western paradigm. *Counselling Psychology Review*, *29*(1), 16–28.

PART 1
Fundamentals

2

Assessment and Formulation in Pluralistic Counselling and Psychotherapy

*John McLeod and
Julia McLeod*

THIS CHAPTER DISCUSSES

- The role of assessment and case formulation in therapy
- A pluralistic perspective on assessment and case formulation
- Client assessment: models and methods
- A framework for collaborative pluralistic assessment
- Case formulation: models and methods
- Collaborative pluralistic case formulation
- Therapeutic challenges and future directions

INTRODUCTION

Client assessment can be defined as a process of information-gathering, usually at the start of therapy or before therapy begins, with the aim of arriving at a decision about such issues as the suitability of the client for therapy, the focus or goals of therapy, and the type or length of treatment that would be most appropriate. Assessment typically also includes some kind of 'history' and exploration of presenting problems. Case formulation or case conceptualisation refers to the process of making sense of information, in relation to the underlying causes of the problem(s) that have been presented, and the factors that might facilitate or inhibit progress in therapy. Assessment and case formulation can be regarded as inter-linked elements in the therapeutic process.

ASSESSMENT

Key principles of pluralistic assessment

A pluralistic perspective introduces a heightened awareness of specific functions that assessment and case formulation might be expected to fulfil. As with any other aspect of therapy, whatever happens should seek to acknowledge and cultivate client agency – the sense that the person seeking help is purposeful and resourceful. A key dimension of client agency, at this stage of therapy, centres on the question of the client's assessment of the therapist. Another key aspect of pluralistic practice concerns therapist transparency – the willingness of the practitioner to share his or her ideas, knowledge and response to the client, and to engage in collaboration and dialogue. A further core aspect of a pluralistic approach is to make use of, and incorporate, multiple theoretical perspectives and ideas about what might be helpful. Finally, a pluralistic perspective invites both client and therapist to consider the relevance and utility of cultural resources that exist outside of the therapy room. The implications of these key principles, for assessment and case formulation practice, are explored in subsequent sections of this chapter.

Models and methods that can be incorporated into a pluralistic approach

The counselling and psychotherapy literature includes descriptions of a rich array of ideas and practices around the theme of client assessment. Good starting points for exploring this topic are Bager-Charleson and van Rijn (2011), Mace (1995) and Milner and O'Byrne (2003). This body of professional knowledge contains many areas that are relevant to a pluralistic approach to assessment.

The ethics of assessment

The process of assessment includes an important ethical dimension. As information unfolds about the life of the client, and the problems for which he or she is seeking help, the practitioner has a moral responsibility to advise on different forms of treatment and support that might be appropriate. Ethical guidelines in the fields of health and social care require that the client be regarded as an autonomous individual, who should have the right to decide. This principle is expressed through the use of informed consent. In practice, informed consent is problematic in counselling and psychotherapy, because it is hard to know what might happen in therapy (and therefore what is being consented to), and because some clients may enter therapy in a state of emotional crisis in which they wish to be guided by the therapist. A study by O'Neill (1999) found that therapy organisations varied a great deal in the extent to which they engaged clients in conversations about alternative types of help that were available for their problem. O'Neill (1999) reported that client involvement in discussion of alternatives appeared to strengthen the client's trust in their therapist. In pluralistic therapy, exploration of alternative types of help is central to the framework for practice, as well as being an ethical requirement. The work of Barry Duncan and Scott D. Miller provides a valuable model of good practice in this area. In their work, assessment and feedback data are collected throughout the course of therapy, in a spirit of openness to the possibility that a positive outcome of therapy might be to 'fail successfully', by working together to identify other pathways of treatment and support that might be more appropriate (see, for example, Miller, Duncan, & Hubble, 2005).

Assessment as a therapeutic process

An important aspect of assessment is that it does not merely serve as information-gathering, but can make a direct contribution to client learning and change. The assessment process can provide an opportunity for clients to reflect on the issues in their life, see the 'bigger picture' and develop a greater level of understanding. In a study by Hunter, Chantler, Kapur, & Cooper (2013), clients were interviewed about their experience of undergoing assessment. Many of them reported that the assessment had a positive impact, in terms of legitimating their distress, off-loading painful emotions, inspiring hope for change, and gaining a sense of being an acceptable, worthwhile person. By contrast, other research participants described assessment as a negative experience, in which they felt shamed and judged, and struggled to be heard.

Assessment as a collaborative activity

There is research evidence, from a number of studies, that practitioner adoption of a collaborative stance, during assessment interviews, leads to a stronger therapeutic alliance and client retention in therapy (Hilsenroth & Cromer, 2007; Riddle, Byers, & Grimesey, 2002). A collaborative approach to assessment can be accomplished by allowing sufficient time, inviting the client to initiate discussion of issues, eliciting the client's understanding, offering feedback, and reviewing the meaning of assessment results (Finn & Tonsager, 1997; Fischer, 2000).

Making use of multiple sources of information

Many therapists and therapy agencies rely solely on clinical interviews as a source of assessment information. While interviews represent a flexible assessment strategy, it is possible to augment them with other sources of information that offer different perspectives. Symptom questionnaires are available that can be used to provide an overall assessment of the severity of a client's problems (Drapeau, 2012). In addition to their use in initial assessment, these brief instruments lend themselves to ongoing monitoring throughout therapy. Comprehensive interview schedules and self-report open-ended questionnaires have been developed by Lazarus (1989), Mace (1995) and

Marquis (2008). Assessment questions that focus on client strengths rather than deficits have been devised by Davidson (2014). Projective techniques, such as the early memories test, can be used to begin to identify relational themes that may be outside the conscious awareness of the client (Clark, 2001). It is possible to explore patterns of family relationships using genograms (McGoldrick, Gerson, & Petry, 2008) and family photographs (Berman, 1993). Some therapists have found it useful to visit the client at home, to gain a better understanding of their everyday-life environment (McElwain, Polizzi, & Polizzi, 2002; Yalom, 2002). It is not necessary to make use of all of these sources of assessment information; there is little point in collecting information that will not be used. Each therapist or therapy agency needs to evolve their own approach to assessment. Mace (1995) discusses how various therapy services, using different models of therapy with different client groups, have developed assessment protocols that are suitable for their specific purposes.

A framework for collaborative pluralistic assessment

A pluralistic perspective invites consideration of particular aspects of the assessment process.

Collaborative style

What happens at the early assessment phase of therapy sets the pattern for what will follow, in terms of setting the scene for collaboration and dialogue. This can be done through offering an explanation of the purpose of assessment, how long it will take, what will happen and how information will be used. The client is invited to initiate topics and provide additional information that they believe might be relevant. It may be useful to chart information on a whiteboard or flipchart, to allow both participants to inspect it together. The client is invited to ask why a particular question or instrument is being used, and told that they may refuse to answer certain questions without needing to give a reason. It is accepted that there may be some aspects of the client's story that they are not yet ready to disclose. The assessor offers feedback and is willing to share their interpretation of what the client has said. The client is invited to offer his or her understanding of events in their life, or answers to questions. At the end, the assessor offers a tentative summary of their conclusions, and invites the client to make comments and corrections. The client is able to see any written reports that are made.

Multiple descriptions and assessments of the client's goals and problems

The aim is to produce a multi-faceted, rich, open-ended description of what has brought the person to therapy, and what he or she hopes to gain from therapy. In the previous section of this chapter, a range of possible sources of information were suggested. Many pluralistic practitioners find it helpful to invite their clients to formulate specific goal statements, as a means of anchoring therapy in a clear, shared understanding of purpose. However, an appreciation of what a problem or goal actually means to a client requires knowledge about the back-story, current and past relationships, and the future time-horizon within which the person operates.

Preferences

Clients have ideas about what has helped (or not helped) in the past, and what they believe might be helpful now. Some of these ideas may be readily articulated, while other preference aspects may be implicit. There are three main strategies that can be used to elicit information in this domain. It is valuable to ask the client what he or she thinks would be helpful, and to emphasise that realisations at a future point of what might be helpful are always welcome. There are scales that can be used to collect information about preferences, such the Patient Expectations scale (PEX; Berg, Sandahl, & Clinton, 2008) and the Therapy Personalisation Form (TPF; Bowen & Cooper, 2012). It is useful to ask about previous episodes of therapy or other forms of help, including self-help, and to invite the client to talk about what it was that was useful (or otherwise) in these activities, and whether this knowledge would be relevant in respect of the current problem. It is essential to keep in mind that client preferences refer not only to in-session activities ('I want to talk about past events that are troubling me', 'I want my therapist to be warm and humorous') but also practical aspects of therapy, such as gender and age of therapist, group vs. individual therapy, frequency and scheduling of therapy, and so on. At the present time, there do not exist standardised forms for collecting this kind of practical information.

Strengths and resources

From a pluralistic perspective, the client is regarded as a co-participant in therapy, who possesses personal knowledge and experience around how to deal with problems in living. When a person enters therapy, he or she is likely to be feeling demoralised and 'stuck', and these strengths and resources may not be at the forefront of their mind. During assessment, and at other points during the opening sessions of therapy, it is useful to invite the client to talk about how they have dealt with difficulties in their life, what they have accomplished in their life, and who in their life believes in them and supports them. Rather than just assembling lists of resources ('I like to walk my dog and read romantic novels'), it is better to show active curiosity around what these activities make possible for the person. Kurt Lewin's concept of the 'life space' (Marrow, 1969) provides a means of thinking about these aspects of the person. When the client allows their therapist (or assessment interviewer) to learn about the territory of their everyday life, the practitioner can begin to build up an appreciation of potential resources that may be available for therapeutic purposes.

> **CASE EXAMPLE**
>
> **Assessment as means of developing understanding**
>
> Tasmin was 23 years old when she entered counselling at her university student counselling service. She was in the final year of a degree in pharmacy, and reported that she was becoming increasingly anxious and worried, unable to sleep, and falling behind with her work. Tasmin had grown up in a traditional Asian community in the UK, but had chosen to attend a university that was far from her home city, and while at university had developed friendships and activities that she realised were in conflict with the cultural values of her family. The assessment phase of counselling comprised a single, extended, 90-minute interview, augmented by the use of a Goals Form and symptom measure, and detailed exploration of personal strengths and cultural resources. At the end of that meeting, Tasmin replied that she could now begin to see how the different parts of her life fitted together.

CASE FORMULATION: MODELS AND METHODS THAT CAN BE INCORPORATED INTO A PLURALISTIC APPROACH

Case formulation takes place after the collection of assessment information, with the aim of making sense of the material that has been gathered, and indicating the direction that therapy might take.

There are many highly useful models of case formulation that are available, for example within the cognitive behaviour therapy (Kuyken, Padesky, & Dudley, 2009) and transactional analysis (Widdowson, 2010) professional communities. These models can be regarded as templates or starting points that can be adapted for pluralistic purposes. Eells (forthcoming) suggests that there are three main functions that a case formulation needs to fulfil:

- describe and take account of the problem(s) for which the client is seeking help;
- provide an explanatory hypothesis, incorporating the immediate and underlying causes of problem(s), and identifying both the resources and obstacles to change;
- an indication or plan of how problem(s) can be alleviated.

Effective case formulations fulfil these requirements in a way that makes sense to the client, and engages the client in an active process of change. Research has shown that, compared to formulations produced by novice therapists, the case conceptualisations constructed by expert practitioners are much more likely to tie observations together in causal sequences (Eells & Lombart, 2003; Eells, Lombart, Kendjelic, Turner, & Lucas, 2005). By contrast, novice formulations tend to be mainly descriptive.

In addition to the general case formulation literature, the emerging model of collaborative pluralistic formulation reflects a range of innovative practices. Omer (1997) describes the activity of 'narrative empathy', which consists of a very simple type of formulation in which the therapist merely re-tells the client's story as he or she has understood it. This simple technique can have a powerful impact on clients, in demonstrating to them that they have been understood by their therapist. It also introduces the idea that a formulation is a story. Other formulation practices that have inspired pluralistic therapists include the use of diagrams and letters in cognitive analytic therapy (CAT; Hamill, Reid, & Reynolds, 2008; Ryle & Kerr, 2002), and the use of letters in narrative therapy (Rombach, 2003). These approaches illustrate the potential value of documenting the formulation in a tangible way, as something that can be kept and consulted (or amended) on future occasions (Oster & Crone, 2004).

A framework for collaborative pluralistic case formulation: the time-line map

There are many ways in which a shared understanding can be developed and discussed, and pluralistic practitioners are encouraged to use their imagination and resourcefulness in this domain. The following description provides an outline of one particular set of procedures that can be used, in the context of a block of time, or whole session, at an early stage in therapy. The therapist needs to lay the groundwork for this session, from the start of therapy and during assessment, by telling the client that he or she would like to share their ideas and understanding at a suitable time. Once this time has been agreed, the therapist takes the initiative by mapping an understanding of the client's life, current issues and future goals, on a large sheet of paper or whiteboard. It is usually best for the therapist to hold the pen, while continually inviting the client to comment and add new information; if the client holds the pen, the process tends to take a lot longer. Sometimes, the client may choose to take over control of the pen, or to take the page home with them to continue at their own pace.

It is necessary for the therapist to rehearse and think about this session in advance, perhaps including use of supervision or consultation with a colleague. However, it is not helpful to come into the session with a pre-prepared diagram – it is essential to allow the client to be able to influence the emerging shared understanding as it unfolds.

The structure that has been found to be particularly facilitative is to use a *time-line* – a horizontal line across the centre of the page that is marked on the left by birth, toward the right end as 'now', and then leave some space for 'future'. Therapists who are interested in inter-generational family patterns may wish to start the left edge of the line before the birth-date of the client. It is best to begin by writing the client's problems around the 'now' point in the line. The therapist then tentatively fills in the earlier life events and turning points, using dotted lines or arrows to offer possible links between these events and current difficulties. It is important to keep talking while doing this, and to use a form of words ('I wondered if some of these fears, now, might be related to the bullying that happened at school – does that make sense?') that invites the client to change, correct or elaborate on what is being mapped. It is important to observe the client's reactions to what is being offered, in terms of interest, agreement and emotional responses. It may be necessary to pause the mapping exercise to allow the client to talk about these reactions.

This approach to using a time-line can be seen as a means of exploring the potential relevance to the client of alternative causal narratives, informed by therapy theories. The problems presented by most clients can be conceptualised in psychodynamic terms ('that was then – to survive, you needed to hide your feelings ... but this is now'), in terms of CBT theory ('you learned to think/feel/act in certain ways'), in humanistic terms ('you chose to fulfil your potential by ...'), in family systems terms, and almost certainly in accordance with any theories known to the therapist. What is being accomplished here is the possibility of considering multiple ways of understanding the problem, in a format that allows for improvisation, and enables the client to 'try out' ideas for size. While this mapping is being carried out, it is possible to add, round the edge, images or labels of personal and cultural resources and accomplishments.

In facilitating this procedure, the therapist needs to leave enough time, either toward the end of the session, or at the next session, to reflect on the map as a whole, and to use it as a basis for deciding on priorities ('there seem to be quite a few areas/tasks we could follow up – where do you want to start?'). One of the distinctive features of pluralistic therapy is that it gives clients the option of pursuing several goals and tasks in parallel. The time-line map provides a way of seeing how different tasks might fit together.

> ## CASE EXAMPLE
> ### Using formulation to explore possible ways of understanding a life
>
> Danny was 30 when he requested to see a therapist at a community counselling service, on the urgings of his mother. He described himself as 'really messed up' and 'just feeling bad a lot of the time'. His goal for counselling was 'to sort myself out'. Five years previously he had been referred for CBT, which he described as having been quite helpful. More recently, he had felt suicidal, and his GP had prescribed anti-depressant and anti-anxiety medication. At the counselling service he took part in an assessment interview, which revealed a troubled and somewhat chaotic life, which included the death of his father when he was a child, moving from one city to another with his mother and stepfather (including periods of time when he was 'dumped' on other family members), and a series of jobs and girlfriends. Reflecting on the assessment information that had been collected, and his own experience of meeting Danny and talking with him during the first two sessions, his counsellor asked if it would be a suitable point for him to share his thoughts on what Danny had told him. At that stage, the counsellor made sense of Danny's issues in terms of a set of tentative and preliminary hypotheses. First, it seemed to be hard for Danny to sustain close relationships – he would get close to a girlfriend or set of work colleagues, and then leave them. The counsellor wondered whether this was a pattern that might have its roots in Danny's loss of his father, which could have left him with an underlying fear that closeness leads to abandonment. The counsellor was old enough to be Danny's father, and was aware of

a countertransference reaction response of seeing Danny as a son, and wanting to take care of him. A second hypothesis related to the way that Danny dealt with stress by turning inward and ruminating, which led to a destructive spiral of becoming more and more hopeless and self-critical. A key element of his coping mechanism appeared to be a tendency to perfectionism. A third hypothesis was concerned with the strongly creative side of Danny (he had trained as a graphic designer) and his pattern of believing that he was 'not good enough' to be a success in this career. In addition to these possible ways of explaining Danny's current problems, the counsellor had identified a number of strengths and resources: Danny's relationship with his step-sister, his creativity and intelligence, and his capacity for hard work. The counsellor and Danny worked together to map these ideas on to a large sheet of paper (Figure 2.1). Danny had three main responses to the picture that emerged. He was immediately struck by the pattern of his life as a whole, in terms of cycles of stress/breakdown and recovery. He became tearful on acknowledging his own strength in always being able to 'bounce back' after a crisis period. Finally, he took charge of the page, and on his own initiative began to create a more detailed mapping (not shown) of what happened during what his counsellor had characterised as a 'rumination cycle'. This issue then became the focus for the next two sessions.

THERAPEUTIC CHALLENGES AND FUTURE DIRECTIONS

At the present time, the majority of counsellors and psychotherapists who have embraced a pluralistic perspective are individuals who have received their initial training in approaches such as person–centred or psychodynamic, which generally do not advocate use of a formal case formulation that is shared with the client. For these practitioners, collaborative case formulation can seem like a big step. What tends to happen is that these therapists discover that this type of formulation is much more productive than they expect, and that clients experience it as meaningful and facilitative. Another challenge, in this area of therapy, concerns terminology. Different organisations use different terms to describe these activities – initial meeting, intake, history, diagnosis, assessment, contracting, formulation, reformulation, conceptualisation. It is important to find a way of talking about these activities that feels right to both therapist and client. A further challenge lies in the achievement of an appropriate balance between therapist 'expert' knowledge and client 'insider knowledge'. Therapists are (or should be) much more fluent and confident than clients in formulating a way of making sense of a set of problems in living. There is a risk that the client may be intimidated or mystified by the therapist's apparent expertise. It is also necessary to keep an open mind, and create opportunities for the case formulation to be reviewed and to evolve as new information becomes available over the course of therapy. A final challenge, at this stage in the development of pluralistic therapy, is to carry out research and innovation around the principles and techniques described in this chapter.

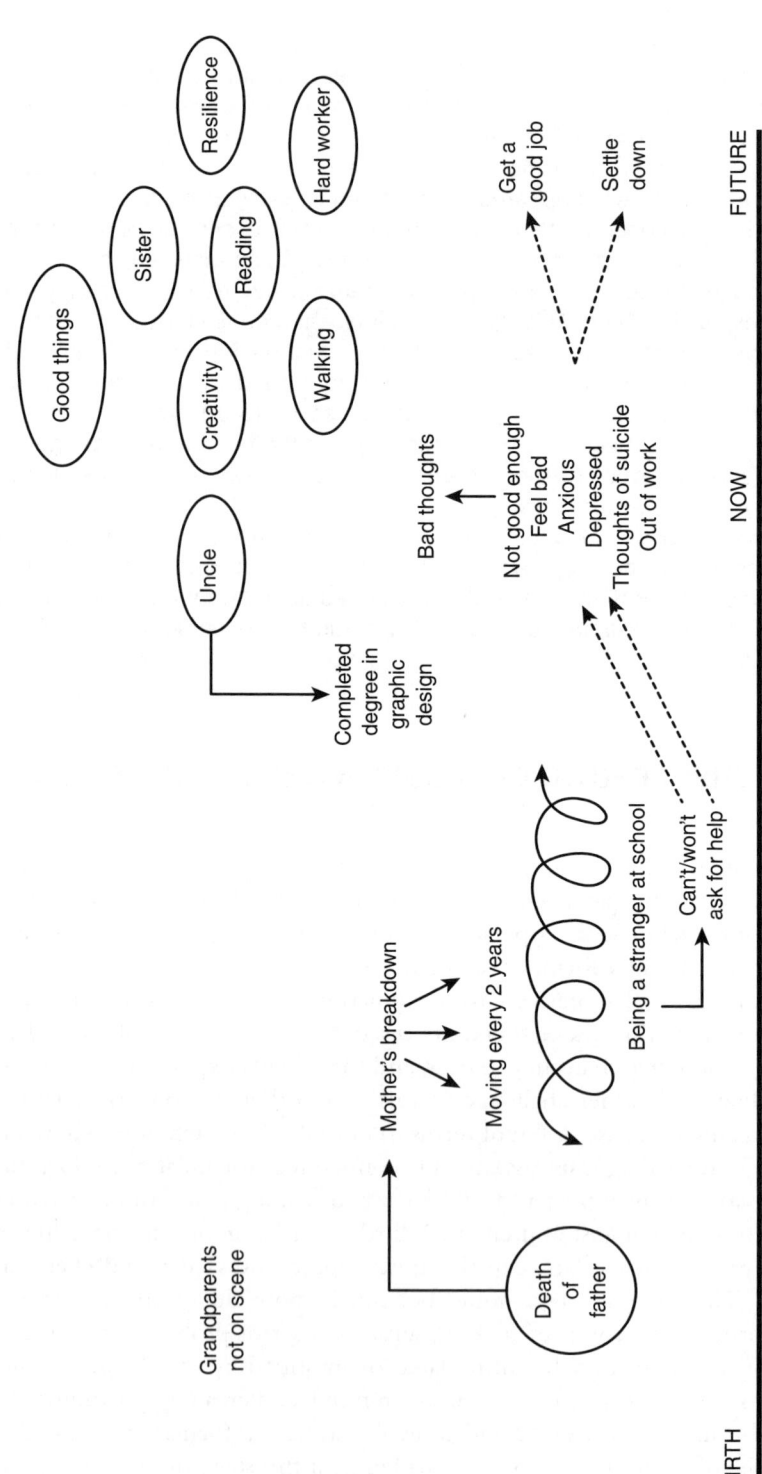

FIGURE 2.1 Danny's case formulation time-line

SUMMARY

The key points of this chapter are:

- A key dimension of pluralistic therapy is shared understanding of the client's problems, and what might help.
- Assessment and case formulation provide specific points, early in therapy, when a shared understanding can be established.
- Within the existing counselling, counselling psychology and psychotherapy literature, there are many ideas and practices that can contribute to pluralistic assessment and case formulation.
- The key principles of pluralistic assessment and case formulation include the adoption of a collaborative, dialogical stance, and consideration of multiple perspectives.

EXERCISES/POINTS FOR REFLECTION

1. What assessment information would you want to collect from clients, in relation to your own ideas about what is important in therapy?
2. In relation to your own work as a counsellor or psychotherapist, and the settings in which you see clients, what terms do you use to describe 'assessment' and 'case formulation'?
3. Identify an issue or problem that concerns you at the moment. Construct a personal time-line formulation around this issue, using at least three contrasting theoretical perspectives. What was your experience of undertaking this exercise? How helpful was it?

FURTHER READING

Finn, S.E., & Tonsager, M.E. (2002). How therapeutic assessment became humanistic. *The Humanistic Psychologist, 30,* 10–22. Moving from a 'medicalised' model of assessment to a collaborative approach.

Johnstone, L., & Dallos, R. (Eds.). (2014). *Formulation in psychology and psychotherapy: making sense of people's problems* (2nd ed.). London: Routledge. An invaluable sourcebook on how formulation is carried out within different schools of therapy.

Kuyken, W., Padesky, C.A., & Dudley, R. (2008). The science and practice of case conceptualization. *Behavioural and Cognitive Psychotherapy, 36,* 757–768. A classic paper, which both describes a CBT model of formulation and questions its relevance and effectiveness.

REFERENCES

Bager-Charleson, S., & van Rijn, B. (2011). *Understanding assessment in counselling and psychotherapy.* London: Learning Matters.

Berg, A.L., Sandahl, C., & Clinton, D. (2008). The relationship of treatment preferences and experiences to outcome in generalized anxiety disorder (GAD). *Psychology and Psychotherapy: Theory, Research and Practice, 81,* 247–259.

Berman, L. (1993). *Beyond the smile: the therapeutic use of the photograph.* London: Routledge.

Bowen, M., & Cooper, M. (2012). Development of a client feedback tool: a qualitative study of therapists' experiences of using the Therapy Personalisation Form. *European Journal of Psychotherapy and Counselling, 14,* 47–62.

Clark, A.J. (2001). Early recollections: a humanistic assessment in counseling. *Journal of Humanistic Counseling, Education and Development, 40,* 96–104.

Davidson, T. (2014). STRENGTH: a system of integration of solution-oriented and strength-based principles. *Journal of Mental Health Counseling, 36,* 1–17.

Drapeau, M. (2012). The value of progress tracking in psychotherapy. Introduction to a Special Issue: 10 tools for progress monitoring in psychotherapy. *Integrating Science and Practice, 2,* 5–6.

Eells, T. (forthcoming). *Integrative evidence-based case formulation in psychotherapy.* Washington, DC: American Psychological Association.

Eells, T.D., & Lombart, K.G. (2003). Case formulation and treatment concepts among novice, experienced and expert cognitive-behavioural and psychodynamic therapists. *Psychotherapy Research, 13,* 187–204.

Eells, T.D, Lombart, K.G., Kendjelic, E.M., Turner, L.C., & Lucas, C.P. (2005). The quality of psychotherapy case formulations: a comparison of expert, experienced, and novice cognitive-behavioral and psychodynamic therapists. *Journal of Consulting and Clinical Psychology, 73,* 579–589.

Finn, S.E., & Tonsager, M.E. (1997). Information gathering and therapeutic models of assessment: complementary paradigms. *Psychological Assessment, 9,* 374–385.

Fischer, C.T (2000). Collaborative, individualized assessment. *Journal of Personality Assessment, 74,* 2–14.

Hallam, R. (2013). *Individual case formulation.* New York: Academic Press.

Hamill, M., Reid, M., & Reynolds, S. (2008). Letters in cognitive analytic therapy: the patient's experience. *Psychotherapy Research, 18,* 573–583.

Hilsenroth, M.J., & Cromer, T.D. (2007). Clinician interventions related to alliance during the initial interview and psychological assessment. *Psychotherapy: Theory, Research, Practice, Training, 44,* 205–218.

Hunter, C., Chantler, K., Kapur, N., & Cooper, J. (2013). Service user perspectives on psychosocial assessment following self-harm and its impact on further help-seeking: a qualitative study. *Journal of Affective Disorders, 145,* 315–323.

Kuyken, W., Padesky, C.A., & Dudley, R. (2009). *Collaborative case conceptualization: working effectively with clients in Cognitive-Behavioral Therapy.* New York: The Guilford Press.

Lazarus, A.A. (1989). *The practice of multimodal therapy.* Baltimore, MD: Johns Hopkins University Press.

Mace, C. (Ed.). (1995). *The art and science of assessment in psychotherapy*. London: Routledge.

Marquis, A. (2008). *The integral intake: a guide to comprehensive idiographic assessment in integral psychotherapy*. New York: Routledge.

Marrow, A. (1969). *The practical theorist: the life and work of Kurt Lewin*. New York: Basic Books.

McElwain, B., Polizzi, L., & Polizzi, D. (2002). Moving psychological assessment: accessing clients' lives at home. *The Humanistic Psychologist*, *30*, 85–101.

McGoldrick, M., Gerson, R., & Petry, S. (2008). *Genograms: assessment and intervention* (3rd ed.). New York: Norton.

Miller, S.D., Duncan, B.L., & Hubble, M.A. (2005). Outcome-informed clinical work. In J.C. Norcross & M.R. Goldfried (Eds.), *Handbook of psychotherapy integration*. New York: Oxford University Press.

Milner, J., & O'Byrne, P. (2003). *Assessment in counselling: theory, process and decision making*. London: Palgrave Macmillan.

Omer, H. (1997). Narrative empathy. *Psychotherapy*, *25*, 171–184.

O'Neill, P. (1999). *Negotiating consent in psychotherapy*. New York: Oxford University Press.

Oster, G.D., & Crone, P.G. (2004). *Using drawings in assessment and therapy: a guide for mental health professionals* (2nd ed.). London: Routledge.

Riddle, B.C., Byers, C.C., & Grimesey, J.L. (2002). Literature review of research and practice in collaborative assessment. *The Humanistic Psychologist*, *30*, 33–48.

Rombach, M.A.M. (2003). An invitation to therapeutic letter writing. *Journal of Systemic Therapies*, *22*, 15–32.

Ryle, A. & Kerr, I.B. (2002). *Introducing Cognitive Analytic Therapy: principles and practice*. Chichester: Wiley.

Widdowson, M. (2010). *Transactional analysis: 100 key points and techniques*. London: Routledge.

Yalom, I.D. (2002). *The gift of therapy: reflections on being a therapist*. London: Piatkus.

3

From Goals to Tasks and Methods

Terry Hanley, Aaron Sefi and Zehra Ersahin

THIS CHAPTER DISCUSSES

- The philosophical and theoretical underpinnings to goal articulation within therapy
- Research issues related to working with therapeutic goals
- Specific practices that therapists might use whilst working with goals in therapy
- Some of the challenges that therapists might encounter when working with goals in therapy
- The move from articulating therapeutic goals to identifying specific therapeutic tasks and deciding upon therapeutic methods

INTRODUCING GOAL ARTICULATION IN THERAPY

Philosophical and theoretical underpinnings of goals in therapy

The goal-oriented approach to therapy, outlined within the pluralistic framework for counselling and psychotherapy, might be viewed as an explicit reflection of its ethically minded positioning. Specifically, this approach is aligned with the work of existential philosophers such as Heidegger and Sartre who view people as future focused meaning-oriented beings (see Cooper, 2015). In holding this position, individuals' actions are viewed as purposeful, even when this purpose might be difficult to comprehend to a person looking in from the outside (such as a therapist). The 'teleological' (teleology literally meaning the study of a person's 'ends'/purpose or goals) assumption here reflects that 'goals' become important in directing people's life choices and are therefore both inevitable within therapy (even if they are not expressed as such) and provide insight into why supporting clients to articulate them might prove useful when considering the intended direction of therapy.

Taking the teleological assumption further, the merits of particular actions to achieve specific goals are commonly judged (by both clients and therapists) by the consequences associated with them. This position might be described as 'consequentialist' in nature and focuses towards what the philosopher Jeremy Bentham classically described as the 'greater happiness [often replaced with 'good'] for the greater number'. Commonly this view is contrasted with other philosophical positions that focus more upon the morality of specific 'acts' (deontological/duty ethics – most often associated with the work of Kant) rather than the 'ends' achieved by it – a crude example may be that, from a consequentialist position, killing one person might be justifiable to save 10; whilst from a Kantian perspective, moral codes such as religious belief systems take precedence and killing might always be viewed as unjust.

Working in conjunction with the perspective that humans are purposeful beings is the pluralistic framework's idiographic understanding of distress. By adopting a position closely aligned to the core principles of humanistic psychology – that people are unique, can exercise choice, and are able to constructively grow (Bugental, 1964) – the framework suggests that the main focus of the therapeutic work should be that which is identified by the client (Cooper & McLeod, 2011b). In doing so, the client is viewed as an active agent in the therapeutic process and is a partner, alongside the therapist, in deciding the direction that therapy will head (Bohart, 2009). The focus of the framework is therefore, not 'What do clients need?', but 'What do clients want?' Such a viewpoint aims to help support the client in providing a more informed consent to the therapeutic work they are entering into. It contrasts with those therapeutic approaches that are primarily directed by theories of psychopathology or therapeutic manuals and commonly act without a great deal of consultation with the client.

Key research findings around goal-oriented approaches

There is a growing body of research supporting goal orientation in therapy. The most significant summary of the literature in this area comes from the American Psychological Association's Division 29 task force (Norcross, 2011 – specifically see Tryon and Winograd (2011) for a summary of the research around goal consensus and collaboration). This group systematically reflected upon the research findings related to numerous topics and concluded that 'the therapeutic alliance', 'empathy' and 'collecting client feedback' were demonstrably effective elements of the relationship. 'Goal consensus' appears in the conclusion's second tier, being noted as 'probably effective' alongside 'collaboration and positive regard', and appears more highly than 'congruence/genuineness', 'repairing alliance ruptures' and 'managing countertransference', which appear as 'promising but insignificant research to judge'.

Ultimately, the review's findings indicate strong links between the client and therapist goal consensus and successful therapeutic outcome.

One of the most commonly cited ways of organising goals is that articulated by Grosse Holtforth and Grawe (2002) in the Bern Inventory of Therapeutic Goals. In their work they have developed a taxonomy of therapeutic goals by thematically examining 1,031 treatment goals of 298 outpatients at a university clinic. From this, five major categories emerged. These were (1) coping with specific problems and symptoms, (2) interpersonal goals, (3) well-being and functioning, (4) existential issues and (5) personal growth. Such a frame has been widely utilised and since its conception it has provided a helpful means for examining what goals people present with in therapy. Table 3.1 provides examples of each of these types of goals.

TABLE 3.1   *Examples of client goals*

Goal type	Examples
Coping with specific problems and symptoms	I want to feel less depressed/anxious
Interpersonal goals	I want my relationship with my partner to be BETTER
Well-being and functioning	I want to feel more comfortable with my body
Existential issues	I want to explore why I don't believe in God
Personal growth	I want to improve my self-confidence

THE PRACTICE OF WORKING WITH GOALS IN THERAPY

Supporting the articulation of goals in therapy: starting the conversation

Identifying goals in therapy can be viewed as the first step towards creating a framework where the client's voice is heard and respectfully attended to. Some suggestions for how this process can be started can be found in Chapter 7 on core counselling skills.

Intrinsic values and goals

When setting goals it is important to consider the issue of values with the client. Goals that are based on values held by the client are more likely to be pursued than goals that are not related to values or are inconsistent with those values. Closely related to this, clients can be driven by their own intrinsic motivations to achieve goals, or by extrinsic motivations derived from others. Intrinsic goals may lead to more efficient goal-oriented behaviour within therapy and more favourable session outcomes – factors that have been observed in research into client motivations

(Michalak, Klappheck, & Kosfelder, 2004). Taking this into account, therapists might aim to explore the source of clients' goals, and whether they are based on clients' fundamental values and are intrinsically or extrinsically motivated.

Creating achievable goals

Importantly, when engaging in conversations about therapeutic goals, it is essential to remain realistic and to identify goals that are achievable within therapy. With this in mind, Doran (1981) introduces the useful idea of 'SMART' goals. This refers to the following acronym:

- S – Specific (the goal is focused upon a particular issue that might be addressed in therapy)
- M – Measurable (there is a means to assessing progress towards the achievement of the goal)
- A – Attainable (the goal is realistic and has an end point)
- R – Relevant (the goal is meaningful for the individual)
- T – Time bound (is it possible to consider a point in time when the goal may be achieved)

Whilst this set of criteria might not explicitly fit with the work of all therapists (its original conception coming from a management perspective), it can serve as a useful aide memoire when considering the nature of the goals set within therapy. Specifically, such thinking might be helpful in considering whether the goals being discussed are unattainable, a factor that may also reduce the well-being of the client (Cohen & Cohen, 2001).

Converting a problem into a purpose

It is not uncommon for attempts to articulate a goal for therapy to be presented in a problem-focused way – for example, 'I want to stop ruining my life'. Such *avoidance* goals have been linked to smaller increases in well-being when contrasted with clients who present with more positively framed *approach* goals (e.g. 'To feel more secure in who I am') (Wollburg & Braukhaus, 2010). The therapist might, therefore, work with clients to redefine avoidance goals into approach goals. For instance, in the example above, the therapist might reframe the statement and ask: 'If you can imagine a time when you're no longer ruining your life, what kind of things will have changed?' or 'What will others notice is different if you're no longer ruining your life?' Questions such as this can help change the focus of the goals being articulated, a factor that has been linked to both stronger alliances and more successful therapy. Law (2013) also suggests that the miracle question used in solution-focused therapy might help with goal-setting: 'Imagine when you go to bed tonight a miracle happens that makes all the difficulties you have go away. When you wake up in the morning, what will you notice is different?' (p. 9). At the same time, supporting the client to remain realistic, as noted above, proves an important element of navigating this process.

Managing multiple goals

In the case of multiple and complex goals, conceptualising goals in a hierarchical structure can prove beneficial; this hierarchy could be defined as *immediate, therapy* or *life* goals. Box 3.1 provides brief definitions for these different types of goals.

Box 3.1   Immediate, therapy and life goals

Immediate goals are the small steps an individual might want to prioritise to achieve longer-term/major goals. These could take the form of an immediate action to an urgent matter (e.g. book an appointment with the GP for tomorrow) or behaviour change around overcoming a barrier (e.g. organise a sleep schedule and keep up with it).

Therapy goals might be viewed as the goals that are to be worked on whilst within therapy. For instance, Gemma may want to improve her relationship with her partner through gaining a deeper awareness of her underlying beliefs and attitudes towards him.

Life goals are the types of goals we strive to achieve in the long term. These might bring ultimate satisfaction to our existential desires in life. For example, Gemma, mentioned above, might hope that the therapy goal helps with a longer-term life goal of having more healthy relationships.

In considering this hierarchy, a client might present with the rather broad life goal of hoping to feel happier. One way of breaking this broad goal into specific goals could be simply achieved by prompting the client by asking 'When you are happy, what will your life look like?' or 'For you to feel happier, what would need to change to bring some happiness into your life?' or 'When do you feel the happiest?' Creating such a conversation and focusing upon the client's responses and expectations will help the practitioner to break down life goals into relevant therapy goals (e.g. 'to develop closer relationships with my friends') and immediate goals (e.g. 'to allow myself to be the real me when I am with Sally next Friday night').

Using goal-related measures in therapy

A final way to consider supporting clients to identify the goals they wish to work on could be by using a goal-based outcome measure (GbOM). The forms used to record these outcomes commonly ask clients to identify the goals they wish to work on in therapy.

Following this, the therapist asks the client to return to these goals at intervals in therapy and rate their attainment to date on a short scale. As well as helping to facilitate the articulation of goals and providing useful information for monitoring progress, GbOMs can also help the client express how things are changing (or not) in a tangible and meaningful way. This might especially be the case with those clients who bring complicated needs and goals to therapy, with GbOMs potentially becoming a useful tool for practitioners to clarify if therapy is heading in the right direction (Law, 2013). Box 3.2 offers some examples of GbOMs.

Box 3.2 Examples of goal-based outcome measures

Goals Form – This is a brief, one-page form in which clients are asked to identify their goals and to rate whether they have achieved them on a scale of 1–7. This is available at www.pluralistictherapy.com.

PSYCHLOPS is a short, one-page mental health outcome measure, assessed under three sub-scales (Problems, Function and Well-being). This asks clients to identify their main problems, when they first became concerned about them and how they have been affected by them over the last week. This is available at www.psychlops.org.uk/index.html.

The Counselling Goals System (CoGs) is a goal identification and monitoring form directed at young people. Originally devised for use online it asks young people to identify goals before rating them out of 10 on a weekly basis. This follows a similar format to the Goals Progress Chart available from the Child Outcomes Research Consortium website and can be found at www.corc.uk.net/resources/measures/child/.

CASE EXAMPLE
Supporting the articulation of therapeutic goals

Sabita is a counsellor working in a GP surgery. Typically, she would see clients for a maximum of 12 sessions. Her client, Jane, was 31 years old, and wanted to work on traumatic memories from childhood. She had been in foster care for a lot of her teenage life, misused substances and had a history of sexual exploitation. Sabita sensitively opened up the issue of goals in the first session with a brief question: 'Jane, I wonder if you might be able to say what you hope to get from coming to counselling?'

As Jane began to talk it became very apparent that there were numerous complex issues that might be addressed within therapy. Sabita did not assume that any of these issues took precedence over the others and cautiously, and with curiosity, asked questions about which issues might Jane wish explicitly to work on within therapy. Jane was also aware of the 12-week limit to the sessions

(Continued)

> *(Continued)*
>
> and asked Sabita questions about her opinion of what might be achievable in the time available. After some open discussion, which included consideration of a referral to a longer-term service, they agreed upon the main focus of the work they would undertake together. Sabita then introduced a Goals Form: 'To keep a track of these ideas sometimes it can be useful to note down such thoughts on a form like this. We can then check-in with how we're doing on them, or if they've changed, as we go along. Might this be something you'll be willing to give a go?'
>
> Jane tentatively accepted this idea, and through careful discussion, it was agreed that she would work towards the goal: 'To be able to come to terms with some of my experiences.' Some of the goals Jane initially articulated seemed unrealistic to Sabita, and she sensitively helped her find a goal that was more achievable in the time they had together. As an addendum to the goal, Jane articulated which specific experiences she wanted to accept most, and this was the springboard for her to discuss these experiences.

COMMON CHALLENGES IN THE PRACTICE OF WORKING WITH GOALS IN THERAPY

When therapist and client goals conflict

When discussing goals, the therapist and client might disagree upon the major thrust of the work to be engaged in. This has the potential to develop into a major therapeutic rupture if not managed sensitively. For instance, in the case of Sabita and Jane above, the therapist may have steadfastly felt that Jane could not achieve the goal 'To understand why all this has happened to me' in the 12 weeks available (e.g. believing that the trauma related to the history of sexual exploitation would not be sufficiently addressed, and be potentially of detriment to Jane, in the time period available), whilst Jane may have been determined to work on this issue. In such instance, the following may be considered:

- *Reflexive practice*: Schön (1983) introduces the concepts of 'reflecting *in*' and 'reflecting *on*' practice. The former relates to the conscious consideration of the processes going on whilst sitting in the room with the client. The latter relates to reflecting upon work after the event itself. Typically this might take the form of writing clinical notes or attending clinical supervision.
- *Metacommunication*: Metacommunication can be a helpful tool where therapy goals might conflict. Here the therapist might initiate a conversation related to the therapeutic process (Rennie, 1998) with a view to considering how each other's goals might conflict, and how a consensus might be arrived at. For instance, Sabita might have said to Jane: 'I get the sense that you would like to use this therapy to be able to understand all the horrific things that have happened to you. While I hope that we can help you towards that goal, it may be setting us up to fail in some way. I wonder if this is the case?'

- *Referring on*: There may be genuine cases where goals conflict and go beyond the competency or comfort zone of the therapist. In this instance, the goal needs to focus on appropriate and well-managed referral onwards to a better-suited intervention.

Working with a client who cannot articulate goals

Many clients come to therapy struggling to articulate the purpose or intent of their reason for doing so. From a pluralistic perspective, it is important to stress that goal articulation is viewed as part of developing rapport and relationship, and should not act in direct contradiction to that process (Cooper & McLeod, 2011b). The experienced pluralistic therapist can help pace the tempo, skilfully supporting the client to discover their internally located goals. Although settings might dictate the duration of therapy, the timescale allocated to such an activity is by no means prescribed. For some individuals this may mean that goals are articulated very easily in a first meeting, whilst others might need many more meetings to identify them. For example, if a client is struggling to articulate any goals for therapy, it can be helpful to make the process feel less onerous. The therapist could suggest 'How about we set a goal for now around simply being able to express your feelings, and see if a more involved goal comes out of that?'

Challenges when working with people who are 'stuck' for goals

It may be that the client is '*stuck*' in a situation that makes goal articulation a seemingly impossible activity. The complexity of the circumstance can inhibit the ability of an individual to articulate a clear therapy goal. For instance, a client might feel that there is no realistic future to look forward to in which they can achieve a goal, and any attempt at goal-setting would be disrespectful to this state of being. In some situations, it might therefore be more helpful for the therapist to *be* with this stuckness, to develop the rapport and the bond. This approach would be in keeping with humanistic principles, particularly the belief that humans will work towards constructive growth given an appropriately fertile environment, which might be viewed as a base for the pluralistic framework (e.g. Cooper & McLeod, 2011a). As a consequence, this in itself might be viewed as the purpose/goal of the therapy at that point of time – notably to help a client reach a point where he can begin to see a direction or trajectory for his life, and for the therapy.

Challenges around 'perverse' goals

Some clients can seemingly have 'perverse' goals. A perverse goal is one that intends to serve a different purpose to the one articulated. For instance, a client might set a complex and highly ambitious goal in the hope that this will enable them to receive a better, or longer service. There can also be a situation where a therapist might help a client articulate a very easy goal to complete so that their outcomes scores look better. All goal-setting requires careful consideration of what is being agreed, and the underlying motives for any goals can be explored.

FROM GOALS TO TASKS AND METHODS: HOW PURPOSE INFORMS ACTION AND RATIONALE

An introduction to theory of tasks and methods in pluralistic thinking

Therapeutic tasks are the particular type of collaborative process which the client and therapist engage with in therapy. This can vary greatly but remains focused upon achieving the goals articulated by the client. *Therapeutic methods* are the specific activities that are utilised to help achieve these tasks. These activities can be separated into two, those undertaken by the client and those undertaken by the therapist.

Each different destination (the identified goal) has numerous potential routes (tasks) and vehicles (methods) that are suitably plausible. Some routes might take longer, however a scenic route might be viewed as more rewarding.

Table 3.2 provides examples of how a therapeutic goal might be unpacked into tasks and associated methods. This example specifically relates to the work with Tony, a young man who lives on his own and has had extreme difficulties leaving his house to do his shopping.

TABLE 3.2 Working with Tony: an example of how goals may link to tasks and methods in therapy

Therapeutic Goal 1: To be less anxious when leaving the house to do his shopping

   Therapeutic Task 1: Talking through what it means to be anxious when leaving the house

      Therapeutic Methods
      Non-directive empathic reflections
      Socratic questioning

   Therapeutic Task 2: Practising relaxation activities

      Therapeutic Methods
      Breathing exercises
      Safe space visualisations

   Therapeutic Task 3: Exploring self-talk

      Therapeutic Methods
      Identifying and highlighting anxiety-provoking thoughts
      Keeping a journal of thoughts and their triggers as they emerge during the day

Practical ways of introducing different tasks and methods

Once a therapy goal has been agreed upon, the therapist and client then need to work together to further tailor the therapeutic process. A key element to this process is the collaborative nature of the therapeutic work being undertaken. The therapist therefore needs to facilitate respectful conversations around the therapeutic tasks and methods with a view to agreeing upon what might be described as a 'process contract' (Lee, 2006) – notably a contract related to what the therapeutic process might look like, rather than the content that it might address. As was outlined at the outset of this chapter, the negotiated nature of this process would be in keeping with the ethically informed foundation of the pluralistic framework. It would also support the development of collaboratively created individualised therapeutic formulations.

An additional area to introduce here is the concept of feedback. As has already been referred to above, metacommunication can be a very useful tool in clarifying that the therapeutic process is fitting for the client and to navigate potential therapeutic ruptures. For instance, a client might feel that they want to work in a particular therapeutic way; after experiencing it, however, they may decide it is not presently helpful. Instigating formal breaks or review periods can provide a useful interlude in which to 'check-in' around this process. Likewise, utilising forms that monitor whether therapy is addressing the client's goals (e.g. the Session Rating Scale) might be used on a sessional basis.

CASE EXAMPLE
Agreeing upon specific methods with a client

James, a counsellor, is meeting with Tammy for the first time in a community counselling service that commonly offers six sessions of therapy. Tammy has discussed getting angry with her partner 'for no real reason' and has identified the primary goal of 'not being so angry with my boyfriend'. They have briefly discussed that the therapeutic tasks to undertake might be (1) to gain a greater understanding of this behaviour, (2) to gain a greater understanding of the events in which Tammy gets annoyed, and (3) learning how to relax when she becomes angry. They begin to work together on what therapeutic methods might be used.

James: So, that's agreed, to start with we'll focus upon gaining a greater understanding of the events that lead up to you getting annoyed with your boyfriend. I wonder if you have any thoughts about how we might do this? I have a number of ideas but I wonder if you have any thoughts first?

Tammy: I'm not sure to be honest. I thought that would be where you come in. I guess I thought it would be helpful to talk it all through to help

(Continued)

(Continued)

                    me get my head around it, but I don't really know. It just seems to come out of the blue.

James: OK [*taking a small whiteboard from the table in front of them*]. Well, let's note that down [*writes down 'talking it all through' on the board*]. There are lots of different ways that therapy can go and one of them is just as you say, it can be a space to talk stuff through. This can be really helpful in sorting out things going on in your head and could be a good way of trying to get a better sense of what happens before you get annoyed.

Here James notes down the first potential method that is suggested by Tammy. He uses a whiteboard as a means of keeping a list of the ideas they come up with. Where possible he uses Tammy's words in the list.

James: Would it be helpful to hear some other possible approaches we might use?

Tammy: Yes please.

James: Well, one idea might be for us to be more focused in our conversation about what happens. For instance, we could take one of the events and unpack it more systematically. You could tell me the story of your day leading up to the arguments and we could then reflect upon whether you see the different things that happen are related to the arguments.

Tammy: OK, so sort of just going through the days when I get angry bit by bit?

James: Yes that's right [*notes down 'go through the days bit by bit'*]. It might be useful to see if there are any patterns we can spot, or it might give us a sense of what we might want to talk in more depth about.

James made several other suggestions to Tammy before asking her if any of the ideas sounded most appropriate to her.

Tammy: They all sound as if they could be useful but I think I'd like to start a bit more focused. Maybe if we go with this one [*Tammy points at the 'go through the days bit by bit' option on the board*] and I can try and remember what happens to wind me up.

James: OK. Well that sounds like a good starting point then. I'm glad we've talked about the different options and come up with a plan. It's really helpful to get a sense of what you want from our meetings. We'll start there but we can check-in as we progress.

James acknowledges the choice of direction and purposefully reminds Tammy that there will be opportunities to redirect the work if it is felt necessary.

SUMMARY

Working with therapeutic goals is in keeping with the philosophical positioning of the pluralistic framework. In particular, the valuing of client agency fits well with the more egalitarian stance of the framework.

- Therapeutic goals can vary greatly in nature. Working with them is, however, supported by theoretical and research literature spreading a variety of therapeutic approaches.
- Starting a conversation about therapeutic goals can be supported by utilising a variety of techniques. These might include becoming familiar with conversations around goals, identifying if the client's goals are intrinsically or extrinsically motivated, developing SMART goals, reframing avoidance goals into approach goals and using Goal-based Outcome Measures.
- Challenges such as disagreements around therapeutic goals, working with individuals who cannot articulate a goal or become stuck doing so, and perverse goals are evident when working with goals in therapy. Therapists might utilise reflexive activities, metacommunication and referral pathways to support this process.
- The way in which goals might be worked with in therapy can be broken down into therapeutic tasks and methods. These need to be sensitively negotiated with clients and might form a 'process contract' that might be reviewed as therapy progresses.

EXERCISES/POINTS FOR REFLECTION

The best way to understand the pluralistic concepts behind goals, tasks and methods is to articulate them in your own words. Imagine a goal you have: for the next week (immediate), for life in general and for your own therapeutic process. Now consider how you might achieve each of these goals – what tasks can be employed to best achieve them, and what methods might be utilised to *contain* these tasks? If you keep all these written in a special place you can refer back to them and see how well each has been achieved. When you do so, you can consider: Did the goals or tasks change? Did the method you proposed work? Also, how helpful was it to articulate them?

FURTHER READING

Bohart, A.C., & Tallman, K. (1999). *How clients make therapy work: the process of active self-healing*. Washington, DC: American Psychological Association. This book provides an excellent introduction to the idea of the active client within therapy. For shorter introductions, many of the authors' papers go into similar territories.

(Continued)

(Continued)

Hanley, T., Humphrey, N., & Lennie, C. (Eds.). (2013). *Adolescent counselling psychology: theory, research, and practice*. London: Routledge. This book includes chapters that focus upon the adoption of goals, tasks and methods within work with young people and young adults.

Law, D. (2013). *Goals and goal-based outcomes (GBOs): some useful information*. London: CAMHS Press. This is a very helpful information sheet related to working with goals in therapy. It is a practical guide and provides lots of useful information for working with young people.

Tryon, G. S., & Winograd, G. (2011). Goal consensus and collaboration. In J.C. Norcross (Ed.), *Psychotherapy relationships that work: evidence based responsiveness* (2nd ed.). New York: Oxford University Press. This chapter is a key summary of the research related to the use of goals in therapy.

REFERENCES

Bohart, A. (2009). The client is the most important common factor: clients' self-healing capacities and psychotherapy. *Journal of Psychotherapy Integration*, 10(2), 127–149.

Bugental, J.F.T. (1964). The third force in psychology. *The Journal of Humanistic Psychology*, 4(1), 19–26.

Cohen, P., & Cohen, J. (2001). Life values and mental health in adolescence. In P. Schmuck & K.M. Sheldon (Eds.), *Life goals and well-being: towards a positive psychology of human striving* (pp. 167–181). Seattle, WA: Hogrefe.

Cooper, M. (2015). *Existential therapies* (2nd ed.). London: Sage.

Cooper, M., & McLeod, J. (2011a). Person-centered therapy: a pluralistic perspective. *Person-centered & Experiential Psychotherapies*, 10(3), 210–223.

Cooper, M., & McLeod, J. (2011b). *Pluralistic counselling and psychotherapy*. London: Sage.

Doran, G.T. (1981). There's a S.M.A.R.T. way to write management's goals and objectives. *Management Review*, 70(11), 35–36.

Grosse Holtforth, M., & Grawe, K. (2002). Bern inventory of treatment goals: Part 1: Development and first application of a taxonomy of treatment goal themes. *Psychotherapy Research*, 12, 79–99.

Law, D. (2013). *Goals and Goal-based Outcomes (GBOs): some useful information*. London: CAMHS Press.

Lee, A. (2006). Process contracts. In C. Sills (Ed.), *Contracts in counselling and psychotherapy* (pp. 74–86). London: Sage.

Michalak, J., Klappheck, M., & Kosfelder, J. (2004). Personal goals of psychotherapy patients: the intensity and the 'why' of goal-motivated behavior and their implications for the therapeutic process. *Psychotherapy Research*, 14(2), 193–209.

Norcross, J.C. (Ed.). (2011). *Psychotherapy relationships that work: evidence based responsiveness* (2nd ed.). New York: Oxford University Press.

Rennie, D. (1998). *Person-centred counselling: an experiential approach*. London: Sage.

Schön, D.A. (1983). *The reflective practitioner.* New York: Basic Books.

Tryon, G.S., & Winograd, G. (2011). Goal consensus and collaboration. *Psychotherapy, 48*(1), 50–57.

Wollburg, E., & Braukhaus, C. (2010). Goal setting in psychotherapy: the relevance of approach and avoidance goals for treatment outcome. *Psychotherapy Research, 20*(4), 488–494.

4
Metatherapeutic Communication and Shared Decision-Making

Mick Cooper, Windy Dryden, Kate Martin and Fani Papayianni

THIS CHAPTER DISCUSSES

- The nature and development of metatherapeutic communication and shared decision-making
- Evidence for metatherapeutic communication and shared decision-making
- Dimensions of metatherapeutic communication in therapy
- Practical strategies for metatherapeutic communication in therapy
- Critical reflections on metatherapeutic communication in therapy

One of the two fundamental principles of the pluralistic approach is that, 'If we want to know what is most likely to help clients, we should talk to them about it' (Cooper & McLeod, 2011: 6). This principle emerges from the ethical driver at the heart of pluralistic therapy: that therapists should engage with their clients in deeply valuing and respectful ways. This means that clients should be engaged with as human beings who – like their therapists – have views and opinions on the therapeutic process that are of worth. This does not mean that therapists should simply agree with how clients see things or comply with their demands. Rather, it means that counsellors, psychotherapists and psychologists should take their clients' views on therapy seriously, and seek to encourage their expression.

Drawing on the work of Rennie (1994), Cooper and McLeod (2011: 46) referred to the process of communicating about communication in therapy as *metacommunication*. These are moments when the participants stand apart from the flow of conversation (i.e., adopt a *meta* position) and talk about what has been said or done. Subsequently, they introduced the term *metatherapeutic dialogue*, or *metatherapeutic communication*, to refer to 'the process of talking to clients about what they want from therapy, and how they think they may be most likely to achieve it' (Cooper & McLeod, 2012: 7). Metatherapeutic communication (MTC) can be understood as one form of metacommunication, in which therapist and client specifically communicate about the therapeutic work itself: in particular, what the client wants from therapy and how this can be achieved.

Within the pluralistic literature (e.g., Cooper & McLeod, 2011), metatherapeutic communication has primarily been described as a means of enhancing the fit of the therapy to the individual client. However, it can also be seen as a therapeutic process in its own right: helping clients to develop skills in interpersonal relating, dialogue and assertiveness; enhancing reflective functioning; and helping to build clients' self-confidence by conveying to them a valuing of their views.

Within the wider healthcare field, a concept that is closely related to metatherapeutic communication is *shared decision-making*. This can be defined as:

> [A] process in which clinicians and patients work together to select tests, treatments, management, or support packages, based on clinical evidence and patients' informed preferences. It involves the provision of evidence-based information about options, outcomes and uncertainties, together with decision support counselling and systems for recording and implementing patients' treatment preferences. (Coulter & Collins, 2011: vii)

In relation to therapeutic practice, metatherapeutic communication can be considered to be synonymous with shared decision-making. However, in some elements of metatherapeutic communication, the decision-making element may be more implicit than explicit: for instance, reviewing with clients how they experienced a session.

The concept of shared decision-making first gained popularity in the United States in the late 1980s (The Health Foundation, 2012), and has become a topic of increasing interest to the present day (Makoul & Clayman, 2006). The shared decision-making approach rejects the traditional, 'paternalistic' model of healthcare – where the professional is seen as knowing best – towards an approach that sees people 'as active partners in, rather than simply passive recipients of, health care' (The Health Foundation, 2014: 28). However, it also rejects a 'consumer choice' approach in which everything is left up to the service user to decide. Rather, the emphasis in shared decision-making is on dialogue, collaboration and mutual involvement across service user and provider (pluralism across perspectives, see Chapter 1).

Shared decision-making has been justified on *instrumental* grounds: as a means of improving outcomes and satisfaction in healthcare. However, like metatherapeutic communication, it has also been advocated as an ethical imperative (The Health Foundation, 2014). Here, autonomous adults are seen as having the right to make informed choices about what happens to their bodies and minds: 'Nothing about me without me' (The Health Foundation, 2012: i). Shared decision-making aims to level the playing field between service users and providers by giving people access to the required evidence-based information about treatment, alternatives and recovery.

Mental health decisions are rarely clear cut and often involve complex, ongoing trade-offs amidst an uncertain evidence base. Under these circumstances, they may be best evaluated and assessed by the service users themselves.

THE NEED FOR METATHERAPEUTIC COMMUNICATION

Therapists may feel that explicit metatherapeutic communication is unnecessary, on the grounds that they already, intuitively, know what clients want and prefer. However, this is challenged by evidence suggesting that therapists and clients can often have very different perspectives on what is going on in therapy. For instance, therapists' and clients' views of the quality of the therapeutic relationship show only moderate correlation; and in just 30–40% of instances do therapists agree with clients on what was most significant in therapy sessions (see Cooper, 2008). Research also shows that clients, at the end of sessions, may tell things to researchers about their therapy that they have not said to their therapists (Rennie, 1994).

Therapists may also feel that they do not need to develop their levels of metatherapeutic communication because they are already doing it. However, research from the wider healthcare field suggests that professionals often think they are doing more shared decision-making than they actually are, or than patients rate them as doing (The Health Foundation, 2012, 2014).

Research also shows that many clients do want greater levels of shared decision-making, with around 50% of mental health service users indicating that they would like more involvement in decisions about their treatment and care (The Health Foundation, 2014). This may be particularly true of black and minority ethnic people, who are less likely to feel that they have been involved as much as they would want to be in decisions about their care (The Health Foundation, 2014).

THE EVIDENCE BASE FOR METATHERAPEUTIC COMMUNICATION AND SHARED DECISION-MAKING

Research suggests that the impact of metatherapeutic communication and shared decision-making on outcomes in mental health interventions, *per se*, may be quite small. In the most comprehensive review to date (Duncan, Best, & Hagen, 2010), shared decision-making interventions had no overall effects on levels of depression, or on symptom severity for patients with schizophrenia. This finding is consistent with research suggesting that matching clients with their preferred therapeutic intervention has only a small impact on clinical outcomes, albeit a significant one (Swift, Callahan, & Vollmer, 2011).

Where the impact of metatherapeutic communication and shared decision-making may be greater, however, is in terms of the process and experience of mental health interventions. Clients with depression, for instance, were more satisfied with their care when it involved a shared decision-making component, and also felt more involved in it (Loh, Leonhart, Wills, Simon, & Härter, 2007). This is consistent with research showing that clients who received a preferred intervention, 'were between a half and a third less likely to drop out of therapy prematurely compared with clients who did not receive their preferred therapy conditions' (Swift et al., 2011: 307). Qualitative research also suggests that clients value having their feedback heard and acknowledged in dialogue with their therapists (Cooper et al., 2015). Interestingly, therapists, too, felt more satisfied when care involved a shared decision-making component (Duncan et al., 2010); and this is consistent with research showing that therapists who are more satisfied with their work report greater levels of metatherapeutic communication (Thompson, 2013).

These findings are very consistent with evidence on shared decision-making across the broader healthcare field. In terms of raw clinical outcomes, the evidence is mixed, with some studies showing that shared decision-making can improve health status but others showing no such effect (The Health Foundation, 2014). However, in terms of the process and experience of care, shared decision-making interventions have been found to:

- Increase satisfaction with care
- Increase active involvement in care
- Reduce drop out
- Increase self-efficacy, self-confidence and self-management
- Improve people's knowledge about their condition and treatment options
- Improve professionals' communication with patients.

(Makoul & Clayman, 2006; The Health Foundation, 2012)

Shared decision-making with children and young people

Although research is limited, studies suggest that many children and young people also want collaborative involvement in their care, where they can be involved in the analytical stages of decision-making, including weighing up the benefits and risks of treatment options (e.g., Simmons, Hetrick, & Jorm, 2011). A quality improvement programme developing shared decision-making in child and adolescent mental health services (CAMHS) found that it brought about a radical change in the relationships between clinicians and young people (Wolpert et al., 2014). This included increased transparency about therapeutic goals and better monitoring of progress or lack of progress. Rapid feedback from clients informed further decision-making and treatment planning, and helped to facilitate more explicit discussion and negotiations. There was also evidence of impact on clinical work and a reduction in challenging behaviour incidents in an inpatient context. Young people felt that they were more valued, more empowered and they experienced their care more positively due to being more involved in managing their own lives.

THREE DIMENSIONS OF METATHERAPEUTIC COMMUNICATION: THE 'WHEN?', 'WHAT?' AND 'ABOUT WHEN'?

What is the nature of metatherapeutic communication in therapy? A recent study (Papayianni & Cooper, 2015), based on post-session notes from 12 therapists practising pluralistic therapy (see Cooper et al., 2015), identified three main dimensions. Table 4.1 presents these findings, augmented by clinical observations.

TABLE 4.1 *Three dimensions of metatherapeutic communication*

Time: When?	Subject matter: What?	Temporal focus: About when?
Pre-therapy	Goals	Previous therapy
Assessment	Methods	Previous sessions
Start of session	Content	Current session
Mid-session	Understandings	Next session
End of session	Contract/boundaries	Therapeutic work as a whole
Review points	Progress	Extra-therapeutic activity
Final sessions	Client experiences	Ending

The first dimension was time: *when* the metatherapeutic communication took place. Most frequently, metatherapeutic communication took place at the start of sessions. However, it could also take place during sessions, at the end of sessions, at review sessions/review points, or at the end of therapy. From clinical observations, metatherapeutic communication also frequently takes place in assessment sessions. It can even occur before this: for instance, in the information that therapists make available on a website or email; or through initial discussions on a telephone call. From conversations with therapists, mid-session metatherapeutic communication seems to be particularly appropriate at a number of points: for instance, when the therapeutic process feels 'stuck', when there is an alliance rupture, after a new method has been tried out, or when the client does not know what to talk about.

The second dimension of metatherapeutic communication was the subject matter of the dialogue: *what* was talked about. This was often the goals of the therapeutic work (for instance, 'What shall we aim to do this session?'), or the particular methods to be used (for instance, 'Would you like to try a relaxation exercise?'). Very commonly, however, therapists also talked to clients about the specific content that they would like to discuss – particularly at the start of sessions. For instance, a therapist might ask, 'What would be good to talk about today?' A fourth subject matter for metatherapeutic communication was the therapists' and clients' *understandings* of what clients' difficulties were. For instance, 'I wonder if it makes most sense to understand your anxiety in terms of childhood experiences or as a biological predisposition?' This is a process of *collaborative case formulation* (see Chapter 2, this volume) which can be considered central to a pluralistic way of working. It may be facilitated through a range of *conversational tools* (see Chapter 12, this volume), such as diagrams on a flipchart page, written reports, or letters. Finally, therapists and clients may also dialogue over contract and boundary issues, clients' progress in therapy, and clients' experiences of therapy to date.

The third dimension of metatherapeutic communication was the temporal focus: for what period, or *about when*, was this for. In some instances, particularly when discussing goals, the focus was on the previous therapeutic sessions: reviewing what had been achieved so far. Very commonly, however, the focus was on the present session (particularly at the start of sessions), the next session (particularly at the end of sessions), or on the future therapeutic work as a whole. Another temporal focus was on clients' activities outside of the immediate therapeutic encounter: for instance, negotiating over the 'homework' that they would do. From clinical observation, the temporal focus of the metatherapeutic communication could also be previous episodes of therapy.

METATHERAPEUTIC COMMUNICATION IN PRACTICE

So how should counsellors and psychotherapists go about initiating, and developing, metatherapeutic communication with clients? Based on the available evidence and clinical experience, the following guidelines can be proposed.

Address metatherapeutic issues from the start of therapy

Generally, it seems a good idea to introduce metatherapeutic communication as early on in therapy as possible – and even before therapy starts (see above). This maximises the likelihood that clients' desires and preferences can shape the therapeutic work, and sets up a culture of feedback and shared decision-making from the start. Indeed, even if clients find it difficult to express their opinions in the early stages of therapy, offering them an opportunity to do so may make them feel more comfortable about doing so at a later date.

Assessment sessions provide a particularly valuable opportunity to initiate a discussion around metatherapeutic issues. With respect to clients' goals, therapists might ask:

- 'Do you have a sense of what you want from our work together?'
- 'So I wonder what's brought you here?'
- 'Where would you like to be by the end of therapy?'

Clients can also be asked whether they would like to set specific goals for the therapy, or whether they would like to work on a more open-ended basis.

With respect to therapeutic methods, clients might be asked whether they have been in therapy before and, if so, what they found helpful and unhelpful. For instance, Gurleen, a client of Mick's, said that she had felt pushed 'into a direction' by previous therapists, and that this time she did not want structure, goals or someone telling her what to do. Clients can also be asked questions like:

- 'What would you want from me as a therapist?'
- 'What do you think I might be able to do to help you achieve your goals?'
- 'Are there things in therapy that you think you'd find less helpful?'

If clients have not been in therapy before, they can still be asked about what they have found helpful in the past when facing difficulties, and particularly from other people.

In the assessment session, there is also an opportunity for therapists to dialogue with clients over contractual issues, such as levels of confidentiality, frequency of sessions, timing of sessions, and contact between sessions.

Actively invite clients to share their views

Given the power dynamic within the therapeutic relationship, and clients' tendencies to *defer* (Rennie, 1994) to their therapists, it cannot be assumed that clients will simply volunteer their goals or preferences for therapy. Rather, clients may need to be *actively* invited to share their views. This can be through questions and encouragement, through processes and outcome measures, and also through reassurance that the views they do share can make a valuable contribution to the therapeutic process.

See metatherapeutic communication as an ongoing process rather than as a one-off event

At the start of therapy, clients may not be able to articulate what they want from it, or how they would like it to be. Their views and preferences may also change over time. So it is important to understand metatherapeutic communication as a process that continues and evolves over the course of therapy, rather than as one-off definitive decisions. Review sessions are an ideal opportunity to reflect back at shared decisions, and building in set times for review – for instance, at every fourth or fifth session – can be a good way of ensuring that time is set aside for this. When Mick and Gurleen reviewed their work at session 10, for instance, Gurleen indicated that she now wanted more structure and goals to therapy and to be challenged more, and so Mick strove to take a more active stance in the therapeutic work. However, ongoing metatherapeutic communication can take place at any time and, as we have seen, this is often clustered at the start or end of sessions. Indeed, at the start of session 13, Gurleen said that Mick's new, more challenging stance was 'pissing her off', and that she preferred him to be more empathic. This is a good example of the iterative nature of metatherapeutic communication: with clients learning, growing and changing their mind as the process unfolds.

Uncertainty is a good predictor of when metatherapeutic communication may be helpful

For therapists, a good indication of when metatherapeutic communication may be appropriate is when they are uncertain about what is going on for clients, or how to take the work forward. Therapists' first responses, in such situations, can be to take such issues to supervision, and this is entirely appropriate. But therapists (and their supervisors) should also consider whether clients can be directly consulted on *their* views. One example of this is Mick's work with a Swiss social worker, Andreas (Cooper, 2015). Andreas was experiencing severe depression, and although there were many reasons why this might be the case – such as social isolation, a sense of meaninglessness and negative thought patterns – neither Mick, nor his supervisor, had a clear sense of which factors were most significant. In Session 26, therefore, Mick took the opportunity to directly ask Andreas what *he* thought: developing, collaboratively, their 'case formulation':

Mick: And we don't know why you feel *that* sadness. It could be … biological … it could be … existential … it could be cognitive … [*Pause*]. Shall I tell you what the different theories are and you can tell me–

Andreas: Yes, OK.

Mick: OK, biological theory: that there's some biochemical imbalance. That means that … um … you – you're more likely to experience low moods than other people. [*Mick goes on to describe a range of different theories of depression.*]

Andreas: I think I relate to … parts of the ones that you said the most: existential one and two, and also interpersonal …

Be part of the dialogue

As the previous example suggests, metatherapeutic communication requires therapists to be willing to share their own views and understandings, and to challenge clients where appropriate. And, indeed, both of these are activities that clients tend to want therapists to do (Aylindar, 2014). Later in the dialogue with Andreas, for instance, Mick said that he also felt Andreas's depression was related to interpersonal themes; but he challenged Andreas's assumption that he was 'stupid' and self-indulgent to be asking the existential questions at the core of his sadness.

Describe what the options might be

As in shared decision-making in healthcare (Makoul & Clayman, 2006), one of the key functions that counsellors and psychotherapists may have in metatherapeutic communication is to present clients with the range of different options, and to discuss the pros and cons of different understandings, therapeutic methods, or therapeutic goals. In presenting different methods, for instance, a therapist might say: 'So I'm thinking that we could explore this issue in a number of ways: we could talk about how it links to your childhood, we could go into some of the feelings, or we focus on the best way of managing it: Do you have a sense of what would work best for you?' Here, it is important to bear in mind that clients may be unfamiliar with the various methods being proposed, and therapists may therefore need to take some time to describe the alternatives, and to check whether the client has a sufficient understanding of them.

In presenting such options, two particular pointers emerge from the literature on shared decision-making. First, it is important that therapists hold 'decisional equipoise' (Duncan et al., 2010: 14). That is, they are able to present the different options in a balanced way, and not make assumptions about what is best for clients. Second, wherever possible, it is good if therapists are able to draw on the available evidence in presenting options to clients. For instance, a therapist might say, 'One option we might want to consider here is two-chair work, and there is good evidence that it can help people who are dealing with internal conflicts.' This means that therapists should familiarise themselves with the evidence on what works in therapy: both at the intervention level and the level of different methods (see, for instance, Cooper, 2008).

Use measures

There are many different outcome and process measures that can be used to support the process of metatherapeutic communication (see Chapter 5, this volume). Some of these have been directly designed to help clients articulate their preferences and goals, such as the Cooper-Norcross Inventory of Preferences (Cooper & Norcross, 2015). These measures provide channels through which clients may be able to say things that they would not otherwise: for instance, that they are having suicidal thoughts, or that they are finding the therapist unsympathetic. It is important to note, however, that it is often not the completion of the measures, in itself, that is a form of metatherapeutic communication – rather, it is the conversation that emerges following their completion.

Tailor levels of MTC to the particular client

Research into shared decision-making shows that not all clients want to be involved in decisions about their care (The Health Foundation, 2012) and the same is almost certainly true of metatherapeutic communication. That is, there are likely to be wide variations in how much clients want to talk at the metatherapeutic level, with some wanting to be asked about their wants and preferences, and others preferring just to 'get on with it.' One client, for instance, stated:

> I felt like she would ask me how the session had been for me at the end of every session as a kind of mini-review and I just felt totally, like, put on the spot, and still trying to process whatever we had been talking about. So it kind of took me out of what I had been thinking about and I lost touch with the process, rather than become absorbed in it. (Andrews, 2011)

There are a range of reasons why clients may not want to engage in metatherapeutic communication and shared decision-making. They may feel, for instance, that too much responsibility is being placed on them, or overwhelmed by the range of possibilities presented, or uncomfortable at giving personal feedback to the therapist. Working pluralistically, then, means being pluralistic about how much pluralism is introduced into the work with each individual client!

Adopt a whole service approach

A final learning from the shared decision-making field is that metatherapeutic communication may be most effective when it is part of a wider service context that emphasises these values (The Health Foundation, 2014). Hence, for instance, if therapists are working within counselling or psychotherapy organisations, it may be important that the whole service – and not just their practice – embodies these principles of shared decision-making. This means ensuring service users have a collective voice and are involved in service level decisions, as well as in their individual support/care. This requires a range of approaches, which may include service users being involved in such areas as staff recruitment, training and governance as representatives on the board of trustees.

CRITICAL REFLECTIONS

On the face of it, what could be problematic about talking to clients about their therapy and involving them in their treatment? Of course, doing so is predicated on the notion that clients can articulate both what they want and what they need therapeutically and that therapists can help them do so explicitly. However, assuming that therapists can help clients do this, there are two situations in which some pluralistic practitioners may struggle with these principles.

First, clients who see effective therapists as experts may regard being asked for their views of therapeutic issues and for feedback about therapy as evidence that the therapist does not know what he or she is doing, and would thus see such practitioners as ineffective. Here, pluralistic therapists who are drawn towards this approach for philosophical and ethical reasons may struggle to eschew, or tailor, this way of working. However, therapists who are more pragmatically pluralistic, and whose therapeutic range incorporates the possibility of practising as an expert, would have less of a problem setting aside metatherapeutic communication.

Second, when clients are asked about their views about therapy and what they may find helpful, they may propose processes and activities about which they feel comfortable but which may not lead to an effective outcome. This may be one reason why the research evidence does not show a stronger association between shared decision-making and therapeutic outcomes. There are, of course, times in therapy when the comfort of clients is paramount. This is particularly the case at the outset when clients will only truly open up to their therapists when they feel safe to do so. However, there are times when it may be helpful for clients to push themselves, or be pushed by their therapists, into zones of discomfort if they are to meet their long-term goals. Here, pluralistic practitioners who go along uncritically with their clients' preferences for comfort may not serve their clients' best interest. On the other hand, therapists who give a clear rationale for clients to go against their preferences for comfort, and who are persuasive in this respect, may be more effective with their clients in the longer term.

SUMMARY

Metatherapeutic communication is a process of talking to clients about what they want and prefer in therapy, and parallels shared decision-making in the wider healthcare field. Metatherapeutic communication is important because, in many instances, therapists do not know what works best for clients in therapy; and many clients want to be more involved in decisions about their care and can make a valuable contribution to metatherapeutic decisions. Talking to clients about these issues can help them feel more satisfied with the therapy, more empowered and less likely to drop out – and it may also make some contribution to clinical outcomes. Metatherapeutic communication can take place at different points in therapy; it can be focused on the therapeutic goals, methods, content or understandings; and it can be about past, present, or future periods of therapy. In terms of practice, it is probably best to address metatherapeutic issues from the start of therapy, but it should be considered an ongoing process. Therapists should actively invite clients to share their views; but should also take an active role themselves: be willing to challenge clients, and encourage them – where appropriate – to move beyond their comfort zones. Therapists can also be particularly helpful in laying out the options for clients, introducing measures and tailoring the levels of metatherapeutic communication to the particular client's needs.

EXERCISES/POINTS FOR REFLECTION

1 When, and how, might it be most helpful to communicate about metatherapeutic issues with clients?
2 How can we, most effectively, create an environment where clients feel able to openly and honestly communicate their metatherapeutic wants and preferences?
3 What is the *process* by which metatherapeutic communication can be beneficial to clients?
4 How can therapists be trained to develop metatherapeutic practices?

> **FURTHER READING**
>
> Cooper, M., & McLeod, J. (2011). *Pluralistic counselling and psychotherapy*. London: Sage. Ch. 3: Building a collaborative relationship. Practical guidance on metatherapeutic communication.
>
> Makoul, G., & Clayman, M. (2006). An integrative model of shared decision making in medical encounters. *Patient Education and Counselling, 60*, 301–312. Classic paper on shared decision-making.
>
> Rennie, D.L. (1998). *Person-centred counselling: an experiential approach*. London: Sage. Ch. 8: Metacommunication. Explores the nature and forms of metacommunication in therapy.
>
> The Health Foundation. (2014). *Person-centred care: from ideas to action*. London: The Health Foundation. Excellent, accessible review of the evidence on shared decision-making.

REFERENCES

Andrews, K. (2011). *Client narratives of perceived helpful factors of person centred therapy.* Doctorate in Counselling Psychology Dissertation, University of Strathclyde/Glasgow Caledonian University, Glasgow.

Aylindar, S. (2014). *The Therapy Personalisation Form.* Unpublished doctoral thesis, University of Strathclyde, Glasgow.

Cooper, M. (2008). *Essential research findings in counselling and psychotherapy: the facts are friendly.* London: Sage.

Cooper, M. (2015). *Existential psychotherapy and counselling: contributions to a pluralistic practice.* London: Sage.

Cooper, M., & McLeod, J. (2011). *Pluralistic counselling and psychotherapy.* London: Sage.

Cooper, M., & McLeod, J. (2012). From either/or to both/and: developing a pluralistic approach to counselling and psychotherapy. *European Journal of Psychotherapy and Counselling, 14*(1), 5–18.

Cooper, M., & Norcross, J.C. (2015). A brief, multidimensional measure of clients' therapy preferences: the Cooper-Norcross Inventory of Preferences (C-NIP). *International Journal of Clinical and Health Psychology.* Manuscript accepted for publication. doi: 10.10.16/j.ijchp.2015.08.003.

Cooper, M., Wild, C., van Rijn, B., Ward, T., McLeod, J., Cassar, S., . . . Sreenath, S. (2015). Pluralistic therapy for depression: acceptability, outcomes and helpful aspects in a multisite open-label trial. *Counselling Psychology Review, 30*(1), 6–20.

Coulter, A., & Collins, A. (2011). *Making shared decision-making a reality: no decision about me, without me.* London: The Kings Fund.

Duncan, E., Best, C., & Hagen, S. (2010). Shared decision making interventions for people with mental health conditions. *Cochrane Database Systematic Review, 1.*

Loh, A., Leonhart, R., Wills, C.E., Simon, D., & Härter, M. (2007). The impact of patient participation on adherence and clinical outcome in primary care of depression. *Patient Education and Counseling, 65*(1), 69–78.

Makoul, G., & Clayman, M. (2006). An integrative model of shared decision making in medical encounters. *Patient Education and Counselling, 60*, 301–312.

Papayianni, F., & Cooper, M. (2015). Metatherapeutic communication: a thematic analysis of therapist-reported moments of dialogue regarding the nature of the therapeutic work. Manuscript submitted for publication.

Rennie, D.L. (1994). Clients' deference in psychotherapy. *Journal of Counseling Psychology, 41*(4), 427–437.

Simmons, M.B., Hetrick, S.E., & Jorm, A.F. (2011). Experiences of treatment decision making for young people diagnosed with depressive disorders: a qualitative study in primary care and specialist mental health settings. *BMC Psychiatry, 11*, 194–194.

Swift, J.K., Callahan, J.L., & Vollmer, B.M. (2011). Preferences. In J.C. Norcross (Ed.), *Psychotherapy relationships that work* (2nd ed., pp. 301–315). New York: Oxford University Press.

The Health Foundation. (2012). *Helping people share decision making*. London: The Health Foundation.

The Health Foundation. (2014). *Person-centred care: from ideas to action*. London: The Health Foundation.

Thompson, A. (2013). *Development of a self-report measure of pluralistic thinking, practice and collaboration*. University of Strathclyde/Glasgow Caledonian University, Glasgow.

Wolpert, M., Hoffman, J., Abrines, N., Feltham, A., Baird, L., Law, D., … Hopkins, K. (2014). *Closing the gap: shared decision making in CAMHs. Final report for closing the gap through changing relationship*. London: The Health Foundation.

5

Systematic Feedback through the Partners for Change Outcome Management System (PCOMS)

Barry L. Duncan[1] and Jacqueline A. Sparks

However beautiful the strategy, you should occasionally look at the results.

Sir Winston Churchill

THIS CHAPTER DISCUSSES

- Systematic feedback and the Partners for Change Outcome Management System (PCOMS)
- PCOMS as a way to truly privilege clients, include them as full partners in decision-making and operationalize social justice and a pluralistic approach

Psychotherapy is a good news, bad news scenario. The good news is that therapy works – the average treated person is better off than about 80% of the untreated sample. The bad news is that, despite overall efficacy, many clients do not benefit,

---

[1] Correspondence should be directed to Barry L. Duncan, Psy.D., PO Box 6157, Jensen Beach, Florida 34957, USA or barrylduncan@comcast.net. Duncan is a co-holder of the copyright of the PCOMS family of instruments. The measures are free for individual use but Duncan receives royalties from licences issued to groups and organizations. In addition, the web-based application of PCOMS, BetterOutcomesNow.com is a commercial product and he receives profits based on sales.

dropouts are a problem, and therapists vary significantly in success rates, are poor judges of client negative outcomes and don't have a clue about their effectiveness (Duncan, 2014).

The Partners for Change Outcome Management System (PCOMS) offers a solution to these problems (Duncan, 2012). PCOMS employs two, 4-item scales: one focuses on outcome (the Outcome Rating Scale; ORS) and the other assesses the therapeutic alliance (the Session Rating Scale; SRS). It includes a real-time collaborative comparison of client views of outcome with an expected treatment response that serves as a yardstick for gauging client progress and signalling when change is not occurring as predicted. With this alert, counsellors and clients have an opportunity to shift focus, re-visit goals, or alter interventions before deterioration or dropout. PCOMS has been shown to improve outcomes in five randomized controlled trials (RCT) and is included in the Substance Abuse and Mental Health Services Administration's (SAMHSA) National Registry of Evidence-based Programs and Practices (NREPP).

PCOMS is one approach of what is called *systematic feedback*. Although systematic feedback systems vary significantly in the measures used, empirical support and clinical processes, all share the desire to measure the client's response to service (the outcome), and feed that information back to the therapist (or to both client and counsellor) to enhance the possibility of a positive outcome. Two other systems are worthy of note and exploration. First is the Outcome Questionnaire-45.2 System (OQ; Lambert, 2010). Michael Lambert is the pioneer of systematic feedback, evolving the idea of outcome measurement to a 'real time' feedback process with a proven track record of improving outcomes. The central measure is the OQ-45, a self-report measure with 45 items targeting symptoms, emotional states, interpersonal relationships and social role performance. With seven RCTs supporting it, the OQ System is the only other system included in the SAMHSA National Registry. For more information, see www.oqmeasures.com. Second is the Clinical Outcomes in Routine Evaluation-Outcome Measure (CORE-OM; Barkham, Hardy, & Mellor-Clark, 2010). This is a practical and widely used system in the UK. The central measure is the CORE-OM, a 34-item self-report questionnaire, tapping the domains of subjective well-being, problems, functioning and risk. It is administered before and after therapy (10- and 5-item versions are used for tracking in between). For more information, see www.coreims.co.uk.

If someone told you that by having your clients answer four brief questions at the beginning and end of each session you triple their chances of having a successful outcome, would you say: 'Na, too much trouble?' That's exactly what PCOMS brings to the table. A meta-analytic review (Lambert & Shimokawa, 2011) of three of the five PCOMS studies ($N = 558$) reported that clients in the feedback group had 3.5 times higher odds of experiencing reliable change and less than half the chance of experiencing deterioration than treatment as usual (TAU). This chapter intends to give you enough about the Partners for Change Outcome Management System to get you started. In addition to its empirical support and feasibility, PCOMS offers a way to operationalize a therapy that privileges the client, prioritizes the relationship and seeks full partnership with clients about all decisions that affect their care – or in other words, a pluralistic approach.

PCOMS AND A PLURALISTIC APPROACH

> To exchange one orthodoxy for another is not necessarily an advance. The enemy is the gramophone mind, whether or not one agrees with the record that is being played at the moment.
>
> George Orwell, 1972

PCOMS boils down to this: partnering with clients to identify those who aren't responding and addressing the lack of progress in a proactive way that keeps clients engaged while new directions are collaboratively sought. Five RCTs, the largest benchmarking study ever conducted in public behavioural health, and a cohort study have unequivocally shown that PCOMS improves outcomes with youth and adults, in individual, couple and group therapy, with both mental health and substance abuse problems, and with the impoverished and disenfranchised (for a review of these studies conducted by the Heart and Soul of Change Project, see Duncan, 2014; to download these studies, visit https://heartandsoulofchange.com).

Although PCOMS is designated as an evidence-based practice, it is not your average evidence-based practice – not a specific treatment model for a specific client diagnosis. PCOMS has demonstrated significant improvements for both clients and counsellors regardless of therapist theoretical orientation or client diagnosis. More importantly, PCOMS is evidence-based at the individual client–counsellor level, promoting a partnership that monitors whether *this* approach provided by *this* therapist is benefiting *this* client. In other words, it is *evidence-based practice one client at a time*.

PCOMS, consequently, lines up very well with both a *pluralistic perspective* and *pluralistic practice* (Cooper & McLeod, 2011). A pluralistic perspective posits that different clients are likely to benefit from different things, and that therapists should work closely with clients to help them identify what they want from therapy and how they might achieve it. *Pluralistic practice* is an approach to therapy based on a pluralistic perspective that draws on techniques from multiple orientations, and is characterized by ongoing negotiation with clients about the goals, tasks and methods of therapy.

PCOMS operationalizes a pluralistic approach in several ways. First, PCOMS does not drag any theoretical baggage to the therapeutic journey – it neither explains client problems nor offers any solutions. PCOMS is consequently pluralistic in its scope and encourages an individually tailored therapy that emerges from the client's idiosyncratic strengths, cultural worldview and theory of change (Duncan, Solovey, & Rusk, 1992). When services are provided without intimate connection to those receiving them and to their responses and preferences, clients become cardboard cut-outs, the object of our professional deliberations. Valuing clients as credible sources of their own experiences of progress and relationship allows clients to teach us how we can be the most effective with them, consistent with a pluralistic perspective.

A pluralistic approach values dialogue and negotiation and PCOMS provides a ready-made structure at the top and bottom of the hour for that to happen. It ensures therapy's match with a client's preferred future via monitoring progress on the ORS.

And it provides a way to ensure therapy's alignment with a client's goals and preferred way of achieving goals via monitoring the relationship with the SRS. Thus, PCOMS promotes the values of social justice by privileging client voice over manuals and theories, enabling idiosyncratic and culturally responsive practice with diverse clientele. Clients determine the fit and benefit of services as well as intervention preferences. This is the essence of a pluralistic approach.

THE PARTNERS FOR CHANGE OUTCOME MANAGEMENT SYSTEM

> The only man I know who behaves sensibly is my tailor; he takes my measurements anew each time he sees me. The rest go on with their old measurements and expect me to fit them.
>
> George Bernard Shaw, 1903

PCOMS embraces two known predictors of ultimate treatment outcome. Time and again, studies reveal that the majority of clients experience the majority of change in the first eight visits (e.g., Baldwin, Berkeljon, Atkins, Olsen, & Nielsen, 2009). Clients who report little or no progress early on will likely show no improvement over the entire course of therapy, or will end up on the drop-out list. Monitoring change provides a tangible way to identify those who are not responding so that a new course can be charted. A second robust predictor of change solidly demonstrated by a large body of studies, is that taken-for-granted old friend, the therapeutic alliance. Clients who highly rate their partnership with their therapists are more apt to remain in therapy and benefit from it.

PCOMS starts with the Outcome Rating Scale (ORS; Miller, Duncan, Brown, Sparks, & Claud, 2003) or the Child ORS (Duncan, Sparks, Miller, Bohanske, & Claud, 2006), which is used for children aged 6–12 and their caregivers. Adolescents use the ORS (both measures are free for individual use and inexpensive for groups; download at https://heartandsoulofchange.com). The ORS and CORS are given at the beginning of a session and provide client-reported ratings of progress (as well as caregiver ratings for youth). An inspection of Figure 5.1 reveals that the ORS and CORS are visual analogue scales consisting of four 10 centimetre lines, corresponding to four domains (individual, interpersonal, social and overall). Clients place a mark on each line to represent their perception of their functioning in each domain. Therapists use a 10 cm ruler (or available software) to sum the client's total score, with a maximum score of 40. Lower scores reflect more distress.

The Session Rating Scale (SRS) (Duncan et al., 2003) and Child SRS, both 4-item visual analogue scales covering the classic elements of the alliance (Bordin, 1979), are given toward the end of a therapy session. The CSRS is for children 6–12 years; adolescents use the SRS. Similar to the ORS, each line on the SRS or CSRS

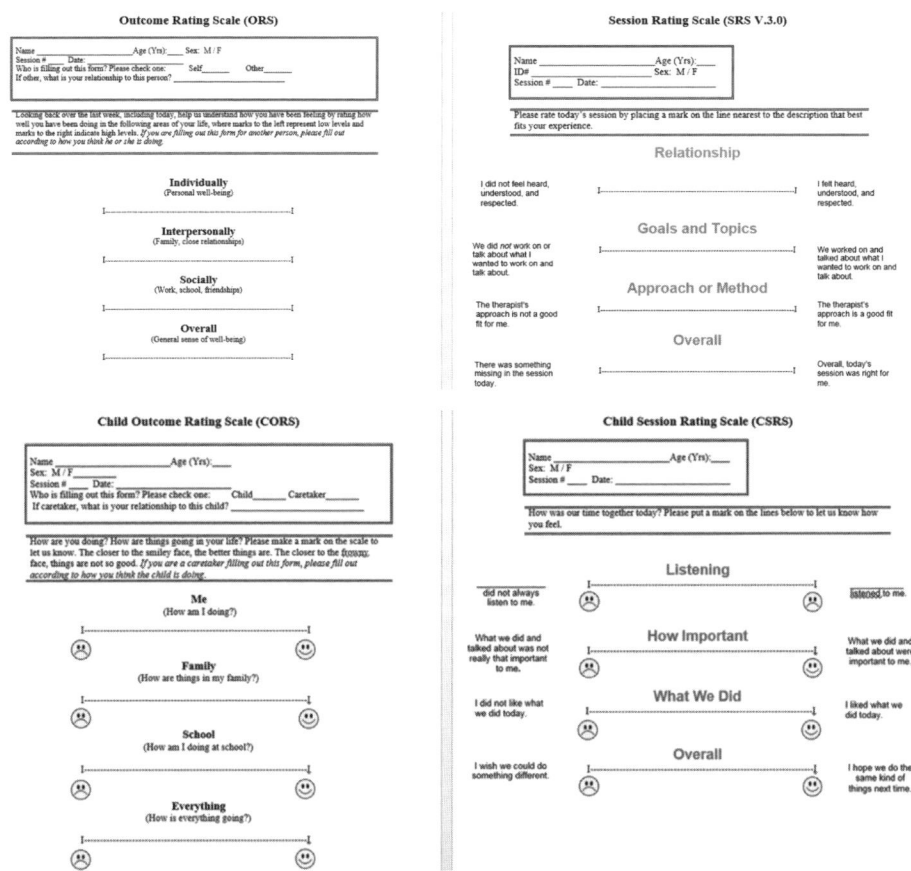

FIGURE 5.1   The Outcome Rating Scale (ORS), Session Rating Scale (SRS), Child ORS and Child SRS. Copyright 2000, 2002, 2003 and 2003, respectively by B. L. Duncan, S.D. Miller (for the ORS, SRS, CORS, CSRS), and J.A. Sparks (for the CORS and CSRS). Reprinted with permission. For examination only. Download free working copies at https://heartandsoulofchange.com

is 10 cm and can be scored manually or electronically. Use of the SRS encourages all client feedback, positive and negative, thus creating a safe space for clients to voice their reactions to therapy and expectations for it.

THE CLINICAL PROCESS

PCOMS is a light-touch, checking-in process that usually takes about 5 minutes but never over 10 to administer, score and integrate into the therapy. PCOMS works best as a way to gently guide models and techniques toward the client's perspective, with a focus on outcome. Besides the brevity of its measures and feasibility for everyday use in the demanding schedules of front-line clinicians, PCOMS is distinguished by its routine involvement of clients in all aspects of counselling; client scores on the ORS and SRS are openly shared and discussed at each administration. Client views of progress serve as a basis for beginning therapeutic conversations, and their assessments of the alliance mark an endpoint to the same. With this transparency, the measures provide a mutually understood reference point for reasons for seeking service, progress and engagement.

Given that at its heart PCOMS is a collaborative intervention, it is important that clients understand two points: (1) the ORS (or CORS) is a way to make sure that the client's voice is not only heard but remains central; and (2) the ORS will be used to track outcome in every session. In the first meeting, the ORS pinpoints where the client sees him- or herself, allowing for an ongoing comparison in later sessions.

Since everything about PCOMS is 100% transparent, the task after the score is totalled is to make sense of it with the final authority – the client. The 'clinical cutoff' facilitates a shared understanding of the ORS and is often a step toward connecting client marks on the ORS to the reason for services. Twenty-five is the cutoff for adults, meaning that, on average, persons seeking therapy will fall below that, and those not typically seeking counselling will score above. For those scoring below the cutoff, the therapist can assure them that they made a good decision to come in. For those scoring above the cutoff, counsellors can simply validate their score by saying that it looks like things are going pretty well, which leads to the next logical question – what are the reasons for meeting now? But importantly, even if clients score above the cutoff there will be one scale lower than the rest that typically signals the reason for service.

> *Therapist:* What I do is I just measure this up, it's four 10 cm lines and it gives a score from 0 to 40 and I just pull out this ruler and add up the scores, and then I will tell you about what this says and you can tell me whether it is accurate or not, and then we will have an anchor point to measure each time and see if you're getting what you came here to get … Okay, you scored a 19.8. And what that means is that this scale, the Outcome Rating Scale, has a cutoff of 25 and people who score under 25 tend to be those who wind up talking to people like me, they're looking for something different in their lives. You scored about the average intake score of persons who enter therapy, so you're in the right place. And it's not hard to look at this and see pretty quickly that it's the family/close relationship area is what you are struggling with the most right now. Does that make sense?
> *Client:* Yes, definitely.
> *Therapist:* So what do you think would be the most useful thing for us to talk about?
> *Client:* Well, I am in the middle of divorce and struggling with figuring this out …

Give the score, say what it might mean, and look for feedback to see if it fits. What you will find in 99 out of 100 administrations in the first meeting is that clients mark lowest the scale that they are there to talk about. The above client did just that. The initial ORS score is an instant snapshot of how the client views him- or herself. It brings an understanding of the client's experience to the opening minutes of a session.

Unlike other outcome scales, the ORS is not a list of symptoms or problems checked by clients or others on a Likert Scale. It is individually tailored by design. This requires that the counsellor ensure that the ORS represents both the client's experience and the reasons for service – that the general framework of client distress evolves into a specific account of the work done in therapy. Clients usually mark lowest the scale that represents the reason they are seeking therapy, and often connect that reason to the mark they've made without prompting from the therapist. Other times, the counsellor needs to clarify the connection between the client's descriptions of the reasons for services and the client's marks on the ORS. At the moment clients connect the marks on the ORS with the situations that prompt their seeking help, the ORS becomes a meaningful measure of progress and a potent clinical tool. And that moment facilitates the next question: 'What do you think it will take to move your mark just one centimetre to the right; what needs to happen out there and in here?'

With the same client as above:

Therapist: If I am getting this right, you said that you are struggling with the divorce, specifically about why it happened and your part in it so you are looking to explore this and gain some insight into what perhaps was your contribution. You marked the Interpersonally scale the lowest [*Therapist picks up the ORS*]. Does that mark represent this struggle and your longing for some clarity?

Client: Yes.

Therapist: So, if we are able to explore this situation and reach some insights that resonate with you, do you think that it would move that mark to the right?

Client: Yes, that is what I am hoping for and that's what I think will help me. I know I wasn't perfect in the relationship and I want to understand my part. I already know his part!

The SRS (or CSRS) opens space for the client's voice about the alliance. It is given at the end of the meeting, leaving enough time for discussing the client's responses. Given that clients tend to score high on alliance measures, a total score below 36 signals the possibility of a problematic alliance and prompts a frank discussion about steps needed to increase client connection to the therapist and the process. Regardless of the score, the SRS focuses attention on the alliance, and therefore helps build strong ones.

After the first session, PCOMS simply asks: are things better? We are hoping for a six-point increase on the ORS, what is called a *reliable change*, or a six-point increase *and* crossing the clinical cutoff, what is called a *clinically significant change*. ORS scores are used to engage the client in a discussion about progress, and more importantly, what should be done differently if there isn't any. When ORS scores increase, a crucial step to empower the change is to help clients see any gains as a consequence of their own efforts. This requires an exploration of the clients' perception of the relationship between their own efforts and the occurrence of change (Duncan et al., 1992). When clients have reached a plateau or what may be the maximum benefit they will derive from counselling, planning for continued recovery outside of therapy can start.

A more important discussion occurs when ORS scores are not increasing. The longer therapy continues without measurable change, the greater the likelihood of drop out and/or poor outcome. The ORS stimulates such a conversation so that both interested parties may struggle with the implications of continuing a process that is yielding little or no benefit. Although addressed in each meeting in which it is apparent that no benefit is occurring, later sessions gain increasing significance and warrant additional action including referral of the client to another counsellor – what we have called *checkpoint conversations* and *last chance discussions* (Duncan, 2014).

In a typical outpatient setting, checkpoint conversations are conducted at the third to sixth session and last-chance discussions are initiated in the sixth to ninth meeting. This is simply saying that the trajectories observed in most outpatient settings suggest that most clients who benefit from services usually show it in sessions 3–6; and if change is not noted by then, then the client is at a risk for a negative outcome. The same goes for sessions 6–9 except that the urgency is increased, hence the term 'last chance'. An available web-based system provides a more sophisticated identification of clients at risk by comparing the client's progress to the expected treatment response of clients with the same intake score.

The progression of the conversation with clients who are not benefiting goes from talking about whether something different should be done, to identifying what can be done differently, to doing something different. Doing something different can include, for example, inviting others from the client's support system, using a team, developing a different conceptualization of the problem, trying another therapy approach, or referring to another counsellor or venue of service such as a religious adviser or self-help group – whatever seems to be of value to the client.

CASE EXAMPLE

Ken

Ken, a 35-year-old construction supervisor, was convinced that he was going crazy because panic attacks were becoming ever more intrusive. He scored a 14.2 on the ORS at intake, indicating a high level of distress. Ken said he was at a loss about what to do and looked to the therapist for something to manage the anxiety. Trying to address his request, the therapist called up training in CBT (see Chapter 9, this volume) and strategic therapy and suggested a combination of relaxation training, challenging the beliefs that led to the panic, and some strategic monitoring (symptom prescription). But nothing happened, and none of these approaches seemed to resonate much with Ken – his scores on the ORS hovered around 14.

> So, in the fourth meeting, the therapist and client renegotiated, via the *approach* scale on the SRS. Ken intimated that maybe he could try to understand why he was having panic attacks. Ken also shared during this quiet negotiation that in tough times he always talked to his dad, but his dad had passed away some 6 months before. He noted that he felt alone in his struggles, although he knew that really wasn't true because his wife was supportive and he had some good friends. The therapist enquired if Ken believed there was a connection between his father's death, his feeling of aloneness and the panic. Ken replied with tears, and a quiet yes.
>
> A different kind of discussion ensued, drawing on the therapist's existential training (see Chapter 11, this volume), of not only Ken's confrontation of his own mortality but also the incredible dread that accompanies the realization of our essential aloneness in the world. A new theory of change evolved, one that seemed to make a lot of sense within the four big existential givens: death, freedom, isolation and meaninglessness. Ken found these conversations useful, and after four more meetings his panic attacks subsided and ultimately stopped; his ORS scores increased to 24.6 (a reliable change nearly to the clinical cutoff).
>
> What PCOMS brought to the table is that it spotlighted the lack of change. Impossible to dismiss, it brought the risk of a negative outcome front and centre. Without the findings from the ORS, the therapist might have continued with the same strategies for several more sessions, hoping that these reasonable methods would eventually take hold. As it was, the evidence obtained through PCOMS pushed both Ken and the therapist to explore different options.

This story, of course, says nothing about the value of CBT, strategic, or existentially informed therapy – all approaches provide useful ideas to pursue. Rather, Ken's therapy illustrates that first identifying clients who are not responding, and then re-exploring the client's perspectives about change, things that resonate better with the client, can enable different, more fruitful directions. This is what pluralistic, or what we have called 'client-directed', counselling is all about.

LIMITATIONS OF PCOMS

Even though the research is compelling, most counsellors do not monitor outcomes. There are several reasons. First, finding out how effective you really are can be a risky business. You might learn something that you might not want to – but the only way to get better is to know where you are now versus where you would like to be; to aspire for the best results, and take action to get them. But the good news here is that we know it works. In our large feedback study with couples, 9 out of 10 therapists improved their outcomes with feedback (Anker, Duncan, & Sparks, 2009).

Another reason is that, on the whole, counsellors don't like the idea of 'assessment' or numbers. But this is different because PCOMS invites clients into the inner circle, amplifying their voices in any decisions about their care. The numbers don't mean reducing clients to statistics. Rather, the numbers represent clients' own assessments of progress. Without them, clients' views do not stand a chance to be part of the real record – that is, critical information that guides moment-by-moment, week-by-week, decisions or evaluates eventual outcomes.

A third reason is that many believe they already know the information PCOMS is designed to provide. In fact, in the couple study (Anker et al., 2009), all 10 of the therapists indicated that they already informally acquired outcome and alliance information and, moreover, that systematic feedback would not improve their effectiveness. Nine of the 10 *did* improve their outcomes, so only one of them was correct.

Finally, a concern sometimes voiced before PCOMS is tried is that some clients won't want to do PCOMS. In truth, clients very rarely say 'no' to PCOMS when a sincere, authentic therapist conveys that the ORS and the SRS are to ensure their voice stays central as well as making sure they benefit. But the therapist has to believe that this is true and use the measures in a way that makes them meaningful to the work. If the ORS is treated as a perfunctory piece of paper that is not related to the therapeutic process, then clients will see it similarly. However, if the client persists in refusal after further clarification of the purpose of PCOMS, then it is likely best to move on with the session.

CONCLUSIONS

At bottom every man [sic] knows well enough that he is a unique being, only once on this earth; and by no extraordinary chance will such a marvellously picturesque piece of diversity in unity as he is, ever be put together a second time.

Friedrich Nietzsche, 1874

Routinely measuring outcome and the alliance with every client ensures that neither issue is left to chance. This allows both transparency and true partnership with clients, keeping their perspectives the centrepiece. In addition, it serves as an early warning device that identifies clients who are not benefiting so that the client and the therapist can chart a different course. This in turn encourages the counsellor to step outside of business as usual, do new things and therefore continue to grow as a therapist. Finally, PCOMS improves focus on what matters most to the client both in terms of what needs to change outside of therapy as well as during the hour. Although it sounds like hyperbole, identifying clients who are not benefiting is the single most important thing a therapist can do to improve outcomes – 12 RCTs (both PCOMS and OQ System) now support this assertion.

But it requires the therapist to show up. If the counsellor doesn't authentically value clients' perspectives and believe that they should be active participants, PCOMS will fall flat. In addition, without therapist investment into the spirit of partnership of the feedback process, little gain is likely to happen. It's not enough to flick the forms in the face of the client – the feedback must be used and allowed to influence the work.

PCOMS and pluralistic practice call for a more sophisticated and empirically informed clinician who chooses from a variety of orientations and methods to best fit client preferences and cultural values. Although there has not been convincing evidence for differential efficacy among approaches, there is indeed differential effectiveness for the client in the room now – therapists need expertise in a broad range of intervention options, including evidence-based treatments, but must remember that, however beautiful the strategy, one must occasionally look at the results.

SUMMARY

The key points of this chapter are:

- Twelve RCTs (both OQ System and PCOMS) demonstrate that systematic feedback improves outcomes by recapturing clients who are headed toward a negative end.
- PCOMS is the only system that includes routine alliance monitoring and that is, by design, intended to be collaborative and transparent.
- PCOMS operationalizes a pluralistic approach (and social justice) by providing a methodology for individually tailoring counselling to client goals and preferences, and privileging client perspectives over model and theory.

EXERCISES/POINTS FOR REFLECTION

1. Download the PCOMS family of measures from heartandsoulofchange.com or pcoms.com. The measures are free for individual use. Simply click on 'Get measures' on the homepage, indicate your understanding of the License Agreement, register your email (no marketing materials sent), and download the measures in 24 languages.
2. Watch the free webinars at heartandsoulofchange.com. Click on 'PCOMS 101' on the cascading slide or on 'Training' on the menu. 'PCOMS Video' is a good place to start and includes the nuts and bolts of using the measures.
3. Reflect whether systematic feedback fits into your value system and can become integrated into your authentic practice of psychotherapy. PCOMS (or anything else) doesn't 'work' without your investment of yourself and your genuine desire to partner with clients and appreciate their feedback.

> **FURTHER READING**
>
> https://heartandsoulofchange.com. Contains more than 250 free resources including webinars, articles, chapters and slide handouts.
>
> Duncan, B.L. (2014). *On becoming a better therapist: evidence-based practice one client at a time* (2nd ed.). Washington, DC: American Psychological Association. 'All in one' source for PCOMS, the common factors, and how to become a better therapist.
>
> Duncan, B.L., & Reese, R.J. (2012). Empirically supported treatments, evidence based treatments, and evidence based practice. In G. Stricker & T. Widiger (Eds.), *Handbook of psychology: Volume 8: Clinical psychology* (2nd ed., pp. 977–1023). New York: Wiley. Comprehensive resource covering the controversy about evidence-based treatments.
>
> Duncan, B., & Sparks, J. (2010). *Heroic clients, heroic agencies: partners for change* (2nd ed.). Jensen Beach, FL: Author. Practical, how-to 'manual' for client-directed work and PCOMS that is consistent with a pluralistic approach. The first edition (2002) presented the original articulation of the clinical use of the ORS/SRS.
>
> Kottler, J., & Carlson, J. (2014). *On being a master therapist: practicing what you preach*. New York: Wiley. Great resource from two renowned psychotherapists.

REFERENCES

Anker, M., Duncan, B., & Sparks, J. (2009). Using client feedback to improve couple therapy outcomes: a randomized clinical trial in a naturalistic setting. *Journal of Consulting and Clinical Psychology, 77*, 693–704.

Baldwin, S., Berkeljon, A., Atkins, D., Olsen, J., & Nielsen, S. (2009). Rates of change in naturalistic psychotherapy: contrasting dose-effect and good-enough level models of change. *Journal of Consulting and Clinical Psychology, 77*, 203–211.

Barkham, M., Hardy, G., & Mellor-Clark, J. (2010). *Developing and delivering practice-based evidence: a guide for the psychological therapies*. Chichester: Wiley Blackwell.

Bordin, E. (1979). The generalizability of the psychoanalytic concept of the working alliance. *Psychotherapy, 16*, 252–260.

Cooper, M., & McLeod, J. (2011). *Pluralistic counselling and psychotherapy*. London: Sage.

Duncan, B.L. (2012). The Partners for Change Outcome Management System (PCOMS): the heart and soul of change project. *Canadian Psychology, 53*, 93–104.

Duncan, B.L. (2014). *On becoming a better therapist: evidence-based practice one client at a time* (2nd ed.). Washington, DC: American Psychological Association.

Duncan, B.L., Miller, S., Sparks, J., Claud, D., Reynolds, L., Brown, J., & Johnson, L. (2003). The Session Rating Scale: preliminary psychometric properties of a 'working' alliance measure. *Journal of Brief Therapy, 3*, 3–12.

Duncan, B.L., Solovey, A., & Rusk, G. (1992). *Changing the rules: a client-directed approach to therapy*. New York: The Guilford Press.

Duncan, B.L., Sparks, J., Miller, S., Bohanske, R., & Claud, D. (2006). Giving youth a voice: a preliminary study of the reliability and validity of a brief outcome measure for children. *Journal of Brief Therapy, 5*(1), 5–22.

Lambert, M. (2010). *Prevention of treatment failure: the use of measuring, monitoring, and feedback in clinical practice.* Washington, DC: American Psychological Association.

Lambert, M., & Shimokawa, K. (2011). Collecting client feedback. *Psychotherapy, 48,* 72–79.

Miller, S., Duncan, B., Brown, J., Sparks, J., & Claud, D. (2003). The outcome rating scale: a preliminary study of the reliability, validity, and feasibility of a brief visual analog measure. *Journal of Brief Therapy, 2,* 91–100.

Nietzsche, F. (1874). Schopenhauer as educator. *Untimely meditations.*

Orwell, G. (1972). The freedom of the press. *The Times Literary Supplement,* 15 September.

Shaw, G.B. (1903). *Man and superman.*

6
Client Strengths and Resources: Helping Clients Draw on What They Already Do Best

Jacqueline A. Sparks[1] and
Barry L. Duncan

Until lions have their historians, tales of hunting will always glorify the hunter.

African Proverb

THIS CHAPTER DISCUSSES

- The empirical evidence supporting a strengths-based approach
- Specific practice guidelines for recruiting client resources to promote change
- The link between pluralistic counselling and a focus on client strengths

Have you ever noticed that the field of psychotherapy is egocentric or, more to the point, therapist-centric? Therapist theories and models fill textbooks and journal articles, dominating everyday practice procedures. From the first days of training, students learn about superstar theorists and therapists. Meanwhile, seasoned clinicians seek out expert-led workshops on the latest techniques. Where does the other half of therapy, the client, come in? True, client problems are well represented in the literature. But the talk is mostly about what *we* do – or what *we* do to *them*. In this drama, clients are little more than passive recipients of therapist interventions, or their contributions are characterized by problematic transference, resistance, cognitive distortions and the like (Bohart & Wade, 2013; Duncan, 2014).

This chapter challenges this view and makes the case that clients are the centrepieces in the counselling process; therapists' interventions succeed to the degree they engage clients and their inherent abilities. To do this, the chapter explores the empirical

---

[1]Correspondence should be directed to Jacqueline A. Sparks, Ph.D., 2 Lower College Road, Kingston, RI 02881, USA or jsparks@uri.edu.

evidence supporting a strengths-based approach and offers specific practice guidelines to help clinicians recruit client resources to promote change. The consistency between pluralistic counselling and a strengths-based approach is noted, and it is suggested that adopting this way of seeing and doing therapy can enhance psychotherapy outcomes.

EVIDENCE SUPPORTING A STRENGTHS-BASED APPROACH

A strengths-based approach views clients as the engines of change (Bohart & Tallman, 2009). Specifically, strengths-based therapists seek and utilize clients' personal, interpersonal, social and cultural resources to assist them in reaching their goals. This requires that clinicians first believe that clients have strengths that are available to resolve difficulties. Second, therapists must be able to recognize client strengths or elicit them when needed. Finally, therapists need to know how to integrate client strengths into effective treatment strategies. The first step is perhaps the most difficult as it involves therapists stepping out of ingrained ways of thinking, engendered, in particular, by psychotherapy's emphasis on client dysfunction. Without this conceptual shift, the ability to perceive and respond to what clients contribute is diminished.

While believing in client strengths may be inherently appealing, without empirical support, it can be easily dismissed as naïve or unrealistic. Researching client contributions to therapy is hampered by the magnitude of idiosyncratic client characteristics and responses to therapy which are difficult to manipulate experimentally. Nevertheless, two primary bodies of research shed light on the extent and quality of client contributions to the therapy process. The first consists of five decades of exploration into factors responsible for change, best known as common factors since they are shared by all bona fide treatment approaches. According to Duncan (2014), as much as 86% of psychotherapy outcome can be attributed to one of these, client/life factors. Client/life factors include all aspects idiosyncratic to the specific client and incidental to the treatment delivered (Lambert, 2013). In other words, they are anything having to do with the client and his or her life that aids in recovery apart from participation in therapy. For example, clients may have successfully negotiated life dilemmas in the past and have a stored set of usable strategies for dealing with their current dilemma. Or, a client may have a supportive grandmother, a strong religious affiliation, or a steady job. Client/life factors also include serendipitous events in clients' lives which create conditions that help them move toward recovery, as illustrated by the following:

> A mother who sought help for her eight-year-old son, Andrew, who regularly wet his bed, described a shift in the family structure when her ageing mother moved into their home. The extra time the mother now needed to tend to this new addition to the household catapulted her son into a new life stage. At his final session, Andrew proudly proclaimed that he could not keep depending on someone else all his life. He had assumed a more 'grown-up' role in the home, including managing his own laundry and his bed-wetting.

In contrast to client/life factors, the proportion of outcome variance attributable to treatment is modest. A casual inspection of Figure 6.1, with the small circle nested within the larger upper left circle representing treatment effects, reveals the disproportionate influence of what the client brings to therapy.

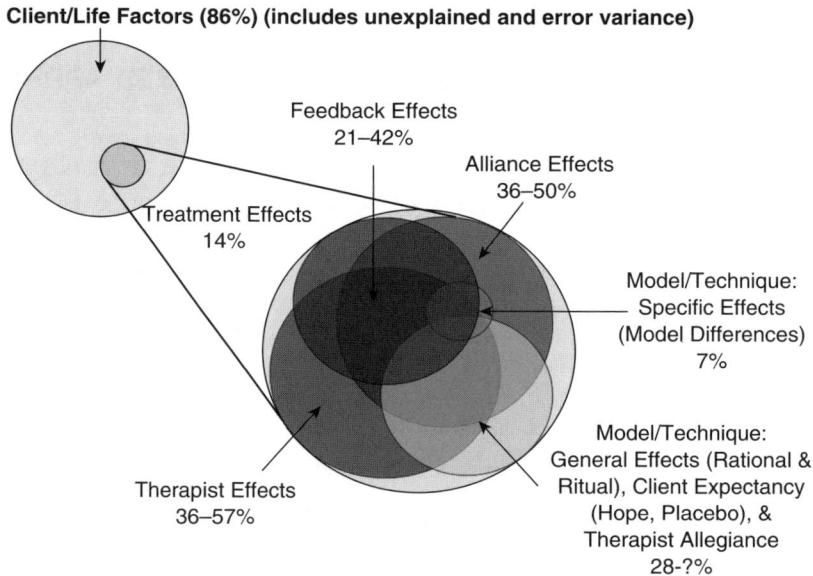

FIGURE 6.1 *Relative outcome variance of client/life factors and treatment effects*

Note: Percentages of common factors for the large bottom right circle reflect percentages relative to treatment effects (the small circle embedded in the large top left circle depicting 14%), not overall outcome variance. They are best viewed as meta-analytic estimates of each factor's contribution to treatment effects. Because of the overlap among these common factors, their separate percentages will not add upto 100%.

Other common factors depicted in the lower right circle include therapist, alliance, feedback, and the general effects of models and techniques, including hope and expectancy. Compare these factors to the specific effects of the differences between models and techniques. In all these factors, clients play major roles. Regarding therapist effects, those effects that represent the variance attributable not to a model but to whom the therapist is, studies have found that clients often assist therapists to meet their needs by such activities as redirecting them when they are not being helpful or modifying therapist blunders that threaten the process (Bohart & Tallman, 2009). Similarly, studies describe how clients use what therapists say or do to fit their unique goals and preferences for help (Bohart & Wade, 2013). Between sessions, therapists' interventions serve as triggers for client generativity, including personal reflection, self-questioning, or preparation for sessions that promote change in clients' everyday lives (Bohart & Wade, 2013).

Clients also play pivotal roles in the formation and maintenance of the therapeutic alliance, the partnership between the client and therapist to achieve the client's goals (Bordin, 1979). For example, instead of the alliance being created by therapists to benefit clients, clients actively participate in alliance-building, including expressing vulnerability, thereby eliciting therapist empathy, being willing to self-reveal to enhance connection, and engaging in prosocial behaviours such as humour and accommodation (Bohart & Wade, 2013). Client cooperation and collaboration have been cited as pivotal in the creation of change (Orlinsky, Rønnestad, & Willutzki 2004). Additionally, clients' perceptions of the therapeutic alliance, not therapists' or observers', are the best predictors of outcome (Bohart & Tallman, 2009; Duncan, 2014). Rather than their views being distorted by pathology, clients accurately assess what is most helpful for them. From this standpoint, it makes sense to gather client feedback about the alliance rather than rely on clinician judgements.

Finally, client hopefulness, sometimes referred to as the placebo effect, is a potent common factor that intersects with therapist and alliance factors to energize and sustain positive therapeutic momentum. Placebo effects involve the belief on the part of clients that therapy will be helpful. According to a review of 40 meta-analytic studies, the placebo effect has an effect size of .44 compared with no-treatment controls (Bohart & Tallman, 2009). Again, this important common factor centrally involves clients – their ability to enter therapy with the belief that it will be helpful and their propensity to maintain that belief as therapy progresses.

An additional body of literature speaks to the capacity of clients to self-heal. This research draws on both clinical and non-clinical studies. As an example, Gurin (1990) surveyed people who had experienced significant health, emotional, addiction, or lifestyle problems in the prior year and found that the vast majority (90%) reported having dealt with these difficulties successfully. Another study revealed that of the 50–60% of persons in the USA exposed to some type of trauma, only 5–10% actually develop posttraumatic stress; the rest find a way to move forward without major life disruption (Ozer, Best, Lipsey, & Weiss, 2008). In many instances, it appears that people never receiving professional help successfully use methods similar to those employed by psychotherapists (e.g., re-exposure after trauma) to restore well-being, without formal knowledge of what they are doing (Bohart & Tallman, 2009).

Even for diagnoses considered chronic and lifelong, recovery is not only possible but common (Bohart & Tallman, 2009). For example, studies show as much as an 88% recovery rate for persons diagnosed with borderline personality disorder over a 10-year period (Zanarini, Frankenburg, Hennen, Reich, & Silk, 2006). In a study of persons experiencing a first psychotic episode treated with the open dialogue approach (Seikkula et al., 2006), 79% were asymptomatic at 5 years. Eighty per cent were working, in school, or looking for work; two-thirds never took medications and only 20% regularly took psychiatric drugs. The possibility of return to health from even dire difficulties is underreported, likely engendering a pessimistic atmosphere among helpers as well as clients. Similarly, the idea that the more difficult the problem, the longer and more arduous the recovery, appears far from universal. The experience of sudden, significant personal transformation is, in fact, well documented and less rare than one would think (Bohart & Tallman, 2009). Prochaska, Norcross and DiClemente (1994) conclude that, in or out of therapy, all change is self-change; therapy change simply has the benefit of a coach.

Far from cardboard cut-outs that therapists target with their interventions, the research makes clear that clients are active, inventive players, pivotal in fashioning a successful psychotherapy process. Despite the evidence, clients still fail to register on the radar screen of most theoretical models of change. Unfortunately, this represents missed opportunities to capitalize on the most potent therapy resource. Given the literature, it only makes sense that counsellors recruit client idiosyncratic contributions to outcome in service of client goals. Indeed, Orlinsky et al. (2004), after a review of more than 1,000 process–outcome studies, observed that 'the quality of the patient's [sic] participation [emerges] as the *most* important determinate of outcome' (p. 324; emphasis added). It's the client's resources and strengths, the client's view of the alliance, the client's hope and expectation for change, and the client's preferences for intervention that drive therapy (Duncan, Solovey, & Rusk, 1992).

IMPLICATIONS FOR CLINICAL PRACTICE

With this knowledge in hand, clinicians can believe in their clients and learn how best to learn from them to construct effective treatment goals and strategies. The following example illustrates just what it means to believe in client strengths, even when it seems counter-intuitive:

> Ty called to make an appointment for himself and his wife, stating it was his last hope for his marriage. At the first session, he and Lisa, who made it quite clear she believed the meeting was a waste of time, described the depressing circumstances of their 10-year marriage. From their wedding day onward (with the exception of the past month), Ty would drink until he passed out. Numerous in-patient treatment programmes, AA meetings, and near misses with accidents and the law, did not deter his addiction. Now, believing that Lisa would leave him for sure this time, he claimed to be on a new path.

Given this couple's presentation, it might be easy to entertain thoughts that go something like: 'Don't get sucked in. Sure, he sounds sincere, they all do. As for Lisa, sounds like a serious case of co-dependency. He won't change unless she does.' A strengths-based narrative allows consideration of other possibilities. First, it makes room for heroic stories (Duncan, 2014). In this case, the counsellor (J.S.) wondered at Lisa's fortitude in the face of great disappointment, even abandonment. This position replaced a deficit-based view that would have communicated to her that she had done something wrong in holding their lives together for so long. Second, the counsellor entertained the possibility that Ty was genuinely remorseful for the hurt he had caused and desired to make amends. Importantly, the counsellor never once believed either was not capable of transforming their lives. This fundamental belief grounded all that was done from the first session forward.

Research indicates that therapists who choose to centre resources rather than problems in their conversations are more effective (Gassman & Grawe, 2006). There are several systems of therapy that include specific questions to help therapists tap into and amplify client strengths (e.g., Cooper & McLeod, 2011; de Jong & Berg, 2008; Duncan & Sparks, 2010). Solution-focused frames locate exceptions to problems and enquire about how those can become more frequent. With Ty, the therapist enquired into the details of how he had achieved an entire month of sobriety. She did this as a resource-based therapist, but also because of her desire to learn why and how people take radically different paths in their lives. She was asking him to teach her. These types of questions and listening to the responses they generate are undertaken in a spirit of genuine appreciation for people's struggles and their triumphs, even if it is a one-month hiatus from addiction.

One resource-based approach for counselling recommends that counsellors serve as witnesses to unrecognized aspects of clients' lives. What counsellors enquire about helps people identify events in their lives not included in 'problem saturated' stories (White & Epston, 1990: 16). For example, Ty's therapist asked who in his life would not be surprised that he could go another month without a drink. In response, Ty thought for a moment and settled on one friend. 'And what is it about you that your friend sees, that perhaps others don't, that tells him you can make it?' The discussion that followed rekindled Ty's faith in himself. Ty and the therapist then speculated whether those attributes could be harnessed to reclaim his life and his marriage. This conversation allowed Ty, with the therapist and Lisa as witnesses, to create a new story about who he was and what might be possible for his future.

The therapeutic alliance serves as a context for implementing a strengths-based approach. Bordin's (1979) classic definition of the alliance – the client's felt connection to the therapist and the agreement on the goals and tasks of therapy – helps to understand how the alliance and a resource focus complement one another. A strengths-based approach begins by respecting what clients bring to the counselling process and their inherent worth as a human being. This is Rogers's unconditional positive regard. A recent meta-analysis of 18 studies examining positive regard and outcome found a significant relationship, an r of .27 (Farber & Doolin, 2011), more potent than any technique. It stands to reason that when clients feel valued by their therapist, they are more likely to participate in therapy and also to revise negative beliefs about themselves. Recall, also, that this participation is the most crucial element of a positive outcome in psychotherapy.

The warm regard between the therapist and client is not enough, however. There must be a match between client goals and the therapist's focus in treatment, as well as agreement between client preferences in therapy and therapist activities. Establishing an understanding of what clients want and what tasks appropriately fit those wants is a crucial early stage of successful therapy (Cooper & McLeod, 2011), one especially challenging with couples:

> Ty wanted Lisa to move on from the past. Lisa's face, in response to this, said it all – 'Seriously?!' The therapist had to find a way to reconcile her view that Ty's recovery might be real, while also appreciating Lisa's reticence to 'just get over it'. She validated both their positions first and then stood in solidarity with Lisa. At the same time, she joined with Ty's goal by suggesting that proving to Lisa that this time was different would be the only way to begin to move toward normalizing his relationship with his wife. This strategy involved many detailed conversations where the balance of her alliance with each of them was always being negotiated.

A key factor in these conversations is the clinician's ability to maintain faith in the client's ability to change while matching their views of how this might happen. Routine tracking of the therapeutic alliance at each session enables therapists to determine if their approach fits for each client and to adjust it as needed (see Chapter 5, this volume). It also ensures clients' goals and preferred ways of working are honoured, thereby securing their active participation.

Finally, highlighting client progress is a hallmark of a strengths-based perspective. Counsellors working from this point of view are hyper-vigilant toward change, however small. Contrast this with deficit-based approaches where incidental mention of change generally gets overlooked as therapists focus on difficulties or setbacks.

> For Ty and Lisa, changes were hard to miss. Ty stopped seeing his drinking friends, painted the bedroom Lisa's favourite colour, and did not drink. Despite a 'wait and see' attitude the therapist adopted to match Lisa's, she commented on Ty's efforts, explored what differences they made, and asked about how he might continue them. She punctuated Ty's change rather than viewing it as insubstantial in light of the severity of his longstanding addiction.

In sum, capitalizing on client momentum means listening for, commenting on and exploring even the smallest change.

Change conversations are facilitated by use of systematic client feedback regarding progress:

> Within 4 weeks, Ty's reported distress level on the Outcome Rating Scale (see Chapter 5, this volume) reached the non-clinical range. At the same time, the therapist tempered her enthusiasm, appreciating the difficulty of the road ahead and not wishing to alienate Lisa who had every reason to be wary of a premature victory lap. Nevertheless, Ty's scores were visual gauges of something happening, prompting the therapist to discuss in session what they meant and how they might be sustained.

This dramatic improvement might easily be dismissed based on common views about recovery from entrenched addiction. Alternatively, it can be considered in light of the literature that attests to early change in psychotherapy (Howard, Kopta, Krause, & Orlinsky, 1986). Self-generated and spontaneous recovery have been identified in numerous studies of personal change apart from professional help (Bohart & Tallman, 2009).

In sum, being strengths-based requires that clinicians align with a strengths-based philosophy, be adept at identifying strengths, and adopt a particular set of strategies. Thus, the approach requires both conceptual, perceptual and executive aspects, each being crucial to successful implementation. The following guidelines summarize these components:

1. *Believe in clients.* Cultivate through study of the literature and clinical experience the belief that all people have invaluable resources waiting to be tapped in the interest of achieving desired goals.
2. *Listen for heroic stories.* Develop an ear for client reports of successes and unique achievements, whether directly related to the presenting problem or to other life experiences, past and present.
3. *Punctuate client strengths.* Comment on client resources when you hear them and enquire more about them. Whether directly connected to the presenting problem or not, consider and discuss how these attributes might shed light on potential solutions.
4. *Ask about client strengths.* Enquire about life events not generally presented in clients' accounts of the problem to help clients re-story their life narratives to include strengths.
5. *Develop a change orientation.* Become attuned to any mention of change and, when hearing it, enquire more about it.
6. *Utilize progress and alliance measures routinely.* Use client self-report progress measures routinely to serve as visual tools for noticing client progress and enquiring about different strategies to begin progress or reverse deterioration. Use alliance self-report measures routinely to ensure fit of therapist focus with clients' preferred modes of help and goals.

IMPLICATIONS FOR POLICIES AND TRAINING

Adopting a strengths-based perspective requires a re-configuring of procedures in most clinical settings. Therapists who naturally gravitate to this way of working as well as those who simply wish to test the waters inevitably will encounter obstacles. For example, the requirement in many settings to diagnose makes it difficult to be strengths-based. Additionally, rote inclusion of strengths assessments that figure little in treatment plans and interventions give mere lip service to being strengths-based. To challenge these practices, clinicians can join together to voice their discontent with deficit-based diagnostic systems. More immediately, clinical staff, from case managers to supervisors and upper management, must believe that clients can succeed. When this is so, paperwork and procedures involve practices that match a strengths-based perspective. As a result, a culture is created that is optimistic, respectful and empowering for all.

While such a transformation may appear 'pie in the sky', movements are under way that offer alternatives to business as usual (e.g., https://heartandsoulofchange.com; Cooper & McLeod, 2011). Centralizing a strengths-based approach throughout graduate training will be required to reconfigure future mental health care. As with client-directed practice, a pluralistic approach instils in trainees a fundamental respect for therapy service users as human beings and as experts in their own lives, possessing both the desire and ability to resolve their difficulties (Cooper & McLeod, 2011). This stance is critical for creating successful client–therapist collaborations. Until clinical practice infrastructure, including policies, procedures and paperwork, is aligned with a fundamental valuing of client strengths, clients, and all they bring to the table, will remain an underutilized force for positive therapeutic change.

CHALLENGES

Therapists committed to seeing clients as prime movers in therapy are likely to encounter two pitfalls that can jeopardize the success of treatment. First, in their zeal to highlight strengths, counsellors may downplay clients' struggles. While some clients respond well to hearing hurrahs and compliments, others may believe that their story has not been fully understood or appreciated. Listening for and highlighting strengths cannot be done at the expense of the alliance. First and foremost, counsellors need to listen to clients' stories and acknowledge their dilemmas. With this as a foundation, a more multi-storied account can enter the conversation and take shape.

Second, while it is true that many clients discover their own solutions via active listening and validation as well as eliciting heroic stories, other clients want something else. Here is where the hard work of learning multiple interventions pays off. Counsellors select an approach that resonates with client preferences, a key element of pluralistic and client-directed practice. Recall that there can be no positive alliance without an agreement regarding the tasks of therapy; this cannot happen without a task or method. Clients often expect their therapist to offer a particular explanation for their problem and a ritual (or intervention) that will resolve it (Frank & Frank, 1991). At the same time, the explanation and intervention must fit the client's theory of change – his or her view about the origins of the problem and a general idea of how it can be resolved (Duncan et al., 1992).

DISCUSSION

> In their eighth (and last) session, Ty and Lisa described their lives as rather boring. Gone was the constant tension of trying to maintain a sense of normalcy amidst the unpredictability many families with active drinkers face. Now, Ty and Lisa went to work, ate their evening meal, watched TV, then settled into bed together at the end of the day – just your average domestic couple. This is what had been missing and this is what they now rejoiced in having. At the last session, they discussed their plans to 're-marry,' followed by a real (sober) honeymoon.

Whether Ty's sobriety continued is not known, though, based on alliance feedback, he likely would have returned in the event of relapse. The point is, believing in clients, trusting in their views of what is needed and in a process that honours those views is not just for some clients; it applies to all, even those with severe distress. Diagnoses like schizophrenia, for example, should not deter a strengths-based approach. People respond to human relationship regardless of diagnosis and extent of symptomatology. While adaptations may be needed (e.g., patience during psychotic episodes until meaningful communication can be established), therapists can feel confident that a focus on strengths is a valid, research-informed position likely to enhance outcome.

The lure of expert diagnosis and prescriptive treatment risks diminishing clients' critical contributions to therapy. Instead, psychotherapy can embrace its own evidence base that supports an idiosyncratic interweaving of therapist and client in relationship, informed by client feedback, with clients in the lead. Consistent with a pluralistic approach, being strengths–based means creating strong alliances by honouring client goals and preferences. And this cannot happen without valuing client resources. Choosing this path, psychotherapy adheres to empirically established and humanistic principles to provide effective and culturally responsive services.

SUMMARY

The key points of this chapter are:

- Client factors comprise the bulk of common factors across all bona fide treatments, accounting for as much as 86% (including client/life factors, measurement error and unexplained variance) of outcome.
- People have a strong propensity to self-heal, including recovery from trauma with and without formal intervention, recovery from serious disturbances such as schizophrenia and personality disorders, and spontaneous and transformative change.
- Clients are not passive recipients of therapist intervention but actively make therapy work for them.
- Believing that clients have resources and can change is the foundation of a strengths-based approach.
- Counsellors who foster hope and who tailor treatments to fit clients' preferences enhance the therapeutic alliance and increase client engagement, the most significant determinant of psychotherapy outcome.
- Strategies such as listening for and punctuating heroic stories, helping clients uncover submerged strengths, attending to and amplifying small changes, and using progress and alliance instruments to demarcate change and ensure fit are key strategies for strengths-based practice.
- Policies, procedures and paperwork either support or undermine a strengths focus in practice settings.
- Therapist cheerleading and passivity are challenges of a strengths-based approach.

EXERCISES/POINTS OF REFLECTION

1 In groups of four or five, choose a client and two counsellors. The client decides on a presenting problem and talks with the first therapist (about 5–7 minutes) who assumes a deficit-based perspective. This counsellor believes the client is defined by his/her pathology and failures and actively searches for and asks about them in the interview. Next, the same client is interviewed by a second counsellor who assumes a strengths-based perspective. The group debriefs by first asking the client about his/her experience in each interview. Counsellors

and observers then offer their experiences of the role plays. Final points for discussion include contrasting the two experiences and considering the therapists' fit with the client, ability to validate the client's concern and provide hope.

2 A front-line counsellor at a busy community mental health agency is attending a routine agency staffing. The team is discussing a mother's diagnosis of bipolar disorder and the impact of this on her family. What obstacles does the counsellor face in being strengths-based in this meeting? What protocols might be instituted to incorporate client strengths into the discussion? Into the agency? What obstacles do you encounter in your workplace being strengths-based? What steps might you take to integrate a strengths-based approach at your workplace?

> ## FURTHER READING
>
> https://heartandsoulofchange.com. The Heart and Soul of Change Project is an international consortium articulating the research and practical objectives of a client-directed, strengths-based, therapeutic paradigm.
>
> Bohart, A. (1999). *How clients make therapy work: the process of active self-healing.* Washington, DC: The American Psychological Association. This book elaborates the essence of a client- and strengths-based therapeutic paradigm, with suggestions for how therapists can promote what clients already do best.
>
> Duncan, B.L. (2014). *On becoming a better therapist.* Washington, DC: American Psychological Association. For therapists and educators, this book details how to use systematic client feedback and incorporate client resources to make clients true partners in therapy and improve outcomes.
>
> Duncan, B., & Sparks, J. (2010). *Heroic clients, heroic agencies: partners for change* (2nd ed.). Jensen Beach, FL: Author. This book is a practical, hands-on manual for including clients in each step of therapy.

REFERENCES

Bohart, A., & Tallman, K. (2009). Clients: the neglected common factor in psychotherapy. In B. Duncan, S. Miller, B. Wampold, & M. Hubble (Eds.), *The heart and soul of change: delivering what works* (2nd ed.). Washington, DC: American Psychological Association.

Bohart, A., & Wade, A. G. (2013). The client in psychotherapy. In M.J. Lambert (Ed.), *Bergin and Garfield's handbook of psychotherapy and behavior change* (6th ed.). Hoboken, NJ: Wiley.

Bordin, E.S. (1979). The generalizability of the psychoanalytic concept of the working alliance. *Psychotherapy, 16,* 252–260.

Cooper, M., & McLeod, J. (2011). *Pluralistic counseling and psychotherapy.* Los Angeles, CA: Sage.

de Jong, P., & Berg, I.K. (2008). *Interviewing for solutions* (3rd ed.). Belmont, CA: Thomson Higher Education.

Duncan, B.L. (2014). *On becoming a better therapist: evidence-based practice one client at a time* (2nd ed.). Washington, DC: American Psychological Association.

Duncan, B.L., Solovey, A., & Rusk, G. (1992). *Changing the rules: a client-directed approach to therapy*. New York: The Guilford Press.

Duncan, B., & Sparks, J. (2010). *Heroic clients, heroic agencies: partners for change* (2nd ed.). Jensen Beach, FL: Author.

Farber, B., & Doolin, E. (2011). Positive regard. *Psychotherapy, 48,* 58–64.

Gassmann, D., & Grawe, K. (2006). General change mechanisms: the relation between problem activation and resource activation in successful and unsuccessful therapeutic interactions. *Clinical Psychology & Psychotherapy, 13,* 1–11.

Frank, J.D., & Frank, J.B. (1991). *Persuasion and healing* (3rd ed.). Baltimore, MD: Johns Hopkins University Press.

Gurin, J. (1990, March). Remaking our lives. *American Health,* 50–52.

Howard, K.I., Kopta, S.M., Krause, M.S., & Orlinsky, D.E. (1986). The dose–effect relationship in psychotherapy. *American Psychologist, 41,* 159–164.

Lambert, M.J. (2013). The efficacy and effectiveness of psychotherapy. In M.J. Lambert (Ed.), *Bergin and Garfield's handbook of psychotherapy and behavior change* (6th ed., pp. 169–218). Hoboken, NJ: Wiley.

Orlinsky, D.E., Rønnestad, M.H., & Willutzki, U. (2004). Fifty years of process-outcome research: continuity and change. In M.J. Lambert (Ed.), *Bergin and Garfield's handbook of psychotherapy and behavior change* (5th ed., pp. 307–390). New York: Wiley.

Ozer, E.J., Best, S.R., Lipsey, T.L., & Weiss, D.S. (2008). Predictors of posttraumatic stress disorder and symptoms in adults: a meta-analysis. *Psychological Bulletin, 129,* 52–71.

Prochaska, J.O., Norcross, J.C., & diClemente, C.C. (1994). *Changing for good.* New York: William Morrow.

Seikkula, J., Aaltonen, J., Alakare, B., Haarakangas, K., Keränen, J., & Lehtinen, K. (2006). Five-year experience of first-episode nonaffective psychosis in open dialogue approach: treatment principles, follow-up outcomes, and two case studies. *Psychotherapy Research, 16*(2), 214–228.

White, M., & Epston, D. (1990). *Narrative means to therapeutic ends.* New York: Norton.

Zanarini, M.C., Frankenburg, F.R., Hennen, J., Reich, D.B., & Silk, K. (2006). Prediction of the ten year course of borderline personality disorder. *American Journal of Psychiatry, 163,* 827–832.

7
Core Counselling Methods for Pluralistic Practice

Mick Cooper

This chapter discusses a range of basic counselling methods that can be used as the foundations for pluralistic practice. These are

- Establishing goals
- Active listening
- Expressing acceptance and care
- Minimal encouragers
- Reflecting, paraphrasing and summarising
- Asking questions
- Using symbols and metaphors
- Working in the here-and-now
- Helping people make sense of why they do things
- Helping people re-evaluate what they do
- Helping people re-decide

Pluralistic practice is based on the assumption that many different therapeutic approaches and methods have the potential to be helpful for clients in achieving their goals. However, given this plethora, the question arises as to where practitioners should start in their training and development. This is a critical question: there is a risk that pluralistic trainees may become overwhelmed by the choices available, and fail to develop a set of coherent, core competencies in therapeutic work.

This chapter is specifically written for trainees in the beginning stages of their development as pluralistic practitioners. It aims to introduce, and illustrate, a set of basic counselling methods that can form the foundations for pluralistic therapy. Consistent with a pluralistic approach, these methods are not drawn from, or aligned to, any one therapeutic orientation. Rather, they are generic counselling skills that can articulate with, and form the basis for, a variety of understandings and methods, both across orientations (see Part 2 of this volume), and across goals (see Part 3 of this volume). These methods are also aligned with a pluralistic approach in that they start by helping clients to identify their goals, and then, through a process of reflection and decision-making, support them to find ways of actualising these goals more fully. Consistent with a pluralistic outlook, most of the methods described in this chapter have also been shown, through empirical evidence, to be helpful to a majority of clients (Cooper, 2008; Williams, 2002).

ESTABLISHING GOALS

From a pluralistic standpoint (Cooper & McLeod, 2011; Chapter 3, this volume), a fundamental skill in any therapeutic practice is to be able to help clients articulate what it is that they want from therapy and from life. In many instances, it is best to initiate this dialogue in a first, or assessment, session (see Chapter 2, this volume). It can be stimulated by a range of questions, for instance:

- 'Do you have a sense of what you want from our work together?'
- 'What do you hope to get out of therapy?'
- 'What kind of things would you like to change in your life?'
- 'Where would you like to be by the end of therapy?'

(see Cooper, 2015: 72)

Clients' responses to these questions can then form the basis for a more in-depth dialogue about where they are trying to get to in their lives. Clients and therapists may want to write these goals down, for instance using the Goals Form (www.pluralistictherapy.com), and evaluate progress on a weekly basis.

An alternative approach is to help clients establish what is the main *problem* or *trouble* that they would like to address in therapy. Given that clients seem to do better when they are trying to achieve something they want (*approach goals*), rather than get away from something they do not like (*avoidance goals*) (see Cooper & McLeod, 2011), this may be a generally less helpful starting point for therapy. However, for some clients, particularly early on in therapy, it may be much easier to articulate what they are unhappy with in their lives than what they positively want to achieve.

Rob was a 34-year-old white musician who will be used as a client study throughout this chapter. At the start of our first session together, I asked Rob what had brought him to counselling and what he might want to talk about. Rob replied that, 'the biggest thing is my relationship with my girlfriend'. Rob said that it was fine on a day-to-day basis, but that there were problems when it came to 'being intimate'.

'I'll find myself avoiding night-times,' said Rob, 'doing work or staying up late or finding excuses not to be around and then she feels bad about it and I feel really guilty.'

Helping Rob to find ways of addressing this problem became the initial focus of our work together. However, as with many clients, Rob's goals for therapy changed over time. By session 4, for instance, Rob felt that he no longer needed to work on his relationship with his partner as things had improved a lot. However, he was beginning to notice that some of his behaviours that were causing problems with his girlfriend – being acquiescent and unassertive (see below) – were also present in other relationships, such as with his sister.

> *Mick:* In the last few weeks, we've been focusing on the pattern with your girlfriend, and how you're tending to be doing things that maybe you don't want to be doing. And it sounds like that's kind of helpful to talk about that [Rob: Yeah], but we're maybe coming to the end of that for now [Rob: Yeah], but there's maybe a kind of deeper pattern that's going on that's actually happening in other relationships in your life [Rob: Yeah]. Do you think that – Would you *like* to focus on that? ...
>
> *Rob:* Well maybe, yeah, because ... it just feels like it's gone in one place and, sort of, come out another one ... I just want to be able, like, to be a bit stronger and say what I want ...
>
> *Mick:* So if we were going to set some specific goals for this work together, what would you say they would be? ...
>
> *Rob:* So I'm really, like, able to say, 'That is— *This* is what I think.'

As this dialogue demonstrates, pluralistic therapists not only need to be able to initiate a dialogue about goals, but also to revisit and follow this conversation up. This requires an ongoing openness to clients and their changing goals over the course of therapy, and a willingness to engage in flexible and responsive ways.

ACTIVE LISTENING

For clients to achieve many of their goals – such as greater self-awareness, more self-acceptance, or behavioural change – they need to have an opportunity to *reflect* on their lives and experiences. One basic way that pluralistic therapists can help clients to do this is by providing them with time to talk through these issues. This requires *active listening*. At its most basic, active listening means we are quiet and allow clients to talk. The existential–humanistic psychotherapist James Bugental (1981), for instance, suggested that therapists should talk about one-twentieth of the time. But active listening is much more than an absence of therapist talk. Rather, it requires us to attend closely to what clients are saying and to communicate this attending to them, both non-verbally and verbally. Egan (2013) suggested some basic non-verbal strategies for conveying active listening to a client: sitting squarely to the client, maintaining an open posture, leaning slightly towards the client, maintaining eye contact and being relaxed. However, as this latter strategy suggests, active listening should not be practised in a rigid or very technical way – it should be a natural expression of being alongside clients as they talk about their lives.

As the initial session with Rob proceeded, he talked more about how he avoided sexual intimacy with his girlfriend. He talked about how he felt frozen when he was in bed with her, how he felt really bad about this, and how he was struggling to find a way through these feelings. Throughout this process, I primarily listened, asking Rob the occasional question to encourage him to say more about his experiencing. Giving Rob this space to reflect formed the basis for all our subsequent work.

EXPRESSING ACCEPTANCE AND CARE

For clients to be able to talk about – and reflect on – their lives and experiences in an honest way, they usually need to feel that they will not be judged or criticised for what they say. So pluralistic therapists need to respond to clients in ways that are *non-judgemental* (Rogers, 1959): that is, that do not put a negative value on their experiences and perceptions.

What may particularly help clients open up, however, is not just feeling that their therapists are *non*-judgemental. Rather, it may be a feeling that we genuinely *care* about them and their lives (e.g., Knox & Cooper, 2010). This is a sense of *mattering* to us: that we are actually interested in their well-being and are willing to 'go the extra mile' for them. Obviously, we cannot generate these feelings towards our clients if we do not feel them. But if we do feel them, we can explore ways of allowing their fuller expression. This might be in small gestures: for instance, a welcoming smile when the client comes through the front door. But it may also be in more explicit ways: for instance, a willingness to try to be flexible around time boundaries if a client really needs more time to talk (see Chapter 23, this volume).

MINIMAL ENCOURAGERS

Minimal encouragers are another very simple way of communicating to clients an active interest and care in who they are and what they are saying. These are brief interjections or gestures that we may make as the client is talking: for instance, 'mm', 'uh huh,' 'yeah' or head nodding. Such utterances communicate to clients, without interrupting them, that what they say has been understood, respected, and that they should say more. Obviously, such encouragers cannot be forced; nor should they be implemented in a mechanistic way. Indeed, counsellors can sometimes have a reputation for over-using such terms. But, as a natural part of the therapeutic dialogue, they can play a key role in helping clients feel more able to talk and reflect. An example comes from the work with Rob as he talks about the experience of going up to the bedroom with his partner.

Rob: It's kind of fear [*Mick nods his head vigorously*]. It's like suddenly I'm scared of her [*Mick*: Right]. Yeah. It's like suddenly she becomes this ... thing that I'm— yeah— that's sort of— dangerous ... not in terms of physical threat, because actually she has sort of tried to touch me a few times [*Mick nods his head vigorously*] and ... actually— I've actually freaked out a little bit [*Mick nods his head*].

REFLECTING, PARAPHRASING AND SUMMARISING

Reflecting, paraphrasing and summarising all essentially involve saying back to clients what they have said, and can be very useful in helping them develop an awareness of their thoughts and feelings. As with minimal encouragers, however, they are probably least helpful when done in a mechanistic or formulaic way (e.g., parroting the client). Rather, they should be a natural expression of our *empathic* understanding of our client (Rogers, 1959): an articulation of how we imagine the client experiences his or her world.

Reflecting is a relatively word-for-word restatement of what clients have said; paraphrasing involves some rewording; and summaries reflect back to clients, in condensed form, what they have said over some period of time. As with minimal encouragers, these responses can support the process of reflection by helping clients feel understood and valued, such that may feel more able to talk about their issues and experiences. They also provide clients with an opportunity to 'stand back' and 'hear' what they have been saying, such that they can go on to develop or articulate it in more nuanced ways.

The following is an example of reflection with Rob:

Rob: I don't want to— to start being intimate with her and then freak out. I know it will mess her up, and so I— I don't start it, but then I know that is messing her up anyway. Yeah, so just sort of frozen.
Mick: So you get frozen about the whole situation really.
Rob: Yeah, yeah, yeah, and then I'll go and smoke a joint or do something else...

Later on in the session, I summarised what Rob has been saying to this point:

Mick: So it sounds like something— you were getting along really well [*Rob*: mm], good sexually [*Rob*: Yeah], and then ... over time ... something's happened [*Rob*: Yeah] that's made you more anxious about it and action about ... being sexual ...

Rob confirmed this, and went on to say that it had been a 'cumulative thing', rather than a one-off event that triggered his fears. Rob then talked about how something similar had happened in a past relationship.

> Rob: It's like a spiral really, because I don't want to tell them that I'm not into them, because that— I worry that they'll get upset. So then I don't … tell them, and then I have a freak out and then they're upset anyway.

I then paraphrased what Rob had been saying:

> Mick: And it's something about telling them that you're not into it [Rob: Yeah] is— just feels difficult to do and … but actually what I'm kind of sensing is that if you're not that into it then it's [Rob: Mm] difficult to kind of get engaged … [Rob: Yeah].

ASKING QUESTIONS

It is sometimes said that therapists should not ask questions. And, indeed, the research shows that they can be experienced as one of the least helpful forms of therapeutic intervention (Cooper, 2008). However, there is other research to suggest that clients *can* experience questions as helpful (Watson, Cooper, McArthur, & McLeod, 2012). From a pluralistic perspective, questions – like all interventions – can be helpful or unhelpful, depending on what different clients want, need and prefer at different points in time. Questions, for instance, may be helpful if they support clients to make better sense of their goals and difficulties, their current ways of doing things, or potentially different alternatives.

Open-ended questions (which invite clients to be creative and expansive in their responses) tend to be more helpful in therapy than *closed questions* (which invite clients to give short, fixed answers). In the early stages of counselling, Rob was asked a number of open-ended questions to help him explore his issues. For instance, when Rob was talking about feeling fear towards his girlfriend, I asked him, 'Do you have any sense of what you are afraid of?' Interestingly, however, it was a relatively closed question that proved particularly helpful in the session. Rob, as we saw above, had been describing how this downward spiral started to emerge when he was not 'that into' a woman, and this begged an obvious question: 'So does that mean,' I asked Rob, 'with your girlfriend at the moment, that there is part of you that is maybe, isn't so … into her at the moment?'

Rob replied: 'Yeah, I think so. Yeah.' From this, Rob then went on to describe how he was feeling quite resentful to his girlfriend and taken for granted. He felt that he was caring for her and looking after her – for instance, giving her lifts to the station every morning – and not getting much in return.

USING SYMBOLS AND METAPHORS

Sometimes, people can find it difficult to describe things in their lives using words alone; and some people just naturally find it easier to describe things through images, symbols, narratives or metaphors. In many cases, clients will just naturally bring in these forms of reflection into the therapeutic work, and therapists can help them expand on them and explore them in more detail. As Rob reflected on his resentment towards his partner, for instance, he began to recognise that part of the problem was that he was not telling her about the things he was unhappy with, because he was afraid that she would get angry with him. Why was that so awful? Rob said that, when other people were angry with him, it felt like he was zooming along a 'railway track', believing what other people were saying, with no control over where he was going and no way of turning off. Developing the metaphor further, Rob said that, at these times, he felt like he was collecting 'parcels' – 'You're bad', 'You've done it wrong' – that he could not even think to throw off.

Listening, empathically, to Rob's metaphor, I had a sense of how frightening it might feel to be zooming down that track without control. 'It sounds pretty scary,' I said to Rob. He replied that it was: 'It feels quite terrifying actually.'

If clients are struggling to find the right words to describe things, it may also be helpful for us to ask them to describe it in symbolic or metaphoric terms. For instance, 'Do you have an image that could describe that?' 'What would that feeling be like if it was a colour?' In some instances, we may also come up with symbols or metaphors for what seems to be going on for the client. These have the potential to be very useful. However, we do need to be tentative in sharing them and ready to withdraw them if they do not fit, so that our understanding of what is going on does not come to dominate over the client's.

WORKING IN THE HERE-AND-NOW

To help clients get a really vivid sense of what goes on for them and how they might change, it can sometimes be helpful for them to look at what they are actually experiencing in the *immediate* therapeutic encounter. Bringing things into the here-and-now may be particularly helpful when exploring feelings and emotions, which people sometimes need to viscerally feel to be able to fully cognise. For instance, you might ask a client, 'You talked about feeling scared, and I wonder if you feel this here too?' Inviting clients to describe what they are experiencing in their body is often a good way of deepening this exploration of feelings and emotions. For instance, you might ask a client, 'You said that you have a sense of shame right now and I wonder where you feel that in your body?'

As with psychodynamic 'transference work' (Chapter 10, this volume), one aspect of the here-and-now experience that may be particularly useful to help clients explore is their feelings and perceptions towards *us*, as their therapist. At the start of the third session with Rob, for instance, I noticed that he was very quiet and did not seem to want to explore anything. As we talked about this, it emerged that Rob had not really wanted to come to therapy that day. However, as we had contracted that he would pay for sessions that he did not cancel within 24 hours of their start he felt 'obliged' to come along – albeit resentfully. Later on in the session, I reflected back to Rob that – as with other relationships – he seemed to find it difficult to say to me that he was unhappy and annoyed about things. Rob agreed. I then asked him if he had a sense at all of what made that so difficult.

Rob: I wouldn't want to … be in a situation where you could get angry about that … that you'd feel, sort of, 'Who is this guy in my— causing problems', you know. I don't feel it's alright to do that, for some reason, like I have to be well-behaved, or … I'll get in trouble or something [*laughs nervously*].

Mick: So it feels like, if you were to— say maybe you wanted some things differently here that it would be about causing trouble, and being badly behaved. It would feel like you'd done something wrong.

Rob: Yeah … and I wouldn't want to sort of upset you ….

Mick: Because I might get angry [*Rob*: Yeah]. And do you have a sense— if I did get angry with you … what would that— might be like, or why would that be a bad thing?

Rob: Well it'd … I'd kind of, um, want to leave, or I'd— then I'd feel like … *guilty*, I guess, as well.

Mick: Right, so it's something about— if other people feel angry with you, then you feel guilty [*Rob*: Yeah, yeah]. And it feels like a really uncomfortable place to be …. Which kind of relates a lot to what you've been talking about with your girlfriend and, um, with other people [*Rob*: mm] …

Through focusing on what happened in our immediate therapeutic relationship, Rob and I deepened an understanding of his fear of angering others, and also the excruciating guilt that he can experience when he believes that others are annoyed with him.

With here-and-now work, it may also be helpful for us to feed back our own experiences of the client. With Rob, for instance, I might have disclosed that, had he expressed anger towards me, I would have actually appreciated his honesty, and looked at how I might have changed my behaviour. Such self-disclosure has the potential to help clients understand more about how others actually experience them, and to experience less of a hierarchy between themselves as client and therapist as 'expert'.

HELPING PEOPLE MAKE SENSE OF WHY THEY DO THINGS

In many cases, clients come to therapy to try to understand more about why they feel and act in the way that they do, and this is something that we can often help them with. With Rob, for instance, we came to see that his problems with being intimate with his girlfriend stemmed from a growing feeling of resentment towards her; and that this resentment partly came about because he was afraid of telling her – as with other people – what he was unhappy about. This *formulation* (see Chapter 2, this volume) emerged through our process of reflection and dialogue and, as a pluralistic formulation, was co-constructed by both client and therapist. Rob talked about his experiences and, simply by doing so, started to make links between different things that he was thinking, feeling and doing. And I – drawing on a range of personal and theoretical understandings (see, for instance, Chapters 8–21, this volume) – shared with Rob my observations, ideas and insights. Through this process, Rob could get a better sense of why he was not getting to where he wanted to in life, and also what the levers of change might be in finding more satisfying and fulfilling ways of being.

HELPING PEOPLE RE-EVALUATE WHAT THEY DO

Through the methods outlined above, clients will often come to an 'intuitive' sense of what are the better, or less helpful, ways of acting and thinking. When Rob talked about not expressing his wants to his girlfriend, for instance, we both had a sense that this was probably not a helpful thing to do. Re-evaluation, however, is also a process that can be stimulated by the therapist. For instance, a therapist might say to a client: 'What do you think is best to do here?' or 'You seem to be doing X because of Y, is that what you want to carry on doing?'

As therapists develop more knowledge and experience, we may also begin to bring a range of theoretical understandings to bear on this re-evaluation. For instance, drawing on humanistic ideas (see Chapter 8, this volume), we might say to a client: 'I can see that it's really important for you to do things that you think others will like, but I wonder if that leaves you sacrificing a lot of your own needs?'

With Rob, I drew on a mixture of cognitive behavioural (Chapter 9, this volume) and existential understandings (Chapter 11, this volume), as well as self-disclosure, to input into this re-evaluation process:

> Mick: I know for myself that when people are annoyed with me and angry with me it— it doesn't feel great, but I guess there is something about, learning to *bear* that, kind of tolerate that, to … accept that sometimes those kind of things are going to happen …
>
> Rob: Yeah. Yeah. I mean when you talk about it like that it sounds sort of normal. Of course people get angry. I just see that I've spent so much time … avoiding it. It's like— the idea of it actually happening now is terrifying.

Drawing on theoretical understandings and insights, therapists can also help clients generate alternative – and potentially more helpful – ideas about how they can think and behave. For instance, drawing on CBT ideas around developing more helpful thinking (Chapter 9, this volume), I said to Rob:

> Mick: So … rather than maybe thinking that: 'If people are angry with me, it's just going to be unbearable', what would be a— maybe a more constructive way of thinking about it, or more helpful for you?

Rob: I guess like, um, 'OK, so …' Just to be like, 'OK, well, they're angry now, and … I don't have to sort of … make myself in the wrong because of it.' 'Just because they're angry, it doesn't necessarily mean that I've done something wrong. They're just angry … They're just pissed off, and they've got a right to be pissed off, but I don't have to, like, assume that that's my fault.'

HELPING PEOPLE RE-DECIDE

Once clients have re-evaluated their choices, they may decide that they want to try thinking or acting in different ways. As with re-evaluation, this may be a natural progression for clients, but it may also be something that we can stimulate. For instance, we might ask, 'So how do you think you can take this forward?' 'How might you make this happen in your life?'

As a first step, clients may decide to try things out in different ways in the therapeutic relationship itself. For instance, with Rob, we joked about the idea of me practising getting annoyed with him, and Rob practising to say to himself, 'Ok, that's alright, that's cool.' Ultimately, however, it may be important for clients to try things out in the 'real world'. After our first session together, Rob decided that he wanted to try to be more upfront with his partner about the things he was finding difficult. He chose to talk to her before our next session and, to his surprise, he reported that she was actually quite receptive, not angry at all, and within a few weeks things were considerably improved within the relationship.

SUMMARY

This chapter has introduced, and illustrated, a range of basic methods for pluralistic therapy. These can form the foundation for the more advanced methods discussed in Parts 2 and 3 of this book, but they can also be a pluralistic form of counselling in themselves: helping clients identify, and progress towards, their personal goals. Most fundamentally, pluralistic therapists can help clients recognise what it is that they want from therapy, and from life. We can then help them reflect on how they think, feel and act in relation to these areas of their lives by actively listening, conveying acceptance, offering minimal encouragers, reflecting, asking questions, using symbols, working in the here-and-now, and helping clients to make sense of why they are doing things. Through this process, clients may naturally come to re-evaluate their ways of thinking and acting and re-decide on potentially better alternatives. But therapists can also stimulate this process of re-evaluating and re-deciding by asking more direct questions and inputting their own perspectives into the process.

EXERCISES/POINTS FOR REFLECTION

1. For which kinds of clients do you think the methods described in this chapter are most likely to be helpful? Do you think, for instance, that they are most suited to clients with particular types of goals or problems?
2. What do you think is missing from this chapter? That is, what other methods do you think are core counselling practices: that can help a wide range of clients achieve a wide range of goals?

FURTHER READING

Dryden, W., & Reeves, A. (Eds.). (2014). *The handbook of individual therapy* (6th ed.). London: Sage. In-depth introduction to a range of different therapeutic orientations.

Egan, G. (2013). *The skilled helper: a problem-management and opportunity development approach to helping* (10th ed.). Belmont, CA: Brooks–Cole. Classic counselling skills text with parallels to the pluralistic approach.

McLeod, J., & McLeod, J. (2011). *Counselling skills* (2nd ed.). Maidenhead: Open University Press. Explores a range of core counselling skills from a pluralistic perspective.

Williams, E.N. (2002). Therapist techniques. In G.S. Tryon (Ed.), *Counselling based on process research: applying what we know* (pp. 232–264). Boston: Allyn & Bacon. A very valuable chapter reviewing the evidence of effectiveness of different counselling techniques.

REFERENCES

Bugental, J.F.T. (1981). *The search for authenticity: an existential-analytic approach to psychotherapy* (Enl. ed.). New York: Irvington.

Cooper, M. (2008). *Essential research findings in counselling and psychotherapy: the facts are friendly*. London: Sage.

Cooper, M. (2015). *Existential psychotherapy and counselling: contributions to a pluralistic practice*. London: Sage.

Cooper, M., & McLeod, J. (2011). *Pluralistic counselling and psychotherapy*. London: Sage.

Egan, G. (2013). *The skilled helper: a problem-management and opportunity development approach to helping* (10th ed.). Belmont, CA: Brooks–Cole.

Knox, R., & Cooper, M. (2010). Relationship qualities that are associated with moments of relational depth: the client's perspective. *Person-Centered and Experiential Psychotherapies, 9*(3), 236–256.

Rogers, C.R. (1959). A theory of therapy, personality and interpersonal relationships as developed in the client-centered framework. In S. Koch (Ed.), *Psychology: a study of science* (Vol. 3, pp. 184–256). New York: McGraw-Hill.

Watson, V., Cooper, M., McArthur, K., & McLeod, J. (2012). Helpful therapeutic processes: a pluralistic analysis of client activities, therapist activities and helpful effects. *European Journal of Psychotherapy and Counselling, 14*(1), 77–90.

Williams, E.N. (2002). Therapist techniques. In G.S. Tryon (Ed.), *Counselling based on process research: applying what we know* (pp. 232–264). Boston: Allyn & Bacon.

TUTORIAL VIDEOS

A series of tutorial videos are available in which Mick Cooper discusses the counselling skills relevant to this chapter, many of which include clips of Mick's counselling sessions with the client, Rob. They are part of the SAGE Counseling and Psychotherapy video collection: https://sk.sagepub.com/video/counseling-psychotherapy

PART 2
Therapeutic Orientations

8

Humanistic Approaches and Pluralism

Terry Hanley, Adam Scott and Laura Anne Winter

THIS CHAPTER DISCUSSES

- The nature, development and schools of humanistic therapy
- The development of integrative perspectives within humanistic therapy
- The commonalities and differences across humanistic and pluralistic perspectives
- The key humanistic understandings that can contribute to a pluralistic practice
- The key humanistic methods that can contribute to a pluralistic practice

BRIEF INTRODUCTION TO HUMANISTIC THERAPIES AND HISTORICAL DEVELOPMENT

Humanistic psychology emerged within 1950s America during a time of great cultural and political change. The traditional establishment was being challenged and new-found freedoms of expression were coming to the fore (Feltham, 2013). It was within this melting pot of new ideas that humanistic psychology gathered momentum and established itself as the 'third force' in psychology (Bugental, 1964). Its evolution led to the explicit questioning of the *status quo* and saw the rise of humanistic psychotherapies that had a shared humanistic base but distinct theoretical identities and therapeutic practices. This movement included contributions from influential figures such as Carl Rogers with client-centred therapy, Fritz Perls with Gestalt therapy, and Eric Berne with transactional analysis. There were numerous other individuals, each leaving their own legacies, however due to limitations in space we will not introduce them here.

The many variants of humanistic therapies proved diverse in description and implementation. They shared a common foundation however, and were each underpinned by the key principles of humanistic philosophy. Briefly, and in summary, these are that humanistic therapists view each person as unique, greater than the sum of their parts, that they have the potential for constructive growth and that they can exercise choice over situations (Bugental, 1964). Although the writings of key authors demonstrate the stark difference between the authors, this is even more evident within the numerous films of practice created during this period. For a very clear example, comparing Carl Rogers's practice with that of Fritz Perls in the film of them both offering therapy to the same woman (Gloria), demonstrates how similar foundations can manifest in vastly different practice.

In recent years it could be argued that humanistic psychology has moved from being a central force in psychology to being perceived as a kindly, but ultimately archaic, alternative to more commonplace practices such as cognitive behaviour therapy (Elkins, 2007). This change in political goodwill can be viewed as unfortunate and primarily reflects that humanistic therapists' priorities have been somewhat different to the mainstream. For instance, humanistic psychology has been closely aligned with strengths-based approaches of therapy (in contrast to the more common pathology-driven model) and has played a key role in the development of qualitative research methods in psychology (rather than focusing upon quantitative methods, which have become so powerful in discourses of therapy). Although both of these remain important issues in humanistic psychology, the pragmatic attitude that pervades the approach has led to an increasing interest in more mainstream research endeavours.

DEVELOPMENT OF INTEGRATIVE AND PLURALISTIC PERSPECTIVES IN HUMANISTIC THERAPIES

The most common variant that comes under the humanistic therapy umbrella is person-centred therapy (PCT), originally conceptualised by Carl Rogers. PCT is far from a homogenous approach and is made up of a variety of 'tribes' (see Sanders, 2012). However, despite their differences, at the heart of all of these approaches is the centrality of the client, their experience and their capacity for personal growth. Thus, it may be argued that whilst therapeutic practices may differ, the underlying principles held towards such work remain the same. It is at this level that many perceive recent developments in humanistic therapeutic integration.

Norcross (2005) suggests that integrative and eclectic practice is the most common therapeutic approach in the English-speaking world. Notably, many of these ways of working align themselves with humanistic theories in some shape or form. For instance, psychodynamic interpersonal therapy, psychosynthesis, transactional analysis, motivational interviewing and the third wave of CBT all make use of literature from the humanistic psychology domain. Further, integrative frameworks that attempt to make use of recent developments around therapeutic 'common factors', for example as Gerard Egan's (2013) 'Skilled Helper Model' and Clara Hill's (2014) 'Helping Skills Model', also make significant links to this way of viewing the world. In both of these models, therapy is viewed trans-theoretically and certain stages are viewed as being inherent in the therapeutic process (e.g. Hill would emphasise the 'exploration', 'insight' and 'action' stages of therapy). Additionally, they both encourage the use of 'skills' from a multitude of approaches; skills that vary in alignment with typical humanistically orientated work.

The pluralistic framework might be considered as following along this trend of therapeutic integration. However, despite this, as the framework has evolved it has been suggested that it itself is a person-centred approach (Cooper & McLeod, 2011a). In making such a statement, the framework might therefore be considered to be an alternative 'tribe' in this nation. However, instead of dogmatic adherence to a particular way of working that prizes specific theoretical consistency, it explicitly acknowledges the potential strengths in other therapeutic approaches, both from inside and outside of the humanistic counselling world. The framework therefore provides scaffolding for what could be viewed as systematic eclecticism underpinned by an attitude based upon pluralistic principles.

ALIGNMENT OF HUMANISTIC AND PLURALISTIC PRINCIPLES

Commonalities

When considering the commonalities and differences between humanistic and pluralistic principles there is much overlap:

- First, both perspectives value the individual as unique. This leads to a position that acknowledges the complexity inherent within each individual, and thus the notion that one size of therapy will fit all is not compatible with either approach.
- Second, both positions value the idea that individuals can exercise choice in the therapeutic process. This may be facilitated by metacommunication in both cases.
- Third, in much the same way that the pluralistic framework outlines the importance of the therapeutic relationship, humanistic perspectives of counselling and psychotherapy share this sentiment.

Differences

In contrast to these commonalities, there are ways in which the pluralistic approach diverges from the humanistic perspective:

- The pluralistic therapist might not view constructive growth as a given for an individual. The belief in the actualising tendency, in which change will occur naturally if provided with an appropriately fertile environment, might not be viewed as an important underpinning principle.

- The pluralistic approach does not always aim to view the individual in a holistic way. Pluralistic therapy may solely focus therapy upon a small area of a client's life and utilise methods that purposefully work around broader processes.
- Whereas a humanistic therapist might prize *principled* non-directiveness in their work (a philosophical position based upon the therapist's positive perspective of the person), the pluralistic therapist is more likely to explicitly direct the content of the therapeutic work. This might specifically be evident when considering the different tasks and methods that might be utilised.
- The explicit focus upon goals within the pluralistic framework is unlikely to sit well with many approaches of humanistic therapy. Placing such an emphasis upon the need for individuals to identify and articulate goals might appear counter to the more organic nature of some humanistic approaches.

KEY HUMANISTIC UNDERSTANDINGS THAT CAN CONTRIBUTE TO A PLURALISTIC PRACTICE

The humanistic psychology movement has contributed significantly to the development of therapy more broadly. Here a number of the contributions that are made explicitly to the pluralistic framework are considered.

Working towards constructive growth: the potentiality model

From a humanistic perspective every individual is viewed as having the potential for constructive growth. This might be described as an actualising tendency (Rogers, 1961). To do so, however, humanistic therapists believe that people need to be provided with an appropriately fertile environment. Creating such a space therefore becomes a major role of the therapist and humanistic therapies commonly focus upon the skills and attitudes needed for developing an appropriate therapeutic relationship. For instance, a person-centred therapist might be guided by the principle that if a person received the right type of conditions in a relationship this would support them in reaching their potential. Therefore, a therapist would attempt to offer clients an empathic, honest and accepting relationship in which the person can explore themselves rather than having techniques or theory imposed on them.

The person is unique and more than the sum of his/her parts: the challenge to pathologically driven systems

Humanistic therapists commonly adopt a holistic perspective of the person. In doing so they are likely to view individuals as unique and incredibly complex in nature. As has been noted earlier, this perspective might be perceived as running counter to the dominant force in therapy which places a great deal of emphasis upon pathology-based models. From this position, diagnostic manuals that purposefully aim to produce lists of symptoms and provide classification systems of distress are viewed critically (Sanders, 2005). This can range from the complete rejection of these manuals to a more dialogic stance in which therapists work flexibly with diagnoses. It could be argued that this latter view fits well with a pluralistic position, whilst the former does not.

The person has choice: valuing client agency

The concept of client agency pervades much of the change literature related to humanistic therapy. This idea emphasises the role that clients have within the therapeutic process and works with the assumption that individuals are fundamentally free and have the potential to choose the direction their lives will take. Duncan, Miller and Sparks (2004) play with this importance in the title of their book *The Heroic Client*. The view here is that, whereas there has been a historical prizing of the skills of therapists (the therapist as the hero of our clients), maybe therapists should be focusing more upon the client's role in therapy. The active role of clients can be seen in literature across therapeutic approaches, with clients withholding information so as not to upset person-centred counsellors and clients reworking homework tasks in CBT to better suit their needs. Importantly this concept strikes at the heart of the view that therapy can be standardised as, although therapist behaviours can be kept relatively consistent, the way in which clients' use therapy might fluctuate greatly.

Research

In addition to therapeutic practice developments, humanistic psychologists have also been associated with significant contributions in the world of research. In particular, the approach has been strongly aligned to the development of qualitative research methods in psychology. Although this is by no means exclusive, there are many overlaps in the holistic attitude held by humanistic psychologists and the desire to capture the rich experiences of people often present within qualitative research. In recent years developments have shifted and also include interests in mixed methods research and quantitative research (e.g. Hill & Elliott, 2014). Such research is commonly critically positioned and capturing a generalisable truth as an end goal is unlikely to be the major task undertaken.

KEY HUMANISTIC METHODS THAT CAN CONTRIBUTE TO A PLURALISTIC PRACTICE

In this final section we now consider what might be construed as specific therapeutic methods that come from humanistic therapies and which might be applicable to the pluralistic framework.

Non-directive working

The concept of non-directiveness has received considerable attention within the humanistic psychology literature. Much of this has been driven by the early work of Carl Rogers and is reflected in the work of many person-centred practitioners. In working in this way the therapist might be viewed as attempting to get out of the way of the client's material at times, as opposed to more directive approaches that purposefully take on what might be construed as a more expert role. Two types of non-directiveness are:

> *Principled non-directiveness:* Underpinning this position is the belief that given the right environment individuals will grow constructively, as guided by the actualising tendency perceived to be within all humans. Such a position might be difficult to conceptualise as a method, however it could be that such a trusting position might be a foundation stone from which some pluralist therapists work.
>
> *Instrumental non-directiveness:* This perspective might prove more fitting with the concept of the therapeutic method. It relates to the times when therapists might specifically utilise a non-directive approach because they feel it may be useful for the client at that particular time. A therapist adopting this position is unlikely to believe wholeheartedly in the actualising tendency of the person.

In the example of instrumental non-directiveness below, the therapist works collaboratively with the client and sensitively attempts to introduce this way of working to the client:

> *Therapist:* Firstly thank you for sharing everything that has been going on recently. As I mentioned earlier there are many ways that therapists might work, and commonly, in the way that I work, at the beginning of our first sessions I will discuss some of the ways that I believe might be helpful with you. Hopefully we can then work out what type of approach you might see as being a good fit for you. Does that make sense?
>
> *Client:* Yes. I'd be interested in knowing a bit more.
>
> *Therapist:* OK. Well one common approach, which might be useful, is for this to primarily be a space for you to talk. I most probably wouldn't say much but I would listen carefully to what you're saying and reflect things back if I thought, or felt, that might be useful. I might also ask you to do certain things with the hope that we can learn together a bit more about the emotions behind them. Although this might sound daunting, or even a little strange, it can often be very helpful for people who come to therapy with issues similar to you. It's sometimes difficult to imagine what this process might be like and I'd recommend that if it sounds like this might be something that you want to try then we give it a go and reflect upon it as our meetings progress.
>
> *Client:* OK

The difference between content direction and process direction (Rennie, 1998) is helpful to introduce here. Although directing the content of the session might not prove fitting for some humanistic therapists, directing the process might prove acceptable. In making such interventions the therapist aims to manage the process around the content introduced by the client. Here they may introduce therapeutic activities (such as those noted below) to support the deepening understanding of the issues that the client has introduced. Additionally the therapist is likely to introduce conversations about the therapeutic process itself (metacommunication). This helps to clarify the appropriateness of the process interventions and supports the development of the therapeutic alliance. It is anticipated that the notions of process direction and metacommunication are well suited to the pluralistic framework.

The therapeutic relationship: offering the core conditions

One area of humanistic therapy that pluralistic practitioners might wish to draw from is the nature of the therapeutic relationship, and specifically Carl Rogers's conditions model from classical person-centred therapy. From this vantage point, a therapist provides the 'necessary and sufficient' conditions, and constructive personality change occurs (Rogers, 1957). These conditions are primarily to offer congruence, empathy and acceptance towards the client. Whilst these conditions are unlikely to be viewed as 'sufficient' in all cases by pluralistic practitioners, Cooper and McLeod (2011b) suggest that they might be methods used within pluralistic practice to facilitate change.

Although viewing the conditions for constructive change outlined by Rogers as technical intervention might prove controversial, rather than viewing it as *a way of being*, it is useful to consider what the therapist *does* to communicate their meeting of these conditions to the client (Merry, 2012). For example, therapists might utilise the following explorative microskills, as discussed by Lent, Hill and Hoffman (2003), to help convey the conditions noted above:

- Using open questions to encourage exploration
- Actively listening to the client – capture and understand the words the clients use
- Reflecting feelings that arise in the session
- Using restatements – repeating or rephrasing what the client has said
- Using attending behaviour – using body language and eye contact to convey warmth.

These microskills receive a great deal of attention within approaches that place an emphasis upon the need for specific skills in the helping professions (e.g. Egan, 2013 and Hill, 2014). One example of reflecting feeling might be as follows:

Client: I was out with my friend for lunch yesterday, and she told me that she can't make the party next weekend. I told her it was fine but actually I was a bit upset … I just had to pretend like it was OK.
Therapist: You were disappointed that she isn't coming to the party.

Individualised formulation

A formulation from a humanistic perspective would take an individualised and tentative approach. It would be purposefully collaborative in nature with the purpose being to develop a shared understanding of the issues being discussed, rather than squeezing them uncomfortably into a theoretical frame and model of practice chosen by the therapist (Gillon, 2013). Rather than providing a road-map for therapy, humanistic formulations may instead provide a tentative framework for the therapist to hold lightly in their mind to aid understanding of the client's presenting issues. This process is exemplified in the case example of Rosanne which follows:

> I (Laura) have met with Rosanne on four occasions now. She is in her early twenties and came to me asking for help with anxiety and difficulties sleeping. Through our discussions it became apparent that she had a very low opinion of herself, and often said things like 'I'm worthless' and 'I'm a bad person' to herself when feeling anxious. In the fourth of our sessions she expressed a desire to go back to work now that her daughter is 1 year old. She described how uncomfortable it felt to share this with me. As part of the ongoing therapeutic process with Rosanne I have reflected on whether or not we can establish a therapeutic relationship meeting all of the six necessary and sufficient conditions for therapeutic change (Rogers, 1957). I have also found it useful to reflect on person-centred theoretical understandings of the self, for example considering the way in which perhaps Rosanne established 'conditions of worth' around only being a good mother if you stay at home, and the resulting incongruence when experiencing feelings such as the one she shared with me. This is something I haven't shared with Rosanne as I feel it would be an unnecessary imposition of an external theoretical point of view, and I am more concerned about her experience and understanding of herself. It also does not form a 'target' in therapy for me. It does, however, when held tentatively, help me to develop my empathic connection with Rosanne, therefore supporting me in meeting the conditions for a healing relationship.

Focusing

The work around focusing provides a specific move into a territory in which humanistic therapists become more explicitly active in the role they adopt. Focusing is a method in which the therapist supports the client in becoming more aware of the immediate felt sense within therapy. Originally outlined by Eugene Gendlin (2003), this process involves attuning to the client's way of being in therapy with a view to picking up on moments where the client might be beginning to express something on the edge of awareness that might be helpful to understand further. Gendlin outlined six stages to this process that might be incorporated into the pluralistic therapist's toolkit. These are:

Clearing a space – first attempt to become aware of each concern that may be around. Welcome them but do not reflect further upon them individually at this stage.

Getting a felt sense – choose one concern that has arisen. Do not go into it, instead attempt to feel the concern as a whole.

Get a handle – attribute a word, phrase or image to the felt sense.

Resonating – check out the handle you have attributed to the felt sense. Change the term if it does not accurately capture the felt sense.

Asking – now ask 'What is it about this whole concern that makes this quality?'

Receive – dwell upon the question and pay attention to the feelings that arise. Accept what arises in response to the question in a welcoming way.

This process has been devised as a means for both self-reflection and work with a therapist. A pluralistic therapist might therefore use it within therapy or suggest it as a form of homework. Below is an example of a therapist introducing the idea into a session:

Client: I have been thinking about it all week. It's been bothering me so much but I can't quite put my finger on what it is. Umm [*pause*]

Therapist: Shall we explore it in more detail?

Client: Well it's confusing. Actually, it's not confusing, I'm angry that I've got myself into this and I can't get out of it.

Therapist: Let's stay with that a little longer, if that's OK?

Client: That's OK.

Therapist: Just take a moment to get more of a sense of the feelings that are around for you. It sounds as if there might be quite a few. If you just sit quietly, close your eyes if you wish, and just notice what comes up. For now, just notice what they are, welcome them, and see if you can put them in a list in your head. Then, once you're ready, maybe you can tell me more about these feelings and we can choose one to focus upon.

[*pause*]

The empty chair and two-chair techniques

Empty chair work and two-chair techniques originated within Gestalt psychotherapy and psychodrama. More recently they have been harnessed in emotion-focused therapy (Elliott, Watson, Goldman, & Greenberg, 2004). The purpose of these approaches is to encourage active expression within sessions by asking the client to enact a conversation between different aspects of the self or others.

The empty chair method

In this method the client is invited to talk to an empty chair within the therapy room (which represents a separate part of the individual or a key person within the client's life).

This might provide a helpful environment to express unexpressed or unresolved feelings. The example below provides an illustration of how this process might start:

[*Psychologist puts an empty chair in front of her client and says*]

Psychologist: I was reflecting on last week's session and what you said about your mother belittling you and beating you ... and that you said you feel 'stuck' because you wanted to tell her the impact of her actions ... did I get that right?

Client: Yes, she was horrible to me and now that she is dead I can't confront her ... now I can never do it ... I feel so trapped ...

Psychologist: Well ... this might sound strange but can I suggest we try something. I would like you to imagine that your mother is in this chair and I wonder whether you could tell her how you feel? Would that be OK?

Client: To be honest, that sounds 'bonkers' but I am willing to give it a go ...

Two-chair work

This approach utilises a similar format as empty chair work, but is a method of exploring *conflict splits*. These are internal struggles between different 'parts' of the person: for instance, their vulnerable side and their self-critical voice. In this approach the client is invited to move between two chairs and have a discussion between the two parts in question, so as to stimulate greater dialogue and understanding at the intrapersonal level.

SUMMARY

This chapter raised the following key points:

- Humanistic therapies have a rich and diverse history that has much to offer pluralistic therapeutic work. This includes the development of numerous therapeutic approaches, including the person-centred approach, Gestalt psychotherapy and transactional analysis, as well as providing a basis for numerous integrative frameworks.
- Humanistic principles might be viewed as a foundation for pluralistic working. In particular, the view that each person has the potential for constructive growth, is unique and greater than the sum of their parts, and capable of exercising choice over situations, proves very fitting with the pluralistic framework.
- Humanistic thinking has helped to develop approaches to research that are in keeping with pluralistic positions. This includes development in qualitative research and more recently mixed methods and quantitative work.

- The notion of non-directive working, the conceptualisation of the therapeutic relationship and individualised formulation provide useful practically applicable positions that can be adopted and integrated into pluralistic therapeutic work.
- The explicit therapeutic methods of focusing, utilising two-chair and empty chair techniques, provide a useful contribution to the pluralistic framework.

EXERCISES/POINTS FOR REFLECTION

Watch Carl Rogers and Fritz Perls working in the 'Three Approaches to Psychotherapy' film involving Gloria (this is widely available free of charge on the internet – www.youtube.com/watch?v=24d-FEptYj8). Whilst watching: (1) consider how different the two humanistic approaches are, and (2) note down any instances where you see the core values of humanistic psychology in their therapeutic practice (i.e. the uniqueness of the individual, that a person is more than the sum of their parts, the personal tendency towards growth and that a client can make choices for themselves).

At the end of the session consider the following questions: (1) What therapeutic goals does Gloria present with in the sessions with Carl Rogers and Fritz Perls?, and (2) What tasks and methods can you identify within each of the sessions?

FURTHER READING

Cooper, M., O'Hara, M., Schmid, P., & Bohart, A. (Eds.). (2013). *The handbook of person-centred psychotherapy and counselling* (2nd ed.). Houndmills: Palgrave. This is an excellent wide-ranging introduction to the person-centred approach. It provides a useful introduction to person-centred theory and considers its practice both in general and with specific client groups.

Duncan, B.L., Miller, S.D., & Sparks, J.A. (2004). *The heroic client: a revolutionary way to improve effectiveness through client-directed, outcome-informed therapy.* San Francisco: Jossey–Bass. This text concentrates on the important role that the client plays in therapeutic change. In doing so it emphasises the importance of methods, such as metacommunication, within therapy. It is a very readable text with numerous examples from practice.

Elliott, R., Watson, J., Goldman, R., & Greenberg, L. (2004). *Learning emotion-focused therapy: the process experiential approach to change.* Washington, DC: American Psychological Association. This is a key text about emotion-focused therapy. It is an approach that values both the relationship and the tasks that therapists might complete in therapy. With this in mind, it outlines numerous methods that might be incorporated into practice.

Hill, C.E. (2014). *Helping skills: facilitating exploration, insight, and action* (4th ed.). Washington, DC: American Psychological Association. This text provides an

(Continued)

(Continued)

abundance of information about the helping skills that humanistic practitioners might incorporate into their work. It specifically relates these skills to the 'exploration', 'insight' and 'action' elements of the therapeutic relationship.

Stewart, I. (2014). *Transactional analysis in action* (4th ed.). London: Sage. This book provides a thorough introduction to transactional analysis. Although this approach has not been greatly present within this chapter, it is one that has many elements that fit well within a pluralistic approach.

REFERENCES

Bugental, J.F.T. (1964). The third force in psychology. *The Journal of Humanistic Psychology*, 4(1), 19–26.

Cooper, M., & McLeod, J. (2011a). Person-centered therapy: a pluralistic perspective. *Person-centered & Experiential Psychotherapies*, 10(3), 210–223.

Cooper, M., & McLeod, J. (2011b). *Pluralistic counselling and psychotherapy*. London: Sage.

Duncan, B.L., Miller, S.D., & Sparks, J.A. (2004). *The heroic client: a revolutionary way to improve effectiveness through client-directed, outcome-informed therapy*. San Francisco: Jossey-Bass.

Egan, G. (2013). *The skilled helper* (10th ed.). Belmont, CA: Brooks/Cole, Cengage Learning.

Elkins, D.N. (2007). Empirically supported treatments: the deconstruction of a myth. *Journal of Humanistic Psychology*, 14(4), 474–500.

Elliott, R., Watson, J., Goldman, R., & Greenberg, L. (2004). *Learning emotion-focused therapy: the process experiential approach to change*. Washington, DC: American Psychological Association.

Feltham, C. (2013). The past and future of humanistic psychology. In R. House, D. Kalisch, & J. Maidman (Eds.), *The future of humanistic psychology*. Ross-on-Wye: PCCS Books.

Gendlin, E. (2003). *Focusing* (rev. ed.). London: Rider.

Gillon, E. (2013). Assessment and formulation. In M. Cooper, M. O'Hara, P.F. Schmid, & A. Bohart (Eds.), *The handbook of person-centred psychotherapy and counselling* (2nd ed., pp. 410–421). Basingstoke: Palgrave Macmillan.

Hill, A., & Elliott, R. (2014). Evidence-based practice and person-centred and experiential therapies. In P. Sanders & A. Hill (Eds.), *Counselling for depression*. London: Sage.

Hill, C.E. (2014). *Helping skills: facilitating exploration, insight, and action* (4th ed.). Washington, DC: American Psychological Association.

Lent, R., Hill, C., & Hoffman, M. (2003). Development and validation of the counselor activity self-efficacy scale. *Journal of Counseling Psychology*, 50(1), 97–108.

Merry, T. (2012). Classical client-centred therapy. In P. Sanders (Ed.), *The tribes of the person-centred nation: an introduction to the schools of therapy related to the person-centred approach*. Ross-on-Wye: PCCS Books.

Norcross, J.C. (2005). A primer on psychological integration. In J.C. Norcross and M.R. Goldfried (Eds.), *Handbook of psychotherapy integration*. New York: Oxford University Press.

Rennie, D. (1998). *Person-centred counselling: an experiential approach*. London: Sage.

Rogers, C.R. (1957). The necessary and sufficient conditions of therapeutic personality change. *Journal of Consulting Psychology, 21*(2), 95–103.

Rogers, C.R. (1961). *On becoming a person: a therapist's view of psychotherapy*. Boston, MA: Houghton Mifflin.

Sanders, P. (2005). Principled and strategic opposition to the medicalization of distress and all of its apparatus. In S. Joseph & R. Worsely (Eds.), *Person-centred psychopathology: a positive psychology of mental health* (pp. 21–42). Ross-on-Wye: PCCS Books.

Sanders, P. (Ed.). (2012). *The tribes of the person-centred nation: an introduction to the schools of therapy related to the person-centred approach* (2nd ed.). Ross-on-Wye: PCCS Books.

9
Cognitive Behavioural Approaches and Pluralism

Terry Boucher

THIS CHAPTER DISCUSSES

- The foundations of cognitive behavioural approaches to psychotherapy
- The development and growth of integrative perspectives within cognitive behaviour therapy (CBT)
- The alignment of CBT with pluralistic principles
- The key CBT understandings that can contribute to pluralistic practice
- The key CBT methods that can contribute to pluralistic practice

FOUNDATIONS OF COGNITIVE BEHAVIOURAL APPROACHES TO PSYCHOTHERAPY

Cognitive behavioural approaches to the psychotherapeutic setting developed through the work of a number of practitioners in the 1960s and 70s, most notably Albert Ellis's rational emotive therapy (Ellis, 1962) and Aaron Beck's cognitive therapy (A. Beck, 1964; Beck, Rush, Shaw, & Emery, 1979). Historic roots can be found in the philosophic teachings of Greek philosophers such as Epictetus and the discourse method of Socrates, and developmental influences include learning theory and the work of behavioural therapists such as Wolpe (1958), as well as the research of Kelly (1955) into cognitive constructs. As a modality it also draws on the understandings and vocabulary of Bartlett (1932) and Piaget (1950). Cognitive behavioural approaches, now often referred to collectively as cognitive behaviour therapy (CBT), have evolved to become firmly established as one of the main orientations of psychotherapy. The approach is supported in the UK by the National Institute for Health and Care Excellence (NICE) for a number of presenting difficulties, and is sanctioned by large-scale organisations such as the National Health Service.

THE DEVELOPMENT AND GROWTH OF INTEGRATIVE PERSPECTIVES WITHIN CBT

From its original theoretical standpoint and focus on the role of underlying cognitions that drive emotional, physiological and behavioural responses, the past 40 years has seen many adaptations, innovations and diversifications within CBT as it has strived to integrate research and evolving therapeutic practices into its approach. Indeed, one could see cognitive analytic therapy (Ryle, 1990), dialectical behavioural therapy (Linehan, Armstrong, Suarez, Allmon, & Heard, 1991), acceptance and commitment therapy (Hayes, Strosahl, & Wilson, 1999), mindfulness-based cognitive therapy (Segal, Williams, & Teasdale, 2002), schema therapy (Young, Klosko, & Weishaar, 2003), and compassion focused therapy (Gilbert, 2005), as all integrative approaches within the broad church of the CBT paradigm. Furthermore, the very name cognitive behaviour therapy belies the earlier and fundamental integration of perspectives, between the behavioural tradition of psychotherapy of the 1950s and the growing awareness of cognitive processes in the 1960s and 70s. With this propensity for *theoretical* development and integration acknowledged, as we will see later, it must also be recognised that the therapeutic *practice* of CBT draws largely on humanistic principles, particularly Rogerian (Rogers, 1957) core conditions, in establishing a working and collaborative therapeutic relationship.

ALIGNMENT OF CBT WITH PLURALISTIC PRINCIPLES

In looking at how CBT can be aligned with a pluralistic approach I will draw on a core text, *Cognitive Therapy: Basics and Beyond*, written by Judith Beck (1995).

> *Personalising therapy*: Judith Beck stresses the importance of a therapist developing an individualised conceptualisation and understanding of a client. She states: 'Cognitive therapy is based on an ever-evolving formulation of the patient and [their] problems in cognitive terms' (J. Beck, 1995: 5). She goes on to outline how this formulation is derived from a comprehensive assessment of an individual client's presenting difficulties that highlights the importance of current thinking patterns; problematic behaviours; precipitating or triggering factors; developmental events; and enduring patterns of interpretation which could have predisposed the client to their difficulties. Later cognitive therapists have stressed the importance of explicitly sharing and developing this individualised and evolving-formulation with the client (Wells, 1997).
>
> *Collaboration*: Beck also emphasises collaboration *with* and active participation *by* the client, where the client's unique cognitive patterns and biases, which emerge from the dialogue, are explored as a 'team' (J. Beck, 1995: 6). Here decisions are made together as to session focus, structure and between-session tasks. In this manner therapy is a 'personalising' experience where if either of the 'others' in the relationship are not genuinely engaged, it is less likely to be effective.

From goals to tasks and methods: 'Cognitive therapy is goal orientated and problem focused' (J. Beck, 1995: 6). From the outset, therapists and clients are encouraged to collaboratively identify therapeutic *goals*. These may focus on particular thought patterns, problematic behaviours, or any other specific issues the client is aiming to manage better. For example, a client might want to feel more confident in social settings. Goal-focused *tasks* are then collaboratively identified, in a graded and systematic manner, with the aim of learning specific cognitive and behavioural *methods* in their attainment.

Metatherapeutic dialogue (see Chapter 4, this volume): It could be said that because CBT sessions are structured, time-limited and focused on the present, it necessitates the foregrounding of metatherapeutic communication in its processes. Indeed, the above three paragraphs could be said to highlight how the CBT practitioner values metatherapeutic communication in conceptualising a client's difficulties from their perspective; sharing and developing with them a cognitive understanding of their difficulties; and working collaboratively towards their goals. To this end the dialogic techniques of *Socratic questioning* and *guided discovery* are deeply embedded in CBT, and aimed at developing a richer understanding of a client's unique cognitive frameworks and the meanings attached therein (Beck & Weishaar, 1989; J. Beck, 1995: 8). These techniques are modelled in an open inquisitive style by the therapist for the client to adopt themselves as they develop greater awareness of their cognitive processes and the cognitive biases that might not serve them well.

Systematic feedback: An emphasis on monitoring therapeutic progress through client feedback is at the core of CBT. Therapists are encouraged to check-in and gather direct feedback from clients regularly in sessions and explicitly at the end of each session. This aims at developing shared understandings and maintaining momentum in the approach taken; identifying any problems that might arise in the therapy and working flexibly towards their resolution; and, through such metacommunicative dialogue, building collaboration that enhances the therapeutic relationship (J. Beck, 1995). CBT practitioners are also encouraged to utilise a number of psychometric tools to monitor the progress of therapy and measure outcomes. In fact the value placed on such measures is clearly demonstrated by the specific psychometrics developed by Aaron Beck himself such as the Beck Depression Inventory (BDI).

Client strengths and resources: From the outset, at the 'assessment' phase, the CBT practitioner aims to elicit client coping skills and 'protective' features in their presentation. As therapy progresses CBT recognises that by identifying and drawing on a client's personal strengths, through metatherapeutic dialogue and specific techniques, so the process of therapy is likely to be enhanced, with clients developing a sense of mastery over their difficulties and building motivation in working towards their goals (J. Beck, 1995). In fact it is CBT's ability to formulate the client, not in terms of the events to which they have been exposed, but in terms of their cognitive and behavioural *responses* to such events, that can be so empowering for clients in taking ownership of their difficulties; drawing on their strengths; developing a framework for adaptation; and building skill sets and internal and external resources, or resilience, for the future in line with their goals and values.

KEY CBT UNDERSTANDINGS THAT CAN CONTRIBUTE TO PLURALISTIC PRACTICE

Essentially, CBT proposes that it is cognitive biases in a person's interpretations of events, not the events themselves, which can lead to distortions and mistakes in the evaluation of such events and consequently dysfunctional reactions to them. It is such cognitive distortions and dysfunctional reactions which are then seen as underlying a number of clinical presentations, such as anxiety and depression, and consequently they become the therapeutic target – the evaluation and adaptation of which leads to modification in a person's presenting difficulties (J. Beck, 1995).

An information processing model to cognitions

In CBT human beings are seen akin to an information processor, evaluating data input in line with a number of background programs and memory systems. Each human being is likely to have differing evaluation processes and memory systems based on their unique experiences and the learning taken from these. CBT foregrounds the assessment phase of the therapeutic process, capturing an individual's cognitive processes though consideration of presenting thoughts often embedded in a client's language. In this way the CBT therapist from the very start of the therapeutic process is attending to a client's language in detail, looking for hints as to how this person might be experiencing life through their cognitive understandings of themselves, other people and the world in general. It is at this level that the therapist is particularly trying to identify potential distortions and biases in interpretations and memory processes – originally termed 'thinking errors' – that may also be shown in the metatherapeutic dialogue. Hillary, on meeting her therapist for the first time, said, 'I'm really not sure I should be here, you'll probably think I'm wasting your time, sorry'. For the CBT therapist, this 'negativity' in language might alert them to potential issues of self-worth, both in terms of self-evaluations and the expected judgements of others.

An appreciation of learning theory for behaviours

Drawing on learning theory, particularly research into classical and operant conditioning, the CBT therapist will attend to a client's behavioural responses, both to external situational stimuli, e.g. a phobic response to seeing a spider, as well as, internal cognitive stimuli, e.g. the thought/image of having a panic attack in public. Behavioural responses might then be framed with a client as either adaptive or maladaptive, and behavioural goals and tasks set to help the client re-learn their behavioural options to reinforce adaptive cognitive/behavioural responses and extinguish maladaptive ones.

Jerry's fear of dogs was really starting to impact on his ability to leave the house. Using graded exposure to progressively more anxiety-provoking 'dog contact' situations – first in picture form, then at a vet's, then walking with a friend's dog – Jerry was able to relearn his response and feel more at ease leaving his home again.

The interconnectedness of thoughts, emotions, physical responses and behaviours

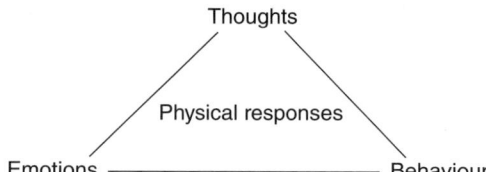

CBT sees the systems of thoughts, emotions, physical responses and behaviours as interconnected and interactive with each other. This is sometimes depicted as a triangle or a 'hot cross bun' (Padesky & Mooney, 1990). In CBT particular attention is paid to the role of 'automatic thoughts' that might arise spontaneously within an individual's constant thought/imagery processes and memory systems, and the impact they might have in triggering emotions, physiological processes and behavioural responses. Every time Jane saw an ambulance she remembered the accident she had. She thought 'you could be dead right now' and became very anxious and panicky, felt hot and sweaty, and sat on the floor thinking she might otherwise collapse. Sitting on the floor then made her feel more self-conscious and vulnerable, thinking other people saw her as 'mad' and 'crazy' – demonstrating a 'vicious cycle' in experience – and so now she rarely went out. The vigorous assessment of such interactions, attending to the cognitive triggers, behavioural reinforcers and the context around an individual, allows for the co-construction of a personalised formulation between therapist and client. From this a suitable approach forward can be developed, targeting unhelpful thought processes and behavioural habits that might maintain the 'vicious cycles' in a client's experience.

A developmental model of difficulties

Early developmental and learning experiences
↓
Schema and core belief development
↓
Assumptions and rules in response to core beliefs

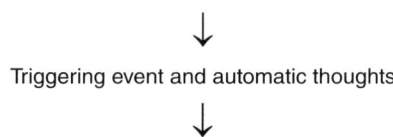
Triggering event and automatic thoughts
↓
Presenting symptoms (emotions, physiology, behaviour)

CBT sees a client's current presenting difficulties as often rooted in a developmental pathway. In line with information processing models and learning theory, the human brain is seen as attempting to make sense of and respond to the environment from the earliest days. As development progresses through each of its 'stages', so the person emerges with their own unique set of understandings or *schemas* based on their unique developmental and learning experiences. These schemas could be said to represent sets of beliefs about the nature of the world in which they live, beliefs about others in that world and beliefs about themselves. Belief formation may have aspects that are very helpful for the growing person, but sometimes they can develop in a way that is more unhelpful! Philip, for instance, had a father who was always harsh and punitive towards him, criticising him for the smallest thing. This led Philip to develop the belief that he was a failure and a burden to others.

In response to their core beliefs, an individual might develop a set of cognitive and behavioural assumptions and rules to ease their existence. Philip reported he persistently avoided social situations and group activities at school, assuming that if he spoke or interacted with others they would see what he called his 'idiotness' and laugh at him, his own company protecting him from this pain. However, this moderately successful strategy faltered when he left school and had to find employment. Being a good artist he secured a job in advertising, but hated it due to the open-plan office and the pressure to socialise with others. He often took time off owing to his anxiety and now was being threatened with disciplinary action for his poor attendance. From the cognitive behavioural standpoint this change in circumstance or triggering event threw into question Philip's assumptions and rules for living (his coping strategies), i.e. 'if I keep out of people's way and don't socialise I will be OK'.

As already mentioned, in CBT automatic thoughts are often seen as the basis of understanding an individual's current and future projected responses. These responses – emotional, physiological and behavioural – to a situation often hold the key to past experiences and belief formation. Consequently, CBT practitioners spend a lot of time and effort with clients identifying their specific unhelpful or negative automatic thoughts (NATs), and helping them to evaluate and modulate them. This is often done by questioning the validity and reliability of NATs in relation to cognitive biases, and by building on a client's own cognitive strengths and resources in nurturing their more adaptive thought processes and evaluations. In discussing Philip's anxiety and avoidance of the work situation it became clear that he often found himself flooded with thoughts – 'they will find you out'; 'you will make a fool of yourself'; 'you will go red and embarrass yourself' – all of which made him anxious and panicky (emotions), raised his heart rate and sweat response (physiology) and caused him to phone in sick (behaviour). These were his presenting symptoms to therapy – which were now jeopardising his future career (environment).

KEY CBT METHODS THAT CAN CONTRIBUTE TO PLURALISTIC PRACTICE

CBT is often:

- Initially focused on here-and-now presenting issues
- Structured in nature, valuing the need for out-of-session tasks ('homework')
- Empirical, taking a 'scientist/experimental' stance to exploring experience
- Brief and time-limited
- Focused on symptom reduction and relapse prevention.

In line with the understandings detailed above, CBT has also developed a number of specific methods and tools to be utilised in the therapeutic context.

Monitoring automatic thoughts

One of the foundation blocks of CBT method is the identification and evaluation of unhelpful automatic thought processes or NATs, and the growth and development of more adaptive ones. To this end 'thought records' are commonplace in the work. Whilst there are many formats to thought records, which can be adapted and personalised to a client's specific difficulties, they are likely to conform, more or less, to the outline shown in Figure 9.1.

			Thought and feelings record			
Date and situation	Initial emotion	Initial unhelpful thought(s)	Evidence for initial unhelpful thought(s)	Evidence against initial unhelpful thought(s)	Alternative helpful thought(s)	Consequent emotion change

FIGURE 9.1 *Example thought and feelings record*

In using thought records, the client and therapist collaborate – initially in sessions, then through setting out-of-session tasks – in identifying situations that provoke strong undesirable emotions, e.g. panic, hopelessness, depression and the thoughts that might be a precursors to such emotions. Time is then spent evaluating the 'validity' and 'reliability' of such thoughts by looking at the evidence for and against them, with the aim of developing a more helpful thought process with consequent change in emotion. In the example in Figure 9.2, John was initially asked to complete the first three columns as a 'homework' task, recording a situation where he felt strong emotion and the thoughts he was having at the time. He returned to the session and with his therapist completed the fourth and the fifth columns; in the narrative the therapist asking open questions as to the evidence that supports or did not support his initial thought. John was then asked to identify, on balance, a more realistic or helpful thought and jot that down in the sixth column, as well as re-rate his envisaged emotional response, given the new thought, in the seventh.

Thought and feelings record						
Date and situation	Initial emotion	Initial unhelpful thought(s)	Evidence for initial unhelpful thought(s)	Evidence against initial unhelpful thought(s)	Alternative helpful thought(s)	Consequent emotion change
01.03.14 Car park outside supermarket	Sadness and fear	I will bump into my ex, and they will see what a loser I am.	They shop there. I was buying food for one. I looked a mess.	I have never bumped into them before. Buying food for one, and not looking smart for the shops doesn't make someone a loser.	It is unlikely I would bump into my ex, and if I did I would look just like other people going about their lives.	More confident and less anxious and down.

FIGURE 9.2 *John's completed thought and feelings record*

Identifying 'thinking errors'

In developing alternative, more helpful thoughts, the therapist is likely to explore *with* the client their cognitive biases or 'thinking errors' embedded within their language or images. The main 'thinking errors' they might look for are:

- 'All or nothing' and 'black and white' thinking:
  - *'I fail at everything'; 'I'm completely useless'*.
- 'Fortune telling' and trying to predict the future, often negatively:
  - *'I won't succeed'; 'They won't want to know me'*.
- 'Linking unconnected events' or 'personalisation':
  - *'My friends haven't phoned because I didn't see them yesterday'* or
  - *'It's all my fault'*.
- 'Dwelling on the negatives' and concentrating on weaknesses and dismissing strengths:
  - *'I passed, but only got 52%. Anyone could do that'*.

- Using 'ultimatum' and 'global' words in language, such as 'shoulds' and 'everyone':
  - *'I should do better; everyone else is cleverer'.*
- 'Mindreading' other people:
  - *'People think I make my pain up'.*
- Labelling oneself or others:
  - *'I'm stupid and useless'; 'They have got it in for me'.*
- 'Emotional reasoning':
  - *'I feel stupid, so I must be stupid'.*
- 'Catastrophising':
  - *'This is terrible, I will never be able to face them again'.*

By identifying and evaluating such biases the CBT practitioner hopes to demonstrate that thoughts are not equal to facts and that clients can develop flexible cognitive and behavioural responses to unhelpful thoughts. This aims to help the client move towards their therapeutic goals, e.g. to be less anxious in social situations.

The 'downward arrow' technique

By following a client's affect in the therapeutic dialogue a therapist might identify a number of key automatic thoughts that trigger strong emotions. The therapist might then gently enquire in a progressively focused manner as to the meaning of such a thought were it to be true. Continuing to follow thoughts in this way, to deeper levels of cognition like a 'downward arrow', the therapist aims at uncovering underlying cognitive interpretations and meanings representing a client's schemas, core beliefs and assumptions. Katherine was very worried about her husband's willingness to stay late at work:

Therapist: What is anxiety-provoking for you about that?
Client: He might be having an affair!
Therapist: And if that were true and he is having an affair, what does that mean?
Client: He's going to run off with her.
Therapist: And if he does run off with her?
Client: I'll be alone, stuck on the shelf.
Therapist: What does that mean to you if you're alone, 'stuck on the shelf'?
Client: That no one wants me, that I'm ugly and useless!

Evaluating underlying cognitions

Once the CBT practitioner has identified with a client their underlying schemas, core beliefs and assumptions, they might employ a number of techniques in evaluating and adapting them. Analysing the *advantages* vs *disadvantages* of a particular set of beliefs or assumptions might highlight how they hold a client back in their goals and aspirations. Then the thought record format (see Figures above) could be used to identify more helpful beliefs for a client. Paul identified a core belief that 'I'm a failure, others are better than me' and the assumption that he must consequently 'please everyone all of the time' just to get by. With his therapist, he reflected that while his efforts at 'people pleasing' could earn him praise in the short-term (advantage), over the longer-term he often felt exhausted, frustrated and avoidant of others – compounding his sense of failure (disadvantage). With this vicious cycle clearly marked out, the evidence for his belief was considered and a number of contexts and achievements that contradicted it were identified. Working in this manner Paul learnt to soften his harsh and self-critical beliefs, noting down on a sheet of A4 paper titled *Positive Data Log* his achievements and strengths, and carrying a summary reminder of these on a pocket-sized portable card (*flashcard*) for regular reading to counteract his engrained negative thought bias. Incorporating *continuum* techniques into the process, Paul was gradually able to reflect on and incorporate broader perspectives into his understandings of success and failure. In one of his last sessions he concluded 'at least I bother, a lot of people don't even try' and 'you can't be good at everything, I've got plenty of friends who like me for who I am'. He consequently was able to move himself up a 'continuum of acceptability' he had drawn out with his therapist, 'A' representing his early self-rating, 'B' his later one.

```
Acceptability                              Acceptability
0%          A           B                  100%
_____
```

Behavioural methods

Given that the CBT therapist is acutely aware of how behavioural responses can exacerbate and maintain a client's presenting difficulties, it is of no surprise that much of CBT practice focuses on behavioural adaptation. The following are some of the main methods.

Goal setting and the use of activity schedules

Here a client and therapist might aim to establish SMARTER (Specific – Measurable – Achievable – Relevant – Timed – Evaluated – Rewarded) goals, in working towards a client's personal aspirations. In so doing they may be encouraged to use 'activity schedules', timetables or diaries to clearly lay out a plan for enacting out-of-session tasks. For example, a client might write in their diary two occasions when they will review their cognitive flashcards prior to attending a social group that they have been avoiding, and then plan in the completion of a thought record immediately after the event relating to their experience and their learning. If their goal were to lose weight due to health concerns and low self-esteem, they might task themselves with regular exercise. On their activity schedule they might then plan regular gym sessions and walks, noting their progress and achievements on a positive data log.

Behavioural experiments and role play

A big focus of CBT is often developing and conducting 'behavioural experiments' in order to evaluate the validity of cognitive predictions, as well as to develop and reinforce new behavioural pathways. Behavioural experiments are usually co-constructed between the therapist and the client, and aim to place a client directly into a situation where they can test out their assumptions and apply adaptive techniques for coping. Anne, with her therapist, co-constructed a behavioural experiment to test out her prediction that she would be rejected by others and embarrass herself in social situations. Anne's experiment tasked her with suggesting to a work colleague that they might go to the pub after work to watch a football game as they both supported the same team. To her surprise her work colleague obliged and during the course of the evening she reported feeling more at ease with her friendly co-worker. Experiment completed, she fed back to her therapist that her assumptions had proved 'false' and perhaps not all of her colleagues were to be feared – demonstrating cognitive adaptation. Anne and her therapist also engaged in a number of behavioural 'role-plays' of social settings, aimed at building on her communication and interpersonal skill sets, as well as raising her confidence in social contexts.

Graded exposure

In progressing the learning from behavioural experiments a client and their therapist might develop a hierarchy of tasks. Each task putting the client into progressively more difficult situations, 'graded exposure', where they need to test out and evaluate their cognitions and behavioural responses. Anne graded up the number of co-workers and the frequency with which she saw them. She came to realise that while there were a few colleagues that were 'very different' to her, most were very friendly and seemed appreciative of her contribution to the team – they also seemed to enjoy her dry humour. In this way Anne came to appreciate a number of her own qualities and strengths, and by the end of therapy admitted that she mostly looked forward to going to work, previously fearing it. Clear progress, also reflected in Anne's feedback and the psychometrics used.

The use of 'mindfulness'

Mindfulness has been taken up by a number of approaches that have developed within the broad church of CBT. Dialectical behavioural therapy (Linehan et al., 1991), acceptance and commitment therapy (Hayes et al., 1999) and mindfulness-based cognitive therapy (Segal et al., 2002) all stress the merits of mindfulness in approaching our experience of our internal worlds. In essence, mindfulness invites a client to adopt a different stance to their internal processes – thoughts, emotions and physiology – and consequently respond (behave) in different ways. The stance suggested is one of open curiosity, acceptance and a non-judgemental approach to experience as it happens in the moment, and moment by moment. Within a secure therapeutic setting, clients are introduced to a number of meditative practices, which are encouraged on a daily basis, bringing them into contact with difficult thoughts, emotions and physical sensations. They are encouraged to try not to suppress or fight them, rather be with them, slowly building up their confidence as to their 'harmless' nature. Over time clients learn to respond to such internal events in a different way: finding they are less reactive to them, more tolerant and accepting of them and, consequently, more able to go about their day-to-day lives without being impacted by them. As an approach mindfulness has been applied to a number of presenting psychological and physical difficulties and has a growing and robust evidence base (Burch & Penman, 2013).

SUMMARY

CBT can be aligned with pluralistic principles with regard to its stance on: personalising therapy; collaboration; goals, tasks and methods; metatherapeutic communication; systematic feedback; and building on client strengths and resources. CBT offers the pluralistic practitioner a number of key understandings as to the human condition, with particular attention on 'information processing' models of cognition and behavioural learning theory. CBT's developmental model highlights the primary role of cognitions in presenting psychological difficulties and the behavioural maintaining factors that can lie therein. The main cognitive methods used in CBT are: monitoring automatic thoughts; identifying 'thinking errors'; using the 'downward arrow technique'; and evaluating underlying cognitions. Behavioural methods include: goal-setting and the use of activity schedules; behavioural experiments and role play; and graded exposure. CBT aims to help a client evaluate their current unhelpful cognitive and behavioural responses to events and, through vigorous application of technique, adapt them so as to modulate their impact and improve their lived experience. The practice of 'mindfulness' has also been incorporated into the CBT tradition to this end.

EXERCISES/POINTS FOR REFLECTION

1 How easy do you find it identifying your own thoughts and the potential biases within them?
2 Do you sometimes question the behaviours you engage in and consider how you might adapt them?

3   Do you have any particular thought biases or make assumptions when it comes to the application of CBT in the therapeutic setting – what has informed them?
4   Would you be willing to test out some of the understandings and methods of CBT in your own practice?

> ### FURTHER READING
>
> Beck, A.T., Rush, A.J., Shaw, B.F., & Emery, G. (1979). *Cognitive therapy for depression*. New York: The Guilford Press. One of the cornerstones of the cognitive revolution and gives a very good overview of the development and orientation of the CBT perspective.
>
> Beck, J. (1995). *Cognitive therapy: basics and beyond*. New York: The Guilford Press. Gives a thorough walk-though of most of the major CBT understandings and techniques.
>
> Padesky, C. (1994). Schema change processes in cognitive therapy. *Clinical Psychology and Psychotherapy, 1*(5), 267–278. Gives a detailed discussion of CBT methods aimed at helping a client identify, evaluate and adapt their underlying cognitive processes.

REFERENCES

Bartlett, F.C. (1932). *Remembering: a study in experimental and social psychology*. Cambridge: Cambridge University Press.

Beck, A.T. (1964). Thinking and depression: II. Theory and therapy. *Archives of General Psychiatry, 10*, 561–571.

Beck, A.T., Rush, A.J., Shaw, B.F., & Emery, G. (1979). *Cognitive therapy for depression*. New York: The Guilford Press.

Beck, A.T. & Weishaar, M.E. (1989). Cognitive therapy. In R.J. Corsini & D. Wedding (Eds.), *Current psychotherapies* (4th ed., pp. 285–320). Chicago, IL: Peacock Publishers.

Beck, J. (1995). *Cognitive therapy: basics and beyond*. New York: The Guilford Press.

Burch, V. & Penman, D. (2013). *Mindfulness for health: a practical guide to relieving pain, reducing stress and restoring wellbeing*. London: Piatkus.

Ellis, A. (1962). *Reason and emotion in psychotherapy*. New York: Lyle Stuart.

Gilbert, P. (Ed.). (2005). *Compassion: conceptualisations, research and use in psychotherapy*. London: Routledge.

Hayes, S.C., Strosahl, K.D., & Wilson, K.G. (1999). *Acceptance and commitment therapy: an experiential approach to behavior change*. London: The Guilford Press.

Kelly, G.A. (1955). *The psychology of personal constructs*. New York: Norton.

Linehan, M.M., Armstrong, H.E., Suarez, A., Allmon, D., & Heard, H. (1991). Cognitive-behavioural treatment of chronically parasuicidal borderline patients. *Archives of General Psychiatry, 48*, 1060–1064.

Padesky, C. & Mooney, K. (1990). Clinical tip: presenting the cognitive model to clients. *International Cognitive Therapy Newsletter*, *6*, 13–14.

Piaget, J. (1950). *The psychology of intelligence*. London: Routledge and Kegan Paul.

Rogers, C.R. (1957). The necessary and sufficient conditions of therapeutic personality change. *Journal of Consulting and Clinical Psychology*, *21*, 95–103.

Ryle, A. (1990). *Cognitive-analytic therapy: active participation in change: a new integration in brief psychotherapy*. Chichester: Wiley.

Segal, Z.V., Williams, J.M.G., & Teasdale, J.D. (2002). *Mindfulness-based cognitive therapy for depression: a new approach to preventing relapse*. New York: The Guilford Press.

Wells, A. (1997). *Cognitive therapy of anxiety disorders: a practice manual and conceptual guide*. Chichester: Wiley.

Wolpe, J. (1958). *Psychotherapy by reciprocal inhibition*. Stanford, CA: Stanford University Press.

Young, J.E., Klosko, J.S., & Weishaar, M.E. (2003). *Schema therapy: a practitioner's guide*. London: The Guilford Press.

10

Psychodynamic Approaches and Pluralism

Laurence Spurling

THIS CHAPTER DISCUSSES

- The ambivalent relationship between psychodynamic therapy and pluralism
- The key psychoanalytic understandings and methods that can contribute towards a pluralistic practice

INTRODUCTION TO PSYCHODYNAMIC THERAPIES AND HISTORICAL DEVELOPMENT

The fundamental assumption of all psychodynamic therapies is that of the unconscious, a part of the mind that is not available to our conscious thinking. The unconscious is seen as an area of the mind that operates according to its own laws (non-discursive thinking, displacement and condensation, etc.) and that 'contains' a host of memories, phantasies, thoughts, feelings, etc., which have been deemed unacceptable or too threatening to become conscious. The psychoanalytic method becomes one of acquainting the client or patient with this unconscious part of their mind, so they can understand the meaning of their pain, symptoms or distress.

But psychoanalytic therapy is not simply an insight-giving exercise. In the course of the exploration of the meaning of their experience the patient will also become acquainted with the part of themselves that does not wish to 'know' about this part of themselves, that is, their resistance. The success of analytic therapy will depend on how well this resistance, manifested through a variety of mechanisms of defence (such as repression) is recognized and 'worked through'. Freud's (1914/1964) description of this process, although written over one hundred years ago, captures well the basic attitude adopted by psychodynamic therapists when they listen to their patients:

> One must allow the patient to become more conversant with this resistance … to work through it, to overcome it … only when the resistance is at its height can the analyst, working in common with his patient, discover the repressed instinctual impulses which are feeding the resistance … the doctor has nothing else to do than to wait and let things take their course, a course which cannot be avoided nor always hastened. (p. 155)

Freud found that the patient's resistance tended to be most pronounced when it concerned their experience of the therapy itself. That is, they 'transfer' their experiences onto the therapy and the person of the therapist. They treat the therapist, and expect the therapist to treat them in terms of their unconscious pattern or template of previous experiences. Typically this transference will involve the patient's most intense and conflictual feelings, namely love (erotic or idealized transference) and hate (negative transference) (Spurling, 2009: 92–112).

Whereas Freud tended to focus on transference when it manifested itself as a form of resistance, the development of psychodynamic therapy since Freud has been characterized by seeing the exploration of the transference as a fundamental part of analytic therapy, and the element that is often the most decisive in leading to understanding and change – 'the analytic setting is unique in deliberately existing to concentrate, observe and make sense of transference, rather than modify and dispel it' (Milton, 2011: 9).

Since Freud, a number of different orientations or schools have developed within the field of psychodynamic therapy, each claiming adherence to Freud's basic ideas, but each developing psychodynamic thinking and practice in distinctive ways (see Figure 10.1). One important development is that of 'object relations' thinking. Unlike Freud, who saw his patients as waging a never-ending battle to master their drives or instincts – so, in the quotation above, the aim of analysis is described as that of uncovering 'the repressed instinctual impulses' that feed the resistance – most psychodynamic therapists think in terms of patterns of interpersonal relating, and the affects and conflicts that arise in an interpersonal context, as the main drivers of our experience and behaviour. In terms of practice, contemporary therapists make extensive use of the concept of 'countertransference', to refer to the emotional sensibility of the therapist and their receptivity to what they are feeling about the patient and the work (Heimann, 1950; Spurling, 2009: 111–116).

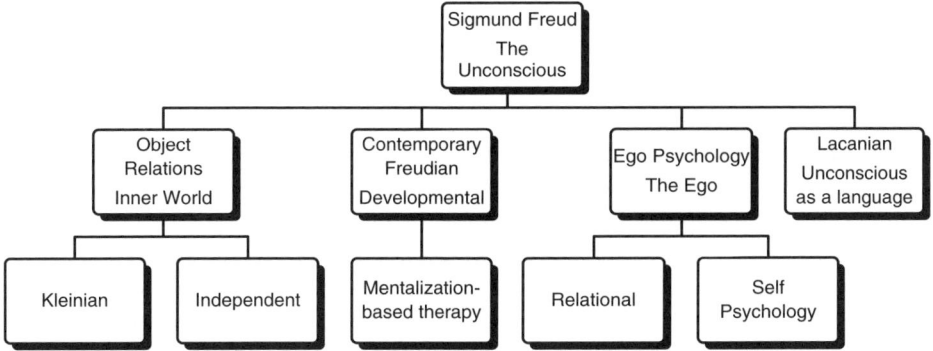

FIGURE 10.1 *A simplified map of the main psychoanalytic schools*

DEVELOPMENT OF INTEGRATIVE AND PLURALISTIC PERSPECTIVES IN PSYCHODYNAMIC THERAPIES

Traditionally, the attitude towards pluralistic and integrative tendencies in the psychodynamic literature has been one of suspicion, seeing them as an attack on the 'purity' of the psychodynamic approach (see, e.g., Milton, 2001). But in more recent years there have been a number of ways in which psychodynamic therapists have started to look seriously at non-analytic approaches and find ways of bringing them together with an analytic approach to produce something richer. One example would be the development of cognitive analytic therapy, as a distinctive blend of cognitive and psychodynamic approaches. Another would be 'mentalization-based therapy', a specific form of therapy for working with borderline patients (Bateman & Fonagy, 2004).

Alongside these developments of more pluralistic thinking, recent attempts within the psychodynamic field to look at how psychodynamic therapists actually practise, rather than how they think they practise, have revealed that their practice is more pluralistic than they think it is. In the words of a member of a working group comparing the way psychodynamic therapists from different orientations worked (Tuckett, 2008):

> Our findings indicate that in nearly all cases there exists a considerable gap between what analysts actually do in clinical practice and what they believe they do ... It was also apparent that in most cases what has been called the 'explicit public theory' was confused with the 'implicit private theory' of the analyst and that this confusion corresponded to a clinical practice that appeared to be only partly connected to theoretical conceptualizations at all. (Diercks, 2013: 1)

In other words, although the analyst or therapist in question might think they are working in accord with a particular psychodynamic school (public theory), when looked at in detail his or her work could be seen to be informed by ideas and thought that were more personal and specific to the work with the particular patient (implicit private theory), and gathered from a variety of different sources.

ALIGNMENT OF PSYCHODYNAMIC AND PLURALISTIC PRINCIPLES

Collaboration and transparency

Comparing the practice of psychodynamic therapy to the pluralistic paradigm as described by Cooper and McLeod (2011), the picture is a mixed one. The key idea in the pluralistic paradigm is that therapy should be *collaborative.* In order to work in a collaborative way the therapist needs to adopt a *transparent* attitude. Adopting these principles means that it is the patient or client who should be given power to determine what kind of therapy is used and how it is conducted.

If we go back to the quotation from Freud and look at it through this lens, it does not seem to be written in the spirit of pluralism. Freud was a doctor and clearly saw the therapist as having the responsibility for conducting the treatment. So the therapist 'must allow' the patient to become conversant with their resistance. Indeed the notions of the unconscious and resistance themselves seem to give the psychodynamic therapist a great deal of power as the person who 'knows' what is wrong with the patient who, by definition, does not know their own mind or the nature of their resistance.

Yet Freud makes clear that it is essential the patient 'becomes conversant' with their resistance. Although the language is different, this is a description of a practice that is collaborative. If the patient is to 'become conversant' with their resistance, this means the patient will have recognized and accepted that what they are doing constitutes a form of resistance. Furthermore, the therapist must work 'in common' with the patient. This is a clear description of collaboration. Contemporary psychodynamic therapists would refer to this 'working in common' with the patient as the establishment of a 'working alliance' to describe this collaborative approach (Spurling, 2009: 97).

Is psychodynamic therapy a transparent practice? It is harder to make a judgement here. Freud's own practice was not particularly transparent; he sometimes gave detailed and elaborate interpretations to his patients, but there is little evidence he was willing to do this in a transparent way, i.e. display for the patient how he came to his ideas. The tendency within much psychodynamic thinking and writing is for therapists to make an interpretation or intervention and then see what the patient or client makes of this, without seeing a need to show how they arrived at what they said. However, more recent trends within psychodynamic therapy have emphasized the need to be transparent in what one says to the patient, so the patient can have the experience of being with a therapist who can think and who is not afraid to offer this thinking to the patient and invite him or her to comment on this thinking (Lemma, 1993).

Seeking meaning and goals

Psychodynamic therapy is here more clearly aligned with pluralistic practice as it sees patients or clients constantly engaged in finding or making meaning in their lives and living their life in accord with certain life goals. These meanings and goals will become the focus of any psychodynamic therapy.

No theory or approach paramount

In their *thinking* many psychodynamic therapists would think of themselves as working within a psychodynamic framework, and within this framework taking one particular orientation as paramount. However, in their *practice* the evidence tends to show that psychodynamic therapists constantly adapt their thinking in the light of the particular clinical situation, and so are able to draw on a range of theories and approaches. (Spurling, 2015; Tuckett, 2008)

No single truth or meaning

An essential part of the pluralistic paradigm is that, when it comes to human experience and behaviour, there is no single truth or meaning. This chimes with a central psychodynamic tenet that the meaning of any event or experience is always 'overdetermined', that is, can be interpreted in a multitude of different ways. It will take time for some of these alternative meanings to become apparent. So, psychodynamic therapists are taught the value of learning to wait; as Freud put it, 'letting things take their course'.

KEY PSYCHODYNAMIC UNDERSTANDINGS THAT CAN CONTRIBUTE TO A PLURALISTIC PRACTICE

Negative capability: managing the frustration of dwelling in uncertainty

Allied to the basic psychodynamic ideas of the overdetermination of meaning and the importance of waiting for meaning to emerge, a key psychodynamic understanding is often expressed in term of John Keats's notion of 'negative capability', the capacity to be 'in Mysteries, uncertainties and doubts, without any irritable reaching after fact and reason' (from Keats's letters, Wadell, 1998: 162). This idea is sometimes expressed in terms of the value of 'not knowing', that is, cultivating an attitude that does not seek the comfort of certainty (Casement, 1985: 3–4).

This way of thinking is illustrated in the following clinical example (the example is based on my own clinical experience with several different patients; I have used the third person to describe the therapy with the intention of making it more applicable to many other clients and situations).

Early on in the therapy Ms A revealed to her (male) therapist that she had been sexually abused as a child by a family relative. Initially this revelation brought a sense of relief and achievement, as Ms A had never before told anyone about the abuse. However, having told the therapist, Ms A then started to speak of feeling stuck and demoralized. It became clear that, having 'confessed' (as she put it) what had happened, she expected to be 'free' from its influence, but she found this did not happen. For his part the therapist tried his best to help Ms A, first of all by encouraging her to speak more about the abuse if she felt safe enough, then by emphasizing her courage in having spoken of this event. But this seemed to make no difference. As the sessions continued, Ms A dropped the subject of abuse and brought more events from her present life, notably the arguments she was having with her partner, which she found very distressing. These arguments not only seemed to be very frequent but, if anything, seemed to have increased in frequency since Ms A had told the therapist of the abuse.

It was only when he spoke to a colleague about the therapy and how stuck he felt that the therapist suddenly realized that he felt frustrated and desperate to try to understand what was happening in the therapy. In so doing, in 'irritably reaching after fact and reason', he realized he had stopped really listening to his client. Once he gave up on trying to know, he was struck by a feature of the way Ms A spoke that he had not seen, or at least not paid much attention to, before. In the way she had spoken about the abuse she used phrases that suggested she felt she had been responsible for what happened. Similarly, in the never-ending arguments with her partner, the therapist also noticed that, despite her often blaming her partner for these arguments, she acted as though she held herself responsible for his actions and his feelings.

This is an example of the importance of learning to dwell in frustration and the value of giving up on trying to grasp at certainties. Only when he was able to look with fresh eyes at how Ms A spoke did the therapist 'see' something that had up until that point in the therapy not been evident to him. This principle finds its most elegant, if enigmatic, expression in Wilfred Bion's injunction:

> The capacity to forget, the ability to eschew desire and understanding, must be regarded as essential discipline for the psycho-analyst. (Bion, 1970: 51–52)

Making an interpretation to provide a provisional meaning

The psychodynamic method is essentially a hermeneutic one, that is, psychodynamic therapists are taught to look for the meaning of the experiences and behaviour of their patients. This method is based on a fundamental principle, that offering an interpretation to a patient or client will give them a tool with which to gather together disparate bits of their experience, providing an experience of understanding and relief.

In the example with Ms A, once the therapist had seen an aspect of her behaviour and experience which he thought she was not aware of it, he decided to offer her an interpretation as a way of sharing this understanding. Choosing his moment, when Ms A had returned to speaking of the abuse but in a flat and lifeless way, he said: 'What X (the relative) did to you was a traumatic event for you, and you feel you have not recovered from it. You can see that what he did was wrong and abusive and was nothing to do with you. But I think what you don't see so clearly is that, although you know what he did was wrong, at the same time you feel responsible for what happened, as though it was your fault. That is why, for instance, when you speak of the arguments with Y (her partner) you characteristically take the blame for what happened, even though when we talk about it you can't see what you have done wrong'.

Ms A listened carefully to this interpretation. She did not say whether she agreed or not with it, but the therapist could see her facial expression becoming softer. Then Ms A started to cry. When she stopped crying she said she did not know whether what the therapist had said was true or not, but for some reason she felt a huge burden had been lifted from her shoulders.

In general, in psychodynamic therapy it is preferable for the patient or client to arrive at their own understanding. But some patients or clients, at particular times in a therapy, find this very difficult or do not yet have the capacity to find this self-understanding. This is when an interpretation – in this case one that links present experiences with past events through the description of an interpersonal pattern of taking responsibility for other people's actions – can prove so effective.

Judging the 'truth' of an interpretation: does it further the therapeutic process?

Although the therapist felt he had arrived at an important piece of understanding, he offered this to Ms A as a provisional hypothesis. As such it might prove to be incorrect, in the sense of not resonating with Ms A, or even if correct of no value in the therapy, being offered at the wrong time or in the wrong way. The therapist therefore listened very carefully to how Ms A responded to what he said. At no time did she say she agreed with what he said, or that he was right. But she had a strong affective reaction, and then described feeling a big sense of relief. The therapist took this as confirmation that the interpretation of her experience was 'true' or 'effective', at least for now. Again he looked in subsequent sessions for further indirect feedback from Ms A. He noticed that in the next few sessions when she reported further arguments with her partner, she was less willing to take responsibility for his actions and was more prepared to stand up for herself.

In other words, psychodynamic therapists widen the notion of collaborative working to include unconscious as well as conscious elements. Freud famously argued that in making an interpretation to a patient, the therapist should not necessarily take the patient's lack of agreement as a sign that the interpretation does not contain some truth (Freud, 1937/1964). However, he also said that the patient's 'yes' to an interpretation is no more accurate a guide. What matters is whether the interpretation engages the patient's interest, whether it furthers the therapeutic process in the sense of allowing the patient to uncover a memory, give expression to a repressed feeling, or have a sense of being understood.

The overdetermination of meaning: adopting a multiplicity of perspectives on an event

At a later stage of the therapy the sexual abuse was re-visited. This time Ms A focused less on the event itself, and much more on the fact that when she told her parents, some time after the abuse had ended, she did not feel they believed her. This was not said in so many words, but Ms A noted that they seemed to do little about it, and seemed to regard it as just something she should 'get over'. As Ms A had gained more trust in the therapist and the therapeutic process, she was now able to arrive herself at another aspect of the trauma. As she put it, 'the abuse was bad enough, but what was worse was that when I told my mother she acted as though she did not believe me'. This re-interpretation of the trauma made sense of why Ms A found it hard to trust anyone, and got into a rage whenever she suspected someone did not believe her.

KEY PSYCHODYNAMIC METHODS THAT CAN CONTRIBUTE TO A PLURALISTIC PRACTICE

Working with resistance

At a later stage of the therapy, after a period where both Ms A and the therapist felt she seemed less burdened by the experience of abuse and had become better able to stand up for herself, Ms A arrived late for a session (she had rarely been late before). The therapist asked her why she had been late, to which Ms. A reacted with anger and hurt (the first time she had responded in this way to anything the therapist had said). Instead of apologizing or defending himself, the therapist tried to explore with Ms A why she was having such a strong reaction. In the course of this exploration Ms A lost her temper, stood up and shouted at the therapist 'I am not putting up with this any more, I have told you why I was late and it is absolutely evident that you don't believe me!' The therapist, feeling it was better to try to meet Ms A on her own terms, also stood up, and said to her 'So, I have become another person who does not believe you.' At this point the force of the therapist's remark got through to Ms A; she sat down and abruptly burst into tears. When she had calmed down, she was able to explore her reaction with the therapist. She could see starkly how powerful her expectation was of not being believed, and how it had nearly resulted in her walking out and ending the therapy in a spirit of discord and grievance.

This is an example of the therapist 'working with resistance'. This means he construed Ms A's behaviour at this point as no longer primarily motivated towards cooperation and a joint exploration of meaning, but, unconsciously, as designed to obstruct the further progress of the therapy – probably in order to protect herself against something which she feared would happen if the therapy developed further. His evidence for thinking of this as resistance was her curt apology (Ms A had never been curt with him before) together with her very strong reaction to his attempt to explore her lateness (she had never reacted with such strength before).

Working directly with resistance can look like a non-collaborative approach. In this case the therapist chose not to back off when Ms A made clear how angry and upset she was with him (he was relying on the establishment of a good working alliance with Ms A; in other situations with other clients he would not have been so challenging).

But working with resistance is done in the spirit of collaboration, with the aim, in Freud's words, of helping the client 'become conversant with the resistance'. As a result of the therapist's persistence, both patient and therapist arrived at an important piece of understanding, and Ms A herself was able to reflect back on her experience and behaviour in the early part of the session and realize she was defending against knowing something about herself.

Working with transference

Resistance on the part of the client can often take the form of experiencing the therapist as a transference figure, that is, as someone seen as an embodiment of past figures and experiences. Working with transference, that is, making the nature of the therapeutic relationship an explicit focus of study, is the most distinctive psychodynamic method. Its value is that it often brings a sense of conviction into the work by giving the client the experience, in the here-and-now with the therapist, of how their mind works and how it influences their experience and behaviour. In the case of Ms A, the session just described proved a breakthrough for Ms A. In subsequent sessions she was able to see how she had got very close to repeating what so far had been what she thought of as the 'story of my life', that men are always shown to be abusers who take no responsibility for their actions, and that she is the perennial victim. Furthermore, following this session Ms A looked back to how she had been in the therapy up until that point, and told the therapist that she thought the nature of her involvement in the therapy had been at times rather superficial – as she put it, 'I was brought up to please other people and I now think I was doing the same in the therapy with you.'

Tuning in to one's countertransference

The capacity to tune in to one's countertransference – that is, become attentive to feelings, thoughts, associations, memories, images, etc., which are related to the work with the particular client – is another method that can contribute to a pluralistic practice. In the example with Ms A, prior to the session described where she was late, the therapist had in fact been paying particular attention to the emotional atmosphere of the work and to his countertransference feelings. He could feel things had gone rather flat in the therapy, and had the suspicion that Ms A was running away from something, but he was not sure what. He found himself feeling less attuned to Ms A, indeed at times was aware of feeling rather irritable with her. He started to wonder whether his occasional irritability might be picking up something Ms A was feeling but not showing, at least explicitly.

Once he was able to recognize these countertransference feelings in himself, the therapist felt more able to try to listen out for indications of resistance and transference. This was why in the session where Ms A had come late, and gave a rather perfunctory explanation for her lateness, rather than simply accepting what she said at face value the therapist had decided instead to explore its meaning with Ms A, and had persisted in this exploration in spite of her protestations.

SUMMARY

The key points of this chapter are:

- Psychodynamic therapies have a number of understandings (negative capability, the value of insight and understanding, how to judge the 'truth' of an interpretation, the overdetermination of meanings) and methods (working with resistance and transference, and tuning into one's countertransference) which can contribute towards a pluralistic practice.
- The main contribution of psychodynamic therapies to a pluralistic practice is in adopting understandings and methods where collaboration has become difficult or is at risk.

EXERCISES/POINTS FOR REFLECTION

One way of thinking about the relationship between psychodynamic therapy and pluralistic practice is to see the most useful or fruitful contribution to be where collaboration with the client has become problematic or is in danger of breaking down. In such situations, the client may need to be challenged, involving the emergence of hitherto hidden aspects of the transference.

However, for those not trained in a psychodynamic approach, or who do not have access to psychodynamic supervision or consultation, simply adopting such methods as part of a pluralistic practice has its dangers. In the example above, in the session where the therapist challenged the client's lateness, and made a transference interpretation as a way of helping her 'see' what she was doing in the session, his use of these methods was based on many years of training and experience. For these reasons it may be best to describe the ways psychodynamic practice can best contribute to a pluralistic practice as ways of thinking that can add further dimensions to one's normal approach. Here are two simple examples of such thought experiments or exercises to practise.

1. COLLABORATION OR COMPLIANCE?

Take a recent example of collaborative work with your client. Now adopt a different perspective, look at this event through the lens of resistance and transference. It is likely that in some areas of the work your client is less collaborative than others. Further, what looks like collaboration can sometimes be a form of compliance or appeasement on the part of the client. How would you be able to tell the difference?

2. LISTENING TO A PATIENT OR CLIENT AS IF THE FIRST TIME

Take a client or patient you think you know well or have worked with for a long time. Now try to listen to him or her as if you have never met them before and you know nothing about them (listening without memory or desire). What strikes you about how your patient or client is talking, how they are describing the people and events in their life, and how they are relating to you? Try to follow up any hunches, thoughts or feelings you may register, even if these seem inconsequential or nonsensical (tuning into one's countertransference). Try to pay particular attention to any thoughts you have that you realize you may not feel comfortable with pursuing – these may be indications of elements of the transference in play that both you and your client/patient are choosing to avoid. If you do get in touch with such thoughts, you are then in a position to bring them to your client's attention, as an area of mutual and collaborative exploration, if you think your client is ready for such an exploration and that it will further the therapy.

FURTHER READING

Holmes, J. (2010). Integration in psychoanalytic psychotherapy – an attachment metaperspective. *Psychoanalytic Psychotherapy*, 24(3), 183–201. A good example of how psychodynamic therapy can foster an integrative and pluralistic approach.

Jimenez, J (2005). The search for integration or how to work as a pluralist psychoanalyst. *Psychoanalytic Inquiry*, 25, 602–634. An account of how a psychoanalyst, working from within the psychoanalytic framework, used an encounter with empirical research to move from one theoretical orientation to another.

Spurling, L. (2012). 'Characters' in psychoanalytic and interpersonal therapy: a comparison. *Psychoanalytic Psychotherapy*, 23(3), 230–244. An example of using understandings and methods from two different types of therapy to enrich one's clinical repertoire and practice.

REFERENCES

Bateman, A., & Fonagy, P. (2004). *Psychotherapy for borderline personality disorder: mentalization-based treatment.* Oxford: Oxford University Press.

Bion, W. (1970). *Attention and interpretation.* London: Tavistock.

Casement, P. (1985). *On learning from the patient.* London: Tavistock.

Cooper, M., & McLeod, J. (2011). *Pluralistic counselling and psychotherapy.* London: Sage.

Diercks, M. (2013, December). *Freud's 'Transference': claim and reality, theory and practice.* Unpublished paper presented at University College London conference: 'Transference, countertransference and enactment', London, UK.

Freud, S. (1964). Remembering, repeating and working through. *The standard edition of the complete psychological works of Sigmund Freud* (Vol.12, pp. 145–156). London: Hogarth Press. (Original work published 1914.)

Freud, S. (1964). Constructions in analysis. *The standard edition of the complete psychological works of Sigmund Freud* (Vol. 23, pp. 255–269). London: Hogarth Press. (Original work published 1937.)

Heimann, P. (1950). On counter-transference. *International Journal of Psychoanalysis*, *30*, 81–84.

Lemma, A. (1993). *Introduction to the practice of psychoanalytic psychotherapy*. Chichester: Wiley.

Milton, J. (2001). Psychoanalysis and cognitive behaviour – rival paradigms or common ground? *International Journal of Psychoanalysis*, *82*, 431–447.

Milton, J., Polmear, C., & Fabricius, J. (2011). *A short introduction to psychoanalysis*. London: Sage.

Spurling, L. (2009). *An introduction to psychodynamic counselling* (2nd ed.). London: Palgrave.

Spurling, L. (2015). *The psychoanalytic craft: how to develop as a psychoanalytic practitioner*. London: Palgrave.

Tuckett, D. (2008). *Psychoanalysis comparable and incomparable: the evolution of a method to describe and compare psychoanalytic approaches*. London: Routledge.

Waddell, M. (1998). *Inside lives: psychoanalysis and the growth of the personality*. London: Karnac.

11
Existential Approaches and Pluralism

Mick Cooper and
Gerhard Stumm

THIS CHAPTER DISCUSSES

- The nature, development and schools of existential therapy
- The development of integrative perspectives within existential therapy
- The commonalities and differences across existential and pluralistic perspectives
- The key existential understandings that can contribute to a pluralistic practice
- The key existential methods that can contribute to a pluralistic practice

EXISTENTIAL THERAPIES: AN INTRODUCTION

Existential therapies are one of the earliest forms of psychological intervention. They emerged in the 1920s through the work of psychiatrists such as Jaspers, Binswanger and Frankl. Existential therapies can be defined as psychological interventions that are informed, to a significant extent, by the teachings of existential philosophers, such as Heidegger, Sartre, Kierkegaard, Buber and Nietzsche, as well as by Husserl and the phenomenologists (Cooper, 2015). Existential and phenomenological philosophy is a broad school of thinking rather than a homogenous set of ideas. However, what unites it is a rejection of systems of thought that are seen as *de-humanising*: that reduce the complexity, uniqueness and inter-relatedness of human lived-existences to a set of impersonal statistics, laws, systems or absolutes. In other words, existential approaches call our attention back to the concrete realities of human existence and experiencing.

Four main schools of existential therapy have been identified (Cooper, 2003), each of which evolved in relative independence from the others:

- *Daseinsanalysis*, developed in the 1930s by Binswanger and then Boss, retains close links to classical psychoanalysis. It provides clients with a 'permissive' therapeutic relationship in which they can express themselves freely, and develop greater openness towards their world (e.g., other people, nature, activities).
- *Meaning-oriented therapies* (e.g., Wong, 2013) began with Frankl's (1986) logotherapy in the 1920s, and focus on helping clients to establish meaning and purpose in their lives. Längle's (2012) existential analysis, which extends classical logotherapy through the integration of psychodynamic elements, is now one of the largest schools of existential therapy across the globe. Meaning-oriented therapies have also been developed to help people with life-threatening illnesses (see Craig, Vos, Cooper, & Correia, 2015).
- The *British school of existential therapy* (e.g., Cooper, 2015; Spinelli, 2014b; van Deurzen, 1998) developed from the work of Laing. It adopts a primarily descriptive, phenomenological stance, with clients encouraged to explore their lived-experiences.
- The *existential-humanistic* approach (e.g., Schneider, 2008; Yalom, 1980) draws on humanistic-supportive practices, as well as those of a more psychodynamic-interpretative nature. It aims to help clients face the 'ultimate givens' of life: in particular mortality, freedom, isolation and meaninglessness.

A recent review of the available research found that existential therapies – particularly the meaning–oriented approaches – had the potential to bring about significant positive changes, particularly in increasing a sense of meaning and in reducing depression and anxiety (Vos, Craig, & Cooper, 2014).

Integrative perspectives in the existential therapies

At the heart of the existential approach is a rejection of the positivistic, nomothetic assumptions that underpin many other forms of psychology and psychotherapy. For this reason, argues Spinelli (2014a: 9), the existential approach does not 'sit easily' with the current dominant models of theory and practice within psychology. And, indeed, historically, existential therapeutic communities (such as the daseinsanalysts and logotherapists) have tended to remain relatively isolated from academic mainstream psychology and from other therapeutic orientations.

Nevertheless, existential therapies have drawn extensively from other orientations, in particular psychoanalysis and the humanistic paradigm. Vice versa, humanistic approaches – like person-centred therapy, Gestalt therapy and Focusing – have distinct existential accentuations (see Chapter 8, this volume). Indeed, Yalom (1980) argues that existential concerns may be taken into consideration by every psychotherapeutic orientation.

Recent years have also seen a range of attempts to develop more integrative forms of existential therapy. There have been efforts, for instance, to integrate existential therapy with brief solution-focused therapy, mindfulness and other 'third wave' forms of CBT (see Cooper, 2015). Wong's (2013: 628) meaning–centred counselling assimilates 'elements of cognitive-behavioural, narrative, cross-cultural and positive therapies' into an explicitly integrative framework. The existential-humanistic field, too, has explicitly described its approach as 'existential-integrative' (Schneider, 2008) and, more recently, 'pluralistic' (Schneider & Krug, 2010: 10); with Schneider (2008: 3) writing that it is 'complementary to and integrative of other practice modalities'. Most recently, Cooper's (2015) *Existential Psychotherapy and Counselling: Contributions to a Pluralistic Practice* directly aims to articulate existential practice within a collaborative integrative framework.

ALIGNMENT OF EXISTENTIAL AND PLURALISTIC PRINCIPLES

Commonalities

The pluralistic approach, as articulated by Cooper and McLeod (2011), was explicitly founded on a number of key existential principles:

- The pluralistic approach rejects nomothetic (i.e., universal) theories of human functioning: that everyone experiences problems for the same reasons, and can be helped in the same way. Rather, as with the existential approach, there is an emphasis on the uniqueness of each individual's wants and preferences.
- There is a rejection of any fixed or definite truths, that any one theoretical orientation has all the answers. Rather, there is an acceptance of the ambiguity, uncertainty and messiness of life.
- In terms of therapeutic practice, the pluralistic approach shares the existential emphasis on the development of a mutual, dialogic, transparent relationship with clients.
- Like the existential approaches (in particular logotherapy), the pluralistic approach holds that human beings are purpose- and meaning-oriented beings, such that an explication of clients' goals may be a key part of the therapeutic process.

Differences

There are also ways in which a pluralistic approach diverges from an existential perspective:

- A pluralistic approach does not consider a wholly existential point of view (as outlined below) as *the* preferred stance towards clients, but as just one that will be useful for some clients some of the time.
- The pluralistic openness to clients' goals could be considered incompatible with some existential approaches, which emphasise 'being with' clients, over 'doing to' (e.g., Spinelli, 2014b).
- While some existential approaches are averse towards techniques, the pluralistic approach is open to a wide range of therapeutic methods and strategies.

KEY EXISTENTIAL UNDERSTANDINGS THAT CAN CONTRIBUTE TO A PLURALISTIC PRACTICE

In rejecting traditional, mechanistic accounts of psychological functioning, the existential approach provides a unique perspective on what it means to be human. The following section describes specific aspects of existential thinking that may make a particular contribution to pluralistic theory and practice.

The primacy of experiencing

As with other phenomenologically based approaches (e.g., Gestalt therapy, person-centred therapy), the existential approach understands human beings primarily in terms of their concrete, subjectively lived flow of experiencing. Experiencing can be defined as all that is going on for the person at any given moment which is potentially available to awareness (Rogers, 1959): our feelings, thoughts, bodily sensations, perceptions and desires. It can be understood to have a number of essential, invariant qualities (Cooper, 2015):

- It is a *dynamic* flow: process-like, as opposed to a static, object-like thing.
- It has an *in-the-moment quality* to it.
- It has the potential to be *consciously* experienced.
- It has a *bodily*, visceral dimension to it.
- It is *intentional*: directed towards something outside of itself.

The freedom of being

From this phenomenological starting point, existential theorists have gone on to say something of what it is like to exist as this experiencing being. A key characteristic emphasised by many existentialists is the human capacity to make choices. Sartre (1958: 25), for instance, writes: 'Man does not exist *first* in order to be free *subsequently*; there is no difference between the being of a man and his *being-free*'. In other words, the capacity to choose is not an add-on to our personality or development, but an intrinsic aspect of our being.

Moreover, for existentialists like Sartre, we are our choices: our identities and characteristics are consequences – and not causes – of the choices that we make. This is not to suggest that people are to blame for their problems: for instance, it is not suggesting that if someone is a victim of domestic violence, then it is their own fault. It also does not represent a voluntarism that everything can be achieved if only wanted. What it does suggest is that the choices we make in our lives have a fundamental effect on who we are and who we become. That is, we are not driven to be any one kind of person: we decide, throughout our lives, on the kind of people we will be. This includes the stance we take towards the existential givens of life.

Being as limited

In rejecting voluntarism, existentialists have argued that human freedom is hedged in in innumerable ways. Key limitations, or 'givens', of existence include:

- mortality: the fact that we are beings-towards-death
- tensions: that we are always pulled in different directions by competing wants
- ontological uncertainty, chance and ambiguity
- social, economic and political givens
- thrownness: that we are born into a world that is not of our making
- temporality: that we live 'in' time.

From this perspective, then, human being is an active choosing-towards-limitations: a constant striving to make the most of our world in the face of givens beyond our control. Marcie, for instance, was a young client with learning disabilities who was looking at what she might do in her life. From an existential perspective, there was no future set for her, no pre-determined path that she must follow. Yet, at the same time, there were definite limitations in her life: such as her cognitive difficulties, her critical parents and the social stigma that existed towards her. She did not choose these, but she could choose how she responded to them.

Being as towards-the-future

In the case of Marcie, her attempts to work out what to do with her life illustrate another feature of existential thought: that it understands human beings as oriented towards their futures. In other words, we look towards a future (for instance, Marcie wanted to work with older adults), and this then shapes how we act in the present (for instance, her therapist explored with her the idea of doing some training in social care work). So, from this perspective, the basic ground for human action is *motives* rather than *causes*: our purposes and future goals can be as important to who we are as our pasts.

For meaning-oriented therapists, this future-directed quality of human being also means that we need purposes and meanings in our lives to thrive (Frankl, 1986). That is, we achieve psychological well-being through making sense of the situations we encounter – whether, for instance, through responding in creative ways or by changing our attitudes towards our suffering – and through having a sense of where we are going in life. Without this, it is argued that we can fall into an existential vacuum: hopelessness, depression and despair.

Being as with-others

Existential writers have also suggested that human beings are fundamentally and intrinsically 'with-others'. Buber (1958) suggests, however, that there are two fundamentally different modes of being with others. In the *I–It attitude*, one person experiences another as a thing-like, determined object: an entity that can be systematised, analysed and broken down into universal parts. By contrast, he describes a deeply humanising, existential form of interrelating, the *I–Thou attitude*. Here, the other is beheld, accepted and confirmed as a unique, unclassifiable and unanalysable totality: as a freely choosing flux of human experiencing. For Buber, such an I–Thou attitude requires a meeting with the other as they are in the present, rather than in terms of our past assumptions or future needs. It is an opening out to the other in their actual otherness – and a loving 'confirmation' of that otherness – rather than a self-reflexive encounter with our own stereotypes and desires.

The tragic dimension of being

Given these assumptions about human being, existential writers have tended to argue that human existence has an inherently tragic dimension. Facing the limitations of human existence – such as transitoriness, death, uncertainty and the paradoxes of life – means anxiety. Existence also means striving to find meanings and purposes in a world that may be devoid of any, but in which we are unable to step off the treadmill of wanting and desiring. And to be human means to be caught up in interpersonal misperceptions, entanglements and conflicts that arise from the very grounds of our being. 'Life', writes van Deurzen (1998: 132), 'is an endless struggle, where moments of ease and happiness are the exception rather than the rule.' Like Sisyphus rolling his boulder up the hill, we must battle to move forward in our lives. There are some successes, but most often they are followed by further failures. And after all that, there is decrepitude and death.

Being as authentic or inauthentic

Because the reality of existence can be so distressing, existential writers have argued that human beings have an inherent tendency to deny it. This may be done in a variety of ways. Yalom (1980), for instance, argues that people may defend themselves against the givenness of their mortality through a narcissistic belief in their own specialness. Similarly, in attempting to deny their own responsibility to choose, people may procrastinate, become apathetic, or behave in fixed, compulsive, obsessive or phobic ways.

Such *inauthenticity* may bring temporary relief but, from an existential perspective, it is suggested that it does more harm than good. This is for a range of reasons. First, if we deny the reality of our human situation, we may be less able to make the most of the lives that we do have. Delegating choices to others, for instance, may bring a temporary sense of relief, but it also means that we are then less able to choose to do the things that we find most rewarding and satisfying. Second, because the reality of existence does not go away, the defences that we erect to protect ourselves against it may falter, such that *existential anxiety* and *existential guilt* (i.e., a natural response to the givens of existence) become *neurotic anxiety* and *neurotic guilt* (i.e., unnecessary and unhelpful reactions to the givens of existence). However painful it may be, then, to authentically face the realities of life, from an existential perspective, it is the key to the fullest, most vibrant existence.

KEY EXISTENTIAL METHODS THAT CAN CONTRIBUTE TO A PLURALISTIC PRACTICE

Existential therapy offers a variety of methods that may support clients towards greater authenticity of being. With adequate knowledge and training, all of these can be incorporated into a pluralistic practice.

Adopting an I–Thou stance

Buber's (1958) concept of the I–Thou attitude (see above) provides an essential starting point for, and articulation of, the existential therapeutic stance; as well as a pluralistic metatherapeutic position. It is also generally well supported by the empirical evidence (e.g., Norcross, 2011). Through being met in this humanising way, clients may come to acknowledge and accept their *own* humanity, and develop the skills to re-connect with others in their lives. Cooper (2015) suggests that this I-Thou stance has a number of characteristics:

- Therapists stand alongside clients as fellow travellers, rather than surveying, studying or analysing them.
- Therapists relate to clients as subjects rather than as objects: engaging with them as sources of agency and experiencing.
- Clients are listened to holistically and in an embodied way: therapists 'breathe in' and respond to the totality of their being.
- Therapists are open to the otherness of their clients.
- Clients are affirmed, but from a place in which therapists hold on to their own differences.
- Therapists relate *as* wholenesses to their clients: bringing their own totality – thoughts, feelings, vulnerabilities, etc. – into the therapeutic encounter.
- Therapists are willing to take risks: allowing themselves to be changed in the meeting with clients in ways they cannot predict.

Working phenomenologically

Closely related to this I-Thou stance is a therapeutic approach that encourages clients to reflect on, and develop awareness of, their lived-experiencing.

Such phenomenological practice is based on two core principles (Spinelli, 2014b). First is the process of bracketing, in which, as therapists, we are encouraged to set aside our initial biases and prejudices of things. This involves suspending our expectations and assumptions, so that we can focus on the actual data of our clients' experiencing. Second is the 'rule of description', the essence of which is '*Describe, don't explain*'. Here, we are urged to refrain from producing interpretations, hypotheses or theories as to what clients are experiencing, and instead to keep strictly to the phenomena as directly visible. So, for instance, if a client was talking about his anger towards his wife, a phenomenological approach would *not* be to wonder, or try to work out, what this was 'really' about. Rather, it would be about helping the client to describe in more detail what that anger was like: How did it feel? What was he thinking? What did it make him want to do?

There are a number of specific therapist activities that may facilitate this process of phenomenological exploration (Cooper, 2015, see also Chapter 7, this volume):

- Actively listening to clients: providing them with sufficient space to talk
- Using minimal encouragers (e.g., 'mm', 'hmm')
- Reflecting, paraphrasing and summarising what clients say, to encourage them to go deeper into their lived-experiences
- Asking open-ended questions: for instance, 'How did you feel?' 'What was going on in your head?' 'How did it feel in your body?' 'What were you wanting?'
- Highlighting contradictions or disparities in clients' narratives
- Using symbols, metaphors or creative methods (e.g., drawing) for clients who find it difficult to verbally describe their experiencing: for instance, 'Is there an image that could express what that bleakness is like?'
- Personification: inviting clients to express different modes, or aspects, of being: for instance, 'What is your critical side saying here?'
- Inviting clients to unpack experiences in the here-and-now, to develop a more vivid and accurate awareness of how they experience things
- Noting, and challenging, clients' blocks to exploration: for instance, 'I notice that, every time we talk about your older brother, you seem to change the topic'.

Challenging clients to accept the freedom of existence

From an existential standpoint, it may also be important to help clients recognise that they are active agents in their lives: that they have the capacity for choice and responsibility. In the following example, Gerhard works with Tom, a young man who has said that he is not sure whether he should have moved in with his girlfriend. Early on in the therapy, Tom had indicated that he was keen to be challenged by Gerhard and not 'let off the hook' – even if it might feel uncomfortable at the time – and so Gerhard took a relatively proactive stance.

> *Gerhard*: So you're saying you're not sure about it: whether you really wanted that.
> *Tom*: Well, actually it's not so much the question of whether we live together. I like her but she's really unpredictable … she's a bit of a drama queen. We fight a lot: one wrong word and she's offended and pulls back for

Gerhard: days. She gives me such a hard time, and I really need to be on top of things at work, so instead of feeling positive things from her …
Gerhard: …You feel annoyed and exhausted, is that it?
Tom: Yeah. And then— 'Let's have a kid together.' But the thought of having one … yeughh. If my girlfriend keeps on being so fragile— I don't know, even the couples therapy didn't work.
Gerhard: So what is it that made you move in with her and choosing to stay?
Tom: I'm hoping that things will get better, but I don't really think so.
Gerhard: You're hoping that things will somehow turn out all right but, can I ask you, are there things you are doing to improve the situation? It kind of feels like you aren't really saying 'yes' or 'no' to the relationship. Are you putting off any real choice?
Tom: Yeah … maybe … In some ways— I think I am probably very vague about things. It's hard to commit to what I want …

Here, Gerhard uses empathic attunement and open-ended phenomenological questions (see above) to help Tom explore his lived-experiencing. Drawing on his existential understandings, however, he also went on to challenge Tom to take responsibility for his choices: to actively decide what he wants to do in this situation rather than positioning himself as a victim of his girlfriend's choices. In this dialogue, we can also see Gerhard use words like 'want' and 'choosing' to try to activate Tom's sense of agency.

Challenging clients to accept the limitations of existence

Existential therapists may also challenge clients to face up to the limitations of their situation. In the following example, 48-year-old Farah has come to therapy to 'accept the reality of the ageing process', but admits that she is really struggling to do so.

Farah: …And now I've got to start wearing specs. I just can't bear it: it's just been too much in the last few months. Hot flushes … I just wonder where it's going to end up.
Gerhard: All these physical and health issues are really worrying you.
Farah: I hate wearing specs. I should have started with them ages ago but I refused it. I'm not even 50 but it feels like 70. I hate it.
Gerhard: From what I've understood before, your state of health is pretty good, but you feel like you're coming to your end?
Farah: Yeah … I've done alright. I got my blood pressure down without using any drugs; and I can still run a half-marathon close to my PB [personal best]. But I just feel— it's too much to handle now. I can't face it and what's to come next.
Gerhard: It sounds like you're kind of desperate that you can't do anything about it to stop these things. It almost feels like some kind of terminal decline for you.

Farah:	Yeah … I don't know. Does it sound like I'm exaggerating? It's not that I want to be a 20-year-old. As old as I am is OK, but in good shape.
Gerhard:	It's hard to accept that your body is causing you problems. You're really working hard to stay fit and in control of things, but I wonder if it's difficult to accept that getting older is something that's outside of your control. Does that make sense?
Farah:	Mm … well … I guess— I do blame my age that I can't do things like I used to.

Consistent with Farah's goals, in this extract we can see Gerhard facilitating a phenomenological exploration, but going on to challenge the client to face a limitation of her life. As the therapy progressed, Farah felt like she was moving closer to her goal of accepting the reality of ageing.

Helping clients to find values, meaning and purpose in their lives

Meaning-oriented methods aim to help clients find greater meaning and purposes in their lives, and have good evidence of effectiveness (Vos et al., 2014). These tend to be more directive and structured than other existential practices. For instance, in Socratic dialogue, therapists ask their clients relatively challenging questions, to help them access deeper feelings about what is meaningful and of value in their lives. An example comes from meaning-oriented therapist Joël Vos's work with a 43-year-old woman, Laura, who had been through treatment for breast cancer (see Craig et al., 2015). In the session, Laura described how she was overwhelmed by feelings of fear and vulnerability, and struggled to develop a more positive sense of meaning. 'I just think about the possibility that it [the cancer] is back,' she says, 'and that I die … I can see myself dying. So much pain, my children will miss me.' Joël responded by suggesting to Laura that it was possible to experience a sense of meaning in life *despite* her feelings of fear and vulnerability. He then went on to suggest to Laura that, from what she was saying, caring for her children and supporting them was how she continued to find meaning in her life. 'I think … it's my children who give me the power,' said Laura, 'And, you know, I'm not the type of person who gives up: I'm persistent, proud, stubborn.' Following this exchange, Joël and Laura went on to look at other specific examples in her life where she did experience a sense of meaning, helping her to reconnect with a sense of purpose and self-worth.

SUMMARY

Existential therapies offer pluralistic therapists a diverse range of understandings and methods that can help clients to acknowledge the concrete realities of their existences:

that we are subjectively experiencing beings, intrinsically related to others, who have the freedom to act towards our futures within a range of limitations. The existential approach reminds us that life is a journey that is filled also with challenge, anxiety and distress; and that, if we try to avoid these feelings, we can end up doing more harm than good. The existential therapies, therefore, propose a range of methods that can be used to help clients face up to the realities of their existential conditions and make the most of their lives. The basic existential approach is an I-Thou stance, in which clients are related to as experiencing subjectivities rather than objective 'things'. This can be supported by phenomenological methods, which aim to help clients unpack their lived experiences. Clients can also be challenged to face up to the freedom and limitations in their lives, and find meanings that are inherently valuable to them.

Within the existential field, there is a strong tradition of integrative practices, and this is consistent with the existential emphasis on fluidity, flexibility and open-mindedness in therapeutic work. Hence, existential ideas provide a strong underpinning for a pluralistic approach to counselling and psychotherapy. In particular, a pluralistic approach is highly consistent with a postmodern reading of existentialism, with an emphasis on reflexivity, deconstruction and a questioning of grand narratives.

EXERCISES/POINTS FOR REFLECTION

1 To what extent do you think existential understandings and methods can be incorporated into pluralistic and integrative therapeutic practices?
2 How easy do you find it to acknowledge a person's freedom and responsibility? In what particular ways might people tend to evade an awareness of their potential for choice?
3 What fundamental limitations for human beings do you acknowledge? How do you resonate with the impact of each of these limitations?
4 Think of a client that you are struggling with: What relationship does he or she have to his or her future? Is there a positive sense of where he or she is going in life, a negative sense, or is there no real sense of the future at all? How do you think this affects him or her in the present?

FURTHER READING

Cooper, M. (2003). *Existential therapies*. London: Sage. Reviews the understandings and methods of the key schools of existential therapy.

Cooper, M. (2015). *Existential psychotherapy and counselling: contributions to a pluralistic practice*. London: Sage. A book on existential therapy specifically written for pluralistic and integrative practitioners who want to draw on these understandings and methods.

Craig, M., Vos, J., Cooper, M., & Correia, E. (2015). Existential psychotherapies. In D. Cain, K. Keenan, & S. Rubin (Eds.), *Humanistic psychotherapies*. Washington, DC: American Psychological Association. Evidence-based review of existential understandings and methods.

> Schneider, K.J., & Krug, O.T. (2010). *Existential-humanistic therapy*. Washington, DC: American Psychological Association. Concise and accessible summary of the existential-humanistic approach, as currently developed in the United States.
>
> Spinelli, E. (1997). *Tales of un-knowing: therapeutic encounters from an existential perspective*. London: Duckworth. A compelling, moving and insightful collection of case studies that gives an excellent introduction to the existential approach.
>
> Yalom, I.D. (1980). *Existential psychotherapy*. New York: Basic Books. Yalom's *magnum opus*, detailing the manifestations of, resistances to, research about and therapeutic work with four 'ultimate concerns' of existence: death, freedom, isolation and meaninglessness. Essential reading for existential therapists of all persuasions.

REFERENCES

Buber, M. (1958). *I and thou* (R.G. Smith, Trans., 2nd ed.). Edinburgh: T & T Clark.

Cooper, M. (2003). *Existential therapies*. London: Sage.

Cooper, M. (2015). *Existential psychotherapy and counselling: contributions to a pluralistic practice*. London: Sage.

Cooper, M., & McLeod, J. (2011). *Pluralistic counselling and psychotherapy*. London: Sage.

Craig, M., Vos, J., Cooper, M., & Correia, E. (2015). Existential psychotherapies. In D. Cain, K. Keenan, & S. Rubin (Eds.), *Humanistic psychotherapies* (2nd ed.). Washington, DC: American Psychological Association.

Frankl, V.E. (1986). *The doctor and the soul: from psychotherapy to logotherapy* (R. Winston & C. Winston, Trans., 3rd ed.). New York: Vintage Books.

Längle, A. (2012). The Viennese School of existential analysis: the search for meaning and affirmation in life. In L. Barnett & G. Madison (Eds.), *Existential psychotherapy: vibrancy, legacy and dialogue* (pp. 159–170). London: Routledge.

Norcross, J.C. (Ed.). (2011). *Psychotherapy relationships that work: evidence-based responsiveness* (2nd ed.). New York: Oxford University Press.

Rogers, C.R. (1959). A theory of therapy, personality and interpersonal relationships as developed in the client–centered framework. In S. Koch (Ed.), *Psychology: a study of science* (Vol. 3, pp. 184–256). New York: McGraw–Hill.

Sartre, J.-P. (1958). *Being and nothingness: an essay on phenomenological ontology* (H. Barnes, Trans.). London: Routledge.

Schneider, K.J. (Ed.). (2008). *Existential-integrative psychotherapy: guideposts to the core of practice*. New York: Routledge.

Schneider, K.J., & Krug, O.T. (2010). *Existential-humanistic therapy*. Washington, DC: American Psychological Association.

Spinelli, E. (2014a). An existential challenge to some dominant perspectives in the practice of contemporary counselling psychology. *Counselling Psychology Review, 29*(2), 7–24.

Spinelli, E. (2014b). *Practising existential psychotherapy: the relational world* (2nd ed.). London: Sage.

van Deurzen, E. (1998). *Paradox and passion in psychotherapy: an existential approach to therapy and counselling*. Chichester: Wiley.

Vos, J., Craig, M., & Cooper, M. (2014). Existential therapies: a meta-analysis of their effects on psychological outcomes. *Journal of Consulting and Clinical Psychology, 83*(1), 115-128.

Wong, P.T. (2013). From logotherapy to meaning-centred counselling and therapy. In P.T. Wong (Ed.), *The human quest for meaning: theories, research, and applications* (2nd ed., pp. 619–647). New York: Routledge.

Yalom, I.D. (1980). *Existential psychotherapy*. New York: Basic Books.

12

Narrative Approaches and Pluralism

Rolf Sundet and John McLeod

THIS CHAPTER DISCUSSES

- The key ideas and practices associated with narrative therapy
- Similarities and differences between narrative and pluralistic ways of working
- Using narrative concepts to contribute to shared understanding between client and therapist
- Using narrative methods to facilitate learning and change

A BRIEF INTRODUCTION TO NARRATIVE THERAPY

Historically, the dominant tradition in counselling and psychotherapy has been based in one-to-one therapy with individuals, informed by psychological theories and concepts. Narrative therapy has emerged from a quite different set of influences. The narrative approaches described in this chapter emerged out of family therapy and community work, and were primarily shaped by ideas from philosophy, sociology, sociolinguistics and social anthropology rather than psychology. As a result, although many contemporary narrative therapists are comfortable about working with individuals, their assumptions and ways of thinking about the process and aims of therapy reflect a critical social perspective that always views the person as existing within a cultural and historical context.

The experience of working with families and communities tends to lead to a realisation that the problems and issues experienced by individuals are shaped by their relationships with other people in their family and community. Models of family therapy have developed many ways of making sense of the inter-connectedness of individual identity and both family and wider social networks and structures. One of the important lines of thought within the family therapy and community work tradition has been that it is helpful to pay attention to the use of language, and the ways that people talk with each other and tell stories about themselves and others. This perspective has been supported by a growing body of theory and research in philosophy and social science, that has been characterised as the 'narrative turn' (McLeod, 1997). From the 1970s onwards, these ideas became increasingly influential within the world of counselling and psychotherapy. The current chapter considers two specific crystallisations of this interest – narrative therapy, developed in Australia and New Zealand by Michael White, David Epston and their colleagues (White & Epston, 1990), and the open dialogue approach, a narrative model developed in Finland by Jaako Seikkula and others (Seikkula & Arnkil, 2006). Although there are distinct differences between these two approaches, we would argue that they represent complementary traditions within a broader narrative therapy movement. In addition to these developments, there have been many other valuable contributions that have followed a similar pathway (Anderson & Gehart, 2007; de Shazer & Dolan, 2007; Paré, 2013).

The starting point for narrative therapy is the notion that the identity of a person, and any problems in living that he or she might experience, are constructed and maintained through conversation. Identity or self is not a fixed entity or set of attributes 'within' the person. Instead, personal reality is created through the stories that a person tells about himself or herself, and the stories that other people tell about him or her. These stories are drawn from a cultural stock of narratives that is available to all members of a culture, for instance stories of being a man or a woman, stories of being mentally ill, stories of redemption. Narrative therapy takes the position that troubles and problems in a person's life can be understood in terms of the experience of being defined by stories that do not match that person's potential as a human being, or their actual experience of day-to-day life, or that create a distance between a person and the possibility of authentic relationships with others. Narrative approaches to therapy aim to create a common language to enable shared understanding of painful dilemmas that may have been inaccessible and unspeakable for the participants.

In general terms, this therapeutic approach makes use of two broad strategies for facilitating learning and change. First, the person is helped to recognise the corrosive and undermining influence of dominant narratives, and replace these stories with alternative narratives that more adequately reflect their strength, resourcefulness and accomplishments. Second, the person is helped to construct alternative social arrangements and structures within their life, that offer supportive and caring environments within which the new story can be sustained. This second element of narrative-oriented therapies (making adjustments to the social world of the person) is an aspect of this approach that is not always fully appreciated by therapists trained within individualistic approaches. The use of concepts such as 'narrative' and 'dialogue' highlights an emphasis on language and talk. However, in practice these approaches also involve active attention to what needs to change in the social world of the client (White, 2003).

Narrative therapy and open dialogue therapy make use of somewhat different practical procedures. These differences are in themselves interesting from a pluralistic perspective, because they illustrate how shared core principles can result in different forms of practice in different contexts. Narrative therapy begins by encouraging the person to 'externalise' the problem ('the problem is the problem; the person is not the problem') as only one among several stories that they might tell. The person is urged to identify 'glittering moments', when he or she had experiences that were not consistent with the problem story. The person is then encouraged to 'thicken' their new story, by finding other examples of innovative actions that they undertook and by exploring the meaning of these actions ('What does it say about you, that you were able to …?'). Alongside these narrative processes, the person is invited to find 'audiences' for this new story, and strengthen their relationships with other people who would appreciate and celebrate their accomplishments. All of this can occur in one-to-one therapy, but may involve working with a couple, a family group, or a community group.

Open dialogue was originally developed as a therapeutic response to the needs of people who have had (or are undergoing) a first episode of schizophrenia, and their families. In most places, such episodes will usually lead to medication and hospitalisation. In open dialogue therapy, a group is convened, consisting of the unwell person and other individuals who are committed to helping them. The group might consist of two or three mental health professionals (such as a psychologist, psychiatrist or nurse), members of the family, and also a friend, employer or teacher. The group meets regularly, for as long as necessary, to arrive at an agreed way forward. The concept of 'open dialogue' refers to the process within the group, in which everyone is encouraged to share their perceptions and ideas, and listen respectfully to others. Over a period of time, this process allows the resources of group members to be brought to bear on the task of supporting the person who is in crisis, through the use of real-world practical support as well as through conversation within meetings. Open dialogue has proved to be a highly effective means of helping a client population that is generally considered as being hard-to-treat. This success has resulted in a widening interest in the potential of open dialogue principles in other therapeutic settings.

This account of narrative-oriented approaches to counselling and psychotherapy offers only a simplified overview of some of the main ideas within this tradition. Interested readers are invited to learn more about this rich source of therapeutic possibilities by consulting texts listed below in the further reading.

PLURALISTIC ELEMENTS WITHIN THE NARRATIVE THERAPY TRADITION

In many respects, narrative therapy and open dialogue can be considered as pluralistic forms of practice, that embody many of the principles outlined by Cooper and McLeod (2011). As in pluralistic therapy, these narrative-oriented therapies are grounded in an overarching philosophical meta-perspective. In pluralistic therapy, the concept of pluralism provides a somewhat generic philosophical anchor-point, that is not closely identified with any specific school of philosophy. By contrast, narrative therapy and open dialogue therapy are informed by poststructuralist and social constructionist ideas that are closely aligned to a critical tradition in philosophy. However, what all of these philosophical positions have in common is a rejection of the possibility of fundamental truth, in place of an acceptance that there are many valid positions that can be adopted in relation to most issues, and that in most situations the best answer arises from a willingness to engage in conversations that allow different voices to be heard.

A further similarity between pluralistic therapy and narrative therapy is that they regard the client as an expert on their own experience and someone who has a lot to offer in respect of finding solutions to problems. A strength-based orientation goes hand in hand with a commitment to collaboration, as a means of finding the best ways to enable strengths and resources to be activated. Both approaches are also characterised by high levels of flexibility and innovation, supported by an attitude of curiosity on the part of the therapist.

Narrative therapy and open dialogue can be regarded as being *more* pluralistic than the versions of pluralistic therapy that have been developed so far, in respect of their openness to the active involvement in therapy of individuals other than the primary client. In open dialogue meetings, and narrative therapy consultations, these other people are not considered as co-therapists, or as clients, but as sources of understandings and methods that are available within the local culture.

There are four main ways in which pluralistic therapy differs from the narrative therapy tradition. First, pluralistic therapy explicitly seeks to make as much use as possible of the entire repertoire of therapeutic ideas and methods that have been devised within the profession. By contrast, narrative therapists have been extremely wary of integrative ventures that involve importing ideas from individualistic, psychology-based forms of therapy such as psychodynamic, person-centred and cognitive behaviour therapy. These mainstream therapies are regarded as reflecting an image of the person as an autonomous bounded 'self', that is at odds with the socially oriented understanding that is favoured within the narrative tradition. In fact, it might even be said that, from a narrative perspective, such individualised concepts of the person actually serve to perpetuate problems.

A second crucial difference between pluralistic therapy and approaches that have been developed within a narrative tradition concerns the status of the client–therapist relationship. Influenced by ideas from psychodynamic and person-centred therapy, the pluralistic approach emphasises the need for the therapist to find a way of relating to the client that matches the client's needs and preferences. In addition, the therapeutic relationship is regarded as a potential source of change. Central concepts within pluralistic therapy (goals, tasks, methods) have been influenced by Bordin's (1979) theory of the working alliance. In comparison, narrative therapy advocates a 'de-centred' relationship. What is important, in narrative therapy, is not the transference/countertransference or authentic connection between client and therapist, but the connection between the client and other people in his or her everyday life. It is not that narratively inclined therapists are cold or distanced in their interactions with clients. There are many descriptions within the narrative therapy literature of deeply caring and playful moments. The difference is that these episodes are not regarded as crucial.

A further significant difference between pluralistic therapy and the narrative tradition is that the latter pays much more attention to issues around power, control and oppression, the origins of these forces within culture and history, and the ways that they are perpetuated within institutions (see, e.g., Denborough, Freedman, & White, 2008; Maisel, Epston, & Borden, 2004; White, 2011). These themes are not explicitly articulated in pluralistic practice, at the present time. A final area of contrast between pluralistic and narrative approaches is that pluralistic therapy explicitly draws on the counselling and psychotherapy research literature, while narrative approaches have struggled to find a relationship with research that is consistent with their values and philosophy. However, there does exist good quality research evidence on the effectiveness of these approaches (Seikkula et al., 2006; Vromans & Schweitzer, 2011).

NARRATIVE UNDERSTANDINGS AND METHODS THAT CAN CONTRIBUTE TO PLURALISTIC PRACTICE

Narrative therapy and open dialogue therapy offer a rich source of concepts, metaphors and theoretical storylines that can be incorporated into pluralistic therapy.

Externalising the problem

One of the central principles of narrative therapy is the idea that 'the person is not the problem; the problem is the problem'. This notion refers to the concept of *externalising* the problem, through finding ways to talk about the problem as a thing in itself, rather than as a part of the person. This strategy implies that 'the problem' is one story that can be told about the life of a person, and that other stories are possible. It also introduces the possibility that the person has the capacity to tell the story in a different way.

CASE EXAMPLE
Integrating an externalising conversation into the flow of pluralistic therapy

Alan was a business manager, age 50, who was referred for counselling by his GP following a series of extreme panic attacks. He was clear that he wanted a practical, no-nonsense approach that would deal with the problem. He knew about CBT, and enthusiastically engaged with homework activities designed to address his negative thoughts and bodily tension. While helpful,

(Continued)

(Continued)

these interventions were not entirely successful in eliminating panic from his life. His counsellor asked if he would be willing to try an alternative approach. Alan agreed that this might be useful. Using a narrative therapy perspective, his counsellor invited Alan to give his panic a name. 'That's easy,' replied Alan, 'I think of it as the "wailing voices" – a terrifying chorus in my head, like one of those Francis Bacon images.' The counsellor then interviewed Alan about how the 'wailing voices' influenced his life, and how he, for his part, was sometimes able to influence them. This conversation unfolded in two directions. Alan quickly appreciated that he could hold a productive conversation with the wailing voices if he listened out for them before they reached a terrifying, paralysing crescendo. This realisation made it possible to take action to prevent the occurrence of full-blown panic. Then, after a while Alan became interested in what the voices were saying to him. At a later session, he talked about how the voices were warning of his death, and his isolation from other people. These themes became the central focus of the remaining sessions of therapy.

Re-authoring

Within narrative therapy, externalising the problem is part of a broader intention to engage in 're-authoring'. The concept of re-authoring implies that some, or most of the stories that are told about a person have been formulated (authored) by others (often 'authority' figures such as parents or teachers). The idea of re-authoring invites the person to be the authority on his or her life, through 'authoring' or telling alternative narratives of who they are and what they stand for. By encouraging the person to consider both the *landscape of action* (what they have done) and the *landscape of identity* (what do these actions suggest about who the client is as a person), the conversation 'thickens' the new story that the person is able to tell about himself or herself.

Dialogue

Recent writing and research from the open dialogue group provides a valuable perspective on work on the process of dialogue, and the conditions under which dialogue can take place (Seikkula & Trimble, 2005). In addition, Sundet (2004) offers examples of how dialogue can unfold within a process of sharing stories. These texts represent an invaluable resource for pluralistic practitioners.

Unique outcomes

The narrative therapy concept of *unique outcomes* refers to the occurrence of actions and experiences which contradict the 'problem-saturated' story that the client tells about himself or herself. For pluralistic therapists, unique outcome stories open up an expanded appreciation of the strengths and cultural resources that are available to the client. Reflection on what made a unique outcome possible, can also lead to the identification of change methods that may be applicable in different situations.

Absent but implicit

The meaning we make of any experience comes from contrasting it with another experience or set of experiences. Many stories that people tell about their lives do not explicitly highlight such points of contrast. In narrative therapy, the notion of *absent but implicit* (Carey, Walther, & Russell, 2009; White, 2000) is used to draw attention to the therapeutic potential of such ways of talking. For example, clients may describe events in which they portray themselves as powerless and depressed. However, implicit in the act of telling such a story is a sense of a person who is already taking positive steps to remedy that situation, and who possesses a vision of a better life. This use of the notion of 'implicitness' is similar in some respects to the psychodynamic concept of the unconscious, the use of reframing in cognitive therapy and the idea of 'edge of awareness' within the person-centred tradition. The particular contribution of a narrative perspective is to anchor 'implicitness' in actual stories that the client tells, and to use these stories as a starting point for further exploration of what is not being said.

Using documents, letters, songs and creative artefacts

Alongside a rich array of theoretical ideas, narrative therapy also incorporates a wide variety of practical techniques that can be used by pluralistic practitioners. Earlier versions of narrative therapy (White & Epston, 1990) placed a lot of emphasis on the use of documents such as letters and certificates, as methods of reinforcing new preferred stories of a person's life. More recently, Denborough (2014) has described further creative techniques, such as *tree of life* drawings and collective song-writing.

Conversational tools

A key feature of pluralistic practice is the use of brief process, outcome and preference scales on a regular basis, as a means of eliciting client feedback and ensuring the input of the client in relation to the goals, tasks and methods being pursued. From a narrative perspective, research and service development conducted by Sundet (2009, 2011, 2012a, 2012b, 2014) has introduced a valuable means of understanding how these measures operate at a deeper level, as 'conversational tools' that do not provide definitive answers or assessments, but instead provide opportunities for conversations that lead to focus and plans (goals/aims and methods/tasks) within a collaborative therapeutic relationship.

> **CASE EXAMPLE**
>
> **Using conversational tools**
>
> Rita had been referred for counselling by her GP, because of depression and social withdrawal. On the basis of the referral letter, I expected to encounter a depressed and withdrawn woman. At the first meeting, Rita completed the Outcome Rating Scale (ORS) (see Chapter 5, this volume). She reported the following scores on the four, 10 cm visual analogue scales of the ORS (Miller, Duncan, Sorrell, & Brown 2005): personal well-being, 7.6 (high positive rating); interpersonal issues (family, close relationships), 5.9; social concerns (work, school, friendship), 2.1 (low rating); and overall (general sense of well-being) 7.8. We then discussed what these numbers meant to Rita:
>
> *Therapist:* Tell me about your scores?
> *Rita:* The first is high because I am a strong person, although I am very tired at the moment. This has to do with me and my son quarrelling a lot, but that again is connected to what I have scored on the third dimension; I have a very bad relationship with the teachers at my son's school.
> *Therapist:* Given these scores, where do you want to focus our collaboration?
> *Rita:* I need to do some things. First of all somebody must talk with the teachers and tell them that everything is not proper and good for my son at school. I cannot do that.
> *Therapist:* Why cannot you do that?
> *Rita:* Because I get so damn angry.

The ensuing conversation around the scores brought forth a plan where we would work on how she could attend meetings at school without getting angry and blaming, and instead use these emotions as energy for keeping the focus on her son's problems.

Witnessing and reflecting

One of the important and distinctive features of the narrative therapy and open dialogue tradition is that it views the person as always in relationship with other persons, and as part of a broader culture. This means that the stories that a person tells are always connected up, in some way, with the stories of other people. A key aspect of this type of therapy, therefore, is to create conditions under which this kind of interlacing of narratives can take place, for instance within open dialogue meetings. These therapy approaches typically use other people ('outsiders'), including but also in addition to the therapist, as 'witnesses' who are willing to share their own reactions to the person's story. This form of practice can have a powerful effect, in such domains as reducing isolation, feeling valued by others, and introducing novel perspectives and solutions.

The narrative concepts and methods that have been introduced in this section have been selected to illustrate some of the possibilities of this approach. Further examples can be found in the sources listed at the end of the chapter. On the whole, the narrative therapy tradition has tended not to emphasise the identification of specific goals and tasks, to avoid the risk (as they would see it) of limiting the conversation. Instead, narrative therapists generally take the presenting problem as a starting point, and seek to create a situation in which this problem can be viewed from different perspectives and talked about in different ways. For pluralistic practitioners, the narrative tradition offers a rich source of methods, such as externalising conversations and use of documents, and ways of understanding, such as the concept of re-authoring and the notion of the 'absent-but-implicit'. Clients can be invited to try out these methods and understandings in the context of virtually any therapeutic task, for example by using a statement such as 'I wondered if it might be useful to try to think about the issue in a different way, by … .'

SUMMARY

Narrative therapy, open dialogue therapy and other similar approaches represent a tradition of therapy that emphasises careful attention to the use of language, storytelling and dialogue.

Narratively oriented therapies draw on philosophical and sociological ideas and evidence, and as a result offer perspectives and ways of understanding that are in contrast to more individual-focused approaches.

Narrative-oriented therapies offer a politically informed perspective that could be regarded as filling a gap within contemporary pluralistic theory and practice.

The collaborative stance espoused by narrative therapy and open dialogue is highly consistent with the values of pluralistic therapy, and has the potential to both extend and deepen this aspect of pluralistic practice.

There are many practical techniques and strategies used in narrative therapy and open dialogue that can be readily assimilated into a pluralistic therapist's 'toolkit'.

EXERCISES/POINTS FOR REFLECTION

1 Listen to the stories that you tell about yourself, or that one of your clients tells about himself/herself. To what extent do these stories seem to be drawn from the words and ideas of people in positions of authority and control? How often do these stories describe moments of creativity and resistance?
2 When someone else is telling a story, pay attention to your own reaction, in terms of memories that are triggered. In what ways does your reaction lead you to a more complete appreciation of events and issues in your own life?
3 What are the main possibilities, and challenges, that are associated for you, when you consider making use of narrative ideas and methods within your work as a counsellor?

> **FURTHER READING**
>
> Denborough, D. (2014). *Retelling the stories of our lives: everyday narrative therapy to draw inspiration and transform experience*. New York: Norton. Recent developments in narrative therapy and community practice.
>
> Morgan, A. (2000). *What is narrative therapy? An easy to read introduction*. Adelaide, Australia: Dulwich Centre. The best starting point for anyone wishing to learn about narrative therapy.
>
> Payne, M. (2006). *Narrative therapy: an introduction for counsellors* (2nd ed.). London: Sage. An influential book, which makes connections between narrative therapy and other approaches, in particular person-centred therapy.
>
> Seikkula, J. (2011). Becoming dialogical: psychotherapy or a way of life? *Australian and New Zealand Journal of Family Therapy, 32*, 179–193. An accessible, personal account of the origins and development of the open dialogue approach.
>
> White, M. (2004). Folk psychology and narrative practices. In L. Angus & J. McLeod (Eds.), *Handbook of narrative and psychotherapy*. Thousand Oaks, CA: Sage. A powerful analysis of the limitations of an over-reliance on psychological ways of thinking.

REFERENCES

Anderson, H., & Gehart, D. (Eds.). (2007). *Collaborative therapy: relationships and conversations that make a difference*. New York: Routledge.

Bordin, E.S. (1979). The generalizability of the psychoanalytic concept of the working alliance. *Psychotherapy: Theory, Research and Practice, 16*, 252–260.

Carey, M., Walther, S., & Russell, S. (2009). The absent but implicit: a map to support therapeutic enquiry. *Family Process, 48*, 319–331.

Cooper, M., & McLeod, J. (2011). *Pluralistic counselling and psychotherapy*. London: Sage.

Denborough, D. (2014). *Retelling the stories of our lives: everyday narrative therapy to draw inspiration and transform experience*. New York: Norton.

Denborough, D., Freedman, J., & White, C. (2008). *Strengthening resistance: the use of narrative practices in responding to genocide survivors*. Adelaide, Australia: Dulwich Centre.

de Shazer, S., & Dolan, Y. (2007). *More than miracles: the state of the art of solution-focused brief therapy*. New York: Haworth Press.

Maisel, R., Epston, D., & Borden, A. (2004). *Biting the hand that starves you: inspiring resistance to anorexia/bulimia*. New York: Norton.

McLeod, J. (1997). *Narrative and psychotherapy*. London: Sage.

Miller, S.D., Duncan, B.L., Sorrell, R., & Brown, G.S. (2005). The partners for change outcome management system. *Journal of Clinical Psychology, 61*, 199–208.

Paré, D.A. (2013). *The practice of collaborative counseling and psychotherapy: developing skills in culturally mindful helping*. Thousand Oaks, CA: Sage.

Seikkula, J., Aaltonen, J., Alakare, B., Haarakangas, K., Keranen, J., & Lehtinen, K. (2006). Five-year experience of first-treatment nonaffective psychosis on open-dialogue approach: treatment principles, follow-up outcomes, and two case studies. *Psychotherapy Research, 16*, 214–228.

Seikkula, J., & Arnkil, T.E. (2006). *Dialogical meetings in social networks*. London: Karnac.

Seikkula, J., & Trimble, D. (2005). Healing elements of therapeutic conversation: dialogue as an embodiment of love. *Family Process, 44*, 461–475.

Sundet, R. (2004). Senses of self and interplay as a metaphor for therapy with adolescents. In A. Johnsen, R. Rundet, & V.W. Torsteinsson (Eds.), *Self in relationships: perspectives on family therapy from developmental psychology*. London: Karnac.

Sundet, R. (2009). Therapeutic collaboration and formalized feedback: using perspectives from Vygotsky and Bakhtin to shed light on practices in a family therapy unit. *Clinical Child Psychology and Psychiatry, 15*, 81–95.

Sundet, R. (2011). Collaboration: family and therapist perspectives of helpful therapy. *Journal of Marital and Family Therapy, 37*, 236–249.

Sundet, R. (2012a). Postmodern-oriented practices and implementation of patient-focused research: possibilities and hazards. *Australian and New Zealand Journal of Family Therapy, 33*, 299–308.

Sundet, R. (2012b). Therapist perspectives on the use of feedback on process and outcome: patient-focused research in practice. *Canadian Psychology, 53*, 122–130.

Sundet, R. (2014). Patient-focused research supported practices in an intensive family therapy unit. *Journal of Family Therapy, 35*, 195–216.

Vromans, L.P., & Schweitzer, R. (2011). Narrative therapy for adults with major depressive disorder: improved symptom and interpersonal outcomes. *Psychotherapy Research, 21*, 4–15.

White, M. (2000). Re-engaging with history: the absent but implicit. In M. White (Ed.), *Reflections on narrative practice* (pp. 35–58). Adelaide, Australia: Dulwich Centre.

White, M. (2003). Narrative practice and community assignments. *International Journal of Narrative Therapy and Community Work, 2*, 17–55.

White, M. (2011). *Narrative practice: continuing the conversations*. New York: Norton.

White, M., & Epston, D. (1990). *Narrative means to therapeutic ends*. New York: Norton.

13

Integrative and Eclectic Approaches and Pluralism

John McLeod and Rolf Sundet

THIS CHAPTER DISCUSSES

- The historical origins and development of integrationist and eclectic approaches
- The idea of pluralistic therapy as a 'meta-integrative' framework
- Similarities and differences between integrationist and pluralistic perspectives
- Making use of integrationist ideas within a pluralistic approach
- How pluralism can enhance integrationist and eclectic ways of working

There exists a long tradition within the field of counselling and psychotherapy of seeking to find ways of combining ideas and methods from different therapy models. The aim of this chapter is to examine the relationship between integrationist and eclectic approaches, and a pluralistic perspective. The chapter considers areas of commonality and difference, and ways in which integrationist understandings and methods can contribute towards a pluralistic way of working.

INTEGRATIONIST THERAPIES AND THEIR HISTORICAL DEVELOPMENT

At the present time, there exists a fundamental tension within the field of counselling and psychotherapy. On the one hand, research and clinical guidelines are dominated by distinct models of therapy, such as psychodynamic, person-centred and cognitive-behavioural (Dryden & Reeves, 2013). However, running alongside the development of these approaches, there have always been theorists and practitioners who have argued that the proliferation of therapy theories is not helpful, and that it makes more sense to combine these ideas into an integrated model. The continued existence of distinct models of therapy reflects a complex set of circumstances (see McLeod, 2013). For example, different therapy approaches reflect different worldviews, change processes, ideas about valid knowledge and political standpoints. These approaches have also become institutionalised, through the creation of professional associations, training programmes and publications. The current situation within the counselling and psychotherapy profession can be regarded as a state of tension. On the one hand, most practice guidelines and research, and many training courses, are organised along single-model lines. On the other hand, the majority of practitioners describe themselves as deploying some kind of combination of approaches (Norcross, Karpiak, & Lister, 2005; Thoma & Cecero, 2009).

One of the challenges facing those who support the idea of bringing together ideas and methods from different therapy approaches is the question of how this can be accomplished. Established single-theory models of therapy offer coherent packages of concepts, techniques and research, that have been 'road tested' with a range of client problems. The act of combining ideas and methods from different approaches runs the risk of ending up with a set of incompatible or contradictory procedures that produce confusion in clients and practitioners. Several strategies have been developed in response to the challenge of how to combine therapy approaches. These include:

- *Eclecticism*. The therapist decides what is best for the client at any particular point in therapy, drawing on a wide repertoire of skills and ideas.
- *Technical eclecticism*. The therapist makes the choice of theory and intervention, based on rigorous assessment of the client's problem, and informed by research findings concerning the relative effectiveness of different methods.
- *Theoretical integration*. A new approach to therapy is created, by constructing a theoretical model that draws on concepts from existing approaches.
- *Assimilative integration*. The therapist is trained in one approach. Then, over the course of their career, they learn about other approaches and gradually incorporate them into their work with clients. Eventually, this results in the emergence of a distinctive personal style of therapy.
- *Holistic integration*. The therapist seeks to develop an understanding of himself or herself as a whole person, encompassing cognitive, emotional, biological, social and spiritual aspects of self. This endeavour enables the therapist to become more responsive to all of these dimensions within the lived experience of their clients.
- *Common factors*. Research has shown that there exists a set of common factors, such as the establishment of a therapeutic alliance, instillation of hope, and expression of emotion, that are found in all successful therapy. The delivery of these factors then becomes an integrative focus for therapy practice.
- *Disorder-specific or problem-oriented integration*. A version of theoretical integration in which a particular set of ideas and interventions is assembled in order to respond effectively to the needs of a client group with a particular problem (e.g., depression, borderline personality disorder).
- *Multicultural and culturally adapted therapy*. Mainstream approaches to therapy inevitably reflect the ideas, values and assumptions of the cultural context in

which they were developed. To use these models in work with clients from different cultures, requires consideration of the indigenous healing practices and beliefs of that cultural group.
- *Feminist therapy.* Within the feminist tradition in therapy, a feminist political stance is used as a basis for selecting and reframing therapy ideas and methods in order to arrive at a way of working that facilitates the empowerment of women.
- *Collective integration.* A group of therapists work together to offer the client a range of therapeutic possibilities, for example within a therapeutic community or personal growth centre.

It is possible to see that there are many possible pathways for accomplishing therapy integration (Gilbert & Orlans, 2011; Lazarus, 2005; McLeod, 2013; Norcross & Goldfried, 2005; Stricker & Gold, 2006). Ongoing reflection, debate and enquiry into the nature of therapy integration can be found in the *Journal of Psychotherapy Integration*, and within conferences organised by the *Society for the Exploration of Psychotherapy Integration* (SEPI).

ALIGNMENT OF INTEGRATIVE AND PLURALISTIC PRINCIPLES

There is a large amount of common ground between the pluralistic framework and other integrative/eclectic approaches to therapy. All integrative approaches share a willingness to be open to new ideas, and a commitment to be responsive to client needs. Pluralism represents a meta-model of therapy integration, which draws on all of the integrative strategies highlighted above (e.g., assimilative integration, theoretical integration, etc.).

There are distinctive features of pluralistic integration, as an integrative model of therapy. Pluralistic therapy invites the client into a collaborative position in relation to deciding what form of therapy would be best for them. Pluralistic therapy is also more inclusive than other integrative approaches, in its willingness to consider the potential relevance of all therapy approaches (rather than a selected sub-set of ideas or techniques), and to make use of cultural resources that are available to the client.

There are also aspects of pluralistic therapy that conflict with widely accepted assumptions about therapy integration. Many integrative training programmes assume that it is necessary to begin training with a grounding in a specific theoretical model, and that integration across models is something that happens later in a career. By contrast, pluralistic training (see Chapter 26) ideally begins with a grounding in pluralistic principles, with later exposure to specific therapy models taking place through a pluralistic 'lens'.

A second area of tension between pluralistic therapy and some approaches to therapy integration arises from the pluralistic position that there can never be one universally valid theory. Pluralistic therapy can be regarded as a form of radical eclecticism. All knowledge and every skill – whether research-based, theory-based, or based in the participant's personal and professional experiences – may be used, within the constraints of the understanding and awareness of the therapist and client. To be radically eclectic means to pick and choose without these choices being dictated or constrained by demands for logical or theoretical coherence (Sundet, 2009). Radical eclecticism lets the choice of method, action, statement, or question be rooted in, and branch out from, the client and her or his response to the interventions of the therapist. The description of therapy is not primarily constrained by theoretical or generalised knowledge, but by feedback from the client and the client's theory of change (Duncan & Miller, 2000). The therapist becomes an active consultant and collaborative-oriented contributor to the construction and development of a therapy tailored to the client. Therapist learning arises when the preferences of the client do not match the knowledge base of the therapist: a pluralistic therapist is committed to a constant knowledge-seeking process.

On the whole, approaches to therapy integration have attempted to construct systems of ideas that cover all eventualities. This leads to bigger and bigger theories. By contrast, a radical pluralist stance regards theories as tools, and seeks to remain open to those things that do not fit together. Being rooted in the preferences of the client, and striving to be helpful for the client, involves a willingness to find the edges of theory, or move outside the range of convenience of any specific theory.

HOW KEY INTEGRATIONIST CONCEPTS CAN CONTRIBUTE TO PLURALISTIC PRACTICE

Proponents of various forms of eclectic and integrative approaches to therapy have spent several decades working out how to combine ideas and methods from different therapy traditions. This body of knowledge has a lot to offer to pluralistic therapy practitioners. Some of the main areas of potential learning are highlighted in the following sections.

Using self-practice to make connections between concepts and techniques from different traditions

Assimilative and holistic approaches to therapy integration place a strong emphasis on the active participation of the therapist in making personal connections between different therapy models. One of the key ways in which this kind of integration takes place is through self-practice: applying ideas and techniques within the therapist's personal life. Research into therapist training, by Bennett-Levy, Lee, Travers, Pohlman and Hamernik (2003) has identified self-practice as one of the main ways in which therapists develop confidence in the utility of new ideas and interventions. A capacity to apply a new technique is enhanced by the experience of knowing that something works, at a personal level, and by being able to refer to a nuanced inner sense of the process of change that is involved. Apart from self-practice of ideas picked up on training courses and workshops, many therapists choose to receive their personal therapy from therapists based in models that are different from their own approach. Self-practice, as a consumer of therapy, represents a core practical strategy for expanding one's 'menu' of therapy methods.

Using the concept of 'markers' as a means of making practical use of new ideas

A 'marker' refers to some kind of pattern of client behaviour that serves as a signal for a theme in the person's life, or a particular type of problematic reaction. The concept of marker has been central to the development of emotion-focused therapy (EFT; Greenberg, Rice, & Elliott, 1993), one of the most influential examples of theoretical integration within the past 20 years. EFT brings together ideas from Gestalt therapy, person-centred therapy, attachment theory and constructivist philosophy. Recent developments within this approach have also made use of concepts from narrative theory and practice (Angus & Greenberg, 2011). Within EFT, different therapy tasks are triggered by identification of such markers as style of emotional processing, mode of engagement, mode of storytelling, occurrence of harsh self-criticism, or voice quality (Watson, 2010). It seems reasonable to assume that all therapy involves being responsive to client markers, but that in most therapy approaches the characteristics of the relevant markers are largely implicit rather than being explicitly identified. For pluralistic therapists, the idea of collaboratively identifying particular tasks or areas of focus for therapeutic work comprises a central element of the framework for practice. Sensitivity to markers allows task-possibilities to be identified, and helps the therapist in timing their invitation to consider the exploration of a specific task. Making use of the concept of marker also allows pluralistic practitioners a means of including potentially new ideas in their work with clients. Learning and training extends the range of markers of which a therapist is aware, and to which he or she might respond.

CASE EXAMPLE
Deliberate self-practice to learn about experiential focusing

Linda was a counsellor who had been mainly trained in CBT, but was keen to develop in a more pluralistic direction. Her work with clients had suggested to her that CBT did not provide her with satisfactory strategies for responding to clients when they told her that they wanted to talk about how they felt about a problem. Linda attended a training weekend in experiential focusing, a model within the person-centred tradition, which involves ideas and practices around paying attention to, and finding meaning in, internal bodily feeling states and processes (Purton, 2004). Following the workshop, she reinforced what she had learned by intentionally paying heed to her own inner 'felt sense', particularly in situations that she experienced as stressful, in ways that allowed the meaning

> implicit within those feelings to emerge into awareness and inform her actions. She reflected on the extent to which an experiential focusing perspective on such episodes was similar to, but also different from, her existing capacity to make sense of such events in terms of the concept of countertransference. In sessions with clients, she also intentionally listened and watched for markers of different aspects of experiential processing, for example moments when the client referred to an unclear felt sense, or gestured in ways that pointed toward areas of feeling with their body. In these ways, Linda engaged in a process of assimilative and holistic integration.

Using the 'common factors' perspective as a framework for understanding the course of therapy as whole

The idea that there exists a set of curative factors that are found in all effective therapies has been at the centre of current debate around the nature of the evidence around therapy outcomes (Tschacher, Junghan, & Pfammatter, 2014). For several decades, outcome research has focused on the question of the differential effectiveness of contrasting models of therapy. Is psychodynamic therapy more effective than CBT? Is CBT more effective than experiential therapy? From a common factors approach, this line of research is ill-conceived, because the various therapy models being compared can be regarded as comprised of the same set of common factors (Wampold, 2001). This issue has resulted in considerable debate around the role of 'specific' vs 'non-specific' factors in therapy. For example, using Socratic questioning to challenge negative automatic thoughts is a specific CBT intervention, while at the same time representing the implementation of non-specific or common factors of engaging in a healing ritual, and acquiring a rationale for the origins of the problem that is being tackled.

For pluralistic counsellors and psychotherapists, an appreciation of the common factors perspective has important practical implications. Thinking about a case in terms of common factors provides a higher-order, theory-neutral framework for understanding what is happening in therapy, and what might need to be done (tasks). For instance, there is likely to be a point in therapy where the client will want to engage in a healing ritual, and will be open to finding a rationale for the development of their problem. A CBT model offers one pathway that might be adopted at that point. However, other therapy traditions, such as psychodynamic, person-centred or narrative, offer alternative pathways. Common factors therefore provide a basis for the initiation of collaborative conversations around client preferences in respect of different tasks and methods.

A common factors perspective can also make a valuable contribution to therapy supervision and other forms of consultation and reflection on practice. The common factors literature can be used as a set of guidelines for all of the ingredients that are necessary for therapy to be helpful. This can be used as a basis for reviewing what might be missing, when therapy is stuck or progress is slow.

A final area in which a common factors perspective can inform practice is in relation to the structure of therapy as a whole. Within the contemporary literature, common factors are typically considered to comprise a list or taxonomy of therapeutic ingredients. However, this was not the approach taken by Jerome Frank (1961, 1974; most recent edition Frank & Frank, 1991) in his book *Persuasion and Healing*, in which the idea of common factors was originally formulated. That volume consists of a critical analysis of both Western and indigenous forms of psychotherapy and emotional healing. What emerged from this endeavour was a model of a generic process of personal change. It is suggested that individuals possess 'assumptive worlds' that reflect their understanding (shared with members of their reference group) of how life should be lived. They seek to resolve personal issues through drawing on their assumptions, and through making use of resources and support that are locally available to them. If, for whatever reason, these resources are not sufficient, and a gap emerges between the assumptive world and the person's lived experience, the individual enters a state of 'demoralization'. This leads to a search for a socially sanctioned and credible healer from outside the person's immediate social circle. This healer invites the person into a sacred, healing space, offers them a confiding relationship, and a credible rationale for the development and resolution of their difficulties. These activities provide hope that the assumptive world can be restored. The healer then initiates a set of healing rituals that involve the expression of emotion, new learning experiences and opportunities for practice. The end-point of this process is the experience of 're-moralization'. An overview of this model of the structure of therapy, and its links to everyday life, is available in Chapter 2 of Frank and Frank (1991). Subsequent chapters of that book provide more detailed accounts of how various stages in this process occur within different healing practices in different cultures.

This more comprehensive understanding of the nature of significance of common factors provides a strong rationale for a pluralistic approach to therapy. For example, client preferences can be seen as rooted in the client's assumptive world, and collaborative communication around tasks and methods and shared understanding can be seen as establishing a credible rationale for the origins and resolution of the client's problem. The ideas in Frank and Frank (1991) offer pluralistic therapists an intellectually rich and challenging means of deepening their understanding of the meaning and interconnectedness of key aspects of therapy practice.

Making use of integration of knowledge in particular problem areas

The field of therapy integration can be divided into two broad camps. In one group, are writers and theorists who are seeking to develop all-encompassing manifestos for integrative practice, in the form of guidelines or theoretical models that account for all types of client and presenting issues. In the other group are writers, theorists and practitioners whose primary interest is to develop effective services for particular groups of clients. Problem-oriented integration is of special interest to pluralistic therapists because it tends to reflect pragmatic ideas that stay close to the actual experiences and needs of clients. The literature within this type of integration allows scope for creative and idiosyncratic contributions from individual therapists. Problem-oriented practice also makes it somewhat easier for the client's voice to be heard, because it is more likely that client and service user support and advocacy groups will be in existence.

There are many domains of problem-oriented integration that have the potential to inform pluralistic practice. The area of bereavement care represents a typical example of this form of integration. In practice, there are many points of connection between bereavement counselling and other forms of professional practice, such as pastoral care, hospice work, nursing, midwifery and funeral directing. This means that it is possible to draw on ideas from different professional communities. Although some specific therapy models have been applied in bereavement counselling, such as CBT and psychodynamic, the structure of training and practice means that most bereavement counsellors are more interested in integrative, flexible models, such as the Worden (2001) task model. This openness to consider anything that will work is also reflected in books such as Neimeyer (2012; see Chapter 17, this volume).

An important aspect of the pluralistic framework for counselling and psychotherapy practice is that it emphasises the importance of therapist personal and professional development. Good therapists are not made by training, or defined by mastery of a specific approach. Good therapists are people who continue to learn over the course of their careers (Skovholt & Jennings, 2004). One of the characteristics of good therapists appears to be that they are more effective with some presenting problems, and less helpful with other issues (Kraus, Castonguay, Boswell, Nordberg, & Hayes, 2011). It is possible, therefore, that movement in the direction of specialisation may be a career development pathway followed by many pluralistic practitioners.

Finding metatheories that are relevant in individual cases

A key aspect of therapy integration that does not receive sufficient attention is the existence of thriving sub-fields of eclectic/integrative practice within such areas as feminist therapy, multicultural counselling and adventure therapy. These are all fields that are organised around superordinate 'metatheories' that provide a basis for deciding between the relevance and merits of competing ideas and methods from therapy research and practice. Feminist therapy and multicultural counselling both draw on political and social metatheories, related to values of equality and empowerment. Metatheories provide a vantage point from which therapists can choose the most appropriate therapy ideas. For example, many feminist therapists find meaning in psychodynamic theory, but mainly in relational rather than classical (drive theory) versions of this approach. At the same time, they may see the relevance of CBT models, around such issues as control of anxiety, as a means of helping women to be more effective and assertive in work situations. From a pluralistic perspective, it can be useful to find the specific ideas or metatheories that have meaning for each client. Some clients may resonate to the underlying assumptions and values of feminist or multicultural therapy. Other clients may build their lives around rational principles, and as a result find that CBT or cognitive therapy makes a lot of sense to them.

Being able to shift the conversation from discussion of practical interventions, and into the area of values and worldview, is a way of 'thickening' collaborative conversations around client preferences.

> ### CASE EXAMPLE
> ### Working together to find the best mix of theories in a particular case
>
> Anne described herself as having lost her spark. Over a five-year period, she had experienced a series of losses, and had gradually become more depressed. She strongly rejected the offer of anti-depressant medication made by her GP. Her therapist was familiar with person-centred and CBT strategies for working with depression. He could readily see that, in common factors terms, Anne did not regard these approaches as providing a credible rationale for her troubles, and was not hopeful that they would do any good. She characterised these models as 'just mind-games'. Holding on to his own hope that there would be something that would work, he facilitated a wider dialogue and search around how they could proceed. Gradually, it emerged that Anne believed that being fit and healthy was the key to living a satisfying life. Between them, they came to the conclusion that the 6-point diet and exercise programme developed by Ilardi (2010) might offer the best way forward. They studied it together, with the therapist adopting a role, as specified by Anne, as supportive coach and trainer. They agreed that he was allowed to ask her about her feelings and relationships, but only as an adjunct to the central priority of completing the programme.

HOW KEY PLURALISTIC CONCEPTS CAN CONTRIBUTE TO INTEGRATIONIST PRACTICE

The main aim of this chapter has been to explore the relevance of existing ideas about therapy integration, for pluralistic practice. It is also possible to identify ways in which the pluralistic model can be regarded as a resource for eclectic and integrative practitioners. The pluralistic framework offers a structure for integrative practice. The emphasis on collaborative dialogue and decision-making around shared understandings and building agreement around goals, tasks and methods, within pluralistic therapy, provides a basis for integrative therapy training, supervision and practice that may be relevant to colleagues who have developed other integrative models. Twenty years ago, Lazarus, Beutler and Norcross (1992) argued that technical eclecticism would gradually come to be the dominant approach within the field of psychotherapy. In many respects, their predictions have turned out to be valid. However, what comes across quite clearly when re-reading their paper in a contemporary context is an absence of any discussion of client preferences and a collaborative stance – the therapist is portrayed as a powerful expert who is able to assess the client and decide on the interventions that are best suited to their problem.

SUMMARY

Pluralistic therapy forms part of a broad movement within counselling and psychotherapy, which aligns itself with a commitment to respect the complexity of human experience and to be responsive to client needs.

It is not straightforward to combine ideas and methods from different therapy traditions. A number of strategies have been developed to facilitate this process.

It is helpful for pluralistic practitioners to be informed by the diversity of ideas that are in circulation about how to combine therapy approaches.

Pluralistic therapy offers a distinctive stance in relation to the question of therapy integration. It provides specific guidelines for integrative practice, based on a collaborative, dialogical stance. It positions itself as a radical eclectic approach, which remains close to the lived experience of the client and regards theories as tools to be used rather than as ultimate truths.

EXERCISES/POINTS FOR REFLECTION

1. What are your own existing strategies for combining ideas and methods from different therapy approaches? Some therapists use ideas from different approaches to help them to think about cases, while only using interventions from one specific model. Other therapists adopt different approaches at different stages of therapy, for example starting with person-centred relationship-building before moving to active CBT behaviour change methods. What do you do?
2. To what extent, and in what ways, do you make use of self-practice during the process of learning about therapy ideas and methods? How helpful is this for you? Are there any ways that you could gain more from this activity?
3. How do you describe your approach as a psychotherapist, counsellor or psychologist? If you describe yourself as eclectic, integrative or pluralistic, how do you explain what you mean, when asked by colleagues or clients?

FURTHER READING

Duncan, B.L., Miller, S.D., Wampold, B.E., & Hubble, M.A. (Eds.). (2010). *The heart and soul of change: delivering what works in therapy* (2nd ed.) Washington, DC: American Psychological Association. An invaluable selection of chapters from therapy practitioners and researchers who share an openness to new ideas. See, particularly, the prologue on Saul Rosenzweig, who was thinking and writing about therapy integration in the 1930s.

Frank, J.D., & Frank, J.B. (1991). *Persuasion and healing: a comparative study of psychotherapy* (3rd ed.). Baltimore, MD: Johns Hopkins University Press. Essential reading for anyone interested in developing a deeper understanding of the meaning of therapy integration.

(Continued)

(Continued)

Omer, H. (1993). The integrative focus: coordinating symptom- and person-oriented perspectives in therapy. *American Journal of Psychotherapy, 47,* 283–295. An example of one of the many contributors to the literature on therapy integration who have not attempted to develop a new overarching scheme, but instead have tried to make sense of how particular challenges to integration can be addressed. This paper explores how a pluralistic 'both/and' stance can be applied within therapy.

Polkinghorne, D.E. (1992). Postmodern epistemology of practice. In S. Kvale (Ed.), *Psychology and postmodernism.* London: Sage. A combination of philosophical analysis and qualitative research, this paper represents one of the few studies that explores the ways that therapists make use of different theoretical perspectives in their work with clients.

REFERENCES

Angus, L.E., & Greenberg, L.S. (2011). *Working with narrative in emotion-focused therapy: changing stories, healing lives.* Washington, DC: American Psychological Association.

Bennett-Levy, J., Lee, N., Travers, K., Pohlman, S., & Hamernik, E. (2003). Cognitive therapy from the inside: enhancing therapist skills through practicing what we preach. *Behavioural and Cognitive Psychotherapy, 31,* 143–158.

Dryden, W., & Reeves, A. (Eds.). (2013). *Handbook of individual therapy* (6th ed.). London: Sage.

Duncan, B.L., & Miller, S.D. (2000). The client's theory of change: consulting the client in the integrative process. *Journal of Psychotherapy Integration, 10,* 169–187.

Frank, J.D. (1961). *Persuasion and healing: a comparative study of psychotherapy.* Baltimore, MD: Johns Hopkins University Press.

Frank, J.D. (1974). Psychotherapy: the restoration of morale. *American Journal of Psychiatry, 131,* 272–274.

Frank, J. D., & Frank, J.B. (1991). *Persuasion and healing: a comparative study of psychotherapy* (3rd ed.). Baltimore, MD: Johns Hopkins University Press.

Gilbert, M., & Orlans, V. (2011). *Integrative therapy: 100 key points and techniques.* London: Routledge.

Greenberg, L.S., Rice, L.N., & Elliott, R. (1993). *Facilitating emotional change: the moment-by-moment process.* New York: The Guilford Press.

Ilardi, S. (2010). *The depression cure: the six-step programme to beat depression without drugs.* London: Vermilion.

Kraus, D.R., Castonguay, L., Boswell, J.F., Nordberg, S.S., & Hayes, J.A. (2011). Therapist effectiveness: implications for accountability and patient care. *Psychotherapy Research, 21,* 267–276.

Lazarus, A.A. (2005). Multimodal therapy. In J.C. Norcross & M.R. Goldfried (Eds.), *Handbook of psychotherapy integration.* New York: Oxford University Press.

Lazarus, A.A., Beutler, L.E., & Norcross, J.C. (1992). The future of technical eclecticism. *Psychotherapy, 29*, 11–20.

McLeod, J. (2013). *An introduction to counselling* (5th ed.). Maidenhead: Open University Press.

Neimeyer, R.A. (Ed.). (2012). *Techniques of grief therapy: creative practices for counseling the bereaved*. New York: Routledge.

Norcross, J.C., & Goldfried, M.R. (Eds.). (2005). *Handbook of psychotherapy integration*. New York: Oxford University Press.

Norcross, J.C., Karpiak, C.P., & Lister, K.M. (2005). What's an integrationist? A study of self-identified integrative and (occasionally) eclectic psychologists. *Journal of Clinical Psychology, 61*, 1587–1594.

Purton, C. (2004). *Person-centred therapy: the focusing-oriented approach*. London: Palgrave.

Skovholt, T.M., & Jennings, L. (2004). *Master therapists: exploring expertise in therapy and counseling*. New York: Allyn & Bacon.

Stricker, G., & Gold, J. (Eds.). (2006). *A casebook of psychotherapy integration*. Washington, DC: American Psychological Association.

Sundet, R. (2009). *Client directed, outcome informed therapy in an intensive family therapy unit – a study of the use of research generated knowledge in clinical practice*. Oslo: Unipub Press.

Thoma, N.C., & Cecero, J.J. (2009). Is integrative use of techniques in psychotherapy the exception or the rule? Results of a national survey of doctoral-level practitioners. *Psychotherapy, 46*, 405–417.

Tschacher, W., Junghan, U.M., & Pfammatter, M. (2014). Towards a taxonomy of common factors in psychotherapy – results of an expert survey. *Clinical Psychology and Psychotherapy, 21*, 82–96.

Wampold, B.E. (2001). *The great psychotherapy debate: models, methods and findings*. Mahwah, NJ: Erlbaum.

Watson, J.C. (2010). Case formulation in EFT. *Journal of Psychotherapy Integration, 20*, 89–100.

Worden, W. (2001). *Grief counselling and grief therapy: a handbook for the mental health practitioner*. London: Brunner/Routledge.

PART 3
Issues and Goals

14

Helping Clients Address Depression

John McLeod

THIS CHAPTER DISCUSSES

- The ways that happiness and unhappiness/depression are understood in contemporary society
- The relevance and practical application of alternative theoretical perspectives
- Therapeutic strategies and methods that can contribute to the recovery of happiness
- Challenges associated with this area of work
- Therapist issues and self-awareness

The aim of this chapter is to consider how the goal of achieving greater happiness and meaning, and amelioration of depression, can be accomplished within a pluralistic approach to therapy.

A BRIEF INTRODUCTION TO THE ISSUE OF HAPPINESS/DEPRESSION IN CONTEMPORARY SOCIETY

The quest for meaning and happiness can be regarded as one of the defining characteristics of modern society. In previous eras, suffering was accepted as an inevitable fact of life. More recently, the 'pursuit of happiness', drive for personal fulfilment, and sense of entitlement to pleasure and enjoyment have emerged as central themes in the ways in which people evaluate their lives. It seems clear that there are several factors that have contributed to this shift. The increasing secularisation of culture has resulted in an absence of external, religious sources of meaning and life satisfaction, and their replacement by a belief that the accomplishment of happiness and meaningfulness is an individual responsibility (and therefore something to worry about). The expanding reach of consumerism as an economic driver has resulted in a proliferation of images of happiness as a marketing strategy.

The growth of depression (negative happiness) as a problem in modern society has been accompanied by an increasing tendency toward the 'medicalisation' of happiness, through the increasing use of anti-depressant medication as a response to individual suffering (Greenberg, 2010; Healy, 2006). Counselling and psychotherapy also make a significant contribution to the societal response to depression. A wide range of therapeutic approaches have been developed for the promotion of happiness and alleviation of depression, stretching from positive psychology to psychoanalysis. The implementation of these therapy models has been accompanied by a substantial amount of research into their efficacy. Reviews of the results of these studies, by Cuijpers, Andersson, Donker and van Straten (2011) and others, have consistently found that different therapy approaches are broadly equivalent in effectiveness. At the same time, evidence suggests that the promotion of happiness and alleviation of depression that occurs as an outcome of both psychological and pharmacological interventions does not always have a long-term effect: if someone has been depressed the chances are that they will get better at some point, whatever help they receive, but will relapse at some point in the future (Judd, 1997).

The existence of multiple causes, perspectives and treatment interventions within the area of happiness/depression (Gotlib & Hammen, 2014), means that this is an issue that is highly amenable to a flexible, holistic, collaborative treatment approach such as pluralistic therapy. From a diagnostic perspective, depression is typically considered to comprise a combination of symptoms that reflect different aspects of life, for example, low mood, guilt, self-critical thoughts, sleep and appetite disturbance, and social isolation. One of the advantages of adopting a pluralistic approach is that it ensures that the therapist takes a curious and open-minded attitude to how the person defines his or her problem. This is vitally important, because there is evidence that 'depression' is not a single entity (see, e.g., Blatt & Zuroff, 1992), and often occurs in combination with other issues, such as anxiety, trauma and substance misuse and long-term health problems (particularly pain). There is also evidence that depression takes different forms in men and women and in different cultures (Jack & Ali, 2010; Kleinman & Good, 1985). A critically informed socio-historical perspective on happiness/depression acts as a reminder that these terms have come to be used in a very general sense, to describe many different patterns of suffering and perceived personal inadequacy.

THE RELEVANCE AND PRACTICAL APPLICATION OF ALTERNATIVE THEORETICAL PERSPECTIVES

Happiness/depression is an area of life that is associated with a huge range of theoretical explanations. From a pluralistic perspective, theories can be viewed as storylines, possible ways of narrating and accounting for personal experience (Hansen, 2006). Some of the happiness/depression narratives that occur most frequently in therapy include:

- I am depressed because I have a biochemical imbalance in my brain (psychiatric/medical).
- I can never find happiness because I am mourning the loss of my mother (psychoanalytic).
- I can never find happiness because I am angry with my mother but am too ashamed to say anything (psychoanalytic).
- I live a boring existence because I have no purpose, meaning or beauty in my life (humanistic/existential).
- I do not matter to anyone (social-psychological).
- Because I am a woman I always need to put other people first/Because I am a man I can never admit my vulnerability (sociological).
- My depression is a journey into myself, to discover a deeper spiritual self (religious).
- There is an endless tape-loop in my head, telling me how worthless I am (cognitive behavioural).
- I am miserable because I am fat (biological/sociological).
- Too many bad things have happened to me and I have just given up (behavioural/learned helplessness).
- I set myself the highest standards, and never live up to them (cognitive behavioural/perfectionism).

One of the early tasks in pluralistic therapy for depression is to begin to identify the storylines that are deployed by both the therapist and client, and finding ways to bring them into alignment. It is also important to be open to the emergence of new storylines, over the course of therapy. Achieving a sufficient degree of shared understanding around ways of making sense of the problem makes it easier to create change methods that are sufficiently plausible and hope-inducing for the client, to mobilise their energy and commitment. There is also a crucial balance to be struck between respect for the client's narrative, and a willingness to suggest alternative ways of framing the problem. Typically, clients prefer solutions that are consistent with their pre-existing worldview (Valkonen, Hanninen, & Lindfors, 2011). However, clients may also appreciate the opportunity to see their problem from a different angle.

> ### CASE EXAMPLE
> #### Developing a shared understanding
>
> Tony was in his mid-40s and described himself as never having been happy. He attributed this to genetic and biochemical factors – his mother had a history of depression, and nobody in his family had ever managed to escape this curse. His therapist was sceptical about biological perspectives on depression, and believed that the condition could be attributed to an interaction between social isolation and dysfunctional thinking. It was apparent from the outset that Tony and his therapist held quite different views about what might be helpful. Somewhat tentatively, the therapist first invited Tony to expand on his understanding, and then talked about his own ideas. Eventually, they were able
>
> *(Continued)*

(Continued)

to build some conceptual bridges between them. They produced a working model, and diagram, organised around three main ideas. First, Tony's underlying illness had resulted in him hiding himself away from others, and so it made sense to work on his social isolation as a means of alleviating this side-effect of the illness. Second, although anti-depressants were helpful, it was clear that his GP would not prescribe them forever, so it was valuable to find alternative strategies for coping with depression in order to retain medication as a way of dealing with particularly bad episodes. Third, the way that the therapist talked about negative thoughts sounded interesting, and Tony was willing to give it a try, while remaining sceptical.

THERAPEUTIC STRATEGIES AND METHODS THAT CAN CONTRIBUTE TO THE RECOVERY OF HAPPINESS

Pluralistic therapy begins by concurrently engaging the client in conversations around their understanding of the problem and their sense of what might help them, and identifying and clarifying goals. At the start of therapy, a client is likely to describe his or her goals in somewhat general terms. The area of work explored in this chapter, tends to be marked by client goals such as 'being happier', 'finding meaning in my life', 'discovering a sense of purpose', 'having more energy', 'being less tired', 'dealing with my depression' and similar statements. A client may find it personally meaningful and helpful to define their troubles as 'depression', or they may not. One of the strategies used in pluralistic therapy, to begin to engage the client in a process of change, is to work together to reformulate broad goals into attainable sub-tasks. For example, it is hard to know what to do to assist a person to 'become happier'. It is easier to have a sense of what to do, when 'becoming happier' is broken down into specific areas of focus such as 'getting more exercise', 'understanding how I put myself down', 'learning how to deal with situations where other people put me down', and 'coming to terms with my divorce'.

In respect of exploring client goals, it is important for the therapist to remain open to the personal meaning of the issues being presented by the client. For example, for some clients, sadness may not be a symptom of depression, but may represent a healthy response to loss and failure. In addition, people respond to their depression in different ways. Some individuals regard it a weakness and personal stain, while for others it can represent a sign of sensitivity.

The process of identifying therapeutic tasks has a number of advantages when working with people who are demoralised or depressed. At the time of entering therapy, it is probable that the client experiences himself or herself as profoundly stuck, to the point of lacking energy or belief around the possibility that things could be better. Talking about attainable tasks introduces the notion that there are small steps that might eventually lead to bigger changes. For some clients, it can also be useful to work on multiple tasks at the same time, or to be able to shift back and forward between tasks. This is an important difference between pluralistic therapy and therapy approaches that make use of case formulation. Most therapy models advocate finding a single focus for therapeutic work. This can be very effective if the client finds it meaningful, and if the subsequent interventions pay off. On the other hand, if a client believes that there is more than one thing that they need to deal with, or if the therapeutic activities associated with that one thing do not progress smoothly, he or she may lose motivation. By contrast, assuming from the outset that there are likely to be multiple tasks keeps the client on board by ensuring that all aspects of their problem are being addressed. It also provides a natural way for the client to control the pace and intensity of therapy – working on tough tasks when they feel strong, looking at less demanding topics at other times, and so on.

> ## CASE EXAMPLE
> ### Identifying and working through different therapeutic tasks
>
> Janet was 55 and had enjoyed a successful career as a classical musician, working in orchestras around the world. She came into therapy following two major losses. Her relationship with her partner had ended in a manner that had been not only emotionally painful but also had left her financially insecure. The orchestra in which she had worked for many years had closed, and the economic down-turn made it unlikely that she would find similar work in the foreseeable future. She felt trapped, living in a small apartment on the edge of the city, lacking confidence and with little to do all day. She longed for the excitement and camaraderie of orchestra life. At the first meeting with her therapist, Janet came across as overwhelmed and defeated. She described her goals as 'moving on' and 'getting my life back'. It was helpful for her to identify a series of issues that might be looked at in therapy, one at a time. These included: brainstorming the pros and cons of various career options, such as music teaching; keeping in touch with former colleagues; being more honest with colleagues and friends about how she felt, and accepting their support; coming to terms with, and making sense of, what had gone wrong in her relationship; being better informed and more assertive around her share of the joint assets from her previous relationship; mourning the loss of orchestra life; learning how to deal with harshly self-critical trains of thought. Janet chose to begin by using therapy as a source of support and planning around meetings with friends and colleagues, and drawing on her therapist's knowledge of cognitive interventions for negative self-talk. At a later stage, the stress of legal proceedings with her former partner brought other tasks into the foreground. Toward the end of therapy, her therapist suggested that it might also be valuable to spend some time looking at how her ways of relating to others had been shaped by her early childhood experience. She agreed that this would be useful, but that it was not a priority for her at that time – it might be something that she would consider 'in a few years, when I feel a bit stronger'.

THERAPEUTIC METHODS AND INTERVENTIONS

In therapy around issues of happiness, meaningfulness and depression, there are many interventions that may be helpful (see also Chapter 7):

Structured methods for modifying self-undermining cognitions

The literature within cognitive therapy, CBT, mindfulness-based CBT, rational emotive cognitive behavioural therapy, metacognitive therapy, acceptance and commitment therapy, and other approaches within this broad tradition, represents an invaluable source of methods. These approaches may involve therapeutic steps such as: psycho-education around the consequences of negative thoughts; identifying and observing the operation of negative thoughts in everyday life, Socratic dialogue that constructively challenges the reality basis of these thoughts, ways of reducing the occurrence of such thoughts, rehearsal of alternative self-statements, rehearsal of mindfulness or relaxation skills, homework assignments to practise new skills and strategies, and monitoring progress. From a pluralistic perspective, a particularly valuable development within this approach to therapy has been a movement away from viewing depression as a single entity, in the direction of devising cognitive behavioural strategies around specific component areas of depression (i.e. therapeutic tasks), such as overcoming perfectionism (Shafran, Egan, & Wade, 2010).

Activation of everyday resources

It is probable that the client has had earlier times in their life when they have engaged in meaningful and pleasurable activities, and made use of social support, but that they have neglected these resources for whatever reasons. The pluralistic concept of 'cultural resources' (Cooper & McLeod, 2011) refers to the therapeutic use of everyday practices such as outdoor activity, reading, art-making, cooking, spirituality and much else. It tends to be most helpful to encourage the client to recall and revisit activities that have held meaning for them in the past, rather than the therapist suggesting or 'prescribing' new activities (Marley, 2011). For example, while attending a fitness centre may be enormously helpful for someone who is depressed, doing this for the first time when lacking confidence and energy is a daunting task that may be more likely to end in a damaging failure experience rather than being life-enhancing. Examples of strategies for activating everyday resources for therapeutic purposes can be found in Flückiger, Wüsten, Zinbarg and Wampold (2010) and Hays (1999).

Life planning and developing a positive future-orientation

A capacity for enjoyment and pleasure requires being able to remain grounded in the flow of here-and-now experiencing. In addition, depression is sustained through rumination about personal inadequacies associated with negative events in the past. In these scenarios, the client may have little or no sense of a positive future that includes moments of pleasurable 'being'. There are several therapeutic models and methods that can be offered to a client, in order to facilitate this kind of shift. At the simplest level, this kind of task can be pursued by inviting the client just to talk about what they are experiencing now, or how they would like their life to be at some point in the future. These methods can be further elaborated through exercises and activities that use guided fantasy, expressive arts techniques, workbooks, journal writing and self-help reading to help the client think about their future.

Facilitating restorative emotional experiences

A central theme within theory and research on the psychology of depression has been the importance of emotion. At the most basic level, people describe themselves as unhappy because of an absence of pleasurable feelings in their life. People describe themselves as depressed because they carry either (or both) a sense of emotional numbness, and/or diffuse emotional pain. It may be helpful, therefore, to pay attention to the emotional life of the client, to listen to one's own emotional response to the client and to invite the client to consider the possibility that a lack of capacity to express certain feelings and emotions may play some kind of role in their predicament. Within the psychotherapy research field, this broad topic has become labelled as the *self-regulation* of emotion. This topic is associated with such questions as: whether a person is aware of what they feel, the capacity to differentiate between different emotions, the capacity to tolerate the expression of emotion, understanding the situations that trigger certain emotions, the ability to express emotion in an appropriate fashion, and so on. These questions provide a starting point and checklist for sub-tasks that might be relevant for particular clients. As well as understanding their emotions, it is also helpful for the person to experience new emotions, and broaden their emotional repertoire. There are many methods that can be used to facilitate emotional experience in-session. Several of these methods have been integrated into emotion-focused therapy (Timulak, 2014), which is notable in describing clear, research-based interventions. Some clients may prefer to create their own restorative emotional experiences in everyday contexts, through techniques such as writing, music-making or sport.

CASE EXAMPLE
Using multiple change methods

Alastair was a successful manager whose life was severely constrained by unremitting self-criticism that undermined his ability to form close relationships and experience pleasure. During the opening stage of therapy, he talked in detail about how his father had never praised him – even the highest exam grades were never good enough. His father's harshly destructive voice lived on as a daily presence in his consciousness. There were several methods that proved

(Continued)

> *(Continued)*
>
> to be useful for Alastair in the therapy he received. It was tremendously important to feel heard, understood and liked. It was best for him if his therapist was highly present and authentic. Only then could he believe that he was accepted. Alastair engaged in a great deal of therapeutic reading as a means of making sense of his life. He found two-chair work and experiential focusing (both are emotion-focused therapy techniques) to be moderately useful, but struggled to let go of his capacity to engage in self-observation and allow himself to fully experience his here-and-now flow of feeling and emotion. Cognitive behavioural strategies for identifying negative thoughts and allowing them to be replaced by other thoughts were also partially helpful. In the end, what made the most difference for Alastair were yoga retreats that required him to painfully enter previously dormant areas of his bodily experiencing. Eventually, and using therapy sessions to process and work through what was evoked in yoga, he came to be able to grow a sense of bodily experience, pleasure and energy for life, and to discover that these attributes allowed him to get closer to other people.

Working constructively and purposefully at the ending stage of therapy is an important aspect of pluralistic therapy. For clients who are seeking happiness, meaningfulness and alleviation of depression, the fact of seeing a therapist on a weekly basis is likely to be beneficial in itself, as a form of social support, a potentially enjoyable way of structuring time and as something to look forward to. In addition, depression tends to be a cyclical condition. For these reasons, it is valuable to use the ending of therapy as a means of planning around how to maintain gains, and how to deal with inevitable crises and relapses. The structure of pluralistic therapy makes it easier to hold these kinds of conversations, because by the end of therapy the therapist and counsellor should have built up a robust shared understanding of how to talk about what might be helpful for the client. There are many strategies that may be relevant for helping clients to carry forward what they have learned in therapy: reviewing what has been useful, and why; writing a 'goodbye' letter or report for the client; the client writing a letter to self; follow-up sessions; periodic email contact; anticipating future difficulties and developing action plans, and so on. The key principle here is to ensure that the resources of both client and therapist are activated as fully as possible during this vital phase of therapy.

THERAPEUTIC CHALLENGES ASSOCIATED WITH THIS AREA OF WORK

A significant challenge arises with clients who do not respond positively to therapy. Some depressed people may present themselves as passive, defeated and too stuck to care. Other clients may have previously tried different therapies, without success, and lack hope. A study by McPherson, Walker and Carlyle (2006) identified two key factors that were frequently observed in intractable cases of depression: longstanding and severe difficulties, and absence of current social support. In some circumstances, involvement of psychiatric services may be helpful, or referral into long-term therapy. Within a pluralistic approach, it is possible to accommodate concurrent use of other resources, such as psychiatric care and medication, and participation in social activities. It is also possible to focus on achievable tasks as part of long-term therapy or while waiting for a referral to a long-term service.

Some people who are depressed are also suicidal, or may have made attempts to harm themselves in the past. Pluralistic strategies for working with these issues are discussed in Chapter 21.

One of the most significant issues for therapists seeking to develop a pluralistic response to clients' issues around happiness and depression is the work that is involved in developing a sufficiently broad and flexible understanding of this topic. There are convincing, evidence-based models of depression that explain this disorder in terms of cognitive processes. There are other, equally convincing, models that highlight the significance of early experience around attachment and loss. There are also influential biologically based and socially based theories of depression. At the present time, there does not exist a single comprehensive handbook or review article that critically analyses and compares all of these theoretical perspectives. Practitioners therefore need to be willing to explore the primary literature in cognitive behavioural, psychodynamic, positive psychology and other relevant approaches. The reference list at the end of this chapter presents some recommended starting points for therapist learning.

It is also important for therapists working with clients around issues of happiness and depression to monitor their inner emotional response to the client. Almost certainly, there will be implicit or hidden emotional themes in the life of the client that are not expressed directly but are nonetheless present in the room. The therapist's awareness of their congruent or countertransferential reaction to the client represents a key resource. It is also important to monitor action tendencies. It may be hard for a therapist to accept and tolerate the depth of demoralisation that can be exhibited by clients who are hopeless or depressed, and there can be a tendency for the therapist to seek a remedy in techniques and exercises, rather than being open to what the client may need to talk about.

A crucial area of therapist self-awareness, with this client group, is to retain a focus on the positive strengths of the client, and the diversity of change processes that may be helpful for them. This can be achieved through reading case studies of therapy for depression, and qualitative research into experiences of recovery from depression. A good example here is a study by Wilson and Giddings (2010), which documents the courage and resourcefulness of women who have recovered from depression.

SUMMARY

The key points highlighted by this chapter are:

- Lack of happiness and meaningfulness, and a sense of being depressed, are issues that are experienced by a growing proportion of people in contemporary society.

- These issues can be understood from a wide range of theoretical and everyday perspectives, which provide a strong rationale for adopting a flexible, pluralistic approach in therapy.
- There are many practical methods and interventions that can be used to alleviate depression, and promote happiness and meaningfulness.
- Therapists need to be aware of their own personal response to these topics, in order to remain focused on the needs and preferences of the client.

EXERCISES/POINTS FOR REFLECTION

1. Identify a time in your life when you experienced low mood or depression for an extended period, or felt that your life lacked meaning and pleasure. What did you, or other people, do at that time to enable you to move forward in your life? What are the implications of this experience, for your approach as a therapist?
2. What are the narratives or storylines that you use in your own life, or that seem most plausible to you, in accounting for the occurrence of depression? Are there any narratives that lack credibility for you?
3. What are your attitudes and beliefs around client use of anti-depressant medication? How might you make constructive use of these beliefs in dialogues with clients?

FURTHER READING

Hidaka, B.H. (2012). Depression as a disease of modernity: explanations for increasing prevalence. *Journal of Affective Disorders*, 140, 205–214. Provides detailed evidence for the social environmental origins of the increase in rates of depression.

Kenny, M.C. (2006). An integrative therapeutic approach to the treatment of a depressed American Indian client. *Clinical Case Studies*, 5, 37–52. Although this case study does not describe an explicitly pluralistic way of working, it nevertheless encompasses many elements that are consistent with a pluralistic perspective on depression.

Levine, B.E. (2007). *Surviving America's depression epidemic: how to find morale, energy, and community in a world gone crazy*. White River Junction, VT: Chelsea Green Publishing. This is an inspiring and informative book, which depicts a critically informed, holistic approach to working with depression.

von Below, C., Werbart, A., & Rehnberg, S. (2010). Experiences of overcoming depression in young adults in psychoanalytic psychotherapy. *European Journal of Psychotherapy and Counselling*, 12, 129–147. An example of a carefully conducted qualitative study, in which depressed clients who received a 'pure-form' approach to therapy nevertheless described multiple change processes that were helpful for them.

REFERENCES

Blatt, S., & Zuroff, D. (1992). Interpersonal relatedness and self-definition: two prototypes for depression. *Clinical Psychology Review, 12*, 527–562.

Cooper, M., & McLeod, J. (2011). *Pluralistic counselling and psychotherapy.* London: Sage.

Cuijpers, P., Andersson, G., Donker, T., & van Straten, A. (2011). Psychological treatment of depression: results of a series of meta-analyses. *Nordic Journal of Psychiatry, 65*, 354–364.

Flückiger, C., Wüsten, G., Zinbarg, R.E., & Wampold, B.E. (2010). *Resource activation: using clients' own strengths in psychotherapy and counseling.* Gottingen: Hogrefe.

Gotlib, I., & Hammen, C. (Eds.). (2014). *Handbook of depression* (3rd ed.). New York: The Guilford Press.

Greenberg, G. (2010). *Manufacturing depression: the secret history of a modern disease.* London: Bloomsbury.

Hansen, J.T. (2006). Counseling theories within a postmodernist epistemology: new roles for theories in counseling practice. *Journal of Counseling and Development, 84*, 291–297.

Hays, K.F. (1999). *Working it out: using exercise in psychotherapy.* Washington, DC: American Psychological Association.

Healy, D. (2006). *Let them eat Prozac: the unhealthy relationship between the pharmaceutical industry and depression.* New York: New York University Press.

Jack, D.C., & Ali, A. (Eds.). (2010). *Silencing the self across cultures: depression and gender in the social world.* New York: Oxford University Press.

Judd, L.L. (1997). The clinical course of unipolar major depressive disorders. *Archives of General Psychiatry, 54*, 989–991.

Kleinman, A., & Good, B. (Eds.). (1985). *Culture and depression: studies in the anthropology and cross-cultural psychiatry of affect and disorder.* Berkeley, CA: University of California Press.

Marley, E. (2011). Self-help strategies to reduce emotional distress: what do people do and why? A qualitative study. *Counselling and Psychotherapy Research, 11*, 317–324.

McPherson, S., Walker, C., & Carlyle, J.-A. (2006). Primary care counsellors' experiences of working with treatment resistant depression: a qualitative pilot study. *Counselling and Psychotherapy Research, 6*, 250–257.

Shafran, R., Egan, S., & Wade, T. (2010). *Overcoming perfectionism.* London: Constable and Robinson.

Timulak, L. (2014). *Transforming emotional pain in psychotherapy: an emotion-focused approach.* London: Routledge.

Valkonen, J., Hanninen, V., & Lindfors, O. (2011). Outcomes of psychotherapy from the perspective of the users. *Psychotherapy Research, 21*, 227–240.

Wilson, J., & Giddings, L. (2010). Counselling women whose lives have been seriously disrupted by depression: what professional counsellors can learn from New Zealand women's stories of recovery. *New Zealand Journal of Counselling, 30*, 23–39.

15

Helping Clients Address Problematic Anxiety

Windy Dryden

THIS CHAPTER DISCUSSES

- Understandings from across the psychological therapies that can be drawn upon in helping clients to understand the major components of their problematic anxiety
- Client goals with respect to problematic anxiety
- The conditions in which problematic anxiety thrives and the conditions in which it withers in the longer term; an analysis that can be used as a basis for developing goal-related tasks with clients
- The development of broad and specific methods that operationalize task-related client goals

In this chapter, I will show how therapy of anxiety embodies the principles of pluralism described by Cooper and McLeod (2011).

THE COMPONENTS OF ANXIETY

Anxiety is perhaps the most common psychological problem for which people seek help, with an estimated one-year prevalence of between 14% and 18% in high income countries across the world (Gulliver, Griffiths, Christensen, & Brewer, 2012).

In this chapter, the term 'anxiety' is used to refer to the entire range of the anxiety disorders (e.g. social anxiety, panic, health anxiety and OCD). Space does not permit a consideration of the complexities of therapy with clients with problematic anxiety. See Sookman and Leahy (2010) for a lengthy consideration of helping anxious clients with co-morbid problems and 'treatment resistances'. See Patterson, Albala, McCahill and Edwards (2010) for a consideration of medication for anxiety.

In this section, I will outline the major components of anxiety.

Interpretation of threat

For anxiety to be present, the person needs to infer the presence of something threatening to them. It is important to bear in mind that the important ingredient here is the person's *interpretation* of a threat, rather than its actual existence.

Threat across the therapies

The central role of threat in understanding anxiety is acknowledged across the therapies. For example:

- *Person-centred therapy*: Carl Rogers (1959) argued that anxiety is felt when the person experiences something that is incongruent with the self-structure and when their attempts to distort or deny the experience have failed.
- *Psychodynamic therapy*: Leichsenring and Salzer (2014) outline a model of anxiety based on the concept of core conflict relationship theme (CCRT). Here, a person's wish, often unconscious, and behaviour related to that wish is associated in their mind with a response from others that is deemed threatening. For example, a person may wish to be affirmed by others and be in the centre of attention, but does not act on that wish because he fears that if he does so he will be humiliated. Symptoms of anxiety will be experienced if the person acts on their wish because the feared response for others will be triggered in their mind.
- *Cognitive behaviour therapy*: Salkovskis (1996) outlined a model of anxiety based on Beck and Emery (1985) according to the following equation:

$$\text{Anxiety} = \frac{\text{Perceived likelihood that a threat will occur} \times \text{its perceived cost or anxietyfulness}}{\text{Perceived ability to cope} + \text{Perceived rescue factors}}$$

Here, the person is more likely to experience anxiety when they don't think they can cope with the threat and when they don't see any rescue factors.

- *Existential therapy*: Wolfe (2005, 2008) shows how existential issues (death, mortality, freedom/security, one's place in the world, meaning and purpose in life) often underly the experience of anxiety. This points to the important distinction between threats that are proximal in nature (i.e. the true threat is close to the surface in the person's mind and is easy to identify) and distal in nature (i.e. the true threat is more deeply embedded in the person's mind and more difficult to identify).

External versus internal threat

An important distinction in anxiety concerns external threat and internal threat. An external threat is external to the person (e.g. your boss indicates that she wishes to see you and you make the threat-related inference that she is going to criticize you) while an internal threat concerns something within you (e.g. you avoid someone because you will experience anger if you see them and you find feeling angry threatening to you). Internal threats are often our own feelings, thoughts and behavioural urges.

Maladaptive responses to the threat

Many theorists argue that anxiety responses are not inherently problematic, but become maladaptive when they don't help the person, *behaviourally*, to deal effectively with the threat if it can be dealt with or, *cognitively*, to make a constructive adjustment when it can't be dealt with. From this perspective the many *physical* symptoms often associated with anxiety are only targets for when they prevent constructive exposure or adjustment. Of course, from a pluralistic perspective, the client's views on this issue need to be taken seriously and clients often do wish to experience less intense physical anxiety symptoms because they are painful.

In addition, problematic anxiety may affect a person's *interpersonal relationships* – although this depends largely on the response of the other (Hoffman, 2014) and it is related to a number of other *emotions*. Thus, if the threat occurs, anxiety gives way to emotions such as anger, shame and hurt.

The maladaptive responses of anxiety can themselves serve as threats

If anxiety and worry is experienced in the context of the person inferring the presence of a threat, then the maladaptive responses of anxiety can, and often do, serve as threats for the development of further anxiety. Sometimes known as anxiety about anxiety or meta-anxiety, it is important to identify what it is about the original anxiety response that is threatening for the person and to determine with the person whether the original anxiety or the meta-anxiety is to be targeted for change first.

The consequences of maladaptive responses of anxiety

It is also important to consider the consequences of the experience and/or the expression of anxiety responses since these responses may make a difference with respect to the prospects of change or the continuation of problematic of anxiety. For example, Jeremy experienced health anxiety and at times when his feelings of anxiety became acute he searched on the internet for evidence that his symptoms were benign. When he found such evidence he immediately felt reassured and his anxiety abated, but this reduction of anxiety symptoms proved short-lived and when his anxiety symptoms increased he returned to searching the internet. This pattern of anxiety responses, searching the internet, initial relief, the return of anxiety responses served to help maintain Jeremy's health anxiety.

Ambivalent features of anxiety

Often when people with anger problems come to therapy, they are ambivalent about change, as they often clearly see the advantages of this emotion as well as its disadvantages. While this is less the case with people experiencing problems with anxiety, it still occurs and it is important to discuss with clients reasons why they might be reluctant to target anxiety for change and what advantages they consider their worry, in particular, may have (e.g. 'Worry protects me from really bad things happening to me'). These are known as positive beliefs in metacognitive therapy (Fisher & Wells, 2009). This approach also points out that people may hold negative beliefs about their thoughts. A common example of such a belief concerns people's beliefs that their thoughts are uncontrollable, thus leading them to conclude that there is little point in targeting them for change.

GOALS IN ANXIETY PROBLEMS

When asked for their goals with respect to their anxiety problems, clients frequently say that they don't want to feel anxious or worried or that they want to feel these states with less intensity. Let's examine each of these in turn. First, what does it mean not to be anxious and worried? Is it humanly possible? If you are facing a threat, isn't it healthy to feel some kind of anxiety or worry if doing so helps you deal effectively with the threat or to discover if the threat actually exists? For these reasons, it is important to discuss with clients alternatives to 'no-feeling' goals. A similar point can be made with less-intensity feeling goals. This may be problematic in that less-intense anxiety goals may not necessarily help the person deal effectively with the threat, for example. As such, it is useful to help clients distinguish *problematic* anxiety that has brought them to therapy and does not help them to deal effectively, with threat from *functional* anxiety, which reflects the fact that they are facing (or think they are facing) a threat and helps them deal effectively with it.

As the above shows, clients are often focused on their feelings when you ask them about their goals. However, as I have discussed, maladaptive responses involve not only feelings, but physiology, interpersonal relationships, behaviour and cognition. The latter two aspects, in particular, often do not feature in clients' goals with respect to their problematic anxiety. It is especially important to ask clients for their behavioural goals if they do not mention them as it is difficult to deal effectively in the long term with anxiety problems if one is not active in doing so. Behavioural goal-setting is best done by taking clients' maladaptive behavioural responses and helping them to articulate a healthy goal for each maladaptive response mentioned. In some cases this process can also be done with maladaptive cognitive responses and goals.

> **CASE EXAMPLE**
>
> **Goal-setting with anxiety**
>
> Malcolm came to therapy for help with public-speaking anxiety. He was particularly anxious about drying up in front of his audience. He dealt with this problem by avoiding giving talks. However, he had just got a job promotion that necessitated him talking in public. As he wanted to keep this new job he recognized that he was going to have to give public presentations. When asked what he wanted to achieve from therapy, Malcolm said that he did not want to feel anxious about speaking in public. I observed that, at present, he was responding to the possibility of drying up with the kind of anxiety that led him to avoid public speaking. I asked him whether it would be best to help him be prepared for the possibility of drying up (i.e. the threat) or leave it and hope that it doesn't happen. He replied that he wanted to be prepared in case he did dry up. I then asked him whether it was more realistic for him not to feel any anxiety or to feel the type of anxiety that would help him give a public talk and deal constructively with the threat (i.e. him drying up). He replied that the latter was more realistic and that he wanted to commit himself to this goal. This led to a discussion of what he could do to achieve this goal. This example shows the importance of working collaboratively. I began by taking seriously Malcolm's initially stated goal and using that as a starting point, then asked questions to help Malcolm choose the most realistic goal.

TASKS EMPLOYED TO ACHIEVE ANXIETY GOALS

Once goal-setting has been carried out, the next stage is to discuss with clients which broad tasks might help them to achieve these goals. I have found it useful in this respect to introduce to clients an exercise that invites them to consider the idea of anxiety as a plant. Table 15.1 details the exercise and, from a review of my

TABLE 15.1 *Exercise to identify tasks to help clients to achieve their anxiety-related goals*

If Anxiety were a Plant

Imagine that your anxiety were a plant. Given that different plants need different conditions to thrive or wither, from your experience what conditions would lead your anxiety to thrive and what conditions would lead it to wither in the longer-term? Please bear in mind that conditions that lead to short-term relief from anxiety are likely to result in anxiety thriving in the longer term

Conditions in which anxiety thrives	Conditions in which anxiety withers (long-term)*
• Attempts to eliminate or suppress anxiety from personal experience • Attempts to avoid public exposure of anxiety	• Understanding anxiety and worry and its often paradoxical nature • Exposure to and acceptance/tolerance of symptoms

Conditions in which anxiety thrives	Conditions in which anxiety withers (long-term)*
• Attempts to avoid the threat and the symptoms of anxiety • Attempts to keep oneself safe from threat without facing up to it • Attempts to neutralize the threat (reassurance, safety-seeking behaviour) • No attempt to test out one's inferences concerning threat • Desperate attempts to control the physical symptoms of anxiety • Self-depreciation (a) should the threat materialize; (b) for experiencing anxiety; (c) for failing to exert self-control • Unrealistic, catastrophic thinking and images • Failing to deal with existential issues (e.g. fear of death) • Intolerance of uncertainty in the face of threat • Others showing intolerance of one's anxiety • Lack of understanding of past contributions to anxiety • Comparing self to others who handle threat well and finding self wanting • No utilization of skills for handling feared situations • No utilization of problem-solving skills • No exposure to good role-model for experiencing, showing and dealing with anxiety	• Exposure to threat[1] • Testing out one's inferences concerning threat[2] • Dealing constructively with threat both cognitively and behaviourally (and learning to develop associated skills)[3] • Constructive adjustment in the face of the continued existence of threat • Self-acceptance (a) should the threat materialize; (b) for experiencing anxiety; (c) for failing to exert self-control • Preparedness to show anxiety symptoms in public (coming out of the closet) • Realistic, non-catastrophic thinking and images[4] • Willing to face up to and dealing effectively with existential issues (e.g. fear of death) • Tolerance of uncertainty concerning threat • Tolerance of lack of self-control • Appropriate use of problem-solving skills • Others showing acceptance and compassion towards self for experiencing anxiety • Understanding the past contributions to anxiety • Having a good role model for experiencing, showing and dealing with anxiety

* The footnotes refer to task-oriented principles put forward by Woody and Ollendick (2006, p. 172) on the basis of their review of empirically supported treatment protocols for anxiety.

[1] 'Use repeated exposure to the feared situation to reduce the intensity of the feared response' and 'Eliminate avoidance of feared situations'.

[2] 'Actively test the validity of erroneous and maladaptive beliefs through behavioural experiments'.

[3] 'Improve skills for handling feared situations'.

[4] 'Challenge misconceptions through discussion and explicitly questioning the evidence'.

case notes, a category list of conditions that a sample of my clients came up with in doing this exercise.

Note that a number of the conditions listed by my clients in the anxiety-withering section (see Table 15.1) are to be found in Barlow et al.'s (2011) *Unified Protocol for Transdiagnostic Treatment of Emotional Disorders*, which comprises a number of modules and has been used as a generic framework for the treatment of a variety of emotional disorders (including anxiety disorders). (There is also a unified psychodynamic protocol designed especially for the treatment of anxiety disorders: Leichsenring & Salzer, 2014.)

Identifying and utilizing clients' strengths in the selection of goal-related tasks

In Chapter 6 of this book, Sparks and Duncan make clear that identifying and utilizing client strengths are key principles in pluralistic approaches to counselling and psychotherapy. It is thus important to bear this in mind when working with clients to help them achieve their anxiety-related goals. The anxiety-withering conditions that you identify with a particular client can inform your therapeutic dialogue here by linking clients' expressed strengths with these conditions.

As Sparks and Duncan (this volume) show, pluralistic therapists can help clients to identify and utilize strengths in dealing with their anxiety problems. As clients with anxiety problems tend to experience themselves as low in resourcefulness, helping them to see that they already have resources to deal with their problems is therapeutic in itself, as well as providing a more specific platform for selecting personalized therapeutic tasks and the concrete therapeutic methods that operationalize these tasks.

METHODS USED IN THE IMPLEMENTATION OF GOAL-RELATED TASKS

Therapeutic methods for helping clients address anxiety vary along a dimension of specificity with the broader methods tending to be derived from the humanistic, psychodynamic and existential therapies and the more specific methods tending to be derived from the cognitive behavioural therapies.

Broad methods I: Helping to lay the foundations of change

Stiles and Wolfe (2006: 157) used the report of the Empirically Supported Relationship (ESR) Task Force (Steering Committee, 2001) to make the following statements about core broad methods that produce change in the treatment of anxiety:

Therapeutic change is most likely when therapists:

- Strive to achieve and maintain a strong therapeutic alliance with anxiety disordered clients
- Strive to be empathic with anxiety disordered clients and communicate their empathy
- Seek to negotiate goals and expectations for therapy on which they and their anxiety disordered clients can agree and should monitor and maintain a mutual sense of involvement in the therapeutic enterprise.

Another broad method that helps to lay the foundations of change is the use of psycho-education. This is particularly helpful for clients who experience phrenophobia (i.e. the fear that their anxiety symptoms mean that they are going mad – Walen, 1982). Offering them a plausible explanation for how anxiety develops and is maintained helps normalize the experience for such clients whose fears of loss of physical and mental control represent meta-anxiety issues (anxiety about anxiety). The broad methods discussed in this section help clients with anxiety problems subsequently to concentrate on dealing with these problems.

Broad methods II: Helping clients to deal with general issues

Earlier I distinguished between proximal and distal threats about which clients have anxiety problems. Being general, broad methods tend to be more suited to dealing with distal threats that tend to be more general in nature. An example would be broad discussion of death anxiety. From an existential perspective, such anxiety is a distal threat that is deemed to underly more real-life proximal threats. By contrast, specific methods are more suited to dealing with proximal threats that tend to be specific in nature. CBT is often seen as the treatment of choice for anxiety problems. However, not all clients with anxiety problems benefit from or resonate with CBT approaches. In addition, the specific focus of CBT may not help clients deal with more distal threats. Thus, Douglas and James (2014) discuss the case of a man who did not respond to CBT for his problematic anxiety, while psychodynamic therapy helped him to identify memories of being unable to react negatively to his critical father for fear of upsetting his mother and thus risking abandonment. This realization helped him to work through his fear of abandonment with beneficial impact on his symptoms.

Also, broader meaning-making methods (see Chapter 11) can be useful to help clients explore the meaning of the gap between how they actually construe themselves and their ideal construction of self where this dynamic is at the root of anxiety, as it commonly is in social anxiety, for example. Two-chair work, derived from Gestalt therapy, can then be used to help clients narrow the gap between ideal and actual self-constructions.

Specific methods

When it comes to using specific methods in the implementation of goal-related tasks in anxiety, many of these are derived from the cognitive behavioural therapies. A good source of such methods can be found in O'Donohue and Fisher (2008). A comprehensive, CBT-based, self-help guide to anxiety detailing specific methods is Shafran, Brosan and Cooper (2013).

Commonly used specific methods are as follows.

Exposure methods

Perhaps the most important thing that clients with anxiety problems need to do is to expose themselves to threat. This may be done in a full way or more gradually, often employing a hierarchy. They may be employed with or without the use of other methods (e.g. relaxation methods or cognitive restructuring methods). It is important for therapists to ensure that clients do not use safety-seeking strategies (i.e. strategies designed to keep them safe from threat, but as a result do not allow them to face up to and deal productively with the threat) while employing exposure methods as these strategies may well interfere with them facing the threat. The exception to this is where safety strategies (e.g. subtle avoidance) are employed to help get the person into the feared situation, at which point the safety strategies are dropped (Rachman, Radomsky, & Shafran, 2008). Exposure can be done *in vivo* (i.e., in actual life) or in imagination. An example of the latter is systematic desensitization, where the client is helped to construct a hierarchy of threats and to imagine facing each threat in the hierarchy while being in a relaxed state (O'Donohue & Fisher, 2008).

In vivo exposure methods are particularly suited to therapy with phobias and if clients are prepared to put up with much discomfort may be successfully employed in a single extended session (Davis, Ollendick, & Ost, 2012; Ellis, 1979).

Cognitive methods

Cognitive methods are employed when clients' anxiety problems are based on what might be generically termed 'maladaptive cognitions and cognitive processes'. Examples of these include inaccurate inferences (e.g. overestimation of threat), selective attention (e.g. focusing on threat in the environment and editing out safety features), maladaptive schemata or irrational beliefs (e.g. I must know for certain that threat does not exist and terrible things will occur if I don't have such certainty) and positive and negative beliefs about anxiety itself (discussed earlier) (see Chapter 9, this volume). The goal of such methods is to encourage the use of more realistic and functional ways of (a) making inferences in situations where threat may occur, (b) attending to threat and safety in one's environment and (c) evaluating self, others and relevant aspects of the world (including anxiety itself) when these evaluations take the form of schemata and beliefs. This is done largely by encouraging clients to stand back and look again at these cognitions and related processes from a more objective and compassionate perspective and to develop more realistic and functional alternatives that are then acted upon in relevant threat-related situations. It is generally agreed that the use of cognitive methods in the therapy room alone without actively employing them in the real world is of limited value (Emmelkamp, Kuipers, & Eggeraat, 1978). A fuller discussion of cognitive methods in anxiety-focused therapy may be found in Leahy (2005, 2009).

I employed two cognitive methods when, as a teenager, I was anxious about speaking publicly due to a pronounced stammer. I heard comedian Michael Bentine on the radio speaking about how he dealt with his stammer. I applied two cognitive methods that he discussed. First, I questioned the idea that I was a stammerer and decided to adopt a more realistic and functional view that I was not a stammerer, but a person who stammered on occasion and was fluent at other times. This is known as 'de-identification'. Second, I questioned the idea that it was terrible to stammer in public; rather, I concluded that it was unfortunate to stammer, but not the end of the world. This known as anti-awfulizing. I acted on these two ideas and took every opportunity to speak in public having rehearsed the ideas. The result was I became more confident and less anxious about public speaking and became more fluent.

Acceptance and mindfulness methods

As opposed to cognitive methods that are designed to help people directly change maladaptive cognitions and cognitive processes that underpin anxiety, acceptance and mindfulness methods are designed to encourage clients to stay with and accept without judgement a variety of anxiety symptoms. Here clients are encouraged to view anxiety as a normal and understandable response to threat and to accept it as such and get on with value-based activity rather than struggle with it. It is the struggle, it is claimed, that is problematic rather than the anxiety symptoms (Flaxman, Blackledge, & Bond, 2011). A variety of personalistic metaphors and analogies are used to make the case with clients for the employment of these methods and how to do them (Blenkiron, 2010).

Imagery methods

It is generally recognized that imagery plays an important part in the development and maintenance of anxiety. It follows, therefore, that imagery methods can help bring about helpful change when this is the case. Examples include repeated review of aversive images until they are no longer aversive; imagining oneself dealing with threat in a resourceful but realistic manner; imagining oneself as an adult going back in time to comfort oneself as a child if one currently has anxiety about the possibility of re-experiencing the childhood event in one's mind's eye. As discussed, imagery is a main feature in systematic desensitization. Hackmann, Bennett-Levy and Holmes (2011) is a good source of using imagery methods in working with clients with anxiety problems.

Physiological control methods

For those particularly troubled by the physiological symptoms that often accompany anxiety, the physiological control methods may useful. Relaxation and biofeedback methods are frequently used in this regard (see O'Donohue & Fisher, 2008). Two points should be borne in mind here. First, such methods should be portable and be able to be employed in situ. Second, if they are used by clients who are desperate in their need to control such symptoms, then they are likely to be ineffective. In such cases, cognitive methods targeted at the desperate need to be in control should be employed first.

Skills learning and application methods

Sometimes a major feature of a person's anxiety is that they lack certain core skills and it is this lack that leads them to be low in the perceived ability of the anxiety equation devised by Salkovskis (1996), which I presented earlier in the chapter. Also, they have such skills in their repertoire but perform them poorly. It follows then that for such clients skills training may be particularly helpful. Examples of such skills that pluralistic therapists may teach their clients include assertion skills, social skills, study and examination skills, and problem-solving skills (see O'Donohue & Fisher, 2008). Such training is rarely the only method employed with anxiety clients but when used to encourage clients to develop greater self-efficacy in specific areas, they can be an important adjunct in anxiety-focused therapy with these clients.

Paradoxical methods

Based on the view that anxiety thrives on attempts to control it, the idea for the use of paradoxical methods is that control is gained not by trying to control anxiety but by deliberately attempting to make anxiety symptoms worse (Fay, 1978). Thus, somebody who fears sweating, for example, is encouraged to drown other people in sweat. By trying to do this, the person learns that paradoxically he sweats far less.

A CHALLENGE FOR PLURALISTIC THERAPISTS IN WORKING WITH CLIENTS WITH PROBLEMATIC ANXIETY

The challenge for pluralistic therapists in working with clients with anxiety problems concerns when to depart from empirically supported tasks and methods. It is important for therapists to have clear professional criteria for suggesting such departures to their clients, which will be discussed fully in the metatherapy dialogue. Thus, I end this chapter by asking you to consider when you might consider departing from Woody and Ollendick's (2006: 177–80) empirically supported treatment recommendations with clients with anxiety problems:

- Recommendation: 'Therapists should be directive, and the therapeutic process should be structured and action-oriented'
  Challenge: When might you consider being less directive and structured and more exploratory and insight-oriented?
- Recommendation: 'Treatment strategies should focus on facilitating behavior change'
  Challenge: When might you consider focusing on facilitating other kinds of change?
- Recommendation: 'Treatment is time-limited and relatively intense'
  Challenge: When might you consider working over time and with less intensity?

- Recommendation: 'Effective treatments for anxiety disorders use emotionally evocative procedures'
  Challenge: When might you consider not evoking emotions?
- Recommendation: 'The focus of empirically supported interventions is primarily intrapersonal'
  Challenge: When might you consider working interpersonally rather than intrapersonally?

SUMMARY

In this chapter, I have made the following key points:

- Helping clients to address their problematic anxiety is best done when it is based on a pluralistic understanding of the major components of anxiety.
- Care needs to be taken when setting anxiety-related goals with clients in case goals are accepted that inadvertently may make matters worse in the long run for clients.
- It is important to help clients distinguish between conditions in which their anxiety thrives and conditions in which it withers. When selecting tasks with clients to help them achieve their healthy goals, it is important to do so based on an understanding of the former and on their pre-existing strengths that have previously been identified.
- Methods that operationalize goal-related tasks may be broad or specific. Both may be employed at different times to help clients achieve their goals with respect to their problematic anxiety.

EXERCISES/POINTS FOR REFLECTION

1. What are you anxious about and/or worry about in your own life? Focus on the anxiety/worry that is problematic for you. What are the threats about which you experience this problematic anxiety? Make a list of these and then choose one to focus on.
2. Identify the major components of your problematic anxiety on this one issue. Use the appropriate section in this chapter as a guide.
3. Identify your goal with respect to your problematic anxiety.
4. Identify the strengths you have that might help you deal with your selected threat effectively.
5. Identify the conditions in which your anxiety might thrive and might wither in the longer term with this threat. Use the 'anxiety as a plant' exercise previously described.
6. Using your list of anxiety-withering conditions as tasks, develop a list of methods that you think might help you achieve your goal and make a plan to carry out these methods if you can.
7. What lessons can you learn from doing this exercise that might help you as a client?

> **FURTHER READING**
>
> Barlow, D.H. (2002). *Anxiety and its disorders: the nature and treatment of anxiety and panic* (2nd ed.). New York: The Guilford Press. Perhaps the most comprehensive text on the anxiety disorders, albeit a little outdated.
>
> Barlow, D.H., Farchione, T.J., Fairholme, C.P., Ellard, K.K., Boisseau, C.L., Allen, L.B., & Ehrenreich-May, J. (2011). *The Unified Protocol for Transdiagnostic Treatment of Emotional Disorders: therapist guide.* New York: Oxford University Press. An outstanding transdiagnostic, empirically derived, CBT-oriented treatment protocol.
>
> Castonguay, L.G., & Beutler, L.E. (Eds.). (2006). *Principles of therapeutic change that work*. New York: Oxford University Press. See Part III, which is devoted to therapy of anxiety disorders.
>
> Leichsenring, F., & Salzer, S. (2014). A unified protocol for the transdiagnostic psychodynamic treatment of anxiety disorders: an evidence-based approach. *Psychotherapy, 51,* 224–245. A psychodynamic alternative to Barlow et al. (2011).
>
> Wolfe, B.E. (2005). *Understanding and treating anxiety disorders: an integrative approach to healing the wounded self*. Washington, DC: American Psychological Association. This excellent integrative book is especially good on combining CBT and existential tasks and methods.

REFERENCES

Barlow, D.H., Farchione, T.J., Fairholme, C.P., Ellard, K.K., Boisseau, C.L. Allen, L.B., & Ehrenreich-May, J. (2011). *The Unified Protocol for Transdiagnostic Treatment of Emotional Disorders: therapist guide.* New York: Oxford University Press.

Beck, A.T., & Emery, G. (with Greenberg, R.L.). (1985). *Anxiety disorders and phobias: a cognitive perspective*. New York: Basic Books.

Blenkiron, P. (2010). *Stories and analogies in cognitive behaviour therapy*. Chichester: Wiley.

Cooper, M., & McLeod, J. (2011). *Pluralistic counselling and psychotherapy*. London: Sage.

Davis, E.T., III, Ollendick, T.H., & Ost, L.G. (Eds.). (2012). *Intensive one-session treatment of specific phobias*. New York: Springer.

Douglas, B., & James, P. (2014). *Common presenting problems in psychotherapeutic practice*. London: Sage.

Ellis, A. (1979). Discomfort anxiety: a new cognitive behavioural construct. Part 1. *Rational Living, 14*(2), 3–7.

Emmelkamp, P.M.G., Kuipers, A., & Eggeraat, J.B. (1978). Cognitive modification versus prolonged exposure in vivo: a comparison with agoraphobics as subjects. *Behaviour Research and Therapy, 16,* 33–41.

Fay, A. (1978). *Making things better by making them worse*. New York: E.P. Dutton.

Fisher, P., & Wells, A. (2009). *Metacognitive therapy: distinctive features*. Hove: Routledge.

Flaxman, P.E., Blackledge, J.T., & Bond, F.W. (2011). *Acceptance and commitment therapy: distinctive features*. Hove: Routledge.

Gulliver, A., Griffiths, K.M., Christensen, H., & Brewer, J.L. (2012). A systematic review of help-seeking interventions for depression, anxiety and general psychological distress. *BMC Psychiatry, 12*, 81.

Hackmann, A., Bennett-Levy, J., & Holmes, E. (2011). *Oxford guide to imagery in cognitive therapy.* Oxford: Oxford University Press.

Hoffman, S.G. (2014). Interpersonal emotion regulation model of mood and anxiety disorders. *Cognitive Therapy and Research, 38*, 483–492.

Leahy, R.L. (2005). *The worry cure: stop worrying and start living.* New York: Harmony Books.

Leahy, R.L. (2009). *Anxiety free: unravel your fears before they unravel you.* Carlsbad, CA: Hay House.

Leichsenring, F., & Salzer, S. (2014). A unified protocol for the transdiagnostic psychodynamic treatment of anxiety disorders: an evidence-based approach. *Psychotherapy, 51*, 224–245.

O'Donohue, W.T., & Fisher, J.E. (Eds.). (2008). *Cognitive behaviour therapy: applying empirically supported techniques in your practice* (2nd ed.). New York: Wiley.

Patterson, J., Albala, A.A., McCahill, M.E., & Edwards, T.M. (2010). *The therapist's guide to psychopharmacology: working with patients, families and physicians to optimize care* (Rev. ed.). New York: The Guilford Press.

Rachman, S., Radomsky, A.S., & Shafran, R. (2008). Safety behavior: a reconsideration. *Behaviour Research and Therapy, 46*, 163–173.

Rogers, C.R. (1959). A theory of therapy, personality and interpersonal relationships as developed in the client-centered framework. In S. Koch (Ed.), *Psychology: a study of science* (Vol. 3, pp. 184–256). New York: McGraw–Hill.

Salkovskis, P. (1996). The cognitive approach to anxiety: threat beliefs, safety-seeking behaviour, and the special case of health anxiety and obsessions. In P. Salkovskis (Ed.), *Frontiers of cognitive therapy* (pp. 48–74). New York: The Guilford Press.

Shafran, R., Brosan, L., & Cooper, P. (2013). *The complete CBT guide for anxiety.* London: Robinson.

Sookman, D., & Leahy, R.L. (Eds.). (2010). *Treatment resistance anxiety disorders: resolving impasses to symptom remission.* New York: Routledge.

Steering Committee (2001). Empirically supported therapy relationships: conclusions and recommendations of the Division 29 Task Force. *Psychotherapy, 38*, 495–497.

Stiles, W.B., & Wolfe, B.E. (2006). Relationship factors in treating anxiety disorders. In L.G. Castonguay & L.E. Beutler (Eds.), *Principles of therapeutic change that work* (pp. 65–81). New York: Oxford University Press.

Walen, S.R. (1982). Phrenophobia. *Cognitive Therapy and Research, 6*, 399–407.

Wolfe, B.E. (2005). *Understanding and treating anxiety disorders: an integrative approach to healing the wounded self.* Washington, DC: American Psychological Association.

Wolfe, B.E. (2008). Existential issues in anxiety disorders and their treatment. In K.J. Schneider (Ed.), *Existential-integrative psychotherapy: guideposts to the core of practice* (pp. 204–216). New York: Routledge.

Woody, S.R., & Ollendick, T.H. (2006). Technique factors in treating anxiety disorders. In L.G. Castonguay & L.E. Beutler (Eds.), *Principles of therapeutic change that work* (pp. 83–109). New York: Oxford University Press.

16

Helping Clients Improve their Interpersonal Relationships

Meg John Barker

THIS CHAPTER DISCUSSES

- The place of interpersonal relationship difficulties in therapeutic practice
- Understandings from across the psychological therapies which can be helpful when working pluralistically with clients' interpersonal relationships
- How collaborative therapeutic relationships can be built with both individuals and dyads who are experiencing relationship difficulties
- Working with life goals and therapy goals around interpersonal relationships in pluralistic counselling
- Methods from across the psychological therapies which can be helpful when working pluralistically with both individuals and dyads in this area

INTERPERSONAL RELATIONSHIPS IN COUNSELLING AND PSYCHOTHERAPY

Most therapeutic approaches agree that humans have a fundamental need for relatedness. Cooper and Joseph (2015) present a compelling review of evidence that interpersonal relationships play a vital role in mental health. This includes the strong correlation between happiness and having close friends and/or partners, the relationship between social isolation and depression, and the fact that people prioritise intimacy goals over other life goals. Quality and quantity of social relationships is one of the very strongest predictors of mortality and physical health (analogous with giving up smoking). Interpersonal relationship problems are frequently found to be the most common issues to be brought to counselling.

The bulk of therapeutic literature in this area focuses on romantic relationships. Indeed, relationship therapy is still often called 'couple' or even 'marital' therapy by the main bodies and journals in the field. In the current Western context, romantic relationships are generally recognised, and experienced, as important, and are also particularly likely to involve – or cause – distress. 'Death of a spouse', 'divorce' and 'marital separation' are the top items on scales of stressful life events, and research finds a strong link between distress in romantic relationships and mental health problems. For these reasons, this chapter focuses on this kind of relationship. However, much of the material here is applicable to relationships more broadly, and we will return to the possibility of broadening out understandings of what constitutes a relationship towards the end of the chapter.

UNDERSTANDING INTERPERSONAL RELATIONSHIPS PLURALISTICALLY

> **Point for reflection**
>
> Before we continue, consider which therapeutic approaches you are most familiar with. How do they understand interpersonal relationships and relationship problems?

Existentialism

Relational conflict is a major feature of existential theories of human experience, notably those of the French existentialists Simone de Beauvoir (1948/1976) and Jean-Paul Sartre (1943/2005). The existential understanding is that one of the universal 'givens' of human experience is the inevitable tension between individual freedom and interconnectedness: throughout our lives we are both fundamentally alone and fundamentally in relation with others. To resolve this tension people often endeavour to objectify the other person, or to objectify themselves, for example trying to turn somebody into your 'perfect partner' or to make yourself into the 'perfect partner' for them. However, freedom always eventually bubbles up to undermine such attempts. This is the thinking behind Sartre's famous quote 'hell is other people'.

Existential understandings can be helpful in normalising the relationship struggles that clients experience between independence and togetherness, such as finding it hard to commit, experiencing jealousy or loneliness, or finding it hard to make decisions between their own goals and those of the other people in their lives. Existential approaches also suggest ways through relationship conflict via a more mutual approach where each person values the other person in all of their difference and freedom, and they help each other to move towards their goals. This requires both cultivating empathy and being open about our own vulnerabilities (see Barker, 2014).

Social constructionism

Social constructionist, systemic and narrative therapy approaches locate people's relationship experiences within wider cultural messages about relationships. It is clear from cross-cultural and historical research that people conduct and experience their relationships in very different ways depending on the social norms around them. For example, consider the vast range of forms of monogamous and polygamous modes of relating that have existed globally and across time (Barker, 2014). One example of the way this currently plays out in client struggles in the West is that there are huge pressures on romantic relationships to meet all of people's needs, and for partners to give and receive an almost 'divine' kind of love in such relationships (Barker, 2013a). Exposure to such ideals of romantic love leads to beliefs associated with problems in real relationships, for example that everybody has a predestined soulmate who will be their perfect match and will be able to read their mind (Holmes, 2007).

A social constructionist perspective would suggest that it is useful to explore the wider cultural messages around relationships – of whatever kind – within which the client is embedded, and how these might feed into their own assumptions, ideals and 'rules' about relationships. Like the existential approach, this approach can take the weight off the individual client feeling that there is something 'wrong' with them, and help them to understand that most people find relationships difficult given the huge cultural pressures and expectations upon them (Barker, 2013a). It is not possible to step outside of culture, but counsellors can encourage a critical engagement with prevailing social norms and cultural ideologies in order that the client can navigate their own way through them. Social constructionist – and related – approaches also demonstrate the need for therapists to have cultural and subcultural competency (or to refer on), given that relationship norms and ideals vary across cultures and communities (see das Nair & Butler, 2012; Richards & Barker, 2013).

Individual psychology

Next, most of the therapeutic approaches offer some way of understanding how people's individual histories of relationships result in certain ways of approaching and experiencing relationships in the present day. For example, a great deal has been written about attachment theory, and the ways in which different attachment styles may play out in adult relationships. Clients may find it useful to consider which kinds of attachment styles seem most applicable to them, or which they find themselves drawn into in different kinds of relationships or situations. In addition to this, or if this psychoanalytic approach is not a good fit for a particular client, it may be helpful to introduce Rogers's person-centred theory of 'conditions of worth' to explore what ways of relating clients had learnt were acceptable or unacceptable growing up. Systemic genograms of family relationship histories and ideas of relationship scripts that have been learnt, can also be useful approaches to explore how clients' own individual ways of doing relationships developed within the wider cultures, communities and families in which they were situated (Barker, Vossler, & Langdridge, 2010).

Relationship dynamics

Finally, a number of therapeutic approaches have something to offer for understanding the ways in which relationship dynamics play out within a specific current relationship, and what may be helpful in shifting stuck or conflictual dynamics. From a CBT perspective, Gottman's (1999) extensive observational research on conflictual couples offers some valuable insight into the common dynamics that occur when couples are in conflict: attacking (criticism and contempt) and withdrawing (defensiveness and stonewalling). Based upon such psychological approaches, clients may explore potentially useful ways of breaking cycles of mutual blame, such as increasing the ratio of positive to negative interactions, or reframing conflict as something circular that is happening between them rather than one person's fault.

Other approaches that many counsellors find helpful in exploring relational dynamics include Karpman's (2007) drama triangle, and the transactional analysis 'parent–adult–child' model (Berne, 1964).

The drama triangle suggests that people in relationships often occupy the roles of victim, perpetrator and rescuer, and move around the triangle between these three in terms of who is taking which role. The 'parent–adult–child' model suggests that each person can occupy a more productive or destructive version of each of these modes of relating. Clients can explore which modes they tend to occupy, and how they might shift between them during an interaction or relationship.

WORKING COLLABORATIVELY ON INTERPERSONAL RELATIONSHIPS

Perhaps an element which all of the approaches covered have in common is that they regard stuck patterns as problematic and see one key task of therapy as loosening such fixed patterns and opening up other options (whether the patterns are located within existential givens and/or wider cultures and/or relationship histories and/or current dynamics). This may well be a useful task to consider with clients, under the goal of improving interpersonal relationships, and with many methods available to assist with it.

Pluralistic therapy aims to engage in a collaborative process with clients to ascertain both their therapeutic goals and their wider life goals through dialogue. However, these goals do need to be considered carefully. For example, it is not uncommon for a client to start therapy with the goal of getting into a romantic relationship or staying together with a particular partner. It may be that the pressures they are placing on romantic relationships are, paradoxically, making these goals more difficult – if not impossible – to achieve. Thus the goals might shift, for example, towards finding ways of meeting people they connect with, or coming to empathise more with their partner whatever the outcome may be for the relationship. In collaboratively coming up with goals with clients it may be helpful to raise this possibility that striving for something can make it more difficult to achieve. I find that the analogy of trying hard to get to sleep is useful to explain how sometimes specific goals can have the opposite effect (Barker, 2013b). Thus negotiation of goals is very much part of therapy, and may usefully be revisited throughout, especially as the client explores some of the different ways of understanding interpersonal relationships.

When addressing interpersonal relationships, we may find ourselves working with individual clients, or with two (or more) people in a relationship. The next two sections take each of these scenarios in turn, exploring kinds of therapeutic methods that might usefully be employed. However, relationship therapy requires a somewhat different skill set to individual therapy and it is worth doing at least some specific training and reading in this area before embarking upon it. For these reasons more space is given here to relationship therapy than to individual therapy on relationship issues.

WORKING WITH AN INDIVIDUAL CLIENT ON INTERPERSONAL RELATIONSHIP ISSUES

The most prevalent practice here is simply talking with the client about relationship issues and helping them to find positive ways forward. However, as will be clear from the overview of different approaches, there are a number of different ways into working with individual clients around interpersonal relationships. It is useful to explore their current relationship situations, and their wider perspectives and experiences around relationships which inform this.

Also, as psychodynamic approaches in particular have highlighted, the relationship between the client and the counsellor is – of course – a relationship, and the here-and-now of what is going on between therapist and client can be valuable information about how they operate in other relationships. It can be useful to explore links between the therapeutic relationship, other present relationships and relationships in the past, for example: 'I noticed that when we were talking just now you didn't seem to acknowledge what I said a couple of times. I wonder if that's similar at all to what you're saying happens with your wife – when she accuses you of not "being there"?' and later, 'Talking about this reminds me of what you said about how as a child you had to become an island. Do you see any links with that?'

Noticing

A useful starting point for any client who wants to improve their interpersonal relationships is inviting them into a project of curiously noticing the dynamics in their relationships. Clients are often very keen to *understand* why they are struggling with their relationships, and/or to find a *fix*. It can be helpful to explain that it is often difficult to understand things, and to fix things (if they need fixing) until we have a clear sense of what is going on. There are various techniques that can be useful for the client to learn in order to slow down and notice how they relate to their partners, family, colleagues, or other people who they are bringing to therapy. For example, mindful meditation can be a useful practice for cultivating the capacity to curiously notice experiences rather than immediately reacting (Barker, 2013b). Focusing can be a good practice for noticing your emotional and bodily responses in relationship (Gendlin, 2012). And the phenomenological approach of producing rich descriptions can also be helpful: some clients may find it useful to write detailed descriptions of their relationship dynamics playing out, for example (see Barker, 2010). Curious noticing of relationship patterns can become helpful client activities to encourage between sessions, whilst curious noticing of the here-and-now of the therapy relationship, and any links, can be a helpful therapist activity.

Self-care

For clients who are experiencing relationship conflict it may also be valuable to introduce the concept of self-care. It can be very difficult to move forward on reducing conflict in relationships if you are not attending to basic self-care needs (eating, sleep, time alone). Also, most therapeutic approaches locate the attacking/withdrawing pattern of relationship conflict in defensiveness about vulnerabilities. A degree of self-care is needed in order to open up about these vulnerabilities. Clients can usefully be invited into a collaborative dialogue about what self-care practices work best, and what blocks may stand in the way of self-care, for them (see Barker, 2010).

Specific techniques

In addition to the possibilities already considered, you might find it helpful to draw on the tools of solution-focused therapy such as asking clients where their relationship is on a scale of 1 to 10 and what it would take to move one point up the scale, or identifying and exploring successful changes that clients have made in their relationships in the past to build a 'history of the solution' to the current issue (de Shazer & Dolan, 2007). Systemic sculpts can be a useful way of getting clients to model the various relationships in their lives, for example choosing stones or buttons to represent different people and placing them on a tray in ways that represent how the relationship is, and then perhaps how they would like it to be (Barker et al., 2010).

WORKING WITH A DYAD ON INTERPERSONAL RELATIONSHIP ISSUES

> **Point for reflection**
>
> In what ways do you think that working with two clients in relationship therapy differs from working with a client in one-to-one therapy (or what is your experience of the difference if you have already done both)? What different skills do you think are required of the pluralistic counsellor in this context?

When conducting pluralistic relationship therapy, key differences are:

- There are two clients, not one, so two sets of backgrounds, and understandings of relationships, are in play.
- The focus is usually on the relationship between the clients more than on either of them as individuals. Problems are usually located within the dynamic between them rather than within one or other individual.
- There are more dynamics in play (between the clients, and between the therapist and each client).

In terms of what is required of the therapist, some authors use the metaphor of a helicopter to suggest that the 'helicopter view' needs to be higher up in relationship therapy in order to see all that is going on. You need to remain aware of what is happening in the various dynamics as well as within yourself so there is more to attend to. The emphasis becomes focused on observing the dynamics between the clients, and sometimes how you are being invited into those dynamics, and reflecting back on this. Therefore the therapist role is even more that of an observer than it is with individual clients. Another key aspect of the role is remaining attuned to each person and ensuring that each is equally involved. A key risk in relationship therapy is becoming more aligned with one person than the other, as we will see.

Collaborative relationship therapy

There are practical decisions to make about how to work with each dyad. Such decisions should be made in a collaborative way. For example, I often find it helpful to start by alternating individual sessions with each person and sessions where they come together. In that way I can explore each person's view of relationships and of the issues separately and get a good sense of where the discrepancies lie, as well as building an alliance with each person individually. From a collaborative perspective it is good to be very transparent about how such an approach would work, inviting the clients – together – to talk about how they would like to proceed, and what ground rules they would like in place, for example about whether material shared in one-to-one sessions will be brought into the dyadic session. Some may prefer not to have one-to-one sessions at all. There are no universal 'rights' or 'wrongs' about how such things are negotiated, but rather the process of negotiation itself is part of therapy, and it is wise for the therapist to know the limits of what they can offer (for example, if they are not willing to hold secrets if one client discloses).

Of course all of the same approaches and methods can be brought into relationship therapy as can be employed in one-to-one therapy, but additional possibilities open up. For example, each person could write a description of a conflict from their perspective, and what they imagine their partner's perspective to be, and they could then compare notes. Or both people could answer some of the questions in the exercise at the end of this chapter alone and then together. Or they could collaborate on a systemic sculpt or genogram. In addition to this, there can be an element, in relationship therapy, of communication training or teaching skills in listening, or conflict management, for therapists who are comfortable weaving a more psychoeducative component into their work. Crowe and Ridley (2000) provide helpful suggestions for how these can be brought in, in their integration of CBT and systemic approaches.

Solving the moment

Wile (2011) presents an explicitly collaborative form of relationship therapy which provides a useful framework for the pluralistic relationship therapist to build upon. He suggests introducing the potential therapeutic goal of 'solving the moment' rather than 'solving the problem'. This can reduce the sense of pressure that big disagreements must be solved by shifting to the smaller goal of increasing intimacy in each moment of therapy, whether or not the problem is resolved. Wile proposes that there are tasks for each part of the relationship therapy encounter at such moments. The therapist's task is to regain empathy, the dyad's task is to regain connection, and the individual's task is to regain their voice about what is alive for them at the moment. The idea is that this will enable everyone to shift from an adversarial or withdrawn cycle (which are the common cycles in relationship conflict) to a collaborative cycle.

In this way, Wile suggests that times when the therapist feels their empathy dropping for one or the other client are important therapeutic moments, rather than something for the therapist to feel bad about. Such an 'empathy drop' helps the therapist to understand how the person they are more aligned to is also struggling to feel empathy for their partner. It also suggests that the partner has not fully expressed where they are coming from, and the therapist can focus on helping them to voice this such that they find their voice, the therapist regains empathy and the dyad regains connection.

CASE EXAMPLE
Claude and Amer in collaborative therapy

An example of this process comes from when I worked with Claude and Amer. I felt an empathy drop when Claude revealed that he sometimes checked Amer's text messages and emails. Like Amer, I felt this was an invasion of privacy and

(Continued)

(Continued)

didn't think much of Claude's explanation that he was the 'couple organiser' so needed the information. I felt that Amer was justified in becoming angry at Claude's behaviour and attacking him for being suffocating and micromanaging.

Following Wile's suggestion, I tried to become a spokesperson for the person I found myself siding against (Claude). I assumed that he was going into the mode of justifying/defending himself because it was hard for him to find, or express, his underlying feelings. Mentally I asked myself, how his behaviour might make sense given what I knew of him, and of the human condition!

In the subsequent conversation I encouraged Claude to reflect on his feelings prior to looking at the texts and emails, as well as voicing some hunches I had that there might be something about his sense of insecurity going on here. Claude admitted that the role of relationship organiser made him feel important to Amer, and that he was ashamed to admit his concern that Amer might not be as committed to the relationship as he – Claude – was, and his underlying fear of losing the relationship. Even though he knew that Amer hated the invasion of privacy, and that it actually made him more distant, he felt that he couldn't help himself because knowing all of Amer's movements made him feel closer and more connected.

Goals in relationship therapy

One challenge for pluralistic relationship therapy is around goals. What happens when the two people you are working with have different goals for life, or different therapeutic goals? In addition to Wile's approach of focusing on 'solving the moment', I find it helpful to explore with clients the possibility that there may be multiple different possible ways forward, and that part of the process of therapy will be about figuring out which way they go on different issues. Here's how I explained it to Amer and Claude.

CASE EXAMPLE
Claude and Amer consider possible outcomes

MJ: We're coming to the end of our first session. I wonder if we can review the different issues we've spoken about today – that you want to make sure we cover over the coming weeks.
C: I think the main ones were how we manage money, and the sex stuff we talked about.
A: And privacy. We often fight about that don't forget.
C: Yep: Money, sex and privacy.
MJ: Anything else?
C: I think that's it [*checking*]
A: That's it for me.

> MJ: So I suggest that we plan to spend about three weeks on each of those issues, giving us time to explore how each of you feel about it and discussing it together.
> C: So will we be trying to find a compromise? Is that the aim?
> MJ: Sometimes that's where it gets to, but it might be different for each thing we're discussing. The way I find helpful to look at it is there's several possible ways through each issue. It might be that when you talk about it you realise you're actually more on the same page than you realised.
> A: Hmm!
> MJ: Or it might be one of you moves closer to the other's position. It might be that you look for a compromise between your positions. Or, alternatively, it might be something that you realise is going to be one of those ongoing tensions that bubbles up from time to time in any relationship. But now you'll be aware of it and notice it more. Or it might be that it's a difference that means you want to make a bigger change to the relationship. All of those outcomes are possibilities we can explore.

Sex therapy

It is worth touching briefly here on sex therapy. Sex and relationship therapy are often combined (in therapy practices, and on training courses) because sexual difficulties are one of the most common problems experienced in romantic relationships. Like relationship therapy itself, sex therapy is something of a different beast to general therapy, because it requires a basic understanding of the more biomedical side of sex, as well as a level of fluency and comfort in talking about sexual matters. For interested readers, Kleinplatz's (2012) book presents a very pluralistic approach to sex therapy, which includes collaboratively working with clients towards different possible goals. For example, Kleinplatz points out that some clients simply want to fix a problem, such as struggling to orgasm, but that it is important to offer other potential goals such as aiming at better sex more broadly, or conducting a deeper exploration of the role that sex has in their lives and relationships.

Beyond the couple

A final important thing to note is that, while relationship therapy has tended to focus on romantic couples, not all love relationships take a couple form (see Richards & Barker, 2013), and not all important relationships in people's lives are partner relationships. Indeed, the Western privileging of romantic relationships could be regarded as part of the problems that many people experience with relationships (Barker, 2013a). As with its stance towards therapeutic approaches, from a pluralistic therapy standpoint it is important to honour all the multiple forms of relating without privileging any one form. It may well be useful to attend to which relationships individual clients focus upon. If you offer relationship therapy it may be worth extending this beyond couples/dyads. Systemic approaches, of course, provide a wealth of information about how larger groups can be worked with (see Barker et al., 2010).

SUMMARY

In summary, the pluralistic approach for working with interpersonal relationships may involve working with individuals, or with dyads (or more). In all cases, it involves the following overlapping stages:

- Forming a collaborative relationship with the client/s
- Exploring different possible goals and outcomes of therapy
- Offering various understandings and methods for making sense of their relationships and for shifting stuck dynamics.

EXERCISES/POINTS FOR REFLECTION

Exercise: Relationships and you

Thinking back to the section of the chapter on understanding interpersonal relationships pluralistically, reflect on your own relationships from the different perspectives presented. It is important, reflexively speaking, to know what your own experiences and assumptions are when you are working with clients around these issues.

- How does the existential tension between freedom and interconnectedness play out in your relationships? Where would you put yourself on a spectrum from valuing independence to valuing belonging? Is this different across different relationships? Has it changed over time?
- What are the wider cultural messages about relationships in the world around you? Think about mass media, political debates and everyday conversations. Which kinds of relationships are most/least valued? What are the rules, for example, about forming, maintaining, conflicting in, and ending, different kinds of relationships? Think about relationships with partners, friends, family, work colleagues, neighbours, etc.
- What is your own history with relationships? What messages did you learn about how to relate to others? What kinds of relationships, and ways of relating, were deemed acceptable, unacceptable, or highly valued? As you grew older did you fit in with those 'rules' and/or resist or reject them in any way? Draw a 'relationship river' of the key relationships in your life (at each bend of the river) and what you learned from them.

What relationship dynamics play out in your relationships today? What roles do you find comfortable in your relationships, and which less so? Which ways of communicating work best for you? Which do you struggle with? Pick one relationship to focus on and think about where it would fit in the drama triangle, or in the parent–adult–child model.

> ## FURTHER READING
>
> Barker, M. (2013). *Rewriting the rules: an integrative guide to love, sex and relationships.* London: Routledge. This is a self-help book aimed at helping people work through their own rules of relationships, within the prevailing cultural norms.
>
> Carson, D.K., & Casado-Kehoe, M. (Eds.). (2011). *Case studies in couples therapy: theory-based approaches.* New York: Routledge. This book provides a rich and practical overview of the diversity of approaches to relationship therapy, including Wile's approach.
>
> Iacovou, S., & Van Deurzen, E. (Eds.). (2013). *Existential perspectives on relationship therapy.* Basingstoke: Palgrave Macmillan. This is a useful edited collection of existential perspectives on relationship therapy.
>
> Welwood, J. (2006). *Perfect love, imperfect relationships.* Boston, MA: Trumpeter. This book presents a valuable development of the theories explored in this chapter around vulnerability and relationships.

REFERENCES

Barker, M. (2010). Self-care and relationship conflict. *Sexual and Relationship Therapy*, 25(1), 37–47.

Barker, M. (2013a). *Rewriting the rules: an integrative guide to love, sex and relationships.* London: Routledge.

Barker, M. (2013b). *Mindful counselling and psychotherapy: practising mindfully across approaches and issues.* London: Sage.

Barker, M. (2014). Open non-monogamies. In M. Milton (Ed.), *Sexuality: existential perspectives.* London: PCCS Books.

Barker, M., Vossler, A., & Langdridge, D. (Eds.). (2010). *Understanding counselling and psychotherapy.* London: Sage.

Berne, E. (1964). *Games people play: the basic handbook of transactional analysis.* New York: Ballantine Books.

Cooper, M., & Joseph, S. (2015). Psychological foundations for humanistic psychotherapeutic practice. In D.J. Cain & J. Seeman (Eds.), *Humanistic psychotherapies.* Washington, DC: American Psychological Association.

Crowe, M., & Ridley, J. (2000). *Therapy with couples: a behavioural-systems approach to couple relationship and sexual problems.* Oxford: Blackwell.

das Nair, R., & Butler, C. (2012). *Intersectionality, sexuality and psychological therapies: working with lesbian, gay and bisexual diversity.* Oxford: Wiley–Blackwell.

de Beauvoir, S. (1976). *The ethics of ambiguity* (B. Frechtman, Trans.). New York: Citadel Press. (Original work published 1948.)

de Shazer, S., & Dolan, Y. (2007). *More than miracles: the state of the art of solution-focused brief therapy.* Binghampton: Haworth Press.

Gendlin, E.T. (2012). *Focusing-oriented psychotherapy.* New York: The Guilford Press.

Gottman, J.M. (1999). *The marriage clinic: a scientifically based marital therapy.* New York: Norton.

Holmes, B.M. (2007). In search for my 'one and only': romance-oriented media and beliefs in romantic relationships destiny. *Electronic Journal of Communication, 17*(3).

Karpman, S.B. (2007, August). *The new drama triangle.* USATAA/ITAA conference lecture. Retrieved from www.karpmandramatriangle.com/pdf/thenewdramatriangles.pdf

Kleinplatz, P.J. (Ed.). (2012). *New directions in sex therapy: innovations and alternatives.* New York: Taylor & Francis.

Richards, C., & Barker, M. (2013). *Sexuality and gender for mental health professionals: a practical guide.* London: Sage.

Sartre, J.-P. (1943 [2005]). *Being and nothingness* (H.E. Barnes, Trans.). London: Verso.

Wile, D.B. (2011). Collaborative couple therapy: turning fights into intimate conversations. In D.K. Carson & M. Casado-Kehoe (Eds.), *Case studies in couples therapy: Theory-based approaches* (pp. 303–316). New York: Routledge.

17

Helping Clients Find Meaning in Grief and Loss

Robert A. Neimeyer

THIS CHAPTER DISCUSSES

- The role of a quest for meaning in adapting to bereavement and loss
- A narrative frame for pluralistic practice, focusing on the 'event story' of the death and the 'back story' of the relationship with the loved one
- Numerous specific clinical procedures that promote integration of the loss
- The evidence base that supports these methods

The death that ends the life of a loved one also punctuates, and frequently perturbs, the life stories of intimate survivors as well. When this disruption is profound and prolonged, and especially when the character of the death or the relationship with the deceased is complicated or problematic, mourners frequently seek professional therapy. They commonly do so hoping to find someone who can hear their accounts of love and loss without providing pabulum reassurance, and who can help them find some means of negotiating a life whose terrain has been made alien by their bereavement. Unfortunately, until recently most therapists were equipped with only rudimentary resources for engaging these accounts, in the form of simplistic stage models of adaptation that carried few practical suggestions beyond the putative value of expressing anguished affect and 'normalizing' the experience. When complicated grief was addressed at all, it was commonly reduced to another diagnosable disorder whose treatment procedures had at best inexact relevance to the unique separation distress at the heart of this condition, and the myriad ways in which this can find expression in the mourner's psychosocial world (Prigerson et al., 2009). In the past 15 years, however, this situation has shifted substantially, as models and methods of grief therapy have proliferated and increasingly garnered research support.

GRIEF AND THE QUEST FOR MEANING

Viewed in a constructivist perspective, grieving entails as a central process the *attempt to reaffirm or reconstruct a world of meaning that has been challenged by loss*. That is, a fundamental feature of human functioning is to seek order, pattern and significance in the events of our lives, and in the course of doing so to construct *a self-narrative*, defined as 'an overarching cognitive-affective-behavioural structure that organizes the "micro-narratives" of everyday life into a "macro-narrative" that consolidates our self-understanding, establishes our characteristic range of emotions and goals, and guides our performance on the stage of the social world' (Neimeyer, 2004: 53–4). Simply stated, we seek to live a life that we can make sense of, and that can make sense of us. The difficulty, of course, is that this quest for coherence poses a constantly moving target, as the conditions of impermanence and unwelcome change repeatedly unsettle our best efforts to scaffold a story with consistent themes, goals and – perhaps most importantly – intimate collaborators in the events of our lives (Neimeyer & Young-Eisendrath, 2015). The death of key attachment figures, especially under conditions that are premature, sudden, violent, or unjust, therefore can massively challenge our assumptive world and its grounding in principles of predictability, beneficence and control. Faced with an anguishing discrepancy between our core presuppositions and the reality of such loss, we are launched into a quest to re-establish abiding life themes or to rework them to find significance in our changed existence. Over the past decade a good deal of evidence has accumulated to support the propositions of this meaning reconstruction model (see Neimeyer & Sands, 2011, for review).

Viewed through a narrative constructivist lens, the acute pursuit of meaning making in loss concentrates on (1) *processing the 'event story' of the death*, and its implications for our ongoing lives, and (2) *accessing the 'back story' of our lives with the deceased loved one*, in a way that restores a measure of attachment security (Neimeyer & Thompson, 2014). Each of these dialectics articulates with a range of contemporary bereavement theories and associated therapeutic practices, in a way that helps organize recent models and methods that can inform pluralistic practice.

PROCESSING THE EVENT STORY OF THE LOSS

When mourners struggle with making sense of the death and its implications for their lives, they may contend with questions like: *What is my role or responsibility in what has come to pass? What part, if any, did human intention or inattention have in causing the death? What do my bodily and emotional feelings tell me about what I now need? How do my religious or philosophic beliefs help me accommodate this experience, and how are they changed by it in turn? Who am I in light of this loss, now and in the future? How does this shape or reshape the larger story of my life? Who in my life can understand and accept what this loss means to me?* (Neimeyer & Thompson, 2014). In other words, the 'effort after meaning' can unfold on any scale from the focal (about a feature of the death itself or an internal feeling) to the global (about one's broader self-narrative or spiritual/ existential concerns), as the mourner seeks to integrate the loss, and reconstruct his or her life. Two contemporary theories of grieving that dovetail with this perspective are Boelen and colleagues' (2006) cognitive behavioral model and Stroebe and Schut's (2010) Dual Process Model of Coping with Bereavement.

From a CBT perspective, grief becomes complicated when mourners *fail to integrate the reality of the death into their autobiographical memory*, in effect, when they are unable to update their schemas to take in the painful circumstance of their loved one's absence (Boelen, van den Hout, & van den Bout, 2006). This situation is often compounded by various forms of *experiential avoidance*, as when mourners attempt to mitigate intense grief by evading memories of the dying, or by no longer engaging in activities that were once associated strongly with the loved one. In operant conditioning terms, such constriction is positively reinforced by a reduction of distress in the moment, but only at the cost of an increasingly untenable posture of suppressing full recognition of the loss and circumscribing the survivor's life.

A second conceptualization that conjoins with a meaning reconstruction approach is the Dual Process Model (DPM), which posits two fundamental orientations in coping with bereavement (Stroebe & Schut, 2010). On the one hand, mourners engage the *loss orientation*, in which they reflect on the death, experience and attempt to modulate grief-related feelings, attempt to reorganize their bond to the deceased, and withdraw from the broader world to seek the support of a few trusted confidants. At other points, they engage in the *restoration orientation*, as they distract themselves from their grief by immersing themselves in work and other activities, step into new responsibilities, and ultimately explore new roles and goals required by their changed lives. Thus, according to the DPM, mourners *oscillate* between these two means of coping with the loss, neither of which is viewed as dysfunctional in itself. Instead, only an inability to engage in one or the other orientation signals concern, though people differ in their degree of engagement with each as a function of personal disposition, gender and culture.

Common to these models is the view that complications in grieving arise when mourners are unable to 'take in' the reality of the loss, and integrate its implications for their ongoing lives. Accordingly, a number of evidence-based procedures have been developed to promote doing so, which are featured in a variety of CBT, eclectic and narrative constructivist therapies, as summarized below.

Restorative retelling of the event story of the death

Survivors of a difficult loss typically seek a context in which they can relate the story of their loved one's death, but rarely do they give voice to its most painful particulars: their mother's gasping for breath at the end of life, their own recurrent helplessness in the face of their child's advancing cancer, the picture of their partner hanging from a pipe in the basement, eyes bulging in a purple face following the suicide. Instead, these often fragmentary images live only as 'silent stories' in their own thoughts and nightmares, persisting as a haunting and unspoken subtext to the highly edited stories shared with others.

In *restorative retelling*, Rynearson and his colleagues (Rynearson & Salloum, 2011) first establish a safe relational 'container' for re-entering the detailed story of the dying, and ground the mourner in a more secure context (e.g., discussing what family members meant to one another before the loss, and what philosophic or religious beliefs they have relied on to deal with difficult times), before inviting a step-by-step recounting of the narrative of the dying, as remembered or, as is commonly the case in violent death, imagined. Like Shear's protocol for *situational revisiting* of the story of the death (Shear, Boelen, & Neimeyer, 2011), Rynearson's procedure encourages the mourner to 'walk through' a slow-motion replay of the events of the dying, often repeating the process on multiple occasions as the person fills in details, modulates difficult emotions with the therapist's assistance, and gradually gains greater mastery of the painful narrative. In both cases the goal is to help the mourner integrate the story of the death in the presence of a compassionate witness, ultimately across several sessions being able to revisit the story with less avoidant coping, less emotional reactivity and greater meaning.

Data from an open trial on restorative retelling are encouraging in suggesting its efficacy in reducing traumatic arousal (Saindon et al., 2014), and Shear's Complicated Grief Therapy (CGT), in which revisiting the situation of the death is a cardinal procedure, has outperformed evidence-based therapy for depression in treating bereaved people in two major randomized clinical trials (e.g. Shear et al., 2014). Related CBT protocols featuring prolonged exposure to difficult details associated with the loss have also garnered support in RCTs (e.g. Bryant et al., 2014).

Directed journaling

Written as well as spoken narratives that bear on the loss experience can promote integration and meaning-making, and have the advantage of being used either as freestanding interventions or as homework to augment the effectiveness of face-to-face therapy. A good deal of evidence supports the use of emotional disclosure journaling, in which writers are encouraged to deeply immerse themselves in the emotions and thoughts connected to a traumatic event for 20–30 minutes over a series of typically three distributed writing sessions. However, research has been less clear about the benefits of this emotionally immersive writing in the context of bereavement, leading clinical investigators to suggest specialized procedures for processing grief (Neimeyer, van Dyke, & Pennebaker, 2009).

Two such forms of *directed journaling* foster *sense-making* and *benefit-finding*, respectively (Lichtenthal & Neimeyer, 2012). In the former, clients who are some months or years into bereavement are encouraged to focus on questions about how and why the loss occurred, and what it portends for their lives. Prompts might include: *How did you make sense of the loss when it occurred? How do you interpret it now? How does this experience fit with your spiritual views about life, and how, if at all, have you changed those views in light of the loss? How has this loss shaped your life, and what meaning would you like it to have for you in the long run?* In contrast, benefit-finding journaling could be prompted by questions such as: *In your view, have you found any unsought gifts in grief? If so, what? How has this experience affected your sense of priorities? Your sense of yourself? What lessons about living or about loving has this loss taught you? Has this experience deepened your gratitude for anything you've been given? Is there anyone to whom you would like to express this appreciation now?* A randomized controlled trial of both forms of directed journaling compared to a standard emotional disclosure paradigm and a neutral control writing condition has established its efficacy and the maintenance of improvement over a three-month follow up, with the impact of such writing being particularly impressive in the benefit-finding condition (Lichtenthal & Cruess, 2010). It is likely that these variations represent only the first of several creative narrative procedures for promoting meaning-making regarding loss, a field that invites greater research to document their efficacy. For example, a recent open trial of a Buddhist-inspired workshop for loss and unwelcome change integrated exercises in deep-listening, hearing one's loss story related to the group by a partner, brief interludes of mindfulness, and imaginative writing about themes of loss from a make-believe, self-distancing viewpoint to promote perspective-taking (Neimeyer & Young-Eisendrath, 2015). Group participants not only reported significantly diminished grief-related suffering, but also greater integration of the loss experience on a validated measure of meaning-making.

> Journaling played an important role in the pluralistic grief therapy I conducted with Gayle in the months that followed the death of her teenage son, Max, in an automobile accident. At various points our in-session work included prolonged retelling of the event story of her learning of the accident, her experiences in the critical care unit of the hospital to which he had been taken, the fateful moment of his dying, and the funeral service that memorialized his life. At other points the therapy was punctuated with imaginal dialogues with Max and with discussion of Gayle's poignant struggle to make sense of her son's sudden and untimely death and her life in its aftermath. Journaling about the loss from a practical, emotional and spiritual perspective between our sessions continued and deepened the work begun together. Increasingly, as time went on, it also eventuated in surprising insights and outcomes, such as her drafting a moving letter of gratitude to the hundreds of people who had attended Max's memorial service, and her drawing on her writing in the years following the loss to offer hope to other bereaved parents.

Behavioral activation

Although reflective processing of the loss experience obviously has a central place in a meaning reconstruction approach to grief therapy, so too does active reinvention of the client's ongoing life. As recognized by the DPM (Stroebe & Schut, 2010), coping with bereavement entails not only loss-oriented strategies for attending to grief-related feelings, but also restoration-oriented behaviors such as renewing movement in the direction of personal goals, and re-engaging the worlds of work and relationships.

Behavioral activation (BA) addresses this latter imperative by using activity scheduling to challenge ruminative and avoidant behaviours that disconnect mourners from valued sources of reinforcement that are unique to each client. It also entails identification of roadblocks to the completion of such activities and the shaping of more effective behaviours for overcoming them. A randomized open trial comparing an immediate start group to a delayed start group documents the clear feasibility and acceptability of BA as a treatment for complicated grief, and suggests its efficacy in reducing prolonged grief, depressive and PTSD symptomatology in bereavement (Papa, Sewell, Garrison-Diehn, & Rummel, 2013).

> When Mark and Sylvia experienced the SIDS loss of their seemingly robust baby, Wallace, they were disconsolate. Despite their devastation, however, they processed the associated emotions and meanings of the tragic loss remarkably well, drawing on Sylvia's emotionally attuned expressiveness as a creative writer, and Mark's unusually reflective, if slightly more reserved, demeanour as a business consultant. But practical adaptation to the loss proved harder to them, as they had fled their small home, so saturated with the very present absence of the third tiny life it had only recently held, to seek refuge in the large home of a generous friend. Now, as weeks merged into months, they began to recognize that they needed to move, at least temporarily, back into their own home and all of the memories it held, until they could make critical decisions about whether they would move to another house and 'try again' for a family.
>
> To approach this forbidding task, we first reviewed the goals they shared about having space of their own and launching a family. We then considered 'baby steps' in that direction in the form of driving, then walking by the house together, being present for each other as they later approached the door and stepped inside. Meaningful dialogue in-session scaffolded these mutually negotiated activities scheduled as literal 'homework', until they were able to remain in the house overnight. Ultimately Mark and Sylvia supported one another through the tearful re-entry into Wallace's room, and through painful but necessary discussions of which of his furniture, toys and clothes they would put in storage until they were ready to try to conceive another child. Though difficult, restoring a 'world of their own' brought with it a sense of healing and hope, even if it also required a graduated confrontation with and mastery of the grief and anxiety that they had long been avoiding.

ACCESSING THE BACK STORY OF THE RELATIONSHIP

In meaning reconstruction terms, bereaved people seek not only reaffirmation or rebuilding of a self-narrative challenged by loss, but also reconnection to the life narrative of their deceased loved one. In sharp distinction to the cultural prescription to 'move on' and 'withdraw energy from the one who has died to invest it elsewhere', such an approach endorses the normative goal of reconstructing the bond to the deceased rather than relinquishing it. When mourners seek to access the 'back story' of their relationship with the loved one, they grapple with implicit questions like: *How can I recover or reconstruct a sustaining connection with my loved one that survives his or her death? What memories of the relationship bring pain, guilt or sadness, and require some form of redress or reprieve now? What memories of the relationship bring joy, security or pride, and invite celebration and commemoration? What lessons about living or loving have I learned during the course of our shared lives? What would my loved one see in me that would give him or her confidence in my ability to weather this hard transition?* (Neimeyer & Thompson, 2014).

A narrative therapy perspective, anchored in the work of Michael White and David Epston, subscribes to a similar view of the continuing bond as a potentially adaptive resource. From this perspective, the dominant cultural narrative that views death only through a lens of loss and presses for 'closure' and 'letting go' does violence to the relational web that sustains love and community, even beyond the physical presence of the other. Thus, rather than advocating 'saying goodbye' as the dominant metaphor for grief work, the goal of bereavement support becomes to 'say hello again', in a sense restoring (and re-storying) a 'conversation' with and about the loved one that was interrupted by death (Hedtke & Winslade, 2004). Support groups conducted along these lines therefore concentrate not solely on expressing and coping with painful grief-related affect associated with those who were lost, but instead on fostering *re-membering conversations* that celebrate the continued relevance of the relationship to the deceased in the lives of survivors. From this vantage point, group facilitators might well prompt members with invitations to 'introduce their loved ones' to the group, using questions such as *Who was _____ to you? What did knowing _____ mean to you? Do particular stories come to mind that _____ would want others to know about his life? What did _____ teach you about life, and perhaps about managing the circumstances you face currently? What difference might it make to keep her memory close to you?* From this perspective the mourner is encouraged to retain a vital connection to the loved one, carrying forward his or her symbolic and social presence in the mourner's own life story.

Imaginal dialogues

In a sense, grief therapy can be considered family therapy *in absentia*. Just as couples or family work typically invites both or all relevant parties into the therapy room for direct work on their relationship, so too can bereavement interventions foster direct work on the relationship of the mourner(s) with the loved one who has died. Invoking an alliance with the deceased in a triadic, rather than merely dyadic, relationship between therapist and client can take many forms, including 'corresponding' with the dead about the mourner's present state, unanswered questions and relational needs (e.g., for forgiveness or the affirmation of love) and guided imagery to conjure the loved one's presence. One particularly potent intervention along these lines draws on *chair work* procedures developed within emotion-focused therapy (Greenberg, 2010), in which the client is encouraged to place the deceased symbolically in an empty chair facing the client's own, and address concerns in the relationship in a first- and second-person, present tense voice (e.g., *'I feel so lost since your death ... You were the only one who really understood and cared.'*). In most cases the client is then encouraged to switch chairs, loan the loved one his or her own voice, and respond as the deceased might to the client's statements. The therapist choreographs the continuing exchange, prompting the client toward emotional immediacy, honesty and depth in each chair, and directing a change of positions at poignant moments in the dialogue.

Research on empty chair monologues by bereaved spouses documents the intimate link between themes of self- and other-blame in the chairing and a variety of adverse outcomes (e.g., guilt, depression, anger) (Field & Bonanno, 2001). Moreover, Complicated Grief Therapy, which uses imaginal dialogues with the deceased as a mainstay intervention to resolve such issues, has proven more effective in the treatment of prolonged grief disorder than evidence-based therapy for depression in two randomized controlled trials (e.g., Shear et al., 2014).

> Now in his early 40s and a successful lawyer, Rob had entered therapy to sort out his life, an effort that had in the last two years moved him to adopt a deeply Buddhist perspective on the role of loving kindness in all relationships. This was a sharp departure from the fundamental religiosity of his parents, with its strong emphasis on sin and the very real threat of eternal damnation. 'Like a wild horse breaking free', Rob recalled jettisoning both his faith and family as he pursued his university and ultimately law school studies with a fierceness and 'ego' that seemed the clearest alternative to the sanctimonious atmosphere of his home. Now, however, Rob realized that his cut-off from family left his little brother, Jimmy, without a 'buffer' from a deeply unhealthy and alcoholic home environment. As Jimmy slipped into an adolescence saturated in substance abuse, Rob recalled that 'I judged him … and he felt it.' Ten years after Jimmy's ambiguous overdose, Rob now felt deep remorse but was stymied how to address it, 'like an itch I can't scratch.'
>
> Having established a strong working alliance in the preceding three sessions, I asked Rob if these were things he would feel ready to address with Jimmy now, were his brother able to join us in the session, fully ready to hear what he had to say. Bravely but uncertainly, Rob nodded his head. Gesturing to the empty chair positioned opposite him, I asked him to close his eyes for a moment and envision Jimmy there, describing to me how he would be dressed (casually), seated (leaning forward, elbows on knees) and engaged (meeting Rob's gaze). I then invited him to open his eyes and using I–you language, speak to the broken heart of their relationship. Rob did so, his eyes growing moist: 'I'm sorry I didn't help you … As 10 years have gone by, my perspective has changed so much. I'm sorry for judging you … I hope my love for you now helps carry you forward. You were always good to me, never judged me. I want to pay that forward with my own children.' 'Try telling him,' I suggested, 'I am loving my kids for you.' Pausing and nodding seriously, Rob repeated this, and responded, 'Yes … Your memory, your essence, are still part of my family; you are forever in my life.' 'Try saying,' I offered, 'You are still my brother.' Tears welling, Rob repeated this, then fell silent with private emotion.
>
> I then gestured to Jimmy's chair, directing Rob to take his seat and respond to his older brother's honest and anguished comments, which I ventriloquized in a few phrases as a reminder. Responding as Jimmy, Rob answered lovingly,

> reassuringly, convincingly: 'Rob, I've missed you greatly. I feel tremendous regret about my addiction ... I just lost the battle. Grieve me ... I'm happy you found beauty and purpose in your life. Love your children ... thanks for keeping me in their minds and hearts ... I accept your apology.'
>
> Moving Rob to a third chair directly across from me and at right-angles to the two he had used in the dialogue, I asked him from this 'witness position' what he had observed about the conversation that had just taken place. Rob responded that he was struck by the 'earnest sincerity in the relationship, the genuine feeling. The relationship is tremendously significant. I think I carry it with me wherever I go.' As we sat with this recognition, Rob was suddenly flooded with profound emotion, and sobbing deeply, stammered out, 'Of all my family, my brother loved me the best. Now I see so much of my brother in me. Jimmy never had my mean streak, my severity.' Recognizing the seeds of love that his brother had planted in him, which were only now growing and bearing fruit, Rob concluded, 'So now I tell my children every time I see them that I love them just the way they are.' Nine months later, as our therapy drew to a close, Rob reflected on that pivotal fourth session, which seemed to resolve a longstanding sense of guilt, install more securely a brother's love, and begin to prompt greater compassion for even those wounded souls – including his parents – who remained physically present for a deeper dialogue.

Legacy work

Grief has been described as a 'biographical emotion,' insofar as it speaks to the near-universal human impulse to recognize and honour the life story of the deceased. In this view, anything that serves to preserve or extend that life story tends to assuage our anguish about the loss, as research on the construction of the deceased person's identity in eulogies and other forms of commemoration suggests (Neimeyer, Klass, & Dennis, 2014). In the context of grief therapy this impulse can take the form of various photographic, scrapbooking, documentary, dramaturgical, ritual and narrative methods as well as a cornucopia of expressive arts techniques (see recommended reading at the end of the chapter).

Among the biographical methods that can be helpful in giving meaning to the loved one's life and impact is the *legacy project*, which can serve to consolidate and communicate the story of the deceased (as in memorial blogs or biographies), or to draw upon his or her life or death to undertake some useful form of social action. In the latter case, legacy projects can be as simple as a random act of kindness in honour of the loved one, as by the bereaved mother who, sitting alone in a restaurant, discovered that the large party at the next table was celebrating a baby shower and, leaving in tears, prepaid the party's bill in honour of her child. Other legacy projects can take the form of sustained social action, as by families of homicide victims taking a stand against violence through pursuing public speaking, promoting safer communities, or offering support to others suffering analogous losses. Indeed, countless charitable and social justice initiatives have their origins in tragic loss and the impulse of survivors to create a positive legacy that honors their loved ones in its wake.

SUMMARY

The key points of this chapter are:

- The death of a loved one may be the most common and significant life stressor, one that often challenges us to find meaning in the loss and in our lives as survivors.
- Several contemporary models of bereavement greatly extend or replace older models focused on the 'stages' of grief, and offer more specific implications for adaptation to loss in general, and for grief therapy in particular.
- A growing evidence base supports a variety of pluralistic procedures for helping the bereaved orient adaptively to the loss, reorganize their relationship to their deceased loved one, resolve problems in the relationship and make sense of their changed lives.

EXERCISES/POINTS FOR REFLECTION

1. **Loss lifeline:** On a blank sheet of paper, chart the course of your life, indicating the important losses of people, places, projects and possessions that have given your life meaning. Consider using a line graph, where 'higher' ratings on the x axis represent times life was going well, and lower points represent times that life was difficult. Then reflect on the role of specific losses in your lifeline, especially those that changed your sense of self or life direction. If you had had access to therapy at any of these points, which of the therapeutic methods described in this chapter might have been most helpful to you, and why?
2. **Making sense of loss:** Consider one important loss in your life. Then answer the *sense-making* journaling questions listed under the 'Directed Journaling' section, either writing out your answers or sharing them with a classmate, friend, or family member. How did it feel to re-engage the story of the loss in this way? What might be the advantages of this in therapy?
3. **Reflecting on life lessons:** Considering the same loss, answer the *benefit-finding* questions listed in the same section, either in writing or with another person. How did this feel different to addressing the previous questions, and what might the therapeutic value be of prompting such reflections?

FURTHER READING

Neimeyer, R.A. (2009). *Constructivist psychotherapy*. London and New York: Routledge. A readable introduction to the principles and practices of constructivist psychotherapy.

Neimeyer, R.A. (Ed.). (2012). *Techniques of grief therapy: creative practices for counseling the bereaved*. New York: Routledge. A compendium of nearly 100 specific techniques of grief therapy, each described in clear detail and anchored in a brief case study.

Neimeyer, R.A., Harris, D., Winokeur, H., & Thornton, G. (Eds.). (2011). *Grief and bereavement in contemporary society: bridging research and practice*. New York: Routledge. Written by collaborating scholars and practitioners, each chapter reviews major models of grief therapy and considers its applications to specific bereavement challenges and populations.

Thompson, B.E., & Neimeyer, R.A. (Eds.). (2014). *Grief and the expressive arts: practices for creating meaning*. New York: Routledge. A compendium of grief therapy techniques providing specific instruction in visual arts, music, creative writing, dance and performance modalities.

REFERENCES

Boelen, P.A., de Keijser, J., van den Hout, M., & van den Bout, J. (2007). Treatment of complicated grief: a comparison between cognitive-behavioral therapy and supportive counseling. *Journal of Clinical and Consulting Psychology*, 75, 277–284.

Boelen, P.A., van den Hout, M., & van den Bout, J. (2006). A cognitive-behavioral conceptualization of complicated grief. *Clinical Psychology: Science and Practice*, 13, 109–128.

Bryant, R., Kenny, L., Joscelyne, A., Rawson, N., Maccallum, F., Cahill, C., ... Nickerson, A. (2014). Treating prolonged grief disorder: a randomized clinical trial. *Journal of the American Medical Association Psychiatry*, 71(12), 1332-1339.

Field, N.P., & Bonanno, G.A. (2001). The impact of self-blame and blame toward the deceased on adaptation to conjugal bereavement: a five-year follow-up. *American Behavioral Scientist*, 44, 764–781.

Greenberg, L.S. (2010). *Emotion focused psychotherapy*. Washington, DC: American Psychological Association.

Hedtke, L., & Winslade, J. (2004). *Remembering lives*. Amityville, NY: Baywood.

Lichtenthal, W.G., & Cruess, D.G. (2010). Effects of directed written disclosure on grief and distress symptoms among bereaved individuals. *Death Studies*, 34, 475–499.

Lichtenthal, W.G., & Neimeyer, R.A. (2012). Directed journaling to facilitate meaning making. In R.A. Neimeyer (Ed.), *Techniques of grief therapy* (pp. 161–164). New York: Routledge.

Neimeyer, R.A. (2004). Fostering posttraumatic growth: a narrative contribution. *Psychological Inquiry*, 15, 53–59.

Neimeyer, R.A., Klass, D., & Dennis, M.R. (2014). Mourning, meaning and memory: individual, communal and cultural narration of grief. In A. Batthyany & P. Russo-Netzer (Eds.), *Meaning in existential and positive psychology* (pp. 325–346). New York: Springer.

Neimeyer, R.A., & Sands, D.C. (2011). Meaning reconstruction in bereavement: from principles to practice. In R.A. Neimeyer, H. Winokuer, D. Harris, & G. Thornton (Eds.), *Grief and bereavement in contemporary society: bridging research and practice* (pp. 9–22). New York: Routledge.

Neimeyer, R.A., & Thompson, B.E. (2014). Meaning making and the art of grief therapy. In B.E. Thompson & R.A. Neimeyer (Eds.), *Grief and the expressive arts: practices for creating meaning*. New York: Routledge.

Neimeyer, R.A., van Dyke, J.G., & Pennebaker, J.W. (2009). Narrative medicine: writing through bereavement. In H. Chochinov & W. Breitbart (Eds.), *Handbook of psychiatry in palliative medicine* (pp. 454–469). New York: Oxford University Press.

Neimeyer, R.A., & Young-Eisendrath, P. (2015). Assessing a Buddhist treatment for bereavement and loss: the Mustard Seed Project. *Death Studies, 39*(5): 263.

Papa, A., Sewell, M.T., Garrison-Diehn, C., & Rummel, C. (2013). A randomized controlled trial assessing the feasibility of behavioral activation for pathological grief responding. *Behavior Therapy, 44*(4), 639–650.

Prigerson, H.G., Horowitz, M.J., Jacobs, S.C., Parkes, C.M., Aslan, M., Goodkin, K., ... Maciejewski, P.K. (2009). Prolonged grief disorder: psychometric validation of criteria proposed for DSM-V and ICD-11. *PLoS Medicine, 6*(8), 1–12.

Rynearson, E.K., & Salloum, A. (2011). Restorative retelling: revisiting the narrative of violent death. In R.A. Neimeyer, D. Harris, H. Winokuer, & G. Thornton (Eds.), *Grief and bereavement in contemporary society: bridging research and practice* (pp. 177–188). New York: Routledge.

Saindon, C., Rheingold, A., Baddeley, J., Wallace, M., Brown, C., & Rynearson, E.K. (2014). Restorative retelling for violent loss: an open clinical trial. *Death Studies, 38*, 251–258.

Shear, M.K., Boelen, P., & Neimeyer, R.A. (2011). Treating complicated grief: converging approaches. In R.A. Neimeyer, D. Harris, H. Winokuer, & G. Thornton (Eds.), *Grief and bereavement in contemporary society: bridging research and practice* (pp. 139–162). New York: Routledge.

Shear, M.K., Wang, Y., Skriskaya, N., Duan, N., Mauro, C., & Ghesquiere, A. (2014). Treatment of complicated grief in elderly persons: a randomized clinical trial. *Journal of the American Medical Association Psychiatry, 71*(11), 1287-1295.

Stroebe, M., & Schut, H. (2010). The Dual Process Model of Coping with Bereavement: a decade on. *Omega, 61*, 273–289.

Thompson, B.E., & Neimeyer, R.A. (Eds.). (2014). *Grief and the expressive arts: practices for creating meaning*. New York: Routledge.

18
Helping Clients Address Addictive Behaviours

Thomas Mackrill and Bettina Jensen

THIS CHAPTER DISCUSSES

- Addiction from a pluralistic perspective
- Reflecting on the client's stage of change
- Working with ambivalence
- Focusing on addictive behaviours as rewards
- Exploring a client's automatic thoughts and beliefs
- Focusing on the client as an agent
- Involving the family
- 12-step approaches

ADDICTION FROM A PLURALISTIC PERSPECTIVE

The term *addiction* has its roots in medical diagnostic thinking. Alcohol addiction has been termed a 'disease of the will' (Valverde, 1998), a disease that relinquishes a person's ability to control an element of their life. Walters (1999) defines addiction as 'the persistent and repetitive enactment of a behavioural pattern involving progression (or increase in severity), preoccupation with the activity, perceived loss of control, and persistence, despite negative long-term consequences' (1999: 10). Whatever the addictive behaviour, whether it is smoking, drinking, drug use or shopping, the term addiction points to a malfunction of a person's willpower; a behaviour that should be controllable, is presently out of a person's immediate control to some extent. From a pluralistic perspective, the disease model that lies at the heart of the term addiction is just one way of understanding a problematic behaviour that a person wants to change, or that someone else wants them to change. As well as understanding an addictive behaviour as a sign of malfunction, it can also be viewed as quite the opposite, as highly functional. Most addictive behaviours have, or have had, functional aspects that a person may be more or less aware of. For example, smoking can offer people a way of taking a break and a deep breath on a regular basis. Drinking can help people become less inhibited and play a role in a person's social life. A regular pattern of heavy drinking can be a way of avoiding a range of challenging situations. People generally have, or have had, good reasons for their addictive behaviours. The behaviours have generally at some point been beneficial to a person in some way in the short term.

As the term addiction is associated with a disease or malfunction perspective on problematic behaviours, we would recommend that pluralistic counsellors consider using the term *problematic behaviour*. In a counselling session, a counsellor might refer to a client's problematic drinking, their smoking too much, or their inability to refrain from shopping, without necessarily using the term addiction, unless the client has introduced the term. By refraining from introducing the term addiction immediately and using more neutral descriptions of problem behaviours that are close to the client's perception of what their problem is, as described above, pluralistic counsellors can more easily draw on a range of ways of grappling with addictive behaviours, and tailor their approach to the individual client in accordance with principles for pluralistic practice. A diagnostic perspective is a professional medical assessment perspective. Some clients may have a diagnostic or disease perspective of their addictive behaviour, but many may not. The term addiction will therefore be appropriate for some clients, but not for all. The pluralistic counsellor should consider how the addictive or problematic behaviour is framed with each individual client.

The notion of tailoring the treatment to the individual client, as emphasised by a pluralistic perspective, has a long history within the addiction treatment field. Bowman and Jellinek (Institute of Medicine, 1990) highlighted the importance of matching the client with the treatment in the first major alcohol treatment review in 1941. Project Match (Matching Alcoholism Treatment to Client Heterogeneity), a major randomised controlled trial that compared motivational enhancement therapy, 12-step facilitation and cognitive behaviour therapy, found no difference in treatment outcomes between approaches (Project MATCH Research Group, 1997). The study also tested hypotheses about outcomes in relation to a range of client characteristics. No evidence was found for outcome variation across treatments in relation to hypotheses relating to the severity of alcohol involvement, cognitive impairment, psychiatric severity, conceptual level, gender, motivational readiness to change, social support for drinking versus abstinence. Studies of addiction treatment have, however, found that the therapeutic alliance is a significant factor in relation to outcomes (Miller, Wilbourne, & Hettema, 2002). The focus on negotiating goals, tasks and methods as prescribed in the pluralistic perspective (Cooper & McLeod, 2011) is therefore relevant in relation to counselling people with addictive behaviours. While there are varying degrees of evidence for the approaches discussed in this chapter, there is, as yet, no evidence for their use as elements in a pluralistic practice.

The pluralistic approach also emphasises client agency. Agency in relation to addictive behaviours has been an object of much research. While counselling can offer clients with addictive behaviours a way out of their problems, counsellors need to be aware of the fact that many people with addictive behaviours change their behaviour without any form of professional help (Sobell, Cunningham, & Sobell, 1996). An enhanced use of alcohol, drugs and cigarettes is associated with life as a young adult in many cultures, and evidence suggests that many young adults with addictive behaviours simply 'mature out', as they settle down into a life with more social responsibilities (Littlefield, Sher, & Wood, 2009). There are of course people who get stuck with their addictive behaviours, and who need professional help.

In the following sections we will introduce some key understandings and methods that various approaches to addiction counselling have to offer the pluralistic counsellor. Most of the ideas presented are connected with rich and well-developed theories and therapeutic practices. Please read the recommended reading to learn more about what the approaches have to offer, as we can only offer you a taste of these understandings and methods.

UNDERSTANDINGS

Reflecting on the client stage of change

'Stages of Change' (Prochaska & DiClemente, 1986) is a trans-theoretical model of self-instigated or therapeutically driven change that has had a huge impact on addiction counselling. The model generates a view of a person's change process and their readiness to change. The model conceives behavioural change as a process that involves progression through five stages: precontemplation, contemplation, preparation, action and maintenance. *Precontemplation* is the stage where a person has no immediate intention of changing their behaviour. For example, John's wife and children think he smokes and drinks too much, but these are not issues for him. He likes drinking and smoking. He is not contemplating changing his behaviour. When working with addictive behaviours, it is important to recognise that many people with addictive behaviours don't experience the addictive behaviour as a problem. Sometimes the person with the addictive behaviour is the last person to see it as a problem. *Contemplation* is the stage when a person recognises that a behaviour is problematic to some extent, and they are considering changing their behaviour, but they are not yet committed to taking action to change their behaviour. After John's boss told him he was concerned about John's drinking, John is now considering drinking less. *Preparation* is the stage when a person intends to change within the next month and begins to try out various kinds of change, but has not yet been effective in changing their behaviour significantly. John has now stopped going to the pub for a pint of beer during his lunch break, and has considered not opening a bottle of wine every evening. He is taking steps to change. *Action* is the stage when a person changes their behaviour or situation to overcome the problem. John's wife has said she will leave him. She has been reading about co-dependency on the internet, and she says she thinks John's drinking has affected the family far more than she was previously aware of. The following day John stops drinking completely and finds a counsellor who specialises in alcohol problems. He does not want a divorce. *Maintenance* is the stage when a person works to prevent relapse and maintains and develops non-problematic or healthy alternative behaviours. John, who used to spend time drinking wine every evening in front of the television, now spends time playing with his children in the evenings and reading aloud for them. He has got his old guitar out and has started playing in a local band. John often still wants to drink, but he starts to think about how important his family is to him, and refrains. Remaining free of the problem and/or consistently engaging in a new incompatible behaviour for more than 6 months are the criteria for the maintenance stage. Prochaska and DiClemente (1986) note that most clients do not pass linearly through the stages of change. Many get stuck on their way, and many may relapse at the maintenance stage and have to start again; so it can be important to include relapse prevention work at the maintenance stage.

The stages of change model can teach us a lot about tailoring treatment to the client. The model highlights the importance of assessing and adapting counselling in relation to the client's stage of change. It draws the pluralistic counsellor's attention to a range of important factors (Norcross, Krebs, & Prochaska, 2011). It is important not to presume that a client is at the action stage. The issue of whether there is a problem at all is central when counselling a precontemplater, but once a client has decided to take action, the client may want another form of more direct support to maintain healthy behaviours. People in precontemplation often underestimate the benefits of changing and overestimate the costs. Addressing the addictive behaviour may be more important in early stages, whereas issues relating to how to lead a satisfactory life without addiction may be more central during the maintenance stage. During the early stages of change, a focus on insight and awareness may be particularly useful, whereas an action focus can be more useful during the preparation and action stages. Norcross, Krebs and Prochaska (2011), for example, propose 'a nurturing parent stance with a precontemplator, a Socratic teacher role with contemplator, an experienced coach with a patient in action, and then a consultant once in maintenance'.

Focusing on the client as an agent

Though people with addictive behaviours generally experience that the addictive specific behaviour is out of control, they usually also experience times when the behaviour is less out of control, or times when the addictive behaviour is completely absent. A key element of the solution-oriented approach (Berg & Miller, 1992) is to draw the client's attention to these exceptions, and to focus on what the client does, and can do, to create similar situations in the future. Like the pluralistic approach, the solution-oriented approach is highly agency-focused. The approach draws attention to what the client is and isn't doing to address their problem. A second key element of the approach is to focus on the client's goals. While some clients may have complete abstinence of the addictive behaviour as their treatment goal, others may have other goals, such as an increased sense of control over the addictive behaviour. This also corresponds with the pluralistic approach, which involves tailoring treatment to the client's specific goals. Asking clients directly what they think will help solve the problem is also central to the approach. These three elements all draw attention to the client as an agent of change.

Henry liked smoking cannabis. He had smoked since he was a teenager and entered counselling because he could see that most of the people he had grown up with had matured out. Like his peers, he was married with young children, but he continued smoking. His wife used to smoke at weekends, but she had stopped when she was pregnant with their first child. Since she stopped, she had become increasingly unhappy about his habit. He now only smoked in the garden shed, behind which he had his plants. He now lied regularly to his wife about his smoking. His counsellor asked him if there were situations when he didn't smoke. It turned out that he never smoked when the family were on holiday. The counsellor asked him what his life would be like if he stopped smoking completely. He said it would mean he would have to grow up. This led to an exploration of Henry's ideas about what being grown up meant to him, and what kind of grown-up he would like to be. He liked being an adult on holiday, but he generally didn't like the kind of stressed-out grown-up he had become. He felt he had become rather like his dad. He sensed there was something seriously wrong with his work–life balance. When his counsellor asked him what he thought it would take for him to quit smoking cannabis, he answered promptly, a different kind of job. Most of his friends were fairly happy with what they did, but Henry couldn't really understand how he had ended up as a key account manager in business telecommunications. Finding a new vocational direction became a key theme in the remainder of Henry's counselling. An agency focus involves getting the client to focus on what works and what doesn't in relation to the addictive behaviour the person wants to change.

Focusing on addictive behaviours as rewards

A lot of addictive behaviours are associated with rewarding oneself. Drinking, using drugs and smoking, for example, are for many people associated with pleasure and leisure. Focusing on behaviours as rewards or reinforcements is central to behavioural therapy. After a particularly industrious day at work where Bill had achieved a range of good results in his job in advertising, Bill poured himself a long drink to celebrate. After a particularly bad day at work, where things had gone wrong, Bill poured himself a long drink, as he felt he deserved a drink. It had been a tough day. In good times and bad, Bill could always find good reason for a drink. When his counsellor asked him whether he could think of other ways of celebrating a good day or consoling himself after a bad day, Bill could not think of anything. Exploring addictive behaviours as rewards and developing other forms of rewards are a key way of helping people with addictive behaviours. Bill's counsellor began to explore other ways Bill could reward himself after successful days at work, with a round of golf for example. They also looked at more functional and rational ways Bill could console himself after a hard day at work. Bill learned to give himself a pat on the back and ask his wife for a hug after both good and bad days at work.

METHODS

Working with ambivalence

Working with ambivalence is a key aspect of working with addictive behaviours. People with addictive behaviours often want to change, and not want to change, at one and the same time. They often have reasons for wanting to maintain their addictive behaviours. Miller and Rollnick's (2012) motivational interviewing is a person-centred approach to counselling that offers the counsellor a way of working with such ambivalence. They define the approach as

> a collaborative, goal-orientated style of communication with particular attention to the language of change. It is designed to strengthen personal motivation for and commitment to a specific goal by eliciting and exploring a person's own reasons for change within an atmosphere of acceptance and compassion. (Miller & Rollnick, 2012: 29)

The approach is based on four general principles. The first principle is about expressing empathy or acceptance (but not necessarily approval) of the client's behaviour, where the counsellor aims to show the client that he or she understands the client's feelings and situation without criticising, judging or blaming the client. Linda's counsellor does not condemn Linda, who loves smoking, for her unhealthy habit. Instead, Linda is encouraged to explore her love of smoking. Ambivalence when changing behaviour is viewed as normal. The second principle concerns developing discrepancy. This is about highlighting and amplifying the client's ambivalence. Linda's counsellor highlights how Linda longs for incompatible outcomes, hoping to change and remain the same at one and the same time. Even though Linda loves smoking, she longs to live a long and healthy life. Developing discrepancy involves exploring both Linda's love of smoking as well as her desire for a long and healthy life, without aiming to confront her with the inconsistency of her desires. The third principle is about rolling with resistance, which is about the counsellor not taking the client's problem on board. When Linda argues against change, Linda's counsellor is supportive and understanding of this perspective, and does not try to persuade or convince Linda to change. When Linda has a relapse and smokes on her birthday after a one-month break, the counsellor doesn't pressure her to stop, but asks her about her experience of smoking on her birthday. Change and resistance are seen as two interdependent and important sides of the change process. The fourth principle is about supporting self-efficacy, which refers to a person's belief that they can change. Linda's counsellor shows she has faith in Linda's ability to change her behaviour throughout Linda's counselling. She attributes change to Linda and not her own 'brilliant' counselling interventions or to other factors in Linda's life. By supporting Linda in her ambivalence about smoking, her counsellor trusts her to find her own way forward. Solving Linda's smoking problem is Linda's, and not the counsellor's, task. The four principles build on humanistic values.

Helping the client weigh up the pros and cons of changing their behaviour is key to motivational interviewing. The counsellor encourages Linda to look at both the costs and benefits of continuing and stopping smoking. Smoking offers Linda something. It makes her feel relaxed, cool and one of the gang; just as it has a price: it is unhealthy and costs money. Similarly, quitting smoking has benefits and costs. Once Linda has stopped smoking, she is less short of breath when she goes up stairs, and she is pleased not to be dependent on cigarettes, but she suffers from severe headaches for the first couple of days after quitting and she misses cigarettes a lot when she drinks coffee in the morning and when she goes out with friends for a drink. Motivational interviewing encourages counsellors to take a balanced view and not side with change. In society, there is a lot of discourse about addictive behaviours, for example about the dangers of smoking. Motivational interviewing aims to create a space where clients can explore an addictive behaviour without being judged or condemned in relation to the behaviour. By giving the client room to reflect, motivational interviewing aims to give the client the opportunity of reflecting and deciding whether they want to continue with the addictive behaviour or not.

Exploring a client's automatic thoughts and beliefs

Exploring a client's automatic thoughts is a method employed by approaches such as Gestalt therapy and cognitive behaviour therapy (CBT). In CBT, a counsellor will typically explore the interrelation between thoughts, feelings and addictive behaviours to find 'irrational' beliefs at play in maintaining a client's addictive behaviour. George was asked by his counsellor to monitor his drinking. When he drank or wanted to drink he was asked to write down his thoughts, feelings and describe the situation. During his counselling, George discovered he held a range of alcohol-related beliefs that he had been unaware of. He believed drinking was central to his social skills and his creativity at work. He told his counsellor that he would never have managed to chat his wife up, when he first met her, had he not had a few drinks. He was convinced that drinking made him fun to be with. He also held the view that his best ideas at work surfaced after a session at the pub. He imagined his life might fall apart if he stopped drinking. He would become boring and a failure and ultimately lose his wife, his friends and his job. George feared ending up alone. Once he had examined his beliefs about drinking, George began to see that he had 'good' reasons for drinking, and that change would be hard. The counsellor challenged George's beliefs. He questioned whether George's wife would leave him, if he stopped drinking. She had, after all, told him she wanted him to cut back and she did seem to enjoy his company when he was sober. She never wanted sex with him when he had been drinking. The counsellor had George describe situations where he had been highly creative without drinking. He challenged the rationality of George's belief in the magical power of alcohol. This process showed George that he was far more sociable, creative and liked than he had thought he was. George also learned to share some of his concerns with his wife. This brought them closer together and he became less afraid of losing her.

Involving the family

Problems relating to addictive behaviours seldom only affect the person with the addictive behaviour. The whole family is often affected. Research suggests that alcohol problems can cause harm to significant others (Laslett et al., 2011). When counselling a person with an addictive behaviour, it is important to consider the implications of the addictive behaviour on other people. When working with addictive behaviours it is always worth considering holding one or more family counselling sessions focusing on the significance of the addictive behaviour on family members. While facing the negative implications of one's behaviour on one's own life can be hard, facing up to the negative implications of one's addictive behaviour on the people you love can be even harder. Exploring the effects of the addictive behaviour on significant others can be a motivating factor for change. Family members of persons with severe alcohol or drug problems often experience ambivalence towards the person with the addictive behaviour. They may, for example, hate the person when they are drunk, and love them when they are sober. Family members may experience feelings of shame and guilt in relation to their ambivalence. In narrative family therapy, families are encouraged to use externalising language about addictive behaviours as a way of dealing with ambivalence (Monk, Winslade, Crocket, & Epston, 1996). Externalising language involves drawing a line between a person with the problematic behaviour and the behaviour. It is not Paul who is the problem. It is the drinking. In family counselling, Paul tells his son, Carl, that drinking has taken over his life, and he can't stop drinking and that drinking is his best friend when he feels sad. The counsellor explores what family life is like when there is drinking and when there is no drinking. Carl tells his dad how much he enjoys evenings with him when they play cards and discuss politics, and how he hates evenings when there is drinking. Carl tells his dad that he never wants to be in the same room as him when he is drinking. He loves his dad, but he hates the drinking. Giving the addictive behaviour a name like 'the drinking' makes it easier for family members to talk about the issue. While externalising addictive behaviours can be useful as a technique in family therapy, there are also times when it can be inappropriate. Five years after the above session with Paul and Carl, Paul still drinks too much. Carl is now in individual counselling. He is angry with his dad and with all the wasted years his dad has spent drinking. Carl no longer sees the drinking as the problem and he gets annoyed with the counsellor, who is still using the technique described above. 'It's not the drinking that's the problem,' Carl tells the counsellor. 'It's my dad.

He's a f***ing alcoholic, and he always will be!' The above example highlights the pluralistic view that a technique that might be highly suited in one context, may be inappropriate in another.

12-step approaches

No chapter on counselling persons with addictive behaviours would be complete without mentioning 12-step approaches. By 12-step approaches we are referring to the work of self-help organisations such as Alcoholics Anonymous (AA) and Narcotics Anonymous. These self-help voluntary organisations do not view themselves as treatment programmes, though there are treatment programmes that draw on 12-step approaches, usually called the Minnesota Model (Spicer, 1993). Key elements of these programmes are:

- Addiction is viewed as a chronic disease. For example, problematic drinking is framed as alcoholism.
- Improvement involves accepting the chronic disease and identifying oneself as afflicted, for example by accepting that one is an alcoholic.
- Improvement involves continued engagement in a community of equals. There are regular meetings and older members of the community help newcomers.
- Though there is no affiliation with a specific religion, the approach does embrace the idea of there being a higher power.
- A series of 12 steps are seen as the way to come to terms with the disease.

The American Psychological Association summarised the steps as involving:

- admitting that one cannot control one's addiction or compulsion;
- recognising a higher power that can give strength;
- examining past errors with the help of a sponsor (experienced member);
- making amends for these errors;
- learning to live a new life with a new code of behaviour;
- helping others who suffer from the same addictions or compulsions.

(VandenBos, 2007)

Alcohol had played a key role in most of Jill's life. She had lost jobs, marriages, friends and even contact with her children to drink. AA meetings were a harbour to her, in an otherwise stormy sea. They were a place where she could always return and where she could always feel understood and accepted whatever she had done. While she wrestled with the notion of alcoholism as a disease, she knew in her heart of hearts that she could not control her drinking. She struggled with the steps. They seemed insurmountable, while at the same time, they made sense to her. A key element of the 12-step approach for Jill was that it offered her a potential life-long support network. This was particularly important as Jill had lost touch with her family. Persons treated according to the Minnesota Model are encouraged to join local 12-step groups after treatment.

Before this chapter draws to a close, it is important to note that some people with severe addiction-related problems have a multitude of other problems. They may live in precarious situations with social problems such as poverty, debt, unemployment, homelessness, poor-quality relationships and a high level of experienced or actual dependency on other people; or they may have other mental health issues such as low self-esteem, depression or other diagnoses. Assessing a person's overall social situation and general mental health is therefore important when working with addictive behaviours.

SUMMARY

The key points made by this chapter are:

- Counselling for addictive behaviours should be tailored to the client's readiness for change.
- Exploring the pros and cons of change and status quo is a key technique.
- Viewing addictive behaviours as rewards, and examining beliefs connected with addictive behaviours can be useful.
- Discuss treatment goals and ask the client what already works or what they think might work.
- Addictive behaviours don't just affect individuals. They can be complex and affect families, friends and even colleagues. Consider involving others in the counselling.

EXERCISES/POINTS FOR REFLECTION

1 Think of someone you know who has an addictive behaviour. Then consider talking to the person about the behaviour. What words do you think would be best to use to talk about the addictive behaviour?
2 Think about someone you know who has an addictive behaviour. Reflect on what stage of change they are at, and how this might influence your way of talking to them?
3 Think about someone you know who wants to change an addictive behaviour. Reflect on what challenges you would face if you did not side with change, but supported the person in exploring both the benefits and costs of change and the benefits and costs of continuing with the behaviour.
4 Think about someone you know who wants to change an addictive behaviour. Reflect on the role of the addiction as a reward in the person's life. What beliefs do you think the person holds in relation to maintaining or stopping the behaviour?

> # FURTHER READING
>
> Berg, I.K., & Miller, S.D. (1992). *Working with the problem drinker: a solution-focused approach.* New York: Norton. This classic book describes a highly collaborative and agency-focused approach to working with alcohol problems. Pluralistically inspired readers will find understandings and methods in the book that help them develop these aspects of their practice.
>
> Velleman, R.D.B. (2011). *Counselling for alcohol problems* (3rd ed.). London: Sage. Written by a key British researcher in the field, this book offers an up-to-date introduction to the field of alcohol counselling.
>
> Walters, S., & Rotgers, F. (2012). *Treating substance abuse: theory and technique* (3rd ed.). New York: The Guilford Press. This book offers an up-to-date guide to substance abuse and its treatment. It presents a range of understandings and methods in the field.
>
> Resources
>
> Alcoholics Anonymous: www.aa.org.

REFERENCES

Berg, I.K., & Miller, S.D. (1992). *Working with the problem drinker: a solution-focused approach.* New York: Norton.

Cooper, M., & McLeod, J. (2011). *Pluralistic counselling and psychotherapy.* London: Sage.

Institute of Medicine. (1990). *Broadening the base of treatment for alcohol problems.* Washington, DC: National Academies Press.

Laslett, A-M., Room, R., Ferris, J., Wilkinson, C., Livingston, M., & Mugavin, J. (2011). Surveying the range and magnitude of alcohol's harm to others in Australia. *Addiction, 106,* 1603–1611.

Littlefield, A.K., Sher, K.J., & Wood, P.K. (2009). Is 'maturing out' of problematic alcohol involvement related to personality change? *Journal of Abnormal Psychology, 118,* 360–374.

Miller, W.R., & Rollnick, S. (2012). *Motivational interviewing: helping people change* (3rd ed.). New York: The Guilford Press.

Miller, W.R., Wilbourne, P.L., & Hettema, J.E. (2002). What works? A summary of alcohol treatment outcome research (pp. 13–63). In R.K. Hester & W.R. Miller (Eds.), *Handbook of alcoholism treatment approaches: effective alternatives.* New York: Allyn & Bacon.

Monk, G., Winslade, J., Crocket, K., & Epston, D. (1996). *Narrative therapy in practice: the archaeology of hope.* San Francisco: CA: Jossey–Bass.

Norcross, J.C., Krebs; P.M., & Prochaska, J.O. (2011). Stages of change. *Journal of Clinical Psychology: In Session, 67,* 143–154.

Prochaska, J.O., & DiClemente, C.C. (1986). Toward a comprehensive model of change (pp. 2–27). In W.R. Miller & N. Heather (Eds.), *Treating addictive behaviors: processes of change*. New York: Plenum.

Project MATCH Research Group. (1997). Matching alcoholism treatments to client heterogeneity: Project MATCH posttreatment drinking outcomes. *Journal of Studies on Alcohol, 58,* 7–29.

Sobell, L.C., Cunningham, J.A., & Sobell, M.B. (1996). Recovery from alcohol problems with and without treatment: prevalence in two population surveys. *American Journal of Public Health, 86,* 966–972.

Spicer, J. (1993). *The Minnesota Model: the evolution of the interdisciplinary approach to addiction recovery.* Center City, MN: Hazelden Educational Materials.

Valverde, M. (1998). *Diseases of the will: alcohol and the dilemmas of freedom.* Cambridge: Cambridge University Press.

VandenBos, G.R. (2007). *APA dictionary of psychology.* Washington, DC: American Psychological Association.

Walters, G.D. (1999). *The addiction concept: working hypothesis or self-fulfilling prophesy?* Needham Heights, MA: Allyn & Bacon.

19

Helping Clients Address Eating Problems

Lynsey McMillan

THIS CHAPTER DISCUSSES

- Key understandings of how eating problems can emerge
- How these understandings can be applied in practice, within a pluralistic framework
- Essential counsellor attributes for working with disordered eaters

INTRODUCTION

Our attitudes towards food, eating behaviours and body image are deeply idiosyncratic. Feeding is inextricably woven into the fabric of our lives from the very moment of birth, and ingrained attitudes towards food, eating and body image are passed down through generations. When problems with eating emerge they can be viewed as 'biopsychosocial' (Engel, 1977) matters that have no single cause, born instead from a combination of personal, social, cultural, biological and genetic factors that are unique to the sufferer yet share broad commonalities to us all.

Eating disorders generally fall into four diagnostic categories: Anorexia, Bulimia, Binge Eating Disorder and EDNOS (eating disorders not otherwise specified) (Grilo & Mitchell, 2010). However, a vast majority will not receive a formal diagnosis of an eating disorder, may not meet the diagnostic criteria or ever present for assessment. Familiarising yourself with the diagnostic criteria (American Psychiatric Association, 2013) will allow you to better assess potential risk factors and ensure best practice.

This chapter is designed for the pluralistic therapist who may encounter clients significantly troubled with eating problems and who may or may not have been diagnosed with an eating disorder. Clients may feel out of control and compulsively over-eat or rigidly control their eating and be on another in a long line of extreme diets. They may under-eat, binge-eat or alternate between both. They might restrict the types of foods they consume or only eat under certain circumstances. Disordered eaters commonly have poor self-esteem and their body image may severely impact on their social lives and relationships regardless of actual body size. Underlying issues with depression, anxiety or past trauma are common and eating problems could be causing or exacerbating existing health conditions. Food becomes a best friend, worst enemy, or both.

Clients often arrive at counselling following exhaustive attempts to alter their behaviours and as a result could have a wealth of theoretical knowledge yet still feel powerless to change. Their food issues may be lifelong or a recent coping strategy in response to new difficulties. Eating and weight issues may be the presenting issue but more frequently it will feature alongside other problems such as depression, anxiety, trauma, abuse, low self-esteem or relational difficulties (Koenig, 2008). Disordered eaters can be overweight, underweight or of normal weight and therapists can overlook eating problems through lack of awareness, knowledge or confidence. Eating problems are frequently shrouded in silence; a private escape that is often experienced as deeply embarrassing and shameful. Eating problems are complex; a pluralistic approach recognises this and allows for a shared understanding to emerge between counsellor and client, drawing from their respective knowledge to generate fresh solutions.

KEY UNDERSTANDINGS

Too often, eating and particularly weight issues are over-simplified or judged in narrow, punitive terms. It is helpful to start with the perspective that food and eating issues are multi-faceted and meaningful, and to encourage the client to adopt a curious outlook.

Psychobiological and genetic factors

There is much ongoing debate around psychobiological and genetic causes of disordered eating. Eating disorders often run in families and research suggests that there may be a significant genetic contribution; for example, female relatives of those suffering from anorexia are 11.4% more likely to develop the disorder and 3.7% more likely to develop bulimia if they have a sufferer in the family (B-eat, 2015). Other research makes connections between personality types and eating disorders. For example, anorexia has been linked to perfectionism traits and incidence of OCD, whilst bulimia has been linked to impulsive and narcissistic personality traits (Wonderlich, 2002: 205). This is a contentious issue; some theorists suggest personality factors predispose a person to having an eating disorder, others argue there is no causal link, whilst others posit that exaggerations in normal personality traits develop as a result of an eating disorder, for example brain changes caused by starvation.

It is thought that some sufferers may have a chemical imbalance in the brain in the areas that govern hunger and appetite. However, the exact meaning and implications of these imbalances remain under debate (Campfield, 2002). There is also growing interest in a possible connection between addiction, eating disorders and serotonin. According to Wansink, author of *Mindless Eating* (2011), we are 'hardwired' to love the taste of fat, salt and sugar. When stressed or anxious, our brain in 'fight or flight' survival mode may instruct us to store fat and we can crave calorie-rich foods. The reward pathways in our brains help to reinforce this particular survival behaviour by producing opioids; a narcotic also found in drugs like heroin and cocaine (Colantuoni et al., 2002). Many people use food as an occasional comforter without it ever becoming a problem; however, for some individuals suffering from low serotonin (or faulty serotonin receptors) food can be utilised as a form of mood enhancer or self-medication. Negative emotions such as boredom, stress, sadness and anxiety are frequently cited as leading to binging (Clyne & Blampied, 2004), and according to Fairburn, 'Mood intolerance is hypothesised to be a critical variable underlying a range of eating disorders' (Fairburn, Cooper, & Shafran, 2003). Targeting mood intolerance therefore is considered an important component in the treatment of all eating problems.

Emotional and psychological factors

For many problem eaters, food is used as an attempt to alleviate and control feelings of overwhelming anxiety (Slowchower, 1987). Emotional eating encompasses a range of behaviours including grazing on small amounts throughout the day, discrete periods of bingeing (often alone and in secret) and frequent overeating. Emotional eaters can be of normal weight or overweight depending on factors such as levels of physical activity, physiology, frequency of compensatory dieting behaviours and levels of restraint.

The degree to which emotional eaters binge, graze or overeat is also a factor; *objective* binging consists of eating an amount of food that general consensus would agree is over-large, whereas a *subjective* binge describes the eating of an amount or even a type of food that is outwith a person's own measure of enough. Regardless of quantity, emotional eaters can feel frustrated, guilty and distressed by their use of food for affect regulation. Stress, anxiety and loneliness are particularly identified as reasons for anaesthetising with food (Bidgood & Buckroyd, 2005; Goodspeed Grant & Boersma, 2005). This sets up a vicious cycle where food is used to manage feelings leading to other meta-emotions that compound or mask the problem.

Because food can act as an emotional analgesic it is unsurprising that there is often a correlation between mental health issues and eating problems. Depression and anxiety commonly occur and may trigger the eating problem or alternatively mental health issues may be exacerbated by an eating or weight issue. For example, a tendency to occasionally comfort eat might be kept under control for years until a situational depression spirals into compulsive eating and weight gain. Clients may also engage in other addictive or compulsive behaviours, such as abusing alcohol or drugs, compulsive shopping or gambling, OCD behaviours or self-harm.

Many disordered eaters experience black-and-white thinking, a cognitive distortion commonly addressed in cognitive behavioural therapies (Neenan & Dryden, 2011). Dichotomous thinking is considered a 'hallmark' of disordered eating (Koenig, 2008) and many clients exhibit all-or-nothing attitudes towards many aspects of life in relation to their eating behaviour. A schema of good or bad foods can emerge generating a cycle of attempted restriction followed by overeating (Seamore, Buckroyd, & Stott, 2008) and is a reason restrictive diet programmes often prove unsuccessful. One of our earliest experiences of autonomy takes place in relation to eating. Restricting eating may be an attempt to find mastery whilst faced with an internal or external chaos; a way to feel some degree of control and success that is often driven by perfectionism and poor self-esteem (Buckroyd, 2011: 37). The internal dialogue of a disordered eater can swing from highly self-critical to persecuted or rebellious. A binge episode illustrates this self-talk: 'Why did I ruin my diet by eating that biscuit? I'm a complete failure, I might as well eat the whole packet then!'

Commonly, those with eating problems have a history of difficult attachments (Buckroyd, 2011). Those with an insecure attachment whose early caregivers were unavailable, abusive or poorly attuned to their emotional needs can struggle, in later life, to self-soothe and form intimate relationships (Gerhart, 2004). These people may have difficulty trusting others, choose unsuitable relationships or avoid close contact (particularly when distressed) and consequently seek out ways to cope alone. Clients may require help addressing difficulties both in their intimate adult relationships and within their own self-concept if they are to successfully overcome their eating problem.

Often an eating problem can develop in response to trauma, loss or abuse (Buckroyd, 2011; Koenig, 2008). Eating can provide a safe place where sufferers can disengage from intolerable distress. In some instances this can become a form of dissociation; during a binge the person may disassociate so much that only the discomfort of being over-full brings them back to conscious awareness. For some, an overweight body may also become a form of defence used, for example, to ward off unsolicited sexual attention or put a boundary around themselves in place of other forms of protection (Koenig, 2008: 46). It is worth considering that a first task may be the creation of alternative safety mechanisms or a 'safe space' where the client can find refuge while traumas are worked through.

Disordered eaters can also typically have poor self-esteem and difficulties with body image, often exacerbated if the individual is overweight or obese (Cash, 2002). The client's relationship to their body can be deeply symbolic; for example, the American author Zadoff (2007) likened his large body to a form of procrastination and described it as hanging out in the locker room but never running the race; his weight protected him from a competitive world that he felt ill-equipped to face.

Given the various unique functions of eating and weight problems, clients may be ambivalent regarding change. Viewing this pluralistically, the therapist can invite the client to share these multiple viewpoints and validate the protective function the problem once served.

Sociological factors

Food is personally and socially symbolic, playing an essential role amongst all of the major cultures and faiths. Food represents nurture, celebration and connectedness; it is life-giving. However, the developed world now presents an unprecedented abundance of food whilst our lifestyles have become increasingly sedentary. Swinburn, Egger and Raza (1999) coined the term 'obesogenic' to describe a first world abundance of calorie-laden food coupled with reduced opportunities to burn off excesses. Additionally, our culture presents us with narrow definitions of beauty, and a glorification of 'thinness' that places value on obtaining the 'perfect body'. Our obesogenic environment increasingly makes this slim ideal impossible for many people. It is therefore unsurprising that food, weight and shape can become a major psychological preoccupation. Rodin, Silberstein and Striegel-Moore (1984) coined the term 'normative discontent' to describe the widespread unhappiness many women feel about their bodies. For many women, body disparagement has become as routine as discussing the weather, and in certain environments, such as ballet, sports and modelling, these pressures are further intensified.

Family factors

Family attitudes to eating and body image may contribute to *or* immunise against body esteem problems (Stice, 2002). Those raised in homes that promote positive messages about bodies and healthy attitudes towards food will be better equipped to cope with external pressures. Disordered eaters often report having parents with excessive appearance or achievement concerns, homes where they may have experienced constant comparisons with other siblings or a history of being ridiculed by family or peers based on their appearance. This can lead to excessive over-valuation of weight and shape and a need to gain control (Fairburn, 2008). Disordered eaters also report upbringings where there were restrictive or rigid rules about foods or conversely frequent use of food as reward, treat or consolation. These family dynamics can often be played out around mealtimes, therefore enquiring about current or past history of family mealtimes may reveal important personal narratives on topics such as power structures, communication and emotional expression.

WHAT HELPS? ESSENTIAL COUNSELLOR ATTRIBUTES

Research has identified three counsellor attributes considered to be helpful: relational qualities, theoretical understanding and personal experience of overcoming an eating problem.

Timulak et al. (2013) and McInerney (2013) both emphasised the vital role of mental health professionals' relational qualities, such as conveying warmth and respect (see Norcross, 2011). It was also considered important that counsellors demonstrated theoretical understanding of eating problems, as this legitimised the counsellor. Counsellors who have personally overcome an eating problem and are willing to self-disclose have also been identified as beneficial (Chan, 2004; Kelley, 2005; Rother & Buckroyd, 2004). Counsellor disclosure normalised the client's experience, humanised the therapist and conveyed hope. This in turn can aid the therapeutic relationship, promote client disclosure, dispel shame, validate the client's experiences and serve as a model for positive change (Knox, Hess, Petersen, & Hill, 1997).

KEY TASKS AND METHODS

Making sense of the problem and its development

This task forms the basis for the initial assessment as well as being an ongoing therapeutic task. Clients can often feel confused and self-critical rather than appreciate their behaviour as meaningful. Increasing understanding can have the effect of raising self-compassion and reducing shame. Jenny entered counselling with a private counsellor, Erica, as a 'last resort' following a lifetime of conflict around food. 'I am fed up with false starts, I know what I should be doing but can't stick to it, I want to know where I am going wrong.' Jenny and Erica agreed a first task was to increase understanding and Erica suggested Jenny keep a 'food and mood' journal to help them begin to connect behaviours and their emotional and situational triggers. She also gave Jenny some questionnaires, which when used to aid a collaborative conversation helped to identify the attitudes, behaviours and emotions behind Jenny's eating. (e.g. Emotional Overeating Questionnaire, Revised; Masheb & Grilo, 2006; Three Factor Eating Questionnaire; Stunkard & Messick, 1985).

Making sense of the problem also includes exploring whether there are barriers such as health, environmental, financial, relational factors, beliefs and attitudes or feelings of fear and ambivalence.

Exploring limiting beliefs and attitudes

Barriers to change can include limiting beliefs and attitudes such as rigid thinking habits and preoccupations, negative self-comparisons, perfectionist beliefs, and self-critical internal dialogues. Methods to address these limiting beliefs can include CBT 'cognitive restructuring' to tackle rigid thinking (Neenan & Dryden, 2011) and transactional analysis approaches that examine critical parent and persecuted/rebellious child 'voices' and seek to strengthen helpful 'adult' responses (Leach, 2006). Ambivalence towards change is characteristic of disordered eaters – solution-focused approaches (de Shazer & Dolan, 2007) offer one way of exploring this possible ambivalence. Erica asked her client Jenny a 'miracle question': 'What would life be like if you woke up tomorrow and the problem had disappeared?' Jenny replied, 'Oh that would be scary! What if I still didn't like myself?', concluding that 'Maybe it's easier to be in a battle over my weight and blame that for absolutely everything.'

Learning the skills to eat 'normally'

Disordered eaters frequently express a desire to be able to 'just eat normally'. Since there is no singular definitive 'normal' the task for client and counsellor is to determine what 'normal' means to them and evaluate whether this goal is achievable.

The task of learning to eat 'normally' focuses on helping the client choose and implement behavioural changes such as increasing awareness of situational eating triggers, replacing old habits with new ones, finding ways to make better choices, for example by meal planning, writing shopping lists, making use of rewards and focusing on incentives to change. Having worked on the task of understanding the problem and what triggers their disordered eating, this task focuses on what achievable steps the client can introduce in order to be more mindful of their eating habits, avoid falling into unhelpful behaviours and make choices more in line with their goals. Sam decided a first step for him to begin to eat 'normally' was to make breakfast every morning. This, he felt, would prevent him from excessively bingeing and vomiting later in the day. He made a plan with his counsellor, Mark, to set his alarm 30 minutes earlier for a week and sit down to eat a nutritious breakfast, noting whether this change made a difference to his bingeing by keeping a daily food diary. Sam became aware that when he did this he made better food choices later in the day. He also discovered that in times of stress he resisted making this extra time for himself and had a 'default' tendency to neglect his own needs.

Self-care and learning to tolerate distress

Many disordered eaters are poor at attending to their own needs and may benefit from learning to self-care and tolerate distress (self-soothe). They can have difficulty prioritising their health or be unable to recognise primary needs, they may allow themselves to be taken advantage of by others and have poor boundaries, or might self-sabotage their attempts at change (Koenig, 2008). Distress tolerance is the ability to endure and accept painful feelings so that problems can be worked through rather than suppressed (Linehan, 1993). It may be important to consider self-care and distress tolerance as foundational tasks and find ways to help the client be more attuned to their feelings. Methods include breathing exercises, meditation and mindfulness, visualisations or the creation of safety plans. Safiya was in counselling to come to terms with childhood sexual abuse. She identified that she used food as a form of self-soothing and that her weight formed a protective boundary for her. The thought of letting go of this coping strategy terrified her. With the help of her counsellor, Safiya devised strategies including the creation of an 'emergency box' (download instructions from www.getselfhelp.co.uk). Safiya was encouraged to put together a box full of resources for when she was feeling anxious and overwhelmed. Safiya chose a poem, some art materials, a soft toy and an mp3 player filled with her favourite songs.

Letting go and healing old wounds

Disordered eating can develop in response to significant loss or trauma, therefore the task at this 'remembrance and mourning stage' (Herman, 1997) is to 'tell the full story of the trauma with the therapist in the role of witness and ally' (Herman, 1997).

Cathartic methods can include paying 'testimony' through writing, talking or art, externalising difficult feelings through two-chair work or sharing memories, photos or mementoes. Safiya was holding on to many painful emotions regarding both her abuser and her mother, whom she felt didn't adequately protect her. With the support of her counsellor, Alice, who encouraged Safiya to set the pace, she began to tell her story and express feelings of shame, anger, grief and fear. Although Safiya enjoyed art she did not want to use this as a method to express her negative emotions as she connected art to feelings of relaxation and comfort. Instead, she chose to write her feelings and later cremated these writings in a ritual she experienced as very empowering and healing.

Finding alternatives to food

A pluralistic approach views the client as inventive and resourceful and the use of food can be understood as a creative response to stressful circumstances that has ceased to be beneficial. This task focuses on helping the client find alternatives to their use of food. This can include conversations about unmet aspirations and researching local resources, but oftentimes clients do not need to discover new resources but remember long-forgotten ones. For example, Steven was a keen golfer but gave up his hobby when his second child arrived, feeling under increased pressure to work, support his wife and spend time together as a family. He entered counselling for work-related stress and mentioned he was regularly bingeing on junk food in the evenings and alcohol at the weekends. Steven hadn't acknowledged the importance of his hobby until he discussed it with his counsellor. He expressed a dichotomous attitude regarding his role as a father and a breadwinner, which eliminated his own separate interests. Golf provided many therapeutic benefits, including outdoor exercise and a sense of accomplishment. Steven particularly identified how much he missed the camaraderie of his golfing buddies.

Social support is essential in maintaining psychological well-being and it is thought that the presence and strength of close relationships with family and peers, along with the support of other sufferers, may play a crucial role in the success or failure of treatments for eating problems. (Timulak et al., 2013).

Improving interpersonal relationships

Making use of social support can be difficult for disordered eaters and improving interpersonal relationships may be a key task in tackling disordered eating. Eating problems can be symbolic of deeper interpersonal issues and sufferers can be highly self-reliant, keen to avoid burdening others or deeply distrustful. Kirsty and Zahra both have difficulties with intimacy and self-expression. Zahra is an emotional overeater, she feels people in her life have always judged her and that by being overweight and wearing her 'armour' she can give them something to criticise. Deep down she fears being thinner because criticism then would 'cut to the bone'. Her goal for counselling was to be less self-critical and find methods to express herself without needing her 'armour'.

Kirsty had many secretive and rigid eating rules; in particular, she felt unable to eat in front of her boyfriend. As Kirsty didn't live with her partner she could allow herself to eat at home but weekends spent together amounted to self-enforced starvation. The couple's plans to live together and eventually marry were being thwarted by her anxiety around eating and intimacy.

Both Kirsty and Zahra felt they needed to learn to express their emotions and explore their trust issues as well as discover better ways to set boundaries and communicate assertively. Both of these clients' stories highlight the potential importance of the therapeutic relationship and the role it could play in helping these women to overcome their relational issues.

SUMMARY

Food is central to everyday life, infused with notions of nurture, connection, celebration and survival, but for many it is also fraught with conflict, confusion and shame. We are biologically designed to crave calorie-rich foods for our survival yet our obesogenic modern society provides countless eating decisions daily whilst also frequently presenting us with unattainable representations of the perfect human form.

Certain foods have been found to act as a pain-relieving 'drug' and some disordered eaters may self-medicate to alleviate intolerable feeling states. Disordered eating can emerge as a response to life's difficulties and sufferers can feel very ashamed and self-critical about their problem. Many have low self-esteem and their body image may be deeply conflicted. Dichotomous thinking, perfectionism and control issues are recurrent themes and disordered eaters can have a history of insecure attachments leading to difficulties with adult relationships. Counsellors who convey curiosity, knowledge and compassion can reduce shame and help clients to make sense of their concerns, explore any ambivalence or limiting beliefs, improve their capacity to self-care, tolerate distress and attend to past 'wounds' and ultimately work towards finding a new 'normal' where food ceases to be a battlefield.

EXERCISES/POINTS FOR REFLECTION

1. How might you include an enquiry into eating as part of your assessment process?
2. How would you describe your current relationship with food? How might this impact on your work with a disordered eater?
3. If eating/body image is difficult for you, how would you deal with transference issues? What are your thoughts on self-disclosure?

FURTHER READING

Buckroyd, J. (2011). *Understanding your eating: how to eat and not worry about it* (4th ed.). Maidenhead: Open University Press. This accessible book is designed for clients, their families and practitioners. Based on years of clinical practice and research, it is designed to increase insight and find meaning behind one's eating behaviour and may be particularly helpfully used in tandem with therapeutic or social support.

Koenig, K.R. (2008). *What every therapist needs to know about treating eating and weight issues*. New York: Norton. This is an excellent first point of reference for trainee and generalist counsellors which covers a wide range of eating and body image issues commonly found in everyday practice and suggests a number of useful techniques, strategies and reflective questions to aid understanding.

Normandi, C.E., & Roark, L. (2008). *It's not about food: end your obsession with food and weight*. New York: Perigee Books. This book is part of the non-diet movement and an antidote to what the authors see as a harmful cultural obsession with food and weight. Their aim is to guide the reader to develop a self-compassionate approach towards their problem, learn to eat intuitively and to attend to underlying emotions.

REFERENCES

American Psychiatric Association. (2013). *Diagnostic and statistical manual of mental disorders* (5th ed.). Washington, DC: Author.

B-eat. (2015). *Facts and figures. How many people in the UK have an eating disorder?* Retrieved from www.b-eat.co.uk/about-beat/media-centre/facts-and-figures/

Bidgood, J., & Buckroyd, J. (2005). An exploration of obese adults' experience of attempting to lose weight and to maintain a reduced weight. *Counselling and Psychotherapy Research*, 5(3), 221–229.

Buckroyd, J. (2011). *Understanding your eating: how to eat and not worry about it* (4th ed.). Maidenhead: Open University Press.

Campfield, L.A. (2002). Leptin and body weight regulation. In C.G. Fairburn & K.D. Brownell (Eds.), *Eating disorders and obesity: a comprehensive handbook* (2nd ed., pp. 32–36). New York: The Guilford Press.

Cash, T.F. (2002). The management of body image problems. In C.G. Fairburn & K.D. Brownell (Eds.), *Eating disorders and obesity: a comprehensive handbook* (2nd ed., pp. 599–603). New York: The Guilford Press.

Chan, C.Y.Z. (2004). *A discovery process-outcome study: the roles of perceived significant events in the changes of anorexia nervosa patients and their families in family treatment* (Doctoral thesis). The Chinese University of Hong Kong, Hong Kong.

Clyne, C., & Blampied, N.M. (2004). Training in emotion regulation as a treatment for binge eating: a preliminary study. *Behaviour Change, 21*(4), 269–281.

Colantuoni, C., Rada, P., McCarthy, J., Patten, C., Avena, N.M., Chadeayne, A., & Hoebel, B.G. (2002). Evidence that intermittent, excessive sugar intake causes endogenous opioid dependence. *Obesity Research, 10*(6), 478–488.

de Shazer, S., & Dolan, Y. (2007). *More than miracles: the state of the art of solution-focused brief therapy*. London: Routledge.

Engel, G.L. (1977). The need for a new medical model: a challenge for biomedicine. *Science, 196,* 129–136.

Fairburn, C.G. (2008). *Cognitive behaviour therapy and eating disorders*. New York: The Guilford Press.

Fairburn, C.G., Cooper, Z., & Shafran, R. (2003). Cognitive behaviour therapy for eating disorders: a 'transdiagnostic' theory and treatment. *Behaviour Research and Therapy, 41,* 509–528.

Gerhart, S. (2004). *Why love matters: how affection shapes a baby's brain*. Hove: Brunner Routledge.

Goodspeed Grant, P., & Boersma, H. (2005). Making sense of being fat: a hermeneutic analysis of adults' explanations for obesity. *Counselling and Psychotherapy Research, 5*(3), 212–220.

Grilo, C.M., & Mitchell, J.E. (2010). *The treatment of eating disorders*. New York: The Guilford Press.

Herman, J.L. (1997). *Trauma and recovery*. New York: Basic Books.

Kelley, J.P. (2005). *What do women in therapy for an eating disorder find helpful? A qualitative study* (PhD thesis). Virginia Polytechnic Institute and State University Blacksburg, VA.

Knox, S., Hess, S., Petersen, D., & Hill, C.E. (1997). A qualitative analysis of client perceptions of the effects of helpful therapist self-disclosure in long-term therapy. *Journal of Counselling Psychology, 44,* 274–283.

Koenig, K.R. (2008). *What every therapist needs to know about treating eating and weight issues*. New York: Norton.

Leach, K. (2006). *The overweight patient: a psychological approach to understanding and working with obesity*. London: Jessica Kingsley.

Linehan, M.M. (1993). *Skills training manual for treating borderline personality disorder: diagnosis and treatment of mental disorders*. New York: The Guilford Press.

Masheb, R.M., & Grilo, C.M. (2006). Emotional overeating and its associations with eating disorder psychopathology among overweight patients with binge eating disorder. *International Journal of Eating Disorders, 39*(2), 141–146.

McInerney, T. (2013). *Helpful aspects of therapy for clients experiencing disordered eating*. Unpublished manuscript.

Neenan, M., & Dryden, W. (2011). *Cognitive therapy in a nutshell* (2nd ed.). London: Sage.

Norcross, J.C. (2011). *Psychotherapy relationships that work: evidence-based responsiveness* (2nd ed.). New York: Oxford University Press.

Rodin, J., Silberstein, L., & Striegel-Moore, R. (1984). Women and weight: a normative discontent. *Nebraska Symposium on Motivation, 32*, 267–307.

Rother, S., & Buckroyd, J. (2004). Experience of service provision for adolescents with eating disorders. *Primary Health Care Research & Development, 5*, 153–161.

Seamore, D., Buckroyd, J., & Stott, D. (2008). Changes in eating behaviour following group therapy for women who binge eat: a pilot study. In J. Buckroyd & S. Rother (Eds.), *Psychological responses to eating disorders and obesity* (pp. 169–186). Chichester: Wiley.

Stice, E. (2002). Sociocultural influences on body image and eating disturbance. In C.G. Fairburn & K.D Brownell (Eds.), *Eating disorders and obesity: a comprehensive handbook* (2nd ed., pp. 103–107). New York: The Guilford Press.

Slowchower, J. (1987). The psychodynamics of obesity: a review. *Psychoanalytic Psychology, 4*(2), 145–159.

Stunkard, A.J., & Messick, S. (1985). The three-factor eating questionnaire to measure dietary restraint, disinhibition and hunger. *Journal of Psychosomatic Research, 29*, 71–83.

Swinburn, B., Egger, G., & Raza, F. (1999). Dissecting obesogenic environments: the development and application of a framework for identifying and prioritizing environmental interventions for obesity. *Preventive Medicine, 29*, 563–570.

Timulak, L., Buckroyd, J., Klimas, J., Creaner, M., Wellsted, D., Bunn, F., … Green, G. (2013). *Helpful and unhelpful aspects of eating disorders treatment involving psychological therapy: A meta-synthesis of qualitative research studies.* Leicester: British Association for Counselling & Psychotherapy.

Wansink, B. (2011). *Mindless eating: why we eat more than we think.* London: Hay House.

Wonderlich, S. (2002). Personality and eating disorders. In C.G. Fairburn & K.D. Brownell (Eds.), *Eating disorders and obesity, a comprehensive handbook* (2nd ed.) (pp. 204–209). New York: The Guilford Press.

Zadoff, A. (2007). *Hungry.* Philadelphia, PA: Da Capo Press.

20

Helping Clients Who Have Health Issues

Julia McLeod, Mhairi Thurston and Kate Smith

THIS CHAPTER DISCUSSES

- The emotional and relationship issues reported by individuals with serious health problems
- Practical challenges arising from working with this client group
- Therapeutic methods that are particularly relevant in this area of practice
- Therapist issues and self-awareness

A BRIEF INTRODUCTION TO THE ISSUES FACED BY PEOPLE WITH LONG-TERM HEALTH CONDITIONS

The term 'long-term condition' refers to a wide range of diagnoses, such as hypertension, depression, asthma, diabetes, coronary heart disease, chronic kidney disease, hypothyroidism, stroke, cancer, mental health, heart failure, epilepsy and dementia (DOH, 2012). Other long-term health conditions which have a substantial and long-term adverse effect on a person's ability to carry out normal day-to-day activities can additionally be categorised as disabilities, such as severe sight loss, HIV and MS (Equality Act, 2010). All these issues differ a great deal in terms of severity, aspects of everyday functioning that are affected, and ultimate prognosis. Nevertheless, from a psychological perspective, all of these conditions share some important characteristics. They have an impact on the way a person feels about himself or herself. They place restrictions on what a person can and cannot do, within their everyday life. They can lead to tensions in relationships with friends, family members and work colleagues. They necessitate regular interaction with physicians, nurses and other health professionals. Finally, these conditions may be associated with financial hardship.

Although the present chapter considers the domain of long-term health conditions as a whole, it is essential, when working with clients, to keep a focus on the unique and distinctive characteristics of the specific condition or conditions with which they are seeking to cope. It is also important to be sensitive to the needs of individuals whose health problems fall outside, or between, diagnostic categories (Creed, Hennington, & Fink, 2011).

There exists a substantial amount of research into the emotional impact of long-term health issues. On the whole, the evidence suggests that physical health conditions tend to generate significant levels of psychological distress, emotional pain, and relationship difficulties (see, e.g., Burmedi, Becker, Heyl, Wahl, & Himmelsbach, 2002). Positive well-being supports good health outcomes (Robertson, Stanley, Cully, & Naik, 2012). It is valuable for pluralistic therapists to become familiar with aspects of this research literature that are relevant to clients with whom they are working, as a means of sensitising themselves to the types of issues that may arise in therapy. There are two types of evidence that are particularly useful. Large-scale studies that invite patients to complete standardised symptom measures provide an overview of the extent and severity of psychological problems that might be encountered with a client group, and the ways in which these difficulties change over the course of a disorder. In-depth qualitative studies and case reports, based on interviews with patients and carers, provide an understanding of what it means to live with a health condition (e.g., Nyman, Dibb, Victor, & Gosney, 2012).

Up to now, the field of counselling and psychotherapy for people with long-term health conditions has been dominated by concepts and methods drawn from cognitive-behavioural, psychodynamic and bio-psycho-social perspectives. Cognitive-behavioural protocols for therapy for stress, anxiety and depression can be readily adapted when these issues occur within the context of long-term health problems. In addition, CBT provides a range of therapeutic strategies in relation to the management of chronic pain. Psychodynamic theory and practice is particularly relevant to an understanding of such questions as the unconscious or underlying meaning of illness for the person, the bodily experience of being ill, and shifts in patterns of relationships. Most practitioners who work in this field are influenced, to a greater or lesser extent, by a bio-psycho-social perspective that emphasises the necessity to take account of physical/biological and social dimensions of the experience of the person, alongside psychological factors (Gilbert, 2002).

Building on these important traditions, a pluralistic approach acknowledges a wider range of therapeutic tasks arising from long-term health conditions, and seeks to make use of the preferences, strengths and capabilities of clients. Compared to CBT, psychodynamic and bio-psycho-social models, a pluralistic framework strives to be more flexible and responsive, and to place a greater emphasis on client–therapist collaboration. In these respects, pluralistic therapy is consistent with current developments in medical care (Mulley, Trimble, & Elwyn, 2012).

The complex and multi-faceted nature of long-term health conditions is illustrated in a study by Omylinska-Thurston and Cooper (2014), based on interviews with people who had received counselling while they were receiving treatment for cancer. All of the individuals who were interviewed reported that they used counselling as a means of coming to terms with overwhelming feelings, such as being vulnerable and frightened. They also wanted to talk about losses, fear of cancer recurrence and longstanding issues that had been re-awakened by the experience of being ill. They also used therapy to explore practical matters, such as going back to work, weight management, sleep problems, relaxation skills and strategies for resolving family tensions.

> ### CASE EXAMPLE
> #### Multiple issues associated with the experience of illness
>
> Isobel was aged 54 at the point when she entered therapy. Nine years earlier, she had received a diagnosis of multiple sclerosis (MS). Having been advised by her GP to see a counsellor, she had little expectation that therapy would be helpful. At the first session, she described herself as unable to accept the reality of the MS, depressed, worried about how people perceived her, and often physically exhausted because she was unwilling to say 'no' to other people. Over the course of therapy, other issues emerged, such as connections between current difficulties and earlier life events and experiences, the possibility of death, issues around sexuality, and anger at the way that she was treated by some doctors. A detailed account of how these issues unfolded and were resolved in this case can be found in McLeod (2013).

PRACTICAL CHALLENGES ARISING FROM WORKING WITH THIS CLIENT GROUP

In this area of work, an essential element of practice is attention to arrangements around how therapy is conducted. People with long-term health conditions may have individual requirements that may need to be taken into account when negotiating such factors as the location of therapy and the duration of sessions. For example, Isobel, the client mentioned above, became a wheelchair user, and needed to be seen in a counselling room that was wheelchair-accessible. At points in her illness when she suffered debilitating relapses, counselling took place at her home or in a hospital ward, or was carried out by telephone. Other clients who are ill may not be able to predict whether they are well enough to attend therapy on any particular day. In some cases, clients may become too tired to continue a therapy session. For pluralistic practitioners, therefore, part of the preparation for working with this client group involves making decisions around what can be offered, in terms of flexible meeting patterns. In most situations, this kind of flexibility will be guided by the needs and preferences of individual clients. In other situations, it may be useful to build in certain arrangements from the outset, which anticipates potential client requirements. For example, in designing therapy provision for individuals with longstanding and intractable issues around irritable bowel syndrome, Guthrie (1991) offered extended first meetings, of two hours or longer, as a means of reassuring clients that the complex reality of their problems was being taken seriously.

Other practical issues are associated with questions around who provides therapy, and who is involved in therapy. In many healthcare systems, patients are only considered eligible for counselling or psychotherapy at the point where they have developed 'clinical' symptoms of anxiety or depression. This kind of procedure fails to offer support at the early stages of medical treatment. On the other hand, offering counselling to all patients at an early stage is costly, and will be viewed as unnecessary by individuals who enjoy good family or community support, or for whom the emotional 'point of impact' does not arrive until much later (Thurston, 2010). In some organisations, doctors, nurses and other health professionals may receive training and supervision in the use of counselling skills (see, e.g., Weaks, Johansen, Wilkinson, & McLeod, 2010). If this occurs, it may be possible for counsellors or psychotherapists to liaise with these front-line colleagues around ways of ensuring that service users receive the level and intensity of counselling that is most appropriate to their needs (McLeod & McLeod, 2015).

Some people with long-term health issues may require the support of carers, who may be members of their family or can be paid support workers. Attendance at counselling may only be possible with the involvement of carers, and on some occasions the primary client may wish their carer to be part of the process of counselling. In other circumstances, or at other points in therapy, clients may prefer to have an opportunity to share their feelings in a private meeting with the counsellor. In recognition of the intense demands of caring roles, it can also be valuable to consider separate counselling support for the carer (Elvish, Lever, Johnstone, Cawley, & Keady, 2013). Beyond the involvement of a specific named carer, there are some situations in which the emotional and practical issues experienced by a person with a long-term health condition have a ripple effect through their whole family network, or are exacerbated by tensions within the family. In such scenarios, it can be useful to explore the possibility of family-based work.

CASE EXAMPLE

Using a pluralistic approach to make use of cultural resources

Silvia lost her sight late in life, following surgery for what had appeared to be a minor eye complaint. As a person who lived alone, she then needed to depend on assistance from a series of paid support workers. In counselling, one of the themes that emerged was Silvia's relationships with these support workers, and the difference in her mood according to which worker has been allocated to her during that particular week. Silvia was able to use counselling to develop a better understanding of her own reactions to different carers, and to devise strategies for making the best use of this resource. Further discussion about how this topic was addressed, alongside other issues that emerged in counselling, is available in Thurston, McLeod and Thurston (2013).

TASKS AND METHODS THAT CAN CONTRIBUTE TO ENHANCED WELL-BEING IN INDIVIDUALS WITH LONG-TERM HEALTH CONDITIONS

The key principle of pluralistic counselling is that there are many things that can be helpful, and that it is therefore a good idea to ask the person what he or she thinks would make a difference to them. The willingness of the therapist to convey a genuine interest in their client's experience, and their knowledge of what has been or might be helpful, is a crucial strategy in its own right. At the point of first involvement in counselling, it may be that a person with a long-term health condition has been immersed in medical and biological explanations and conversation around their problem, and has been engaged in a search for medical solutions. It may also be the case that he or she has a sense of being crushed or overwhelmed by the immensity of what has befallen them. In such a situation, an invitation to engage in a conversation around goals and tasks may provide a structure that allows the person to see that there may be some possible ways to begin to move forward again in their life.

Typical therapeutic tasks that arise in counselling for health issues

The list of generic counselling tasks outlined in Cooper and McLeod (2011) encompasses many different types of therapeutic activity, ranging from general exploratory conversation through to more tightly focused decision-making and behaviour-change initiatives. In working with a particular client group, such as people with health issues, it is helpful to develop a list of therapeutic tasks that are specific to that group. Such a list should not be used in a prescriptive way, but instead serves as a means of sensitising the therapist to issues that may be relevant.

In working with clients who have long-term health conditions, typical therapeutic tasks may include:

- telling the story of what happened (having time and space to reflect on events);
- expressing and coming to terms with difficult emotions (fear, despair, hopelessness);
- exploring identity issues (Who am I now?);
- examining and challenging negative self concepts (being a burden, being useless);
- negotiating roles and relationships (How do I ask for help? What is my role in the family now that I am no longer the breadwinner?);
- coming to terms with the experience of pain, or the possibility of death;
- developing strategies for dealing with healthcare professionals, and the healthcare system;
- identifying and using cultural resources (local groups, carers, relationships, religion).

Examples of how these tasks can emerge within therapy for people living with different types of long-term health condition can be found in studies by McLeod (2013), Thurston et al. (2013), and Weaks, McLeod and Wilkinson (2006).

The therapeutic relationship

For many clients with long-term health conditions, the relationship with their counsellor may have a healing capacity. In an interview-based study of experiences of counselling in people with cancer, MacCormack et al. (2001) found that the theme that was mentioned most often was that the counsellor was 'someone who cared'. At a point in life when a person could easily see himself or herself as worthless and a burden, or as little more than a 'diagnosis', there is a lot to be said for knowing that there is someone who cares. This relationship can also become a reference point and resource in everyday life, as the client comes to use it to anticipate and prepare him or herself for difficult upcoming events, or to debrief following such events.

A collaborative stance, a capacity to break big unmanageable challenges into smaller do-able chunks, and a willingness to offer a caring relationship, are essential general elements of pluralistic counselling. A further generic aspect of therapy is *time*. There are several ways in which time can have a powerful impact on clients who are struggling to cope with states of ill health. The health professionals with whom they are in contact may not be able to offer them enough time to talk, because of pressure of work. Members of their family, or friends, may be willing to spend time doing things, such as driving them to the shops, but less willing to take time to listen, because what needs to be said is hard for them to hear. Compared to these experiences, even short-term counselling allows enough time to talk about significant and painful issues. Another way in which time has a meaning is if counselling continues long enough for the therapist to accompany the person through phases of relapse or crisis. An additional way in which time can be helpful is through providing some structure to a day, or even a week.

THERAPEUTIC METHODS AND INTERVENTIONS

There are many specific activities or methods that are used within counselling sessions that can make a difference to someone with a long-term health condition. For reasons of space, within this chapter it is possible to describe only a selection from the many methods and activities that have been found to be effective in this field of work.

Talking

Providing an opportunity to talk and express feelings can be facilitative in a number of ways. Living with a serious health condition is often associated with worry and rumination. Telling one's story, to a counsellor, offers a means of externalising these recurring thoughts, and reflecting on what they mean and what can be done. Within such a conversation, the client and counsellor can engage in a collaborative effort to understand and 'get a handle' on what is happening for the person. Appropriate use of counselling skills, such as reflecting emotional themes, challenging contradictions and inviting consideration of the implicit meaning of images and metaphors, can enable the person to talk in more depth than would be possible with family members or health workers. Further exploration of the ways in which 'just talking' can be helpful, can be found in McLeod and McLeod (2011).

Writing

There are many situations in counselling where it can be valuable to invite a client to write about his or her experiences and feelings around their illness, or in relation to underlying pre-existing issues (such as loss, trauma or abuse) that are re-awakened by the stress of living with a long-term health condition. Clients may find it helpful to keep a diary or journal, write in a focused way about specific events and episodes, or write 'unsent' letters to key people in their lives. The work of James Pennebaker is a particularly useful resource, in combining creative ideas about different writing styles, along with research that analyses how and why writing can have significant health benefits (Pennebaker & Evans, 2014).

Reading

The experience of illness is frequently accompanied by an effort to understand the impact and implications of the condition, as a means of re-establishing some degree of control over one's life. Reading can also enable a person to realise that they are not alone in their suffering, which in turn can encourage them to reach out to other people. There are many fictional, autobiographical and research-based accounts of the experience of illness that offer useful perspectives. There are also many self-help texts and workbooks that offer practical guidance on how to cope with various illnesses, or with depression, anxiety, low self-esteem and other consequences of such conditions.

CASE EXAMPLE
Exploring existential issues

Donald had received a health scare when he suddenly collapsed with a brain haemorrhage, and was then told that he would need to be monitored on a regular basis for the rest of his life, as well as taking medication. Although he was soon able to resume many of his work and family activities, Donald continued to worry, and sought help from a counsellor. At the beginning of therapy, he was mainly interested in acquiring anxiety management techniques, and renegotiating his relationship with family members. In later sessions, Donald began to identify a different set of therapeutic tasks. More and more, he found himself wanting to talk about what death might mean, and how he could make sense of it. On the suggestion of his therapist, he started to read some of the work of Irving Yalom, and found that his book on mortality (Yalom, 2008) was extremely helpful in allowing him to gain a deeper perspective on this topic.

Assertiveness skills

A common theme in counselling with people who have health issues concerns the difficult task of asking other people for help and information. A person who is ill may lack energy or confidence in respect of standing up for their rights and wants. There can also be a sense of being dependent and grateful for the help and assistance that is already offered by others. Nevertheless, there may well be occasions when a person who is unwell does need to be assertive, for example when their doctor is not listening to them, or a family member is ignoring their disability or fatigue level. The social skills, CBT and assertiveness training literature includes a wealth of ideas about how to support clients to be clearer and more forceful in negotiation with others. Typically, these strategies involve looking closely at how the person currently deals with such situations, then brainstorming and rehearsing alternative responses. These new responses are then tried out in everyday life, in the form of carefully constructed homework exercises. The outcomes of these new initiatives are then reviewed at the next counselling session.

Stress management techniques

Living with a long-term health condition can be highly stressful. It can be hard to predict how well one will function from one day to the next. Everyday tasks may become problematic. There may be background concerns about possible relapse or deterioration. Counselling interventions around stress management can therefore play a key role in counselling with such clients. Examples of relevant methods that can be used include cognitive interventions designed to reduce negative self-attributions, and various forms of relaxation and breathing training.

Cultural resources

The pluralistic tradition in counselling places a strong emphasis on the likelihood that clients will have knowledge and access to cultural resources that can contribute to the alleviation of life difficulties (Cooper & McLeod, 2011). Often, the most valuable cultural resources consist of activities that the person has utilised at earlier stages in their life, but has allowed to lapse. These can be quite simple things. For example, low mood and social isolation can be reduced or transformed by walking in a park and meeting other people, or by finding opportunities to join with others in singing songs. In addition to these personal accomplishments, there are also many self-help groups and internet sites that have been developed specifically for people with health issues (Adamsen, 2002). In counselling, clients can be encouraged to identify cultural resources that may be relevant to them, and then supported through the process of engaging with these activities.

When using a pluralistic approach, it is important to make sure that methods and interventions are linked to therapeutic tasks, and ultimately to the client's goals. Routine use of process and outcome feedback tools, and therapeutic communication, also play a key role in ensuring that therapeutic activities are tailored to the needs and preference of the client at different points in therapy.

THERAPIST ISSUES AND SELF-AWARENESS

Pluralistic counselling and psychotherapy is not merely a set of guidelines for working collaboratively and responsively with clients. Being a pluralistic therapist also involves being open to learning from clients. There are two main ways in which this commitment to learning with and from clients takes a key role in counselling for long-term health conditions. It is important for counsellors to possess a sufficient level of knowledge about the health condition(s) of their client, or to be willing to acquire such knowledge. This does not mean that counsellors need to be experts, or to have backgrounds in nursing or other health professions. What is necessary is for the counsellor to be able to join the client in conversations about their illness or health condition, at a level that is meaningful for that client. Qualitative research studies on patient experiences of specific illnesses offer a useful entry-point to relevant knowledge. Typically, such articles include a succinct summary of the main medical characteristics of the condition, before moving on to explore the personal experience of individuals.

Another significant dimension of therapist self-awareness is concerned with the therapist's attitude to illness. On the whole, people do not readily talk about such matters as their fear of cancer or dementia, or death, or their sense of what it would be like to depend on another to fulfil everyday needs. Yet, most people will have minimally processed childhood experiences of witnessing illness in family members, or hearing stories about such events. From a psychodynamic perspective, such experiences provide a basis for powerful unconscious countertransference responses to clients who have serious health issues. This factor means that it is necessary for therapists who work with such clients to be willing to make appropriate use of personal therapy, supervision and consultation with colleagues.

SUMMARY

Research has found that the experience of living with a long-term health condition is associated with psychological symptoms and distress, exhibited as anxiety and depression, in a significant proportion of patients. However, there are major individual differences in relation to the stage at which these effects occur, and the specific pattern of difficulties that is expressed. A pluralistic perspective provides a means of responding flexibly to the diversity of client needs.

- Practical issues around location and timing of therapy, and collaborative involvement of carers and other professionals, represent important topics for exploration with this group of clients.
- The collaborative structure adopted within pluralistic therapy provides a valuable framework for establishing an alliance with the client, managing distress and conveying hope.

- There exists a wide range of techniques and methods that can be helpful in work with clients with long-term health conditions.
- The emotional intensity of this kind of work means that it is essential for counsellors and psychotherapists to make effective use of supervision and consultative support.

EXERCISES/POINTS FOR REFLECTION

1. What is your own experience of having a health problem, or receiving a health intervention that was uncomfortable, painful, embarrassing or life-limiting in some way? In what ways have these experiences enabled you to be open to the stories of clients with long-term conditions? In what ways might your own experiences lead you to be reluctant to hear certain stories?
2. A client, with whom you have a good therapeutic relationship, tells you that he cannot cope with what lies ahead, at a later stage of his illness, and has started to make enquiries about assisted suicide. How do you respond?

FURTHER READING

Farber, E.W. (2009). Existentially informed HIV-related psychotherapy. *Psychotherapy Theory, Research, Practice, Training*, 46, 336–349. A powerful account of the value of exploring existential themes in health-related counselling.

Frank, A. (1995). *The wounded storyteller: body, illness, and ethics*. Chicago: The University of Chicago Press. A hugely influential book that explores the ways in which receiving a diagnosis produces a fundamental shift in personal identity and the story one tells about oneself.

Healthtalk.org (www.healthtalk.org). Invaluable website that gives access to video interviews with patients with a wide range of conditions, talking about the meaning of their illness and what it has meant for their lives.

McLeod, J. (2013). Process and outcome in pluralistic Transactional Analysis counselling for long-term health conditions: a case series. *Counselling and Psychotherapy Research*, 13, 32–43. Detailed case analysis of pluralistic counselling with three clients with different long-term health conditions.

Nichols, K. (2003). *Psychological care for ill and injured people: a clinical guide*. Maidenhead: Open University Press. A classic text – provides an overview of all aspects of this area of work.

Ogden, J. (2012). *Health psychology: a textbook* (5th ed.). Maidenhead: Open University Press. This book offers a comprehensive introduction to the health psychology literature – a valuable source of ideas and evidence for counsellors working with long-term health conditions.

Qualitative Health Research. The leading journal for qualitative research into the lived experience of health care.

REFERENCES

Adamsen, L. (2002). From victim to agent: the clinical and social significance of self-help group participation for people with life-threatening diseases. *Scandinavian Journal of Caring Sciences, 16*, 224–231.

Burmedi, D., Becker, S., Heyl, V., Wahl, H.-W., & Himmelsbach, I. (2002). Emotional and social consequences of age related low vision: a narrative review. *Visual Impairment Research, 4*, 44–71.

Cooper, M., & McLeod, J. (2011). *Pluralistic counselling and psychotherapy.* London: Sage.

Creed, F., Hennington, P., & Fink, P. (Eds.). (2011). *Medically unexplained symptoms, somatisation and bodily distress: developing better clinical services.* Cambridge: Cambridge University Press.

DOH. (2012). *Long term conditions compendium of information* (3rd ed.). Leeds: Department of Health.

Elvish, R., Lever, S., Johnstone, J., Cawley, R., & Keady, J. (2013). Psychological interventions for carers of people with dementia: a systematic review of quantitative and qualitative evidence. *Counselling and Psychotherapy Research, 13*, 106–125.

Equality Act. (2010). London: HM Government.

Gilbert, P. (2002). Understanding the biopsychosocial approach: conceptualization. *Clinical Psychology, 14*, 13–17.

Guthrie, E. (1991). Brief psychotherapy in patients with refractory irritable bowel syndrome. *British Journal of Psychotherapy, 8*, 175–188.

MacCormack, T., Simonian, J., Lim, J., Remond, L, Roets, D., Dunn, S., & Butow, P. (2001). 'Someone who cares': a qualitative investigation of cancer patients' experiences of psychotherapy. *Psycho-Oncology, 10*, 52–65.

McLeod, J. (2013). Transactional Analysis psychotherapy with a woman suffering from multiple sclerosis: a systematic case study. *Transactional Analysis Journal, 43*, 212–223.

McLeod, J., & McLeod, J. (2011). *Counselling skills: a practical guide for counsellors and helping professionals.* Maidenhead: Open University Press.

McLeod, J., & McLeod, J. (2015). Research on embedded counselling: an emerging topic of potential importance for the future of counselling psychology. *Counselling Psychology Quarterly, 28*, 27–43.

Mulley, A., Trimble, C., & Elwyn, G. (2012). *Patients' preferences matter: stop the silent misdiagnosis.* London: The King's Fund.

Nyman, S.R., Dibb, B., Victor, C.R., & Gosney, M.A. (2012). Emotional well-being and adjustment to vision loss in later life: a meta-synthesis of qualitative studies. *Disability and Rehabilitation, 34*, 971–981.

Omylinska-Thurston, J., & Cooper, M. (2014). Helpful processes in psychological therapy for patients with primary cancers: a qualitative interview study. *Counselling and Psychotherapy Research, 14*, 84–92.

Pennebaker, J.W., & Evans, J.F. (2014). *Expressive writing: words that heal.* Enumclaw, WA: Idyll Arbor.

Robertson, S.M., Stanley, M.A., Cully, J.A., & Naik, D. (2012). Positive emotional health and diabetes care: concepts, measurement, and clinical implications. *Psychosomatics, 53,* 1–12.

Thurston, M. (2010). An inquiry into the emotional impact of sight loss and the counselling experiences and needs of blind and partially sighted people. *Counselling and Psychotherapy Research, 10,* 3–12.

Thurston, M., McLeod, J., & Thurston, A. (2013). Counselling for sight loss: using systematic case study research to build a client informed practice model. *British Journal of Visual Impairment, 31,* 102–122.

Weaks, D., Johansen, R., Wilkinson, H., & McLeod, J. (2010). Training nurses to deliver post-diagnostic dementia support. *Healthcare Counselling and Psychotherapy Journal, 10*(3), 26–31.

Weaks, D., McLeod, J., & Wilkinson, H. (2006). Dementia. *Therapy Today, 17*(3), 12–15.

Yalom, I. (2008). *Staring at the sun: being at peace with your own mortality: overcoming the terror of death.* London: Piatkus.

21
Helping Clients Who are Suicidal or Self-Injuring

Andrew Reeves

THIS CHAPTER DISCUSSES

- What we mean by the terms suicide and self-injury
- How therapist concerns about suicide and self-injury can negatively shape the therapeutic alliance
- How a pluralistic approach can contribute to a collaborative position around risk between therapist and client
- How a pluralistic approach can help the client develop resilience and capacity to take responsibility for their own well-being and safety
- Several interventions that may be of benefit to clients who are suicidal or who are self-injuring

INTRODUCTION

Clients who present with suicidal thoughts, or with self-harm, are not uncommon in therapy settings. Such situations present therapists with a number of difficult challenges to consider in their work, including: the expectations of the working context; personal responses; contractual challenges; and ultimately deciding whether or not the situation is safely containable to continue with the therapy, or to refer to more specialist services for assessment. The nuances in the management of risk situations can often detract from the therapy itself, with the client's experiences and behaviour taking a back-seat to the management of procedural expectations.

However, it is important the therapist does not lose sight of the therapeutic relationship in the face of suicide risk, or of self-injury, so as to ensure therapy remains a viable and trusted option for the client. The disclosure of suicidal thoughts or self-harm by the client can often be accompanied with a great sense of shame or embarrassment, and it is easy for the therapist to lose sight of the intrapersonal dynamic when balancing the needs of a seemingly endless number of considerations. Additionally, the therapist can easily be drawn into 'changing' the client, as a mechanism of coping with their own anxiety, rather than facilitating a process whereby the client takes ownership of their own change process. From a pluralistic position our aim instead should always be to check with the client as to the meaning they attribute to change and how, if change is experienced positively, they can bring about further change using their knowledge and experience as resources.

The purpose of this chapter is to consider how we might use a pluralistic understanding of therapy to help maintain focus on the therapeutic alliance, and how a pluralistic approach can make an important contribution to the well-being and safety of the client.

DEFINITIONS AND PREVALENCE

Definitions

De Leo, Burgis, Bertolote, Kerkof and Bille-Brahe (2006: 12) define suicide as, 'an act with fatal outcome, which the deceased, knowing or expecting a potentially fatal outcome, has initiated and carried out with a purpose of bringing about wanted changes'. Defining self-harm is a little more complex in that it takes into account a number of different behaviours and actions with different levels of immediacy of impact. The National Institute for Health and Clinical Excellence (NICE, 2011: 3) states that self-harm is: '*any act of self-poisoning or self-injury carried out by an individual irrespective or motivation. This commonly involves self-poisoning with medication or self-injury by cutting.*' Self-injury includes behaviours with direct and immediate consequence, such as cutting, burning, banging, ingesting dangerous substances (including medication), while self-harm includes behaviours with indirect and deferred consequence, such as over-exercise, eating disorders, smoking, alcohol and drug use, and sexual risk-taking.

Current challenges in practice

There is extensive evidence (Leenaars, 2004) that speaks of high levels of anxiety therapists can experience when working with higher levels of risk, including anger, feelings of incompetence, professional impotence, fear and anxiety. Some evidence points to the level of trauma therapists can experience not only following the death of a client through suicide, but also in ongoing work with suicidal clients (Fox & Cooper, 1998). The same can be true for working with self-harm. It seems that a threat to the integrity of the client's well-being can be strongly paralleled in that of the therapist. Other challenges can include: therapist personal perspectives and responses; organisational policy; viable alternative support options; and the current evidence base that informs practice.

- **Therapist personal perspectives and responses:** the personal impact on the therapist of working with suicide risk and self-injury can have a profound impact on the nature of the therapeutic relationship, if not acknowledged.
- **Organisational policy:** therapists need to be aware of and adhere to any organisational policy in place to inform work with clients at risk of suicide or self-injury. These can be consistent with the therapist's own views or, instead, present ways of thinking or working inconsistent with the therapist's perspective.
- **Viable alternative support options:** the temptation might be to continue to work with clients at risk beyond the competency of the therapist given a lack of alternative referral options, or difficulties accessing high-demand specialist services.
- **The evidence base:** the evidence base tends to focus on demographic information (the 'who' of risk), rather than a range of viable therapeutic interventions beyond cognitive behaviour therapy (CBT).

WORKING PLURALISTICALLY WITH SUICIDE POTENTIAL AND SELF-INJURY

One of the challenges faced by therapists in working with clients who present with suicide potential and self-injury is that the imperative of risk assessment sits heavily on their shoulders and, as a consequence, can pose a danger of moving them away from a relational process with their client (Leenaars, 2004). That is, therapists, alongside other mental health workers, are expected to draw on the principles of risk assessment to determine the likelihood of the client acting on their suicidal thoughts, or of their self-injury becoming life-threatening. The primary purpose of risk assessment is to identify those factors that make harm more likely (risk), those factors that make harm less likely (protective) and reach a conclusion as to the best course of action. Consider Tom:

CASE EXAMPLE
Tom

Tom is 27 years old. He has experienced a breakdown in his relationship and has little social support. He lives alone with no contact with his family. He is quite depressed, has been prescribed anti-depressants, but also drinks heavily at times and uses recreational drugs to cope with his feelings but has started to attend a support group for his alcohol use. In the past he used to cut himself, but has not done this for three years. He is unemployed. He has come to therapy with a wish to change several factors in his life, however he also talks about sometimes 'wanting to go to sleep and not wake up', when his problems feel overwhelming.

How are we to respond to Tom? There are several risk factors identified here:

- Male
- Age
- Relationship breakdown
- Little social support
- Lives alone
- No family support
- Access to means of suicide (anti-depressants)
- Use of alcohol (self-harm)
- Use of drugs (self-harm)
- Previous self-injury (cutting)
- Unemployment
- Expressed suicidal ideation

There are also a small number of protective factors:

- Attending a support group
- Self-referral for therapy
- Wanting to change things for the better
- Early evidence of a therapeutic alliance

Purely on risk assessment terms, we have a dilemma: there are more risk factors than protective factors, thus suggesting that Tom is at risk of acting on his suicidal thoughts. Further exploration would be needed to try to determine the intensity or degree of factors to evaluate their weighting in terms of risk. However, given Tom's willingness to engage in therapy and evidence of him trying to change things in his life we might be minded to respect the confidentiality of the relationship and work with him, rather than refer him on to other services.

The basic principles of risk assessment, as applied here, are helpful to a point but much more needs to be done. There is a tendency in practice to take on a responsibility *for* our clients, rather than a responsibility *to* our clients. Unless our clients permanently or temporarily lack capacity to make informed decisions for themselves, we can only ever be responsible to them; we cannot control what happens outside the therapy room. Increasingly this approach to working with risk is taking the predominance in practice, particularly in organisational settings that might be risk-averse, where the belief that an application of 'science' can help predict human behaviour. Risk assessment is an important starting point, but is insufficient if it is the end point too.

Responding to risk: a shared process

An unavoidable truth is that it is not us, as therapists, that will keep our clients safe, but rather it will be the client (unless the client is not in a position to make informed decisions). Our contact with clients at risk of suicide or self-injury is a difficult juxtaposition of two realities: we have contact for only 40, 50 or 60 minutes for example, and can therefore influence so little; however, in that space we have the potential to help the client change so much. Collaboration around risk is therefore less of a theoretical nicety, but rather about life and death (if that does not sound too dramatic). The pluralistic frame in this context, therefore, provides an important philosophical and theoretical model through which we might begin to structure our work around suicide and self-injury in that it promotes the principle of collaboration and shared responsibility around the risk of suicide. The client is positioned within a pluralistic approach as an active participant in the therapeutic process, rather than the therapist 'doing to' the client from a risk management perspective. Fundamentally, the client is helped to identify what might work for them and, in doing so, helped to take responsibility for their own process of change. While there will be several aims to consider in working with suicide risk and self-injury, from a pluralistic position we might draw usefully on three:

- To work collaboratively with the client to help reduce the potential for harm
- Helping the client who is suicidal or self-injuring 'position' themselves differently in relation to their harmful experience
- Drawing on the client's interpersonal *and* intrapersonal resources for self-support at times of greater risk

To work collaboratively with the client to help reduce the potential for harm

If we begin with the process of risk assessment, that then leads us into the next process of risk exploration, which perhaps is more attuned to our work as therapists. While demographic information helps inform our thinking, it is the explorative process where we are brave enough to talk to our clients about their fears, thoughts, ideas, anxieties, feelings and behaviours around suicide and self-injury that will transform our thinking into the three-dimensional, from the two-dimensional. I use the word 'brave' here deliberately, in that my own research (Reeves, 2013; Reeves, Bowl, Wheeler, & Guthrie, 2004) pointed to reluctance by therapists to talk with their clients about suicidal thinking and self-injury, very likely because of their own feelings of anxiety and fear. Consider two brief narratives with Tom:

Talking with Tom about harm (1)

Tom: Sometimes it all just feels so rubbish. I step back from my life and think ... well ... what is left. Really?! Honestly, sometimes it just feels so hopeless, like overwhelming.

Therapist: You feel overwhelmed by what you see as rubbish – like you cannot see anything of value?

(Continued)

(Continued)

Tom:	There is nothing of value. Sometimes I think I want to just go to sleep and ... well ... you know.
Therapist:	Go to sleep and ...?
Tom:	Sort of go to sleep and not wake up – then it all goes away, all the crap and the rubbish and the feelings. All gone.
Therapist:	It would be a way to deal with all of this.
Tom:	Yes. All gone.
Therapist:	It sounds really hard for you to feel all this is rubbish.
Tom:	Yeah, really hard.
Therapist:	Hopefully counselling might help to make it not feel so rubbish? Maybe there is some hope too?
Tom:	OK. Maybe. I don't know to be honest.

In this scenario Tom alludes to his wish to die as a means of dealing with what feels overwhelming. The therapist begins to engage with this dialogue, but then moves away from it and instead focuses on the potential for change. While holding hope for a client at risk can be profoundly important, including the chance that therapy might help, it might be that Tom could go away from this session with the view that it is not OK to talk about his feelings of wanting to be dead. What if the therapist was brave enough to 'go there'?

Talking with Tom about harm (2)

Tom:	Sometimes it all just feels so rubbish. I step back from my life and think ... well ... what is left. Really?! Honestly, sometimes it just feels so hopeless, like overwhelming.
Therapist:	You feel overwhelmed by what you see as rubbish – like you cannot see anything of value?
Tom:	There is nothing of value. Sometimes I think I want to just go to sleep and ... well ... you know.
Therapist:	Go to sleep and ...?
Tom:	Sort of go to sleep and not wake up – then it all goes away, all the crap and the rubbish and the feelings. All gone.
Therapist:	Can you tell me a bit more about that feeling Tom? That feeling of not wanting to wake up?
Tom:	I don't know what it would be like. It frightens me in some ways but helps in others ... y'know, not being around any more.
Therapist:	The feeling of not being around – of not being alive – is frightening and also soothing? Like it helps you feel calmer as well.
Tom:	[*crying*] – I don't feel there is anyone there for me. It's like it would be a way of taking care of myself.

> *Therapist:* You feel really alone, Tom. I can really feel how overwhelming this might be for you. You're left at times with not wanting to be here any more. Tom, I wonder how you have managed to not end your life? What has kept you going?
>
> *Tom:* [*pause*] … I don't think I really want to die. When you say 'end your life' it really brings home what it means. I don't think I want that, but I don't really know how to live either.

Several things have been achieved through this dialogue:

- The therapist has a clearer sense of what Tom means by 'going to sleep and not waking up'.
- Tom has a clearer sense of what that means too.
- The therapist has communicated to Tom that talking about his suicidal feelings is OK, that the therapist can 'hear' it.
- The degree of suicidal intent has been more openly explored and understood by both.
- The information gained in considering risk and protective factors has become more meaningful.
- A foundation has been laid for both of them to begin to consider alternative ways for self-support.

So often in work with suicide potential and self-injury the therapist, often as a consequence of their own anxiety, will either disconnect from the client's feelings that relate to risk (as illustrated in the first transcript) or will begin to take all the responsibility for the client's well-being. The imperative of risk 'management' – where the therapist works to ensure the client's safety – can feel onerous. Working pluralistically provides the opportunity to talk with the client about what works for them and how they might make use of a variety of approaches through which they can begin to take responsibility for their own safety.

Helping the client who is suicidal or self-injuring 'position' themselves differently in relation to their harmful experience

The second dialogue above has begun to highlight how Tom 'positions' himself in relation to his suicidal thoughts: what the thoughts might mean for him experientially and practically. When working pluralistically with suicide risk or self-injury it is essential that the client is helped to consider their relationship with their own harm as, in doing so, they are then facilitated to begin to think about what might help them at times of crisis. Put simply, a therapist might draw on ideas or approaches they think will help the client, such as writing down a list of support options in a crisis plan, but unless the client has been helped to consider the strategies that work for them, and thus take ownership over their own crisis self-support, the danger is that the client's own agency for change will be bypassed and the client remains in a passive, and potentially risky, position.

> ### Talking with Tom about harm (3)
>
> *Therapist:* You don't want to die, but you don't know how to live either. Sounds like being caught between a rock and a hard place [*Tom laughs*]. What are you thinking as we're talking?
>
> *Tom:* I think that sounds about right [*laughs again*]. No, I don't want to die but I do feel desperate.
>
> *Therapist:* How does that feel when you say 'I don't want to die'?
>
> *Tom:* It feels kinda alright, y'know. It feels a bit stronger.
>
> *Therapist:* It feels a bit stronger?
>
> *Tom:* I do. Maybe I feel a bit stronger.
>
> *Therapist:* So let's start to think about ways in which you might support yourself with these feelings. Can you talk about how you have managed to not hurt yourself? You haven't cut yourself for nearly three years and, even though you want to go to sleep and not wake up, you have managed to cope with these feelings. What has worked for you Tom?

In the third section, Tom has been helped to move from a position where his thoughts are vague, frightening, soothing, but, to a degree, sit outside his awareness and control, to a point where he feels much clearer and stronger in relation to them. This is both an important therapeutic shift, but also one that helps him begin to help himself. Previously, and commonly, people can feel overwhelmed by their suicidal thinking and can struggle to imagine it being any different. Clarity and strength provides Tom with a much stronger base from which he might begin to self-support. From a pluralistic perspective, Tom's therapist has helped Tom not only to begin to re-think his relationship with his suicidal thinking, but then moves on to asking Tom what has helped. There may be many things that work for Tom and it is important to help him think more carefully about those, so that they can be incorporated into the therapeutic process.

HELPFUL APPROACHES TO SUICIDE RISK AND SELF-INJURY

Developing a therapeutic approach when working with clients who are suicidal, or who are self-injuring, needs to focus on work they can do in the therapy room, things they can do outside the therapy room and, fundamentally, how they will keep themselves safe during that process. An exploration of risk needs always to be collaborative and engaging of the client's own resources. While at times of crisis clients may well need a greater degree of containment to help keep themselves safe, therapy needs to be defined by the client's goals, tasks and the therapeutic approaches that might facilitate them. Thinking of the latter point here, I will offer three different approaches that might be useful to clients: a cognitive behavioural approach, a narrative approach and the development of a crisis, or 'keep safe' plan.

A cognitive behavioural approach

Approaches based on cognitive behaviour therapy (CBT) can be very useful in helping clients to change behavioural patterns and ways of thinking about their problems. With specific reference to suicidal thoughts or self-injury, CBT can help clients to consider:

1. The **triggers** for harmful feelings (events, feelings, situations).
2. How feelings **build** and **develop** toward harming.
3. What happens at the **moment of crisis** (when suicidal feelings are overwhelming, or they self-injure).
4. How clients **feel post-harm** (such as relief, shame).
5. How clients **move on** thereafter and what their **internal narrative** is about what they have experienced.

In re-visiting these five stages with clients, it is helpful to then consider alternative choices, to help break the cycles that shape and influence at points of crisis:

1. Knowing the triggers and developing strategies for self-care at these points.
2. Increasing self-awareness (emotionally and physically) during the build-up of feelings, using strategies such as mindfulness, etc.
3. Providing information regarding alternatives to harmful feelings (such as alternative to self-injury information, which can be freely download from organisations such as MIND, or the Royal College of Psychiatrists).
4. Ensuring clients adopt good self-care strategies during, and immediately after, crisis points (e.g., such as ensuring injuries are cared for and given appropriate attention, which can be used as a wider metaphor for self-care).
5. Re-structuring internal narratives so that they are more self-respectful and self-compassionate, informed by an understanding of the cycle of behaviour.

This form of CBT draws on a number of perspectives, including: attention to thinking patterns; increasing emotional and physical sensation; mindfulness; behavioural changes; self-care; compassion-based approaches; and attention to the client's self-dialogue.

It is worth noting that, for some clients, a specific focus on their 'behaviour' of self-injury will be rejected, instead wanting to focus on the factors in their life they consider to be the cause of their distress. This is an interesting point, in that it tends to be others (such as family, friends, professional 'helpers', etc.) who tend to be more worried about self-injury than the client themselves, who instinctively sees it as a symptom of distress rather than the primary problem. Ensuring therapy remains focused on the goals and tasks of therapy, as defined by the client, is important.

A narrative approach to working with suicide risk and self-injury

Hill and Dallos (2011) developed some interesting ideas with young people in helping them identify and frame a narrative around their self-injuring behaviour. Space does not allow for a full consideration here, but the authors argued for the importance of helping the client to tell their story about the *meaning* of their self-injury, without judgement or pathology, to facilitate a deep understanding and, importantly, to find expression for the anger the authors believed often sat behind the behaviour. This, they believed, provided for an important opportunity for clients to reintegrate previous traumatic experiences with their current sense of self and, in doing so, equipped them to make positive change.

The work of Hill and Dallos is equally transferable to suicide potential. As I have discussed in this chapter, the temptation can be for therapists to move into risk *management*, and run the risk of moving away from the goals of therapy as defined by the client. The client's relationship with their own self-harming thoughts, feelings and experiences needs to be carefully explored so that the client can find a narrative – a personal account – of what their suicidal feelings or self-injurious behaviours are communicating.

Developing a crisis, or 'keep safe' plan

With the shift that has occurred for Tom, important therapeutic opportunities have emerged to explore. However, Tom's safety should not be overlooked as his thoughts might continue to be overwhelming and frightening when on his own. Drawing on Tom's resources is important in helping him to begin to manage his own feelings – his own level of risk – and, as such, perhaps make the other changes he is hoping for. This can be achieved through the therapeutic dialogue, and can be adjusted for different clients at different times (such as age and understanding of the process).

It may be tempting to assume that simply because strategy 'A' worked for a previous client it will inevitably and always work for subsequent clients. Pluralistic working is about drawing on the client's own experience, perspective and expertise to help determine the nature and shape of therapy. In relation to suicide risk and self-injury, a pluralistic approach should aim to help the client engage with the concept of self-support, particularly at times of crisis, so they can keep themselves safe.

Writing down some of the key points can be drawn together into a 'keep safe plan', or 'crisis plan'. This is a written plan the client can take away to use as a resource to help manage suicide potential. This is different to 'no harm' contracts, which focus more on the client making promises not to harm themselves. Some have suggested these can be emotionally coercive, can introduce the potential for a therapeutic fracture if the client is not able to keep to the 'promise', and are often more about the therapist's reassurance (Buelow & Range, 2001).

Important elements of a keep-safe plan might include (Reeves, 2015: 53–4):

- The actual risk being considered (e.g., thoughts of taking an overdose)
- The times when the risks are likely to be at their highest, (e.g., at night)
- 'Red flags' the client might be aware of that could trigger such thoughts, (e.g., when they are alone)
- Factors that make the feelings worse, being as specific as possible (e.g., alcohol or drugs)
- Factors that make the feelings better, being as specific as possible, (e.g., being around people)
- Who is available to offer informal support (e.g., family, friends)
- Who is available to offer formal support (e.g., a crisis team, Accident and Emergency, a telephone helpline), and ensuring details such as telephone numbers are recorded on the plan
- What might make accessing support less likely (e.g., not wanting to wake someone up)
- What might make accessing support more likely (e.g., agreeing contact with someone in advance)
- Intrapersonal mechanisms for self-care (e.g., meditation, breathing techniques, distraction, etc.)
- A date for review (which will usually be the next session).

Such a plan can achieve several things, but for the purposes of this discussion I shall highlight two: client-directed therapy, and a mechanism for self-support and self-responsibility.

Client-directed therapy

In acknowledging there is probably no single 'right way' for all clients, the development of the crisis plan helps the client to bring into their collection of resources a range of different factors that they have been able to identify as of benefit to them. They are, in effect, creating their own toolkit, drawing on a number of different approaches and possible interventions, to help them meet their own self-determined goals and tasks of therapy.

A mechanism for self-support and self-responsibility

Following on from the point above, the crisis plan provides the client with the mechanism through which they might begin, sometimes for the first time, to build confidence in resources – both external and internal – to care for themselves. Additionally, and over time, this can help the client build capacity to take responsibility for their own well-being and safety.

EXERCISES/POINTS FOR REFLECTION

1. What are your views about the statement, 'An unavoidable truth is that it is not us, as therapists, that will keep our clients safe, but rather it will be the client'?
2. What do you consider to be the key advantages and disadvantages of working pluralistically with a suicidal client, or with someone who self-injures?
3. How might you help a suicidal or self-injuring client feel able to collaboratively engage in therapy, when they might just want you to help them feel safer?

SUMMARY

We have seen in this chapter how valuable working pluralistically with clients who may be experiencing suicidal thoughts, or who self-injure, can be. As we have explored, too much of practice with clients who present at risk is driven by individual and institutional anxiety and, as a consequence, the temptation can be to be more directive, or controlling, than is helpful (Leenaars, 2004; Reeves, 2013). A pluralistic approach allows for the therapist and client to engage in a collaborative, relational process that helps position the client so that they are best able to take responsibility for their own safety. By encouraging the client to think about what might work best for them, and to participate in directing the focus of therapy, the client may be more able to take ownership of the strategies explored and, therefore, may feel more equipped to make use of them at times of crisis. Such strategies might include: cognitive behavioural approaches; psycho-education; the development of a 'keep safe' plan; and a narrative approach to help explore the meaning behind suicidal thoughts and self-injury.

FURTHER READING

Leenaars, A.A. (2004). *Working with suicidal people: a person centred approach*. Chichester: Wiley. An evidence-based text that discusses contextual and theoretical aspects of working with suicide risk.

Reeves, A. (2010). *Counselling suicidal clients*. London: Sage. An evidence-based text that focuses specifically on therapeutic interventions with suicidal clients.

Reeves, A. (2013). *Challenges in counselling: self-harm*. London: Hodder Education. An evidence-based text that considers important therapeutic considerations with people who self-injure.

Spandler, H., & Warner, S. (2007). *Beyond fear and control: working with young people who self-harm*. Ross-on-Wye: PCCS Books. A text that draws on practice considerations for working with young people who self-injure.

REFERENCES

Buelow, G., & Range, L.M. (2001). No-suicide contracts among college students. *Death Studies, 25,* 583–592.

De Leo, D., Burgis, S., Bertolote, J.M., Kerkof, A.J., & Bille-Brahe, U. (2006). Definitions of suicidal behaviour: lessons learnt from the WHO/EURO multi-centre study. *Crisis, 27,* 4–15.

NICE (National Institute for Health and Clinical Excellence). (2011). *Self-harm: longer term management.* Clinical Guidance 133. London: Author.

Fox, R., & Cooper, M. (1998). The effects of suicide on the private practitioner: a professional and personal perspective. *Clinical Social Work Journal, 26,* 143–157.

Hill, K., & Dallos, R. (2011). Young people's stories of self-harm: a narrative study. *Clinical Child Psychology and Psychiatry,* 17, 1–17.

Leenaars, A.A. (2004). *Working with the suicidal patient: a person-centred approach.* Chichester: Wiley.

Reeves, A. (2013). *Challenges in counselling: self-harm.* London: Hodder Education.

Reeves, A. (2015). *Working with risk in counselling and psychotherapy.* London: Sage.

Reeves, A., Bowl, R., Wheeler, S., & Guthrie, E. (2004). The hardest words: exploring the dialogue of suicide in the counselling process – an exploratory study. *Counselling and Psychotherapy Research, 4,* 62–71.

PART 4
Professional Issues

22
Difference and Diversity in Pluralistic Counselling and Psychotherapy

Laura Anne Winter, Feng Guo, Katarzyna Wilk and Terry Hanley

THIS CHAPTER DISCUSSES

- What difference and diversity means within a therapeutic context
- The importance and impact of difference and diversity in therapy (both broadly and within the pluralistic framework)
- The potential problems with traditional models of counselling in relation to issues of diversity and difference
- The potential impacts diversity and difference may have on the therapeutic encounter
- The implications of diversity and difference on the various elements of pluralistic counselling practice, including the therapeutic alliance and collaboration, goals, tasks and methods

BRIEF INTRODUCTION TO DIFFERENCE AND DIVERSITY IN COUNSELLING AND PSYCHOTHERAPY

What do we mean by 'difference and diversity'?

'Diversity' simply means variety. In the context of society it refers to the fact that although as humans we are all alike in a number of ways (for example biologically, and sharing a similar environment), individuals and groups vary and differ considerably

(Thompson, 2011). This simplistic definition is considered as a starting point, as issues of diversity are necessarily bound up with power and inequality, which we reflect upon below. Society is inescapably diverse, and difference is a common experience. Difference and diversity become important considerations of counsellors and psychotherapists because counselling and psychotherapy take place within a cultural and societal context, and the individuals and groups with whom therapists work almost inevitably come from diverse social, cultural, political and economic backgrounds. This can prove both challenging and very rewarding for therapists.

In what ways do individuals and groups vary in society? Needless to say the list we could create in answer to this question could be endless, but examples include differences in:

- Gender and sex
- Sexual orientation
- Social class
- Disabilities
- Race and ethnicity
- Age
- Religious beliefs

Each of these loose categories of 'diverse' people is likely to have their own associated cultures and politics.

Definition

Diversity simply means differences that exist. On a societal level this encapsulates the idea that individuals and groups, whilst having lots of things in common, also vary and differ in lots of different ways. Diversity issues are intertwined with inequalities and power imbalances across society.

THE PLURALISTIC FRAMEWORK AND DIVERSITY AND DIFFERENCE

The pluralistic framework emphasises the centrality and importance of diversity and difference (Cooper & McLeod, 2011). The embracing of different perspectives present within the pluralistic philosophy underpinning the approach offers clear potential for putting diversity at the centre of counselling theory and practice. A prizing of diversity and difference is therefore at the heart of the pluralistic framework. All of the themes that are important to a diversity and difference perspective are vital to the pluralistic approach, and for practising pluralistic therapy.

The pluralistic framework might therefore be conceptualised as positioning itself within a broader social justice movement. This more systemic approach emphasises equality and fairness, and encourages therapists to take a holistic view of the people that they meet and work towards increasing social justice through the work that they do. Clients are viewed in their wider social and political environments rather than in isolation as individuals. As part of this, therapists are encouraged to consider the social and political factors that might go some way to explaining an individual's distress, in addition to (or instead of) individual psychological factors. Therefore a social justice approach requires counsellors to recognise the links between wellness and fairness (Prilleltensky, 2013) and to consider how their work tackles unfairness or injustice as well as focusing solely on increasing individual well-being. A social justice position is potentially challenging for therapists, because it involves a call to challenge the unjust status quo, and can involve a realisation that sometimes therapists might inadvertently promote or maintain injustices through their work.

When considered from this social justice perspective, diversity and difference becomes about recognition of power differentials, oppression and inequalities in society (Proctor, 2011). As listed above, individuals differ in lots of ways. But when we talk about diversity we are talking about differences in relation to value and status, and commonly we refer to groups who have experienced historical or current marginalisation and oppression. 'Difference' is determined by the majority cultures, those that hold the greater amount of power and resources within society (Lago, 2011). Social power allows one group of society to control another through limiting their access to resources and opportunities. Challenging the status quo means challenging the unequal distribution of social power. A diversity perspective for therapists therefore means recognising and acting to 'level the playing field' where possible in their work. How this diversity perspective might be embedded within pluralistic therapy in practice is elaborated on below.

> ### Definition
>
> *Social justice* means fairness and equality on a societal level, so that groups and individuals are given equal access to resources, opportunities and benefits.

The following case example is a relatively crude illustration of some of these potential areas of difference, and the ways in which a counsellor and a client may both be very diverse, and different from each other.

> ### CASE EXAMPLE
> #### Ishtar and John
>
> Ishtar is a woman in her forties, living in the North of England. She is originally from Syria, and came to England in 2005 with her husband and three children. She is experiencing a significant amount of distress following a recent miscarriage, has been feeling very emotional and has been struggling to look after the home and her children, which she identifies as being her full-time job. She contacted a local counselling service and has made an appointment to meet
>
> *(Continued)*

> *(Continued)*
>
> with John, who is a counsellor in his early twenties. John has lived in the North for the past 10 years, originally being from the London area. He identifies as a white, homosexual, working-class male. He lives with his partner, Dominic.

Later in the chapter we will consider the implications such diversity may have on the therapy as it progresses, with a number of different case studies.

Beyond personalisation: recognising both individual and group differences within pluralistic therapy

A diversity and difference approach shares with the pluralistic framework the need to tailor therapy to the particular client we are working with, rather than adopting an approach of 'with these clients do X' or 'with clients from this background do Y'. In addition to this, a diversity perspective also highlights the importance of people's cultures and contexts. The need to tailor therapy to the particular client remains of fundamental importance, alongside an acknowledgement that the range of goals and ways of working in therapy may be related to elements of diversity and difference. That is to say, the range of therapeutic methods which an individual from a particular social class, for example working class, may choose or find useful might overlap to a greater degree with another working-class individual than with someone from a higher social class.

A diversity and difference perspective therefore considers the idea of group differences in addition to individual differences. Multicultural counselling movements foreground the idea that individuals presenting in therapy bring with them multiple group identities that impact on the way in which they interpret life experiences and act (Ivey, D'Andrea, & Ivey, 2012). These identities are the ways in which individuals identify as members of different groups, for example groups of individuals from a particular race/ethnic background or those from a particular social class. Therefore both individual and group differences should be recognised and prized within pluralistic therapy. In the same way as clinical diagnoses may be a useful source of information if held lightly and not taken for granted, diversity and difference can then inform our therapeutic practice. The need for a dialogue about this as part of the process of therapy is therefore important. This is something that is elaborated on below.

THE IMPORTANCE AND IMPACT OF ISSUES OF DIFFERENCE AND DIVERSITY IN THERAPY

Having introduced difference and diversity in relation to therapeutic practice, we now go on to explore the importance of diversity and difference, and the impact these issues might have in therapy.

The importance of diversity in therapeutic practice

Fundamentally, the consideration and recognition of diversity and difference is important in counselling and psychotherapy for ethical reasons. On the level of professional ethics, professional bodies such as the British Psychological Society (BPS) and the British Association for Counselling and Psychotherapy (BACP), as well as their international counterparts, all make reference to the importance of respecting issues of diversity and difference in their ethical frameworks. Nevertheless, in addition to professional ethics, it can also be argued that on a moral level it is important to attend to issues of diversity and difference. One's ethnicity and race, culture, sex, age, religious beliefs and social class will all have an impact on a particular individual's identity, life story and reasons for presenting in therapy. Therefore, to ignore these issues is to ignore the uniqueness of the individual(s) that attend therapy. This is the same principle on which the pluralistic framework builds: the client is the 'common factor' in therapy, and as such the particular client's needs and goals should be taken into account in therapeutic practice, rather than reducing the client to their symptoms or potential diagnosis whilst ignoring their unique presentation.

Despite the ethical importance of attending to diversity and difference issues in therapy, traditional models of psychotherapy and counselling have been criticised for their lack of attention to these matters. Counselling itself as a process might be viewed as a very Western, white, middle-class venture. The three main theoretical schools within counselling and psychotherapy – psychodynamic, humanistic and cognitive-behavioural – have all been criticised for taking an approach that is overly focused on the individual rather than taking into account wider social and cultural forces. Thus, historically, diversity and difference issues have typically been considered as additional information rather than fundamental to how one understands the individual or group you are working with. This has led to many critiques of the therapy industry broadly which have suggested that counselling and psychotherapy only maintain the status quo, and serve to maintain the unfair social power differences we discussed above (e.g. Moloney, 2013). Having said all this, movements have been made to address diversity and difference issues within the traditional unitary models, for example the work of Proctor, Cooper, Sanders and Malcolm (2006) in person-centred counselling, and Wheeler (2006) in psychodynamic therapy. In the United States, the multi-cultural counselling and social justice movements have been named the fourth and fifth forces in counselling respectively, following on and developing the psychodynamic, humanistic and cognitive-behavioural models (Ratts, 2009).

THE IMPACT OF DIVERSITY ON THERAPEUTIC PRACTICE

One very explicit way in which issues of diversity may negatively impact upon therapy is when miscommunication or misunderstandings between the therapist and client lead to disillusionment with the therapeutic process. The reasons behind such discontent could include content orientated issues, such as an irritation that the counsellor is not understanding the depth of impact of a particular issue upon the client (e.g. religious beliefs, parental pressures, etc.), or process orientated issues (e.g. despair at the counsellor's inability to explain why they won't provide advice related to the presenting issue, which is an issue that might be heightened by an individual's cultural expectations of the therapist as 'expert'). Such an occurrence might be described as a therapeutic rupture and manifest in a multitude of ways. For instance, a client may prove confrontational towards the therapist or they may withdraw from the therapy (by not engaging in the session or by leaving it all together). Where a therapist becomes aware of such an issue, it can be incredibly helpful to engage in a dialogue around it. Taking this stance proves compatible with the way of working emphasised within the pluralistic framework and further discussions are noted in the following sections.

With the above in mind, issues of diversity and difference are likely to have some significant impact on the processes within the therapy room. Furthermore, these issues might also have an impact on the type of choices that are made regarding the commissioning of therapeutic services. The movement of 'evidence-based practice' in counselling and psychotherapy is associated with delivering standardised models of therapy which research (typically randomised controlled trials) has shown to be effective for particular problems or diagnoses to individuals who are assessed as having those problems. Individuals are therefore treated as fitting into specific boxes with others who have the same symptoms as them (and therefore should have the same treatment). One might argue then that this approach does not pay enough attention to diversity and difference, given it assumes you can prescribe a treatment for a client based on their symptoms, rather than their individual background, including reference to things like their social class, religion, ethnicity, etc. Instead, an approach led by diversity and difference would put the individual at the centre of the process, and work to tailor the therapeutic process to them. Such a more responsive approach is therefore more likely to be consistent with a pluralistic perspective.

Ishtar and John continued: The potential impact of diversity on therapeutic encounters

Ishtar found the initial meeting with John challenging. She felt unsettled by the fact that her therapist was a man, as she wondered whether he would really be able to understand her worries about looking after the home and her children.

Compare the two following scenarios:

1. John had a sense throughout the first session that Ishtar was uncomfortable. He assumed at this stage that this was due to her presenting issues, rather than any dynamics in the relationship because of their differences. As a result of this assumption, he did not voice his feelings and instead continued with his assessment.
2. John had a sense throughout the first session that Ishtar was uncomfortable. He decided to explore this sense in supervision and as a result in a subsequent meeting voiced his feelings with Ishtar. This meant that she was able to share her concerns, and they were able to come up with strategies

> for managing in therapy, such as using a greater amount of metacommunication (for example by John checking out how Ishtar had experienced things he had said and Ishtar sharing specific concerns with John about their communication in therapy).

These two possible scenarios demonstrate the difference in therapy when diversity issues are borne in mind, in contrast to when they are ignored or dismissed. When John assumed that diversity was not an issue in the therapy Ishtar was likely to have been left feeling unsettled and may have eventually disengaged from the therapy. When, instead, John was open to a discussion about diversity, Ishtar was able to process and reflect upon her unsettled feeling.

At the same time as emphasising the impact of diversity on therapeutic practice, we would argue that diversity issues are not *always* the salient issue at the heart of someone's presenting problems. In some cases, the important issue might be something that can be addressed in therapy with little or no reference to diversity issues. Indeed, it may have been the case that Ishtar did not have any concerns about the differences between her and John. The *potential* impact, however, means that diversity issues should always be considered. Therapists play an important role in offering the space to explore whether or not a particular individual feels that diversity issues are what is important for them.

THE IMPLICATIONS OF CLIENT AND THERAPIST DIFFERENCE AND DIVERSITY FOR PLURALISTIC PRACTICE

The therapeutic alliance and collaboration

The therapeutic alliance has been shown in numerous outcome studies to be the most robust predictor of positive therapeutic outcomes (Norcross, 2011) and is a core component of pluralistic practice. How is collaboration enhanced and a therapeutic relationship developed when encountering a client who is very different to yourself? Let's take the following example:

> ### CASE EXAMPLE
> #### Mariah and Claudia
>
> Mariah is a middle-aged woman in her forties who comes from South Africa and is living in the UK. Her personal identity is highly attached to her religious Christian beliefs and this shapes the way she views herself, other people and
>
> *(Continued)*

> *(Continued)*
>
> the world at large. She has begun working with a counsellor – Claudia – who is in her twenties and an atheist and does not have a great deal of knowledge about Christianity. Mariah came to counselling to help explore her unhelpful patterns and to also develop 'a closer relationship with God'. Within the first session, Mariah begins asking Claudia about her own personal beliefs, stating that it's important for her that her counsellor understands her beliefs and how this relates to her goals in therapy.

How might Claudia react to such a client from a pluralistic perspective in relation to building a positive therapeutic alliance and collaborating? Here we can already see that a core component for the client is to have the therapist understand her worldview, which is shaped by her religious beliefs. The therapist might therefore utilise one or a number of different responses, which might include:

- being reflexive and self-aware of her own biases and beliefs and communicating this to the client if appropriate – in this case, it might be useful for Claudia to reflect on her own beliefs and assumptions about Christianity and faith with the support of her supervisor or on her own
- learning about the client's religious beliefs from the client as a way to understand the client and glimpse into their world – in this case, asking questions and being curious about Mariah's identity and experience of Christianity
- identify the shared values they both hold in addition to acknowledging the differences – again, in this case this would come through open dialogue about Mariah and Claudia's religious beliefs
- metacommunication about each other's differing beliefs and how this might shape the process of therapy – in this case, talking to Mariah about the process and experience of having this conversation
- deciding collaboratively how to navigate the process of therapy given the differences and whether this would be a suitable therapeutic match – in this case, this might involve Claudia initiating a conversation about how Mariah feels about working with an atheist therapist
- considering ethical boundaries to the work, and where necessary being able to refer on appropriately.

You might be able to identify several other ways of how Claudia could establish and maintain a good therapeutic alliance with this client and how she can work collaboratively with her, given their differences. If a therapist is to adapt his or her responses to the needs of the client, then they might find that each client has their own unique needs within therapy and that means that different responses are needed with different clients. It is not uncommon to have misunderstandings between client and therapist who have different worldviews and beliefs and, as noted earlier, these may develop and create ruptures in the therapeutic relationship. Importantly, a strong alliance and communication about potential negative feelings or issues that arise in therapy are important for overcoming such ruptures (Safran, Muran, & Shaker, 2014).

Being able to communicate openly about difference and diversity with clients in relation to their needs will help to solidify mutual understanding and trust, which in turn will foster a stronger alliance.

Goals

Some challenges might arise with goal-setting when working with diverse and different clients. For some cultures that identify as more collectivist in perspective, it might be difficult to define personal goals, when there is a traditional focus on group/collectivist consensus (which can be familial, organisational, societal) over individualistic goals, which is a more Western ethnocentric point of view (Laungani, 2004). This can also reflect on a client's expectations of the therapist in relation to being more of an expert rather than a guide and wanting more concrete solution-focused advice over exploratory expression of issues (Wong, 2013). It is therefore useful to discuss a client's goals and expectations for therapy just as much as their own personal life goals.

A client's cultural background can shape their approach and expectations towards therapy. Dismissing the client's reasons for having difficulties with autonomous goal-setting in this case is unlikely to be helpful. From a pluralistic perspective then, the therapist would work with the client's expectations in a way that was meaningful *for the client* and perhaps have explored both of their views towards goal-setting in their own respective cultures. Even the pluralistic framework is just that – a framework, which can be adapted to meet the client where they are at any given moment.

Tasks and methods

How might difference and diversity affect the choice of tasks and methods a therapist might use with his/her client? The case examples below illustrate the implications diversity and difference may have on the methods used and the dialogue we might have about these. After presenting the two cases, we reflect upon the different things we can learn about tasks and methods when working with diversity in pluralistic therapy.

> ### CASE EXAMPLE
> #### Danielle and Mia
>
> Danielle is from a deprived area in the north of Manchester. She left school at 13 with no qualifications and struggles with reading and writing. Mia is a middle-class therapist who, although working in a deprived area, lives in a popular and relatively wealthy area of the city. In initiating a conversation about
>
> *(Continued)*

(Continued)

methods they might want to make use of to work on Danielle's goal of reducing her anxiety levels, Mia was aware of the dynamics that their different social classes may have on both the therapeutic relationship and the process of therapy. She had discussed this in supervision, which helped her become aware of the importance that the difference in social class may have. When discussing ideas for possible ways of working, she was aware of the potential feelings and concerns that might be raised in Danielle if they were to consider a method that involved writing (such as recording worries and monitoring any 'negative automatic thoughts'). Whilst this did not mean that she refrained from talking about this as a potential way of working, it meant that when it was discussed Mia was able to initiate a dialogue about Danielle's thoughts about that particular option and engage in metacommunication about this process. Danielle was reassured that Mia started this conversation, and was able to share that whilst she could see it was potentially a useful method, she was worried about her writing skills and how Mia, someone who was 'obviously middle class', might 'judge' her.

CASE EXAMPLE

Martin and Daniel

Martin is an 18-year-old man who identifies as bisexual, and has recently 'come out' to his family and friends. He told his heterosexual therapist, Daniel, that the goal he wanted to address in counselling was to become more comfortable with his sexuality. Through dialogue, metacommunication and collaboration, Martin and Daniel decided on various things they could do to address this goal in therapy. These fell into two categories: tasks that focused more on Martin as an individual, and tasks that addressed the wider societal issues which were present in his story. These included exploring Martin's feelings and perception of his own identity, both in relation to his sexuality and more broadly; Martin getting in touch with his local LGBT group with the support of Daniel; and role play and rehearsal in sessions of having conversations with and talking to others about his sexuality (including challenging homophobic comments by peers), which Martin could then 'test out' in behavioural experiments outside of the counselling. Daniel provided empathy and acceptance of Martin, and outside of the therapy he utilised supervision and self-supervision to reflect on his experience of his own and others' sexualities, and his heterosexual identity.

The case of Danielle and Mia shows how diversity issues will mean that some tasks and methods are potentially more appropriate than others. As discussed above, we need to consider both individual and group factors when thinking about this. Building on this, the case of Martin and Daniel demonstrates the breadth of tasks and methods that are open to pluralistic therapists when considering diversity, and the need to consider not only methods for within therapy, but also broader, social level tasks and methods in some cases.

SUMMARY

This chapter has highlighted the following key points:

- *Diversity* in society refers to the idea that individuals and groups, whilst having lots of things in common, also vary and differ in lots of different ways. Diversity issues are intertwined with inequalities and power imbalances across society.
- A social justice perspective in counselling and psychotherapy encourages us to see the individual in their context, and consider how societal issues, including issues of diversity, have impacted upon the individual.
- The pluralistic framework puts diversity at the heart of practice, and encourages us to consider both the importance of the individual and personalisation, as well as taking account of group differences.
- There are several implications of diversity and difference for pluralistic practice, including those that impact upon the therapeutic relationship, goal setting and choices around tasks and methods in therapy.
- Counsellors and psychotherapists practising pluralistic therapy can work more effectively with diversity and difference by reflecting on diversity issues in supervision, engaging in open dialogue and communication with clients about potential diversity issues, and collaborating on a range of tasks and methods both within and outside of the therapy room.

EXERCISES/POINTS FOR REFLECTION

The following exercises are designed to help you reflect on your own diversity and difference and how this impacts your understanding of yourself and the world, and how you might work from a diversity and difference perspective in your therapeutic work.

Exercise 1

Write down your:

1. Age
2. Gender
3. Sexual orientation
4. Race/ethnicity
5. Faith or religious practice (if you have one)
6. Social class
7. Disability (if applicable)

Now, notice how each of these categories of difference and diversity might influence you on both a personal and societal level:

- What kinds of perceived benefits and disadvantages can you think of for belonging to these groups of society?
- Do any of these categories feel particularly important in terms of your identity? In what way?

Exercise 2

Now following on from the first exercise, have a look at your completed list again of your own diversity factors:

- How might you perceive or relate to someone who was different from you on **every** single category of difference you listed above?
- How would you work with such a client in your therapeutic practice using the pluralistic framework? Think about the relationship, goals, tasks and methods.

FURTHER READING

Lago, C., & Smith, B. (Eds.). (2010). *Anti-discriminatory practice in counselling and psychotherapy*. London: Sage. This text explores a variety of diversity issues specifically within counselling and psychotherapy.

McLeod, J. (2013). *An introduction to counselling* (5th ed.). Maidenhead: Open University Press. Chapter 13 'Multicultural counselling' and Chapter 21 'The politics of counselling' are a useful couple of chapters in this book which focuses on diversity, difference and multiculturalism, specifically within counselling generally. They are good overviews and introductions to some of the issues in this area.

Thompson, N. (2011). *Promoting equality: working with difference and diversity* (3rd ed.). Basingstoke: Palgrave Macmillan. Whilst this isn't a text specifically for counsellors and psychotherapists, it provides food for thought about issues of equality, diversity and difference in general and gets into some of the theoretical and conceptual issues.

Resources

The American Psychological Association Multicultural Competencies: www.apa.org/pi/oema/resources/policy/multicultural-guidelines.aspx. These are useful to look at when considering competency practising from a multicultural or diversity and difference perspective as a counsellor or psychotherapist.

REFERENCES

Bachelor, A., & Horvath, A. (1999). The therapeutic relationship. In M.A. Hubble, B.L. Duncan, & S.D. Miller (Eds.), *The heart and soul of change: what works in therapy* (pp. 133–178). Washington, DC: American Psychological Association.

Cooper, M., & McLeod, J. (2011). *Pluralistic counselling and psychotherapy*. London: Sage.

Ivey, A.E., D'Andrea, M.J., & Ivey, M.B. (2012). *Theories of counseling and psychotherapy: a multicultural perspective*. Thousand Oaks, CA: Sage.

Lago, C. (2011). Diversity, oppression, and society: Implications for person-centered therapists. *Person-Centered & Experiential Psychotherapies*, *10*(4), 235–247.

Laungani, P. (2004). *Asian perspectives in counselling and psychotherapy.* Hove and New York: Brunner–Routledge.

Moloney, P. (2013). *The therapy industry: the irresistible risk of the talking cure, and why it doesn't work.* London: Pluto Press.

Norcross, J.C. (Ed.). (2011). *Psychotherapy relationships that work: evidence-based responsiveness.* New York: Oxford University Press.

Presnell, A., Harris, G., & Scogin, F. (2012). Therapist and client race/ethnicity match: an examination of treatment outcome and process with rural older adults in the deep south. *Psychotherapy Research, 4,* 458–463.

Prilleltensky, I. (2013). Wellness without fairness: the missing link in psychology. *South African Journal of Psychology, 43*(2), 147–155.

Proctor, G. (2011). Diversity: the depoliticization of inequalities. *Person-Centered and Experiential Psychotherapies, 10*(4), 231–234.

Proctor, G., Cooper, M., Sanders, P., & Malcolm, B. (Eds.). (2006). *Politicizing the person-centred approach: an agenda for social change.* Ross-on-Wye: PCCS Books.

Ratts, M.J. (2009). Social justice counseling: toward the development of a fifth force among counseling paradigms. *Journal of Humanistic Counseling, Education and Development, 48,* 160–172.

Safran, J.D., Muran, C., & Shaker, A. (2014). Research on therapeutic impasses and ruptures in the therapeutic alliance. *Contemporary Psychoanalysis, 50*(1–2), 211–232.

Thompson, N. (2011). *Promoting equality: working with difference and diversity* (3rd ed.). Basingstoke: Palgrave Macmillan.

Wheeler, S. (2006). *Difference and diversity in counselling: contemporary psychodynamic perspectives.* Basingstoke: Palgrave Macmillan.

Wong, C.W. (2013). Collaborative empiricism in culturally sensitive cognitive behavior therapy. *Cognitive and Behavioral Practice, 20,* 390–398.

23

Boundaries: A Pluralistic Perspective and Illustrative Case Study of the Patient-Led Approach to Appointment Scheduling

Timothy A. Carey

THIS CHAPTER DISCUSSES

- The purpose of therapy as well as what boundaries are and why we have them
- Different types of boundaries including professional boundaries such as ethical and professional codes of practice, contextual boundaries such as the duration and frequency of therapy sessions, and interpersonal boundaries such as touch, self-disclosure and multiple relationships
- Applying boundaries flexibly and responsively to promote the effectiveness of therapy

The pluralistic approach to counselling and psychotherapy offers an opportunity to consider therapeutic boundaries flexibly and responsively to ensure that boundaries promote, rather than inhibit, therapeutic activity. Therapeutic boundaries are important for the effective and efficient delivery of counselling and psychotherapy but a rigid approach to boundaries could unnecessarily restrict the therapeutic options that might otherwise be available. Given the explicit pluralistic stance of the client as an active agent in therapy (Cooper & McLeod, 2011), it is important to review therapeutic boundaries by reflecting on the client and the client's purposes in any therapeutic situation.

The usefulness of therapeutic boundaries is clearly recognised in the pluralistic approach to therapy. It would be a mistake to assume that the pluralistic approach advocates a 'boundary-less' approach to psychotherapy and counselling. Boundaries are essential but, in many instances, their application could be more nuanced than it currently is. For some boundaries, such as sexual relationships with clients, it is important to have firm, clear and immutable limits; however, for many other boundaries, such as the timing and duration of sessions, a great deal of flexibility can be incorporated to accommodate and honour client differences.

I begin this chapter by briefly considering the purpose of therapy from a pluralistic perspective. This is important because it is the purpose that guides the way in which boundaries are applied. Then I will introduce one way of conceptualising boundaries as professional, contextual and interpersonal. I will briefly describe the boundaries in each category but will devote far more attention to the way in which these boundaries can be applied adaptively from a pluralistic perspective. To this end, I provide a series of questions that therapists can use to think through any boundary dilemmas that arise in their practice. Finally, I will describe the client-led or patient-led approach to treatment as a case study application of a pluralistic perspective on therapeutic boundaries.

THE PURPOSE OF THERAPY

A core tenet of the pluralistic approach to counselling and psychotherapy is that it is the client who makes therapy work with the therapist acting as a catalyst (Cooper & McLeod, 2011). From this point of view, therapy could be viewed as a resource that clients use to promote their own self-healing processes (Bohart, 2000) and an aspirational common purpose of therapists might be *to help the client to get along without the therapist*. Therefore, with an understanding that change occurs naturally and universally (Duncan, Miller, & Sparks, 2004), it is important that therapists adapt the provision of their counselling and psychotherapy to the different preferences, expectations, characteristics and aptitudes of each client.

Considering counselling and psychotherapy as a resource to be used by clients for their own purposes provides a useful vantage point from which to consider the boundaries within which any therapeutic encounter must occur. Boundaries should not be thought of in a limiting or restricting way but, rather, as guides to keep both therapists and clients safe, so that clients have the best chance possible of making the changes they seek in therapy.

Ethical codes are frequently written in a guiding, non-prescriptive way. The *APS Code of Ethics* of the Australian Psychological Society (Australian Psychological Society, 2007), for example, is written as a set of three fundamental principles. From these principles, ethical standards are formed which therapists can use to guide their practice. The British Psychological Society takes a similar stance with their *Code of Ethics and Conduct* (British Psychological Society, 2009). They describe four ethical principles and explicitly state that 'Moral principles and the codes which spell out their applications can only be guidelines for thinking about the decisions individuals need to make in specific cases' (British Psychological Society, 2009: 4). Ethical codes, therefore, do not appear to tell people what to do in the sense of acting in particular ways in different circumstances. Rather, these codes advise people on *how to think* about various situations so that people can reason appropriate courses of action for themselves. A position of helping people think through different situations rather than telling them how to think is completely consistent with a pluralistic stance which advocates for observance of ethical codes and a mindset of flexibility and responsivity so that, in a therapeutic context, the codes can be applied to promote the effectiveness of therapy. Ethical codes and therapeutic boundaries, therefore, should be used to help the client efficiently and effectively learn to get along without the therapist.

A PLURALISTIC APPLICATION OF THERAPEUTIC BOUNDARIES

The potential number of boundaries that have relevance and applicability to counselling and psychotherapy is very large. Therapists work in diverse settings, such as schools, prisons, work places, private practice, hospitals and aged care facilities. In each setting there are considerations that are specific to that setting but also general principles that apply across settings. I have not attempted to provide an exhaustive list of all of the boundaries to account for, but it might be helpful to consider boundaries in three broad areas: *professional boundaries*, *contextual boundaries* and *interpersonal boundaries*. Table 23.1 lists some of the boundaries therapists may be confronted with according to the categories I have suggested here. In this section I will briefly describe some of the areas that might be included within each grouping and I will provide examples of the pluralistic application of different boundaries from each of these categories.

TABLE 23.1 *Examples of different types of boundaries*

Professional boundaries	Contextual boundaries	Interpersonal boundaries
• Right to withdraw from treatment • Informed consent • Family members and treatment • Confidentiality • Management of risk	• Scheduling of appointments • Duration of appointments • Location of appointments • Contact between appointments • Appointment reminders	• Multiple relationships • Physical contact • Use of language including swearing • Self-disclosure • Meeting outside therapy

Since flexibility, adaptability and responsivity are key features of working pluralistically it is not possible to specify precisely how boundaries should be specified in any given situation. The pluralistic application of boundaries will necessarily accommodate the individual preferences of the client in order to maximise the effectiveness of therapy for the client. Table 23.2 provides a series of questions that therapists can use to guide their pluralistic decision-making when reflecting on their use of boundaries. When discussing the different boundaries below I will illustrate with examples the way in which Table 23.2 can be used for each boundary category.

TABLE 23.2 *A decision-making guide to the flexible and responsive application of therapeutic boundaries*

Information gathering	Planning an approach	Monitoring and evaluation
• What is the issue? • What does the client want? • What does my profession say? • What does the law say? • What does the research say? • What would a respected colleague say?	• What are my options? • What are the short- and long-term consequences of these? • Which ones will help my client learn to get along without me? • What are the legal, professional and ethical implications of these? • What's the best way forward?	• What happened? • What was effective? • What could be improved? • What else needs to be done? • What have I learned? • How would I handle a similar situation in future?

Professional boundaries

The category of professional boundaries covers many of the ethical considerations mentioned earlier. Professional boundaries include those standards and provisions that are associated with acquiring and maintaining professional affiliations. Psychologists have standards that apply to their practice because of the responsibility afforded to them through their professional registration: for example, the ability to administer and interpret certain kinds of tests and assessments. Some of the professional boundary areas include: the right to withdraw from or refuse treatment; including family members in treatment; payment for sessions; and confidentiality and its limits. Professional boundaries also incorporate the competence and expertise of the therapist in terms of therapists acting within the scope of practice for which they have had training. Some boundaries, therefore, may vary from profession to profession. A therapist with prior medical training, for example, may have a wider scope for the provision of advice and guidance on medication than a therapist with no medical training.

The issue of whether or not to include family members in the client's treatment could be used as an exemplar when considering the pluralistic application of boundaries. The questions in Table 23.2 can inform decision-making for any particular client. Initially, a therapist could consider the problem the client wants to resolve as well as what the client's opinion is regarding having family members involved. Professional guidelines such as the *National Practice Standards for the Mental Health Workforce 2013* (Victorian Government Department of Health, 2013) endorse the inclusion of families in a person's treatment when the person gives permission for this to occur. Research, too, often demonstrates the benefits of social support, including family members, with regard to treatment outcomes. The law may vary from place to place so it is important that therapists are aware of any legal considerations that are relevant. For example, a solicitor from the state of South Australia explained to me that it is a 'finable offence' to discuss with other people, including family members, a patient's care or treatment, without that patient's explicit consent. Colleagues may also vary in the extent to which they emphasise the involvement of families, so soliciting the views of peers and reflecting on these perspectives can be useful.

Once therapists feel they have gathered sufficient information they will be in a good position to discuss with the client the different options available as well as the potential consequences of different decisions. Whatever decision is made it is important to monitor and evaluate the effects of the decision and include this information when considering similar situations in future. It is likely that it will be useful and effective to include family members in the treatment of some clients but not others. Moreover, the way in which family members are included may also vary even for clients who seem to present with similar problems. Decision-making such as that which has just been described, that is sensitive to the particular distinctive aspects of each case, is very much the flavour of pluralistic practice.

A non-pluralistic stance would be to either always insist that family members participate in the client's treatment or, conversely, to insist that they never do. Either position is likely to create problems on different occasions and may alienate clients and their families. In the context of the ultimate purpose of therapy, a decision about whom to include in clients' treatment can be made most effectively by considering clients as individuals and recognising the importance to treatment outcomes of the circumstances pertaining to their particular difficulty. Again, it is necessary to emphasise that any decision that is made should acknowledge and incorporate the particular legal, professional and ethical codes governing a therapist's practice. The pluralistic approach does not advocate working outside the parameters of one's professional practice.

Contextual boundaries

There are many boundaries, both implicit and explicit, that exist because of the context of therapy. Haley (1990), for example, argues that the context of the therapeutic hour was established when therapists decided to charge clients for units of time rather than results. The specific context within which therapists work may introduce boundaries in different ways. The context of therapy itself as well as the context within which the therapy is being provided may influence factors such as: how long therapy lasts; how frequent the sessions are; how many sessions there are; the duration of each session; the location of sessions; contact outside of sessions; appointment reminders such as SMS messages; and the format of therapy such as individual or group, face-to-face, or by telephone or internet.

The contextual boundaries of the scheduling of therapy appointments will be addressed in detail below as a general case study example of a pluralistic approach to therapy delivery. The use of SMS reminders, however, could be used as a specific example to consider the way in which contextual boundaries could be approached pluralistically. Some services have adopted the use of SMS text reminders as a way of increasing attendance at therapy appointments. The general attitude seems to be that if people are reminded of their appointment they will be more likely to attend.

Often, however, this attitude seems to be formed in the absence of any empirical evidence and, perhaps more importantly, without consulting the people who will be receiving the reminders.

Text reminders, for instance, might be sent to a person's mobile phone the day before a scheduled appointment. Again, Table 23.2 could be used to guide decision-making with regard to the use of these reminders. Does the client want an SMS reminder for every appointment? What is the attitude of your colleagues to SMS reminders? Are there any legal factors to consider? Will the reminder be sent from your personal mobile phone or will it be sent generically from the service? In terms of research, Clough and Casey (2014) conducted a randomised controlled trial of the use of SMS appointment reminders and found no significant differences between the SMS and no SMS conditions with regard to appointment attendance. They also found there were more client dropouts in the SMS condition compared to the no SMS condition (Clough & Casey, 2014).

By obtaining answers to the questions in column one of Table 23.2 and synthesising the information collected from different sources, a therapist will be able to make a decision for a particular client concerning the use of SMS reminders. It may be that, even if SMS reminders are used, they are not needed for every session for some clients. When the therapist decides on a course of action and implements it the outcomes can be monitored and evaluated and used as part of the information for future decision-making. Given the time that it takes to send reminders to clients it is important to ensure that this strategy will help to promote the effectiveness of therapy.

Interpersonal boundaries

Many interpersonal issues occur just by the very nature of therapy provision. Issues such as: physical contact, self-disclosure, multiple relationships and language use, including the therapist's use of slang or swearing, need to be considered. Furthermore, consider my own example: I live in a small country town, which is also where I operate a psychology clinic; many interpersonal issues can arise in this setting. Seeing clients at the grocery store, or at a restaurant, or at the local swimming pool; having your child in the same class as a client's child and your child inviting the client's child over to your house to play; going to an interagency meeting and finding that one of your clients is also at the meeting; discovering that one of your clients works closely with one of your friends; and finding that the partner of a client is the receptionist at the GP practice you attend; all these situations require careful thought and management.

In situations such as those described above, once again taking a pluralistic approach can be immensely helpful. It is important to consider the client's experience and preferences, to consult with colleagues and to consider any legal and empirical guidance that may exist. Again, what a therapist does in any given situation will depend on the client and the situation. I generally have a discussion with clients in the first session regarding the possibility of being in the same place socially and I suggest that my approach is to be guided by the client on how

I should react. If the client acknowledges me and says hello then I will respond with a similar greeting but if the client prefers to act as though we do not know each other then I will respond in the same way. Clients seem to appreciate being able to control unpredictable situations in this fashion.

The issue of appropriate touch can also be used pluralistically. Again, the questions provided in Table 23.2 will be a useful guide in helping therapists consider how to use touch from a pluralistic perspective to enhance therapeutic outcomes. A non-pluralistic stance would be to adopt an absolute position of maintaining that it is *never* appropriate to touch a client or that a therapist should, for example, *always* shake hands with a client at the beginning and end of a session. I often shake a client's hand at the end of a session although one middle-aged Indigenous man with whom I was working gave me a hug at the end of the first session. While I do not routinely hug clients, I reasoned that it would have been detrimental to the therapeutic relationship if I had stopped this man from expressing his thanks in this way. Again, however, this is an entirely individual decision. A young, female therapist in a similar situation might come to a different conclusion and find another way of relating to this client to achieve the same therapeutic benefit. The emphasis here is that a responsive and flexible approach that considers the ultimate aim of therapy is likely to be most useful.

Case study of the pluralistic application of boundaries: the patient-led approach

The way in which therapy is delivered in terms of how appointments are scheduled, how frequently they are scheduled and so on, is, very frequently, an unquestioned and almost invisible aspect of service provision. I discovered, however, that decisions therapists make in the area of appointment scheduling, can have a significant impact on the access of clients to services. In this section I will outline the approach to therapy that I developed in terms of appointment scheduling as well as some of the results that have been obtained empirically through this approach. As I describe this approach the pluralistic nature of this way of working will become evident.

After I completed my training in clinical psychology I spent five years working in the National Health Service (NHS) in Scotland. When I first started in the position, in the district within which I worked, there was a 15-month waiting list for NHS patients to see a psychologist in the adult primary care service. My line manager explained that it was standard practice to offer fortnightly appointments in this particular service. Although this was a rather benign remark it seemed odd to me only because I had been used to scheduling weekly appointments during my training in Australia.

I began to wonder what the 'right' appointment protocol might be. I consulted the literature and began to search extensively for information about the timing of therapy appointments. The further I searched the more I realised that the duration of therapy in terms of the number of appointments offered was also an important component to consider.

Essentially, I discovered that there was no empirical justification for any particular treatment protocol (Carey, 2005). There were certainly many studies demonstrating that a particular number of sessions (e.g., 12 or 16) was associated with favourable treatment outcomes but I could not find any justification provided for why a certain number (e.g., 12 or 16) had been chosen for the duration of therapy. I also realised that demonstrating that 12 sessions of treatment *could* result in favourable outcomes was *not* a demonstration that 12 sessions of therapy were *necessary* for favourable outcomes (Carey, 2011). I also discovered a long-standing discrepancy in the literature in that most treatments are designed to be *more* than 10 sessions but most clients attend for *fewer than* 10 sessions (Carey, Tai, & Stiles, 2013).

As I gathered more information about the timing and duration of treatment I discovered a lot of support for affording greater autonomy to clients. NHS policy documents supported patients having greater control over their healthcare, ethical guidelines highlighted the importance of clients' right to withdraw from or refuse treatment, and there was also empirical and theoretical support for promoting greater client control over their healthcare (Carey & Spratt, 2009). Empirically, for example, Barkham, Stiles and their colleagues had suggested that clients and therapists regulate treatment duration responsively by continuing treatment only until the clients had achieved a 'good enough level' of change (Barkham et al., 2006; Stiles, Barkham, Connell, & Mellor-Clark, 2008).

The context of the service I worked in was an important consideration because this was a primary care service and the clients were voluntary clients. I discussed the pragmatics of appointment scheduling with colleagues and many of them provided some balance to the information I was gathering in other ways. Some colleagues were concerned about patients becoming dependent on the service or, conversely, not having the skills to schedule their own appointments if the structure of routine appointment scheduling was removed. I wondered, given the problems with client non-attendance at appointments, whether clients might not already be making their own decisions about appointment attendance.

How it works in practice

Given that I was not able to find solid empirical support for any particular treatment protocol being necessary for effective treatment outcomes, I set out to investigate what might happen if clients, rather than therapists, took control of appointment scheduling. Initially, I established systems so that clients could book their own appointments at the clinics where I worked and I began to collect data on appointment attendance and therapy outcomes. I explained to clients at the first session that, now that they had been referred, they could make appointments as they required them. Essentially, clients made appointments to see me in the same way they would make an appointment to see their GP.

After a period of time of working this way on my own, and gathering data about its effect, some colleagues became interested in what I was doing and began to adopt this approach to appointment scheduling also. At one GP practice a colleague and I provided two sessions a week each. A session was typically a block of half a day with four or five hourly appointments. We informed clients that they could come four times a week if they wanted to, or once a week, or whatever they thought was appropriate. We also told clients that they could see one therapist or both of us at their discretion. Furthermore, if clients thought that a one-hour appointment was too brief, they could schedule two appointments in a row to give themselves more time. We continued to collect data on the approach, including qualitative data regarding the clients' and the GPs' experiences of working in this way.

Empirical support for the patient-led approach

Over time, the patient-led approach has been demonstrated to be an effective and efficient approach to treatment delivery (Carey et al., 2013). It has been used now by different therapists, in different clinics, in both primary and secondary care, over different periods of time, with different clients, and in different health systems in different countries. Data from GPs and clients indicate that they appreciate the increased choice and flexibility (Carey & Mullan, 2007). One of the fundamental differences with this method of therapy provision is that the number of non-attended appointments reduces dramatically while the average number of attended appointments stays about the same as it would be when therapists determine the appointment schedule. The effect of more clients attending more of the time can have a dramatic effect on waiting times and access to services. Although there was a 15-month waiting list in the area within which the patient-led approach first started, in less than five years, the waiting time between referral and first appointment was no more than one month. In one GP practice, when the switch was made from conventional to patient-led appointment scheduling, we found that the service could accommodate an increase in referrals from 52 to 93 for the same period from the previous year and, in that time period, a seven-month waiting list that had existed at the beginning of the period was eliminated by the end of the period (Carey & Spratt, 2009).

Despite its benefits, the patient-led approach does take some adjusting to get used to. In some ways it is a 'messy', unpredictable approach where the therapist can never be completely certain as to when clients will return for subsequent appointments. Some therapists also become concerned about clients who do not attend for as much therapy as the therapist thinks the clients should have. From a pluralistic perspective, however, if we are to genuinely embrace the agency of the client, then this must include respecting clients' decisions about how much therapy they need. Even if they get that decision wrong, it is their right to do so, and, by leaving the door open for them to return when they need to, therapists may be doing as much as they can to help the client get along without them and live the life they would like to live.

CONCLUDING COMMENTS

The pluralistic approach to counselling and psychotherapy offers a refreshing opportunity to consider important therapeutic boundaries in a flexible and responsive way to promote rather than impede the core business of therapy. By recognising the agency of clients and by gathering information, making informed decisions, and monitoring and evaluating those decisions, therapists will be able to ensure that the relevant boundaries are enabling the effective and efficient provision of therapy. Very few therapeutic boundaries need to be applied rigidly (although there are some that do need to be applied this way), and the alternative to an inflexible application is not to disregard boundaries completely. Instead, undertaking a pluralistic approach to the consideration of therapeutic boundaries will enable therapists to successfully navigate the important decisions they will be regularly confronted with in the day-to-day practice of therapy provision.

SUMMARY

The key points made in this chapter are:

- Pluralistic therapy is not a 'boundary-less' approach but does invite a considered and flexible approach to the use of boundaries in therapy.
- The job of a therapist is to help the client learn to get along without the therapist and our use of boundaries should be to promote a client's successful functioning independently of therapy.
- Therapy should not be considered as a treatment that is applied to clients but, rather, as a resource that clients can access whenever they want to resolve problems in their life to make their life more like the way they would like it to be.
- Different boundaries will be important for different clients.

EXERCISES/POINTS FOR REFLECTION

1. Ethical and professional codes endorse a client's right to withdraw from treatment or refuse treatment. How does one decide, therefore, whether clients have dropped out of treatment or whether they've exercised their right to withdraw from treatment?
2. How should one decide how much therapy to provide for any particular client? Who should be primarily responsible for making this decision?

FURTHER READING

Carey, T.A. (2011). As you like it: adopting a patient-led approach to the issue of treatment length. *Journal of Public Mental Health*, 10(1), 6–16. A paper that compares and contrasts the Dose–Response and the Good Enough Level models of treatment provision by considering the development of the patient-led model and the results generated through four different evaluations.

(Continued)

(Continued)

Carey, T.A. (2006). *The Method of Levels: how to do psychotherapy without getting in the way.* Hayward, CA: Living Control Systems Publishing. A book describing the Method of Levels (MOL), which is a transdiagnostic cognitive therapy that has the hallmarks of a pluralistic approach in its flexibility and responsivity.

Carey, T.A. (2010). Will you follow while they lead? Introducing a patient-led approach to low intensity CBT interventions. In J. Bennett-Levy et al. (Eds.), *Oxford guide to low intensity CBT interventions* (pp. 331–8). Oxford: Oxford University Press. A chapter that describes the patient-led approach in detail, including challenges that might be encountered when it is established.

Mansell, W., Carey, T.A., & Tai, S.J. (2012). *A transdiagnostic approach to CBT using Method of Levels therapy: distinctive features.* London: Routledge. A book outlining both the theory and practice of the Method of Levels (MOL) which provides another theoretical perspective for the strength of the pluralistic approach as well as providing practical suggestions for incorporating pluralistic methods into one's clinical approach.

Resources

Method of Levels (MOL): www.methodoflevels.com.au. A website about the MOL, with vignettes, publications and other related information. It provides accessible information for clinicians wanting to adopt a more pluralistic style of therapeutic delivery.

REFERENCES

Australian Psychological Society. (2007). *APS code of ethics.* Melbourne: Author.

Barkham, M., Connell, J., Stiles, W.B., Miles, J.N.V., Margison, J., Evans, C., & Mellor-Clark, J. (2006). Dose–effect relations and responsive regulation of treatment duration: the good enough level. *Journal of Consulting and Clinical Psychology, 74,* 160–167.

Bohart, A. (2000). The client is the most important common factor: clients' self-healing capacities and psychotherapy. *Journal of Psychotherapy Integration, 10,* 127–149.

British Psychological Society. (2009). *Code of ethics and conduct: guidance published by the Ethics Committee of the British Psychological Society.* Leicester: Author.

Carey, T.A. (2005). Can patients specify treatment parameters? *Clinical Psychology and Psychotherapy: An International Journal of Theory and Practice, 12*(4), 326–335.

Carey, T.A. (2011). As you like it: adopting a patient-led approach to the issue of treatment length. *Journal of Public Mental Health, 10*(1), 6–16.

Carey, T.A., & Mullan, R.J. (2007). Patients taking the lead: a naturalistic investigation of a patient led approach to treatment in primary care. *Counselling Psychology Quarterly, 20*(1), 27–40.

Carey, T.A., & Spratt, M.B. (2009). When is enough enough? Structuring the organisation of treatment to maximise patient choice and control. *The Cognitive Behaviour Therapist, 2,* 211–226.

Carey, T.A., Tai, S.J., & Stiles, W.B. (2013). Effective and efficient: using patient-led appointment scheduling in routine mental health practice in remote Australia. *Professional Psychology: Research and Practice, 44,* 405–414.

Clough, B.A., & Casey, L.M. (2014). Using SMS reminders in psychology clinics: a cautionary tale. *Behavioural and Cognitive Psychotherapy, 42,* 257–268.

Cooper, M., & McLeod, J. (2011). *Pluralistic counselling and psychotherapy.* London: Sage.

Duncan, B.L., Miller, S.J., & Sparks, J.A. (2004). *The heroic client: a revolutionary way to improve effectiveness through client-directed, outcome-informed therapy.* San Francisco, CA: Jossey–Bass.

Haley, J. (1990). Why not long-term therapy? In J.K. Zeig & S.G. Gilligan (Eds.), *Brief therapy: myths, methods, and metaphors* (pp. 3–17). New York: Brunner–Mazel.

Stiles, W.B., Barkham, M., Connell, J., & Mellor-Clark, J. (2008). Responsive regulation of treatment duration in routine practice in United Kingdom primary care settings: replication in a larger sample. *Journal of Consulting and Clinical Psychology, 76,* 298–305.

Victorian Government Department of Health. (2013). *National practice standards for the mental health workforce 2013.* Melbourne: Author.

24
Ethics in Pluralistic Counselling and Psychotherapy

Lynne Gabriel

THIS CHAPTER DISCUSSES

- What pluralistic philosophy can bring to the ethics of a pluralistic therapeutic practice
- Key ethical challenges for pluralistic therapists
- A pluralistic ethical decision-making frame
- Key implications for practice using this frame

PLURALISTIC PHILOSOPHY: WHAT DOES IT OFFER ETHICAL PRACTICE IN PLURALISTIC COUNSELLING AND PSYCHOTHERAPY?

The philosophy of pluralism is consistent with postmodern and poststructuralist positions, in that there is no foundational truth, rather it is a question of 'both/and', rather than 'either/or' (Cooper & McLeod, 2011; McLeod, 2013). Pluralism holds considerable promise for the pragmatics and ethics of an everyday pluralistic therapy practice. In ontological terms, pluralism is predicated on the notion that *an approach to human experiences and perceptions cannot be reductionist, as there are multiple modes of being.* This fundamental premise of pluralism is core to pluralistic therapy. Ethical thinking and relating stemming from the philosophy of pluralism will manifest as systematic reflection upon our therapy work and relationships (Berlin, 2013), as we aim for 'precarious equilibrium' (Berlin, 2013: 18) that can mitigate any harmful consequences. Pluralism recognises that several values or principles may equally apply in any given scenario. In the context of pluralistic counselling and psychotherapy, this requires therapist and therapeutic equipoise, in pursuit of an apt response or intervention with a given client, in a given session, or setting, or day.

The ethical principles of fidelity (which here refers to trust within the therapy relationship) and justice (with its subsumed concept of informed consent) resonate with pluralism and translate well into pluralistic therapy through relational collaboration and consultation between client and therapist. Fidelity and justice can be fostered in pluralistic therapy through iterative cycles of communication, feedback and negotiation, thereby developing a truly reflexive client–therapist relationship. Pluralistic therapy's active and iterative approach elicits a *dialogical* perspective on therapy relationships and processes (Gabriel, 2005; Gabriel & Casemore, 2009). Pluralistic therapy provokes a dialogical, interactional way of being in relationship, epitomising what I would define as *process ethics* – a relational, evolutionary, responsive way of working, which evolves through client–therapist interaction. Ethical reasoning and actions take place in this relational process and regular reviews generate opportunities to address any issues.

Pluralism recognises cultural diversity, heralding multiple domains of meaning-making. Pluralistic therapy will cross cultural boundaries, bringing inevitable communicative issues and concomitant ethical challenges. Translating this into therapy work, the therapist will view factors outside the individual (not just intra-psychic, intra-personal dynamics), or between the individual and their social, cultural and political environment, as significant dimensions of the client's world and of the material and meaning-making they bring into therapy. Whilst pluralism acknowledges multiplicity and diversity, it does not condone ad hoc relativism (Berlin, 2013), but rather, advocates for the application of disciplined intent in pluralistic practice.

Central to pluralistic practice is critical awareness of our *intentionality*. The concept of intentionality is a central tenet in Husserl's conceptualisation of phenomenology. Here, we can define it pragmatically as *reasoned thoughtfulness and agency in any given decision or action*. The act of deconstructing our intentionality in any given therapy relationship, or therapeutic intervention, or aspects of our professional lives and practices, can be challenging and requires a capacity for flexibility and reflexivity, along with an ability to reach out to others for support and critique of our work. Significant here is a capacity for the mediation and repair of misunderstandings or ruptures in a mutually respectful client–therapist relationship. Essentially, the entire pluralistic therapy endeavour, becomes an ethical journey, co-created by client and therapist.

ETHICAL CHALLENGES FOR PLURALISTIC THERAPY

Whether seeking to enter training, or struggling with day-to-day practice issues, pluralistic therapy faces a number of professional challenges and concomitant ethical issues. These range from integrity of practitioner training through to the challenge of practitioner self-care.

Training challenges

A criticism levelled at pluralistic therapy is that the demands placed upon the trainee, in relation to the required theoretical and practical learning, exceed the scope of any core practitioner training. Arguably, no practitioner training can ever fully equip a therapist, including specialist single-theory training, for the ethical complexities and challenges of professional practice. Nevertheless, until pluralistic therapy training courses are more widely available (see Chapter 26, this volume), there are a number of principles that should be core to an ethical provision of pluralistic therapy:

- our capacity to recognise our theoretical and practical limitations;
- our ability to refer clients on when our practice limits are reached;
- our use of supervision to inform our ethical pluralistic decisions and practices;
- our provision of true client-focused therapy;
- our ethical conceptualisation and operationalisation of multiple theoretical strands into therapy content and process.

The capacity to form ethical pluralistic therapy alliances

The development of productive, co-constructed therapy relationships forms the bedrock of the pluralistic encounter between client and therapist. Agreeing therapy aims (goals) along with the therapeutic models and means (tasks and methods) through which the transition to those goals could be effected, forms the praxis for ethical engagement. This relational process can be ethically complex. For instance, where a client enters therapy imagining or wishing for a 'magical fix', the therapist must work swiftly to elicit their participation in goal-setting and in identifying pragmatic, meaningful tasks to reach those goals. Eliciting client engagement and agency in the day-to-day minutiae of therapy process and content, as well as in any intense ethical challenges that arise, sits well with pluralistic therapy. According to Beauchamp and Childress (2013: 101), fostering a client's autonomy can elicit their 'self-rule that is free from both controlling interference by others and limitations that prevent meaningful choice, such as inadequate understanding'.

Pluralistic therapy provides an element of training and mentoring for the client and, to that end, in our ethical endeavours, we must attend to our every action and thought as we foster client agency and change. As Berlin (2013: 2) notes,

> The goals and motives that guide human action must be looked at ... their roots and growth, their essence, and above all their validity, must be critically examined with every intellectual resource we have. This urgent need, apart from the intrinsic value of the discovery of truth about human relationships, makes ethics a field of primary importance.

Meaning-making and change agency in the pluralistic client–therapist dyad requires engaged and constant '*communicative transactions*' (Manson & O'Neill, 2007: 184), to facilitate a richly lived ethical encounter that epitomises integrity and sincerity. This generates an evolving relational ethic through which positive change is more likely to occur.

Boundaries: the challenge of being a boundary rider

Arguably, role and boundary management is core to successful therapy. The pluralistic therapist will engage in various developmental activities to enhance their boundary 'tool kit' (for a helpful range of boundary management tool kit resources see Bond, 2015; Gabriel, 2005; Gabriel & Casemore, 2009; and Syme, 2003). Essentially, the pluralistic practitioner will become a *boundary rider* (Gabriel, 2005), constantly attending to both theoretical and relational boundaries throughout the course of any given session or client–therapist relationship.

The boundary is 'a limit line, with inherent fluidity and permeability, as well as safety and security ... that requires the thoughtful actions of the boundary rider, the counsellor, to monitor and repair where necessary in order, as far as is possible, to ensure security and safety' (Gabriel & Davies, 2000: 37). The pluralistic emphasis on flexibility raises challenges and risks around boundaries. For the myriad ethical challenges that inevitably arise in day-to-day practice, a comprehensive understanding of boundary issues and violations in pluralistic therapy practice is crucial. A key issue in complaints to professional bodies is therapist inability or inadequacy when managing therapeutic boundaries.

In some instances, unconsidered, ad hoc therapy activities and interventions can lead to diminishing boundary awareness or control. For example, Paul (see Case Example 1, below) integrated in his pluralistic approach a loosely person-centred and Gestalt perspective. Here, there was no clear pluralistic framework, no case formulation, or the identification of goals and tasks, and the therapy relationship with Sally deteriorated to the point of a serious complaint.

CASE EXAMPLE 1
Paul and Sally

Paul worked with Sally on a once-weekly basis. Shortly before commencing work with Paul, Sally was diagnosed with dissociative identity disorder. At times Paul was challenged by Sally's multiple personalities, which variously manifested themselves in the counselling work. Paul worked to facilitate Sally's understanding of each of these 'personalities' and help her identify transitions between them. The work was intense, demanding and elicited an intimacy in the working relationship. Paul found himself becoming increasingly drawn to changing the usual therapy work and routine and allowed sessions to run beyond the contracted 60 minutes into two-, three- and sometimes four-hour meetings.

(Continued)

> *(Continued)*
>
> Sally began to feel the need to revisit some of the places she had lived in, in order to heal the damage of experiencing sexual abuse during infancy and childhood. Paul offered to take her to the locations and Sally accepted. Paul chose not to discuss this development with his supervisor. He also chose not to consider the use of extra-therapy contact or its potential impact upon Sally and the counselling relationship. Nor did he invite critical and collaborative discussion with Sally, to think through how the visits and external contact might impact upon the therapy work. As he involved himself more deeply in Sally's revisiting of past places, he found himself becoming increasingly sexually attracted to her. Rather than use supervision to process his attraction, he withheld information on how the relationship and the work had changed. Neither did he and Sally process the purpose, benefits or impact of the visits within their counselling context. Ultimately they ended up in a sexual relationship. A relative of Sally's became aware of the relationship and told Sally it was wrong and abusive. Sally complained, the complaint was upheld, and Paul was removed from membership of his professional body.
>
> Consider how you would have worked with Sally, using the ethical processing model shown later in the chapter.

The challenge of therapist self-care

As pluralistic therapists, it is essential we attend to our well-being. Whilst, arguably, this applies to all therapists, as pluralistic practitioners we intentionally integrate, manage and monitor multiple aspects of diverse theories and practices. Consequently, we require a degree of agility, a particular 'fitness to practise'. Embedded in the British Association for Counselling and Psychotherapy's (BACP) Ethical Framework, are notions of practitioner self-respect and self-care. The idea of applying the principles of that framework (being trustworthy, autonomy, beneficence, non-maleficence, justice) to oneself makes good sense since, arguably, the capacity to care for oneself and to elicit self-evaluative and reflexive practice is fundamental to providing ethical pluralistic therapy.

According to BACP, the principle of self-respect 'means that the practitioner appropriately applies all … principles as entitlements for self … there is an ethical responsibility to use supervision for appropriate personal and professional support and development, and to seek training and other opportunities for continuing professional development' (BACP, 2013). Recent review and development of BACP's Ethical Framework (in part, to address the post-Francis report health and social care context) saw the concept of 'candour' in helping practice given prominence. BACP's ethical framework review and consultation, led by Tim Bond (2014), conveyed:

> the explicit commitment to 'put our clients first' by making them 'our most important concern during our work together' is an expression of the values and principles that underpin current practice. The duty of candour recommended by

the 2013 Francis report[1] is also substantially present in the current framework but is made more explicit in the revised draft as a commitment to promptly inform a client if anything 'occurs that may cause you harm and quickly limiting or repairing that harm as far as possible'.

Candour – the capacity for frank, sincere communicating and relating – is fundamental to ethical practice in pluralistic therapy. Pluralistic therapists, with their emphasis on collaborative client–therapist communication and work, are well-positioned to facilitate the necessary frank and meaningful discussions, to foster ethical therapy work and relationships.

DEVELOPING AN ETHICAL FRAMEWORK FOR PLURALISTIC PRACTICE

As pluralistic therapists, the concept of '*questing*' (Gabriel, 2005, 2009) provides a heuristic tactic to foster ethical engagement. In questing, we are meaning-making through collaborative searching with our clients, in the pursuit of new insights and understanding. Questing is a useful metaphor, as a means to reflect on how we identify, espouse and maintain ethical pluralistic practice. Questing requires us to invoke a spirit of courage and congruence in our often messy and conflicted therapy work. For example, in my own practice, I use metaphors or images as a means through which to conjure up my internalised 'warrior woman', to help me create pathways through tricky clinical terrain.

The Socratic process of asking '*what if*' questions supports questing and provides a way to support decision-making in the context of ethical issues in pluralistic practice. Consider the following Socratic prompt examples:

- *What if ...* my client decides they do not want to engage in collaboration and feedback within our therapy work and relationship?
- *What if ...* .my client refuses to engage in resolving an ethical issue in our work or relationship?
- *What if ...* .my client wants to know details of my personal life?

A number of *ethical* decision-making models exist to help us navigate our way through difficult therapy processes or relationships. The pragmatic pluralistic model offered here is derived from earlier work (see, e.g., Gabriel, 1996; Bond, 2000; Gabriel & Casemore, 2009) and informed by Beauchamp and Childress (2013: 409), who posit the following core components for ethical thinking:

- *Consistency:* non-contradiction in the decision-making process
- *Coherence* with warranted non-moral beliefs, that is, empirical evidence; well established scientific theories and inferences from both of these

---

[1] The Francis report, based upon findings from a review of healthcare failings in Mid-Staffordshire NHS Trust, advocates a duty of candour in health and social care.

- *Comprehensiveness:* addressing appropriate territory in the moral domain
- And ... the *absence of bias, the presence of argumentative support, and the restriction of starting premises to considered judgements.*

AN ETHICAL DECISION-MAKING MODEL FOR PLURALISTIC PRACTICE

In the following sections, through the medium of two case examples, Sarah and John, we engage with a pragmatic pluralistic decision-making model for ethical practice.

CASE EXAMPLE 2
Sarah

Sarah works with you in your private practice, attending weekly sessions to explore the impact of the recent loss of her partner. As part of managing through-flow in your practice, you have contracted for up to 12 sessions. You use your core training in person-centred therapy as the basis for development of the therapy relationship with Sarah. From her initial presentation and the therapy conversations with Sarah in early sessions, you facilitate her to identify therapy goals. You discuss with her the ways in which you might reach those goals. As the work develops, it is evident that Sarah values your capacity to be-in-relationship, as well as your solution-focused and cognitive behavioural-based interventions. She also values the weekly contact with you and arrives early for sessions, keen to engage with you. Sarah asks if she can meet for lunch and have further contact with you when therapy is finished. How might you respond and work with Sarah?

CASE EXAMPLE 3
John

You work in a GP practice offering short-term counselling of up to 10 sessions, depending upon the client's presenting problems. You've been working with John for two weeks. John presented with issues about his long-term relationship with Ian. John experiences Ian as bullying and is concerned about the lack of control he now has over his life. Ian deals with all the decision-making, finances and friendships. John feels his confidence and joy in life is being gradually eroded. It is evident from the two sessions to date that John is reluctant to engage with you in identifying goals and tasks, apparently preferring to defer to you in your role as therapist. How might you respond to John?

In reflecting upon and responding to John's and Sarah's cases, use the steps of the pluralistic ethical decision-making model outlined below.

Decision-making for ethical practice

1. Stop, think and identify the situation or problem
2. Construct a description of the situation
3. Consider 'whose ethical issue or challenge is it?'
4. Review the situation in terms of your ethical framework or code of ethics
5. Consider moral principles and values
6. Reflect upon the relational processes that have played out in the situation; refer to relevant psychological theories
7. Identify what support is available
8. Identify and critique potential courses of action
9. Choose a course of action
10. Evaluate the outcome
11. Check for personal impact

---

1 Stop, think and identify the situation or problem

Avoid becoming over-anxious by actively and intentionally reflecting upon the situation or issue. Bringing a logical, reasoned approach to reflecting on the problem helps to defuse or minimise the likelihood of any 'knee-jerk' or inflammatory responses.

In working with Sarah's case, a pluralistic practitioner might worry about how to respond to her request for contact beyond the end of therapy, or feel compelled to offer what the client asks for. A substantive body of knowledge exists on dual relationships (see, e.g., Gabriel, 2005, in relation to dual and multiple role relationships associated with counselling and psychotherapy, or Dunnett, Jesper, O'Donnell, & Vallance. 2013, in relation to dual relationships within a supervisory context). However, clear resources, logic and ethical intentionality can be lost in the midst of an acutely felt ethical challenge. This is the moment to pause and gather your thoughts, without any 'knee jerk' reactions. Sarah has evidently responded well to you and she imagines the benefits of having further contact. You recognise that your proactive, engaging and dynamic pluralistic approach can positively influence client engagement. Whilst the work has been short term, you also suspect that to extend the boundaries of your therapy relationship into social or friendship territory could perpetuate some form of dependency.

2 Construct a description of the situation

Give yourself time to write down the key features of the situation. Do this in relation to both case studies. This step really does help to diminish initial anxieties and to identify key details. The notes will also inform discussions in supervision.

3 Consider 'whose ethical issue or challenge is it?'

It may not be immediately obvious as to whose issue or challenge it is. The process of creating a detailed description of the situation will have helped you to identify the key protagonists or players in any given scenario. Where joint or multiple responsibility for a situation exists, for example where there is a case within an organisational setting, then roles, responsibilities and relationship boundaries need to be carefully clarified and negotiated. Where there are multiple and complex features involved, consider the following:

- Who are the main players and stakeholders and what personal and/or professional issues do they bring?
- What values, assumptions, attitudes, tensions, or conflicts prevail?
- What roles, responsibilities, obligations or expectations exist?
- Are there any relevant contractual or legal matters?

In the case of John, the therapist can facilitate conversations focused upon their roles of 'therapist' and 'client', in the process identifying expectations and obligations in each of those roles. For John, in the 'grip' of what he perceives to be a controlling relationship, he finds it especially challenging to fully engage in identifying and deciding priorities, responsibilities and expectations in his therapy relationship with you. However, to facilitate and appropriately challenge and engender John to do so may elicit his sense of agency in his relationship with Ian. In facilitating conversations with John about agency, or about developing confidence and the capacity to challenge and be self-acting, draw out parallels in the roles and lines of relational responsibility within the client–therapist relationship. You invite/facilitate a visual representation of, or metaphor for, John's situation. You elicit comparisons and parallels, between the therapy work and relationship, thereby providing a model that John can translate into other contexts. Essentially, you and John are co-creating and rehearsing different ways of being within his relationship with Ian, using goals, tasks and methods to move to a positive therapeutic outcome for John.

4 Review the situation in terms of your ethical framework or code of ethics

Professional bodies produce ethical frameworks (e.g., BACP Ethical Framework, UKCP Code of Ethics) to inform and support members' practice, as well as to provide points of reference for any complaints received. Consider the situation in relation to your ethics code or framework and identify criteria or points of relevance to your current scenario. Be clear about how your professional body's code of ethics or ethical framework can inform the situation.

In reviewing the issue or situation against the ethics code or framework, consider how they can inform your thinking about Sarah and John. For example, the BACP

Ethical Framework counsels caution in relation to dual relationships. In working with Sarah, you will need to consider the limit or extent of any proposed extension of your interaction beyond the end of the therapy – if indeed you do reach an informed and mutual decision to continue contact in a different context. Dual or multiple role relationships with clients can have a powerful positive or negative impact upon those involved. With Sarah, there does not appear to be any drive for sexualised contact. Whilst some dual relationships are unavoidable, there are those where we can exercise reason and choice; sexual dual or multiple roles with current or past clients would usually be taboo. With Sarah, it is important to give both of you the opportunity to reflect on the potential implications of extending your relationship into other contexts or roles (see Gabriel, 2005, for additional resources).

5 Consider moral principles and values

Moral principles offer a way of reviewing the key relationship, context and stakeholder dimensions of a given ethical and professional problem or dilemma. Principles and values can compete or conflict, and reaching a decision on an issue can demand considerable courage and commitment on the part of the practitioner. It is important that you can clearly account for any decision reached and actions taken. Ultimately, you live with the decision and its impact.

For John, eliciting his capacity for agency, along with growth of a sense and perception of competence and confidence, can form a key part of the therapy. Fidelity and trustworthiness will be essential here. Consider how you might enable John to engage with you in goal-setting:

- What tasks might he be encouraged to engage in between sessions?
- What theoretical concepts could help? For instance, might CBT's ABC model be useful to bring engagement and insights within the context of a therapeutic activity?

With Sarah, you can work collaboratively to 'unpack' the variables associated with moving from a therapy relationship into friendship contact (see Gabriel, 2005, for comprehensive resources to support this type of work).

6 Reflect upon the relational processes that have played out in the situation

How has the situation impacted upon the therapy relationship? The pluralistic therapist draws upon a range of concepts, including the psychodynamic notions of transference, countertransference and projective identification, to support your reflections. In this phase of the model, refer to relevant theories and concepts, using supervision/consultation to inform your processing.

7 Identify what support is available

Consider what advice and guidance is available that can help you with the decision-making process. For example, the BACP has an *Ethical Helpline* (aimed at practitioners) or its *Ask Kathleen* service (aimed at clients). Regard your code of ethics or ethical framework as a working document that you and the client can engage with in the therapy context. Use it to inform your conversations about any ethical matter that arises in the therapy work or relationship. For example, in the case of Sarah, in the spirit of upholding your duty of candour, you would prompt conversations that explored the potential impact of taking the therapy relationship into a social one.

8 Identify and critique potential courses of action

Pluralistic approaches advocate seeing things from multiple perspectives. Think creatively when identifying courses of action. Consider the following:

- the contextual and relational features of the situation
- the ethical and moral dimensions
- the available literature (including codes of ethics)
- the consultation process with all involved in the situation
- the review of the situation in a supervisory context
- consideration of the likely consequences of action/inaction in the short, medium and long term.

From the multiple options you identify, consider *what is the best and most appropriate course of action to take*. In relation to John and Sarah, this phase can be collaboratively engaged with as part of the therapy process. A supervisory context is also an appropriate place in which to creatively and constructively explore options for actions. With Sarah, to inform your deliberations, consider the impact post-therapy contact could have upon any positive effects or changes arising from the therapy work and relationship.

9 Choose a course of action

When deciding upon the courses of action to take with John and Sarah, consider:

- Could your course of action be recommended to others in the same/similar situations?
- Would you take the same course of action with another client in a similar context?
- Would your decision be influenced by a client who was famous or influential?

10 Evaluate the outcome

When you are reviewing John and Sarah's cases consider the following prompts. If your answer to any of them is unfavourable or unexpected, reflect upon what you might do in the future if a similar situation should arise.

- Taking the situation through to a potential conclusion, was the outcome as you had anticipated or hoped for?
- Had you considered all relevant factors, with the result that no new or surprising aspects emerged?
- Would you take the same course of action in the future?

11 Check for personal impact

Consider the impact on you and on your therapy work. Your practitioner reflexivity and associated capacity to manage iterative cycles of practice experience, learning from those experiences and the feed-forward of key learning into future work, will become a key feature of your work.

SUMMARY

The philosophy of pluralism underpins ethics in pluralistic therapy practice in fundamental ways and guides us to a pragmatic and relational frame for ethical practice. The pluralistic ethical decision-making model we have considered here can be transported into our day-to-day practice.

EXERCISES/POINTS FOR REFLECTION

Reflect on the following points that we can take forward from this chapter:

1. The pluralistic principles of collaboration, feedback and client agency offer key concepts for ethical therapy practice and for thinking in action within the context of counselling and psychotherapy; melding pluralistic and ethical principles through a reasoned decision-making model epitomises good practice.
2. Client–therapist collaboration is central to ethical practice in pluralistic therapy.
3. Generating reflexive client and therapist conversations contributes to counselling content and to sustaining and informing client–therapist collaborations on therapy goals and tasks.
4. Metacommunication (Rennie, 1998) is core to the process of agreeing goals, tasks and methods for ethical therapy.

5 Facilitating client agency and autonomy is core to reflexive pluralistic practice and builds client capacity and resilience.
6 The use of an ethical decision-making model to support decisions and actions in counselling and psychotherapy practice provides an invaluable support framework.
7 Consult, consult, consult … true to pluralistic principles, engage in multiple consultative conversations – with colleagues, supervisor, mentor, ethics resources from your professional body/bodies; make consultation a central feature of your pluralistic therapy practice.

FURTHER READING

Bond, T. (2015). *Standards and ethics for counselling in action* (4th ed.). London: Sage. This is an excellent, exemplary text and will be a core component for your ethics 'toolkit'. This latest edition has additional online resources and is a great investment for the pluralistic practitioner.

Gabriel, L., & Casemore, R. (2009). *Relational ethics in counselling and psychotherapy*. London: Brunner–Routledge. This edited textbook offers richly detailed and diverse narratives on ethical practice from a range of theoretical and practical perspectives. Again, a core exemplar for your 'toolkit'.

Gergen, K., & McNamee, S. (1991). *Therapy as social constructionism*. London: Sage. Gergen's work clearly and cogently outlines social constructionist philosophy and how it relates to therapy; a classic.

Lambert, M. (1992). Psychotherapy outcome research: implications for integrative and eclectic therapy. In J.C. Norcross and M.R. Goldfried (Eds.), *Handbook of psychotherapy integration* (pp. 94–129). Lambert's chapter and the Handbook itself offer excellent early exemplars on the integration of thinking and practice in therapy.

Manson, N.C., & O'Neill, O. (2007). *Rethinking informed consent*. Cambridge: Cambridge University Press. Onora O'Neill's work has made a significant contribution to ethics and this accessible book provides informed and informative material on informed consent.

Proctor, G. (2014). *Values and ethics in counselling and psychotherapy*. London: Sage. A rich resource for trainee and newly qualified practitioners. This textbook offers case studies and exemplars for pragmatic, meaningful ethical practice, providing another 'toolkit' essential.

REFERENCES

BACP. (2013). *Ethical framework for good practice in counselling and psychotherapy*. Lutterworth: Author.

Beauchamp, T.L., & Childress, J.F. (2013). *Principles of biomedical ethics*. Oxford: Oxford University Press.

Berlin, I. (2013). *The crooked timber of humanity*. London: Fontana.
Bond, T. (2000). *Standards and ethics for counselling in action* (2nd ed.). London: Sage.
Bond, T. (2014). Editorial, in *Therapy Today*, December 2014.
Bond, T. (2015). *Standards and ethics for counselling in action* (4th edn). London: Sage.
Cooper, M., & McLeod, J. (2011). *Pluralistic counselling and psychotherapy*. London: Sage.
Dunnett, A., Jesper, C., O'Donnell, M., & Vallance, K. (Eds.). (2013). *Getting the most from supervision: a guide for counsellors and psychotherapists.* London: Palgrave.
Gabriel, L. (1996). *Boundaries in lesbian client–lesbian counsellor relationships*. M.Ed. thesis, University College of Ripon and York St John, York.
Gabriel, L. (2005). *Speaking the unspeakable: the ethics of dual relationships in counselling and psychotherapy*. London: Brunner–Routledge.
Gabriel, L. (2009). Relational ethics, boundary riders and process sentinels: allies for ethical practice. In L. Gabriel & R. Casemore (Eds.), Relational ethics in practice: narratives from counselling and psychotherapy (pp. 9-22). London: Brunner-Routledge.
Gabriel, L., & Davies, D. (2000). The management of ethical dilemmas associated with dual relationships. In C. Neal & D. Davies (Eds.), *Issues in therapy with lesbian, gay, bisexual and transgender clients*. Buckingham: Open University Press.
Gabriel, L., & Casemore, R. (Eds.). (2009). *Relational ethics in practice: narratives from counselling and psychotherapy.* London: Brunner–Routledge.
Manson, N.C., & O'Neil, O. (2007). *Rethinking informed consent*. Cambridge: Cambridge University Press.
McLeod, J. (2013). Developing pluralistic practice in counselling and psychotherapy: using what the client knows. *European Journal of Counselling Psychology*, *2*(1), 51–64.
Rennie, D. (1998). *Person-centred counselling: an experiential approach.* London: Sage.
Syme, G. (2003). *Dual relationships in counselling and psychotherapy: exploring the limits.* London: Sage.

25
Supervision in Pluralistic Counselling and Psychotherapy

*Mary Creaner and
Ladislav Timulak*

THIS CHAPTER DISCUSSES

- A pluralistic approach to supervision
- The supervision of pluralistic practice
- Supervisor competency and training from a pluralistic perspective

In recent years the provision of supervision has been seen as a core competency in professional psychology and as a distinct professional practice (Falender et al., 2004). Clinical supervision has also been recognized as a cornerstone of counselling education and a key component in trainee competency development (Bernard & Goodyear, 2014). Beyond the training context, supervision is frequently a mandated career-long professional requirement by a number of counselling and therapy organizations (e.g., The British Association for Counselling and Psychotherapy – BACP).

Contemporary supervision literature (cf. Creaner, 2014) speaks to effective or good supervision, to research-informed best supervision practices (Borders, 2014) and supervisor competencies (Falender et al., 2004). Good supervision is respectful of supervisees' learning needs, seeks to empower supervisee autonomy and builds on their strengths and resources (Ladany, Mori, & Mehr, 2013). Moreover, as a collaborative enquiry, good supervision facilitates many forms of knowledge, perspectives and resources (e.g., theory, research, professional experience, personal knowledge, clinical wisdom, etc.) to be coherently blended and brought to the supervisee's therapy practice (Bernard & Goodyear, 2014; Cooper & McLeod, 2011). Good supervisors are flexible in their approach (Borders, 2014), ethical in their practice (Thomas, 2007), promote a research attitude to the work (Bordin, 1983), advocate inclusive practice and attend to outcomes for both the supervisee and the client (Falender et al., 2004).

As the process of supervision may be understood in terms of a 'double matrix' (i.e., the supervisor–supervisee context and the supervisee–client context; Hawkins & Shohet, 2012: 86), both of these matrices need to be considered in the context of a pluralistic approach.

PLURALISTIC APPROACH TO SUPERVISION

The key principles of the pluralistic approach are congruent with the key principles of good supervision. While a variety of supervision models and frameworks are available to supervisors, a pluralistic framework with its focus on the domains of goals, tasks and methods (Cooper & McLeod, 2007) allows the supervisor to coherently draw on existing supervision models to provide a flexible and best practice approach to supervision. Furthermore, in the training context, in particular, the supervisor needs to have knowledge of the area under supervision (Falender et al., 2004).

In considering how the pluralistic approach presents itself in supervision, a unique feature of pluralism lies in its premise that there is 'no one right way of doing things; different people need different things at different points in time' (Cooper & McLeod, 2011: 6). Just as there is no one way to provide therapy, there is no one way to supervise (Cooper & McLeod, 2011). Moreover, in the context of supervision, learning needs change over time and supervisors need to respond flexibly to such changes as supervisees gain experience (Magnuson, Wilcoxon, & Norem, 2000). Every encounter with a supervisee is unique, the starting point of which is with the supervisee's learning needs (Bordin, 1983; Creaner, 2014). Cooper and McLeod (2011) propose that in determining what people need, we need to ask them and then commence the encounter based on their *goals*. On the assumption that different supervisees need different things it is thus essential to establish a collaborative supervisory relationship that allows supervisor–supervisee dialogue about the best approach (agreement on supervision *tasks*) for the supervisee at their developmental level. This overall strategy (the tasks of supervision that optimally facilitate the achievement of the articulated goals) of tailoring supervision for a particular supervisee, is then supplemented by particular *methods* of supervision delivery (e.g., listening to therapy sessions and reflecting on the recordings).

Building on the principles of pluralistic supervision as outlined by Cooper and McLeod (2011: 6–9), the following offers an elaboration of the key principles grounded in supervision research and literature.

The supervisory relationship

The relationship is at the core of a pluralistic approach to supervision (Cooper & McLeod, 2011). Whether in reference to trainee or post-training supervision, there is wide acceptance that the quality of the supervisory relationship is a critical component in good supervision outcomes (Ladany et al., 2013). The relationship concept of the working alliance (Bordin, 1983) has been widely adopted as a pan-theoretical construct in supervision literature (Watkins, 2014). Defined as a working alliance, the supervisory relationship comprises mutually agreed goals and tasks within the context of an emotional bond between the supervisor and supervisee (Bordin, 1983). Watkins (2014) suggests that the nature of the emotional bond is characterized by a rapport between the supervisee and supervisor that is 'collaborative', 'facilitative' and 'respectful' (p. 156). The work of pluralistic and indeed of any good supervision begins with the supervisee's frame of reference regarding what is most pertinent for them to bring to supervision (Bordin, 1983) and is supportive of supervisee autonomy (Ladany et al., 2013).

Supervision is ideally a collaborative learning relationship (Creaner, 2014). However, the supervision relationship is also a hierarchical relationship — wherever one person monitors or evaluates the work of another, power dynamics will be present in that relationship (Bernard & Goodyear, 2014). In that context, Rousmaniere and Ellis (2013) suggest that trainees may not feel sufficiently empowered to form a truly collaborative supervision relationship. The onus, therefore, of promoting collaboration lies more on the shoulders of the supervisor.

A good-quality supervisory relationship, particularly in the training context, has been demonstrated as contributing to supervisee development in terms of encouraging necessary self-disclosure (Sweeney & Creaner, 2014); increasing self-awareness (Ramos-Sánchez et al., 2002) and supporting self-efficacy beliefs (Efstation, Patton, & Kardash 1990). In contrast, poor supervisory relationships have been seen to contribute to less disclosure of relevant material by supervisees (Ladany et al., 2013), and lower levels of supervisee satisfaction (Ramos-Sánchez et al., 2002). In summary, the quality of the supervisory relationship is paramount to good supervision (Ladany et al., 2013) and can be considered as the container for all supervision processes (Watkins, 2014), including the goals, tasks and methods of pluralistic supervision.

Developing personalized goals and agreement on tasks and methods

The initial contracting phase in supervision is a point of orientation where the expectations, roles and responsibilities of both the supervisee and supervisor can be explicated. It is a place to initiate the supervisory alliance and negotiate the goals, tasks and methods of supervision (Ladany et al., 2013). The supervision contract may be considered as a method of gaining informed consent (Thomas, 2007) and as a negotiated learning agreement that clarifies the learning needs and goals of the supervisee throughout supervision (Creaner, 2014). Clear contracting may also facilitate meta-communication with the supervisee regarding the process of supervision and how they are experiencing this.

Wallace and Cooper (2015) have developed two useful tools to negotiate forms (tasks) of personalized learning in supervision – the *Supervision Personalisation Form – Assessment* (SPF-A) and the *Supervision Personalisation Form* (SPF).

The SPF-A is recommended for use in the initial supervision session and may be considered as a means of assessing the supervisees' preferences for the type of supervision they require and the supervisor's willingness and/or ability to meet those needs. The SPF-A provides a 10-point Likert scale of options for 11 supervision dimensions such as '*provide more structure*' vs '*provide less structure*' and '*talk more*' vs '*listen more*'. The SPF then can be used as a tool for reviewing and developing the initial assessment throughout the supervision arrangement.

A number of challenges can arise for a supervisor approaching supervision from a personalization perspective. For example, frequently in the training context rather than post-qualification phase, beginning supervisees often find it very challenging to identify their learning needs or preferences, and need to be facilitated to do so (Creaner, 2014). Challenges can also arise with reference to balancing the supervisees' learning preferences with the gatekeeping task of supervision, training requirements and also the particular supervisor's style (Bernard & Goodyear, 2014). For instance, with reference to the SPF, a supervisee may wish for a supervisor to '*focus less on the relationship between us*' while the supervisor may deem this a necessary focal point for working through an alliance rupture. Similarly, a supervisee may have a preference for focusing more on their problems and difficulties rather than on their strengths and abilities, whereas facilitating balanced self-assessment and evaluation is typically considered an important supervision competency (Falender et al., 2004). By the same token, in terms of supervision methods, reviewing a client audio/visual recording in supervision may not be a preference of the supervisee, however, it is still considered an effective supervision method (Bernard & Goodyear, 2014).

While in an early point of development, the intent of the Supervision Personalisation Forms is to provide the basis of a collaborative dialogue between the supervisor and supervisee (Wallace & Cooper, 2015). The authors acknowledge that the focus is not about meeting every need of the supervisee and rather propose the SPFs as a method to frame a supervision conversation about tailoring supervision, insofar as possible, to the supervisee's professional development goals, identify the tasks in supervision that would allow these goals to be achieved, and consider the actual methods used in supervision to fulfil those tasks. In the context of supervising pluralistic practice, the use of the SPFs in supervision also provides modelling to the supervisee for the use of the *Therapy Personalisation Form* (TPF) or similar measures in their therapy practice and helps the supervisee to prioritize the client's perspective and personalize therapy to the individual client (Cooper & McLeod, 2011).

The SPFs are also useful tools for incorporation into the overall supervisory learning agreement, which also incorporates preferences for feedback and evaluation (Creaner, 2014). Clear collaborative contracting at the outset and throughout the supervisory relationship can also help build a culture of feedback within supervision (see below). The intent of personalization promotes the supervisee's active engagement and ownership of their supervision experience and encourages the supervisee to take responsibility for their learning. The key point is that supervisors need to discuss and negotiate with the supervisee how best to facilitate their learning, and also how best to evaluate that learning.

Predicated on the assumption that different supervisees have different learning needs and preferences and that these will change and develop over time, a one-dimensional approach to the tasks and methods of supervision will have limited effect (Magnuson et al., 2000). Cooper and McLeod (2011) offer a number of supervision prompts for the supervisor to collaboratively explore supervision goals, tasks and methods with the supervisee. For example, such questions as 'what do you want to get out of our work together?' can help the supervisee to focus on and clarify their learning goals; 'what would you like to work on today?' encourages the supervisee to identify the most pertinent task for them in a particular session; and 'what way(s) of working would be most helpful to you in our supervision sessions?' can focus the supervisee on how and by what methods they wish their learning to be facilitated (Cooper & McLeod, 2011: 136). Such prompts serve to tailor supervision to the individual supervisee and promote a collaborative supervisory relationship. In essence, a pluralistic approach to supervision is supervisee–centred and communicates to supervisees that they are active agents in supervision and in order to make the most of their supervisory experience they will need to embrace this responsibility. The following example highlights the use of prompts to help the supervisee clarify their in-session goals.

> ### CASE EXAMPLE
> #### Maureen and Tina
>
> Maureen is a beginning trainee on a pluralistic counselling course and this is her first experience of clinical supervision. She has attended supervision with Tina for three sessions during which time they have discussed the practicalities of supervision and have begun to negotiate a learning agreement. Since her last supervision session, Maureen has met with her first therapy client and prepares a case presentation to bring to supervision. She is a little nervous about it and not exactly sure what she needs from the supervision session.
>
> *Supervisor:* What would you like to bring to supervision today?
> *Supervisee:* Well, I met with my first client and would like if we could go through that session, if that's OK?
> *Supervisor:* Of course. Well done on meeting your first client. In bringing this client, what do you hope to get from supervision?
> *Supervisee:* I'm not sure ... I guess I want to know that it was OK, that it was helpful to my client, that I didn't do any harm, that I'm working in a pluralistic way.
> *Supervisor:* OK. So within those hopes, you have a number of goals for this session. Let's look at those a little closer and see how you would like to achieve those goals and how you would like me to facilitate that ...

As an educational endeavour, a broad range of supervisory methods are available to facilitate supervisee learning. In their empirical review of 24 supervision articles,

Milne, Aylott, Fitzpatrick and Ellis (2008: 179) identified 26 supervisor interventions. Among these, *teaching* was the most prevalent intervention, cited in 75% of the studies. Other frequently mentioned interventions included giving feedback; reviewing live or recorded therapy sessions; setting goals; modelling; providing support; role-playing; and discussion. The authors note that typically multiple interventions were used and emphasize the need to do so to optimally facilitate supervisee learning. This is not to suggest that the supervisor needs to have an infinite repertoire of interventions or that they should not use interventions that have been demonstrated to be necessary in best practice supervision (e.g., reviewing audio recordings with supervisees), but rather, should encourage supervisors to be flexible in their approach and discuss a menu of options with the supervisee to facilitate collaborative enquiry.

Helping supervisees develop their strengths

Supervisees come to supervision with their lifetime of experience together with their specific training. Many trainees in counselling and psychotherapy pursue such qualifications as a second career and hence have a variety of transferable competencies to bring to their training context. However, the breadth and depth of their experience is often tacit for them and they may fail to recognize this experience as a rich resource for their training. While it is important that supervisees feel psychological safety to bring their doubts and mistakes, it is also important that they are encouraged to identify their strengths and resources. Engaging in a dialogue with supervisees about their strengths in the work provides modelling for balanced self-evaluation. For example, asking such questions as 'what went well in your work with this client?', and 'what did you appreciate about how you worked with this client?', can help the supervisee focus on their strengths in this regard.

Creating a culture of feedback

Providing feedback is one of the main methods of facilitating learning in any educational endeavour and no less so in clinical supervision (Creaner, 2014). As mentioned, giving corrective feedback is one of the most frequently cited supervisory interventions (Milne et al., 2008), and the lack of quality feedback is reported as hindering to supervisee learning (Magnuson et al., 2000). Optimally, useful feedback is directly related to the goal, objective or task at hand and is given in a timely and respectful manner (Bernard & Goodyear, 2014). At times, the content of feedback may be challenging for a supervisor to deliver, particularly if such feedback relates to personal or professional difficulties of the supervisee, if the supervisee is not open to feedback (Hoffman, Hill, Holmes, & Freitas, 2005) or if the supervisor is not sufficiently skilled (Magnuson et al., 2000). The following vignette provides an example of the latter.

> **CASE EXAMPLE**
>
> **Robert and Tracy**
>
> Tracy is a supervisor working in an adult therapy centre and provides supervision for counselling trainees. Robert is a first-year trainee, in his late twenties and has a background in volunteer telephone counselling. Robert and Tracy have met for six supervision sessions. Tracy has noticed from the beginning that Robert's manner of dress is very casual and not appropriate to the setting. At the end of their seventh supervision session, Tracy broaches the subject with Robert and says; 'Before you go, Robert, I have noticed since you started here that you dress very casually – you do look very untidy! It doesn't comply with the dress code of the agency and I am concerned that our clients will think it very unprofessional.' Robert feels embarrassed and reacts defensively. He becomes angry and asks why Tracy hadn't mentioned this as an issue before. He says it was never a problem in his previous role and that this is the first time he has heard of a dress code in the agency.

In the above case example, unfortunately, due to a number of factors – for example, lack of supervisor skill in providing feedback, lack of sensitivity to the supervisee's developmental level, delayed feedback and poor timing of the intervention – the supervisor missed an opportunity to facilitate a valuable discussion on professionalism. Furthermore, the initial contract should include an orientation to the protocols of the agency and explicate the expectations of the placement. There was also a missed opportunity to explore the supervisee's previous experience, noting the resources to build upon and also the differences between the contexts.

Creating a climate and culture whereby not only feedback from the supervisor to the supervisee, but also reciprocal feedback is the norm, may serve to heighten learning for both the supervisor and supervisee and perhaps mediate the supervisee's evaluation anxiety (Creaner, 2014). It can also model the skills of providing and seeking feedback from the client to enhance therapy outcomes. Encouraging supervisees to provide feedback to supervisors optimally promotes democracy in the supervisory relationship. Wheeler, Aveline and Barkham (2011) propose a number of measures that can be used in supervision practice and indeed supervision research to facilitate supervisee feedback (e.g., Helpful Aspects of Supervision, Llewelyn, 1988). In addition, reviewing client feedback also needs to be a focus of a pluralistic approach to supervision.

THE SUPERVISION OF PLURALISTIC PRACTICE

Further to the points considered above for developing an optimal learning environment in a pluralistic approach to supervision (e.g., establishing a good supervision relationship, personalizing the supervision experience, helping supervisees develop their strengths and creating a culture of feedback), a number of other considerations are necessary when supervising pluralistic practice. In working with a supervisee who is a pluralistic practitioner, the supervisor should not only approach supervision in a pluralistic way, but should also have knowledge of the pluralistic model as conceptualized so far (see Cooper & McLeod, 2011). This allows the supervisor to ensure that the supervisee is developing their mastery of this particular approach. This also allows the supervisor to monitor and ensure that learning specific to the pluralistic approach is also focused on in supervision.

The supervisor may, for instance, ensure that the supervisee does not overlook the basic foundations of the model. The supervisor may invite the supervisee to reflect how the basic tenets of the model (e.g., that the client is an active agent of change, that there are different pathways to change, that preferences and predilections may differ from client to client, etc.) are present in particular moments of the supervisee's therapeutic work with a client. The supervisor may actively encourage that a collaborative relationship, flexibility and negotiation (metacommunication) are held at the centre of the supervisee's work. Specifically, in terms of the supervisee's work with the client's goals (cf. Cooper & McLeod, 2011), the supervisor may need to ensure that the supervisee helps the client to articulate and differentiate his or her goals (including unconscious goals). It is important that the goals are achievable, that they also include aspirations and that they build on the client's strengths and resources. The role of the supervisor in this regard is to facilitate the supervisee to explore their client's strengths so they may identify the most congruent methods to help the client achieve their goals. The supervisor may also encourage the supervisee to use some of the existing structured methods for eliciting therapy goals (such as a Goals Form, see Cooper & McLeod, 2011).

With regard to the use of various tasks in therapy (cf. Cooper & McLeod, 2011), the supervisor may support the supervisee to consider and offer the client a range of possible ways of working in therapy (e.g., work on behaviour change, focusing on emotions, problem-solving, meaning-making, etc.) and that these are explicitly offered to the client, negotiated and renegotiated throughout the process of therapy. It may be useful if the supervisor helps the supervisee to build their 'therapy menu' (Cooper & McLeod, 2011), a menu of tasks that they feel comfortable with and competent to provide. This is a personalized and unique menu that a supervisee/therapist can offer the client with confidence.

Similarly, as it is expected that the supervisee will be building their therapy 'task menu', it is also expected that they will identify and develop the ingredients of those tasks (specific methods). It is expected that a pluralistic therapist (supervisee) would be familiar with and competent in a variety of specific therapy methods developed across various therapy approaches (schools) and that the supervisor will facilitate the supervisee to critically reflect on these while fostering an attitude of theoretical flexibility (McLeod & Cooper, 2012). The supervisor may further encourage the supervisee not only to consider various methods in their work and how they can be offered to the client to support engagement in therapy, but the supervisor may also see the building of a portfolio of methods as a legitimate goal in the supervision of pluralistic practice. The supervisor may then ensure that the supervisee is building his or her portfolio and gains specific competence in the various methods.

As previously mentioned, it is important that the supervisor facilitates the supervisee to attend to client outcomes. Supervisees should be assisted to routinely monitor their work with clients to identify what is and is not working (McLeod & Cooper, 2012). While many therapy outcome measures and scales are currently available for this purpose, the intent again is to encourage the supervisee to continue a dialogue of collaboration with their clients, to personalize therapy, to provide another opportunity to enhance the client's active participation in therapy and to evaluate their therapy work with a particular client (McLeod & Cooper, 2012).

Finally, when supervising a pluralistic practitioner, an attitude of further learning and openness, particularly to the evolving world of research-informed practice, needs to be fostered (cf. Cooper, 2008; Timulak, 2008). It is important that supervisors encourage supervisees to regularly consult and familiarize themselves with research literature pertinent to the pluralistic approach (one can expect that most of the research literature would be relevant). Studies that explore how clients can better use therapy may be of particular interest and relevance (Cooper & McLeod, 2011).

SUPERVISOR COMPETENCY AND TRAINING FROM A PLURALISTIC PERSPECTIVE

Recent years have seen attention being paid to supervisor competency and training (Creaner, 2014). Considering that supervision is a professional activity, distinct from therapy, it is reasonable to assert that different competencies are required for the supervisor (Falender et al., 2004), which may be every bit as difficult to acquire and develop as those of the therapist (Watkins, 1993). Much like therapy, supervision practice has preceded empirical enquiry (Creaner, 2014). While core supervision competencies are being developed (Falender et al., 2004), we are still in need of research-informed pedagogical models for supervisor training and supervision training curricula (Borders, 2014). In terms of supervisor training and competency development, the pluralistic perspective presents a valuable framework in this context also. Drawing on the criteria of pluralistic therapy practice as detailed by Cooper and McLeod (2011: 146–7) and applying these to supervision, the broad competencies of the supervisor are outlined in the summary below.

SUMMARY

In summary, the key considerations in the supervision of pluralistic practice are as follows:

- The supervisor needs to reflect upon how pluralistic principles are at the heart of good supervision and how supervision practice may be conceptualized within a pluralistic framework.

- In working with a supervisee who is a pluralistic practitioner, the supervisor needs to reflect on how the supervisee's learning can be best facilitated collaboratively within the pluralistic framework to personalize therapy and provide for the best therapy outcomes with their clients.
- The broad competencies of the supervisor may be seen as (adapted from Cooper & McLeod, 2011: 146–7):
  - The ability to create a collaborative supervisory relationship and working alliance that values the supervisee as an active agent in their learning
  - The ability to create a culture of feedback in supervision
  - The ability to discuss and agree with supervisees' appropriate personalized goals, tasks and methods
  - The ability to implement a range of supervisory methods
  - The ability to help supervisees draw on their strengths and resources to achieve their goals for their professional development and the welfare of their clients.

EXERCISES/POINTS FOR REFLECTION

For supervisees:

1. How would you identify your supervision learning needs and preferences?
2. What do you need from supervision to facilitate you to work within a pluralistic framework?
3. What are your thoughts on developing a collaborative supervision relationship with your supervisor?

For supervisors:

1. What do you consider the key strengths of and challenges in holding a pluralistic perspective in supervision?
2. What do you consider the key strengths of and challenges in facilitating a pluralistic approach with supervisees in their client work?
3. How might you create a culture of feedback in supervision?

FURTHER READING

Bernard, J.M., & Goodyear, R.K. (2014). *Fundamentals of clinical supervision* (5th ed.). Boston, MA: Pearson. This provides a comprehensive research-informed text covering all aspects of supervision theory and practice for mental health professionals.

Cooper, M., & McLeod, J. (2011). *Pluralistic counselling and psychotherapy*. London: Sage. This text is essential reading for practitioners working within a pluralistic framework. A discussion on a pluralistic approach to supervision can be found in Chapter 8.

Creaner, M. (2014). *Getting the best out of supervision in counselling and therapy: a guide for the supervisee*. London: Sage. Drawing on current supervision

(Continued)

(Continued)

literature and research, this book explores the supervisory relationship as a learning relationship and provides resources for supervisors and supervisees to optimize their supervisory experience.

Milne, D., Aylott, H., Fitzpatrick, H., & Ellis, M. (2008). How does clinical supervision work? Using a 'best evidence synthesis' approach to construct a basic model of supervision. *The Clinical Supervisor, 27*(2), 170–190. This article proposes a basic model of supervision constructed on an empirical review of 24 supervision articles that identified pertinent contextual variables, interventions and outcomes in good supervision.

REFERENCES

Bernard, J.M., & Goodyear, R.K. (2014). *Fundamentals of clinical supervision* (5th ed.). Boston, MA: Pearson.

Borders, L.D. (2014). Best practices in clinical supervision: another step in delineating effective supervision practice. *American Journal of Psychotherapy, 68*(2), 151–162.

Bordin, E.S. (1983). A working alliance model of supervision. *The Counseling Psychologist, 11*(1), 35–42.

Cooper, M. (2008). *Essential research findings in counselling and psychotherapy: the facts are friendly.* London: Sage.

Cooper, M., & McLeod, J. (2007). A pluralistic framework for counselling and psychotherapy: implications for research. *Counselling and Psychotherapy Research, 7*(3), 135–143.

Cooper, M., & McLeod, J. (2011). *Pluralistic counselling and psychotherapy.* London: Sage.

Creaner, M. (2014). *Getting the best out of supervision in counselling and psychotherapy: a guide for the supervisee.* London: Sage.

Efstation, J.F., Patton, M.J., & Kardash, M. (1990). Measuring the working alliance in counsellor supervision. *Journal of Counseling Psychology, 37*(3), 322–329.

Falender, C.A., Cornish, J.A., Goodyear, R., Hatcher, R., Kaslow, N.J., Leventhal, G., … Grus, C. (2004). Defining competencies in psychology supervision: a consensus statement. *Journal of Clinical Psychology, 60*, 771–785.

Hawkins, P., & Shohet, R. (2012). *Supervision in the helping professions* (4th ed.). Maidenhead: Open University Press.

Hoffman, M., Hill, C.E., Holmes, S.E., & Freitas, G.F. (2005). Supervisor perspective on the process and outcome of giving easy, difficult, or no feedback to supervisees. *Journal of Counseling Psychology, 52*(1), 3–13.

Ladany, N., Mori, Y., & Mehr, K.E. (2013). Effective and ineffective supervision. *The Counseling Psychologist, 41*(1), 28–47.

Llewelyn, S.P. (1988). Psychological therapy as viewed by clients and therapists. *British Journal of Clinical Psychology, 27*, 223–37.

Magnuson, S., Wilcoxon, S., & Norem, A. (2000). A profile of lousy supervision: experienced counselors' perspectives. *Counselor Education and Supervision, 30*(3), 189–202.

McLeod, J., & Cooper, M. (2012). Pluralistic counselling and psychotherapy. In C. Feltham & I. Horton (Eds.), *The Sage handbook of counselling and psychotherapy* (pp. 368–372). London: Sage.

Milne, D., Aylott, H., Fitzpatrick, H., & Ellis, M. (2008). How does clinical supervision work? Using a 'best evidence synthesis' approach to construct a basic model of supervision. *The Clinical Supervisor, 27*(2), 170–190.

Ramos-Sánchez, L., Esnil, E., Goodwin, A., Riggs, S., Touster, L.O., Wright, L.K., ... Rodolfa, E. (2002). Negative supervisory events: effects on supervision and supervisory alliance. *Professional Psychology: Research and Practice, 33*(2), 197–202.

Rousmaniere, T.G., & Ellis, M.V. (2013). Developing the construct and measure of collaborative clinical supervision: the supervisee's perspective. *Training and Education in Professional Psychology, 7*(4), 300–308.

Sweeney, J., & Creaner, M. (2014). What's not being said? Recollections of nondisclosure in clinical supervision while in training. *British Journal of Guidance & Counselling, 42*(2), 211–224.

Thomas, J. (2007). Informed consent through contracting for supervision: minimizing risks, enhancing benefits. *Professional Psychology: Research and Practice, 38*(3), 221–231.

Timulak, L. (2008). *Research in psychotherapy and counselling*. London: Sage.

Wallace, K., & Cooper, M. (2015). Development of Supervision Personalisation Forms: a qualitative study of the dimensions along which supervisors' practices vary. *Counselling & Psychotherapy Research, 15*(1), 31–40.

Watkins, C.E., Jr. (1993). Development of the psychotherapy supervisor: concepts, assumptions, and hypotheses of the supervisor complexity model. *American Journal of Psychotherapy, 47*(1), 58–74.

Watkins, C.E., Jr. (2014). The supervisory alliance as quintessential integrative variable. *Journal of Contemporary Psychotherapy, 44*(3), 151–161.

Wheeler, S., Aveline, M., & Barkham, M. (2011). Practice-based supervision research: a network of researchers using a common toolkit. *Counselling and Psychotherapy Research, 11*(2), 88–96.

26

Training in Pluralistic Counselling and Psychotherapy

Julia McLeod, Kate Smith and Mhairi Thurston

THIS CHAPTER DISCUSSES

- The objectives and elements of therapy training
- Basic principles of pluralistic training
- How pluralistic training is organised
- The importance of ongoing personal and professional development for pluralistic practitioners

TRAINING IN COUNSELLING AND PSYCHOTHERAPY: KEY OBJECTIVES AND ELEMENTS

The content and style of training received by counsellors and psychotherapists, and the length of training, varies enormously across different countries and different professional communities. However, there exists broad agreement that a satisfactory training curriculum needs to contain certain key elements: theoretical understanding, practical skills, capacity to deal with professional issues, use of supervision, appreciation of the role of research knowledge, cultural sensitivity and the development of self-awareness. The relative weighting of each of these elements will depend on the particular philosophical and professional traditions within which a training programme locates itself. For example, in some programmes, trainees are required to engage in weekly personal therapy, while other courses may recommend personal therapy as an optional activity.

From a research perspective, there is very little reliable evidence around the impact of different training activities and how they are delivered. Because training activities tend to be offered in the context of a whole programme, it is hard to determine the effectiveness of specific elements of that programme. It is also difficult to control for factors other than training (for instance, life experience) that might have an impact on effectiveness. As a result, the best that can be done is to draw on a judicious mix of whatever research evidence is available, along with professional experience and a willingness to engage in critical monitoring of current practice.

Pluralistic counselling and psychotherapy can be regarded as an 'integrative' approach (Stricker, 2010), which brings together ideas and methods from 'pure-form' therapy models such as psychodynamic, cognitive behavioural and person-centred. The provision of integrative training has been regarded as problematic by some members of the counselling and psychotherapy professional community. For example, one of the leading figures in psychotherapy research and training, Louis Castonguay (2005: 385), has stated that:

> one can only integrate well what one knows well. This means that ... students should, in my view, have a deep understanding of the theoretical, clinical, empirical, and epistemological bases of each single orientation prior to using or to creating an integrative system of intervention.

At the present time, there is no consensus around how integrative training should be structured (Consoli & Jester, 2005).

It can be seen, therefore, that there exists a complex set of challenges associated with therapy training in general, and then more specifically with integrative or pluralistic training. It is necessary for anyone designing a pluralistic training programme to give careful consideration to these issues, and for anyone embarking on such training to reflect on the fit between the nature and demands of pluralistic training, and their own personal needs and preferences.

It is widely recognised that it is not at all easy to learn different therapy models that may have conflicting ideas, or to move from one model to another when working with clients. In the UK, all counselling psychology training programmes are required to provide grounding in at least two contrasting therapy approaches. Ward, Hogan and Menns (2011) interviewed trainees from these programmes around their experience of coping with these requirements. One participant observed that 'at first it felt really stressful having all these different views around ... but in the end I think I came to understand the different approaches more because of having to make sense of it all'. Overall, the general view of trainees was that while there had been times when it had been hard to come to terms with an integrative or pluralistic approach, in the end it was worth it. What they found helpful was being offered an overarching explanatory model of how different therapy approaches could fit together.

BASIC PRINCIPLES OF PLURALISTIC TRAINING

The basic ideas that underpin a pluralistic approach to therapy can be found in Cooper and McLeod (2011). Using that text as a primary source, it is possible to identify a set of basic principles of pluralistic practice that can be used to inform the construction of training in this approach.

Recognition of the diversity of cultural discourses and practices around 'mental health' and healing

Contemporary culture in advanced industrial societies is characterised by the co-existence of a wide range of ideas around how to make sense of problems in living, and what to do about them. For example, depression can be understood as arising from a biochemical imbalance in the brain, unconscious rage, social inequality, dysfunctional thought processes, and many other factors. Pluralistic practice acknowledges and embraces this diversity, and assumes that trainees are at some level familiar with all of these ways of thinking as a result of being a reflective member of such a culture. In single-theory training programmes, students are encouraged to focus on a single explanatory framework, and disregard other possibilities. By contrast, pluralistic practice involves finding ways to harness and apply the specific ways of thinking and talking about problems that have most utility for the client.

Adoption of a critical philosophical perspective

The concept of pluralism represents the anchor-point of the approach. This is a philosophical construct, and training needs to allow space for students to explore the epistemological, relational and ethical implications of this idea. One example of this critical philosophical effort occurs in respect of the meaning and use of 'theory'. Rather than regarding theories of therapy as 'true' mirrors of reality, trainees are invited to consider multiple ways in which theory functions in relation to science and practice, drawing on such sources as Hansen (2006) and McLeod (2013: ch. 4).

Maximising the use of personal and cultural resources

A pluralistic perspective on therapy takes account of the many ways in which people make use of everyday activities, available in their social world, to support them through troubled times and accomplish life goals. Such activities include, but are not restricted to, reading, outdoor activities, art making, spiritual practice and political engagement. In order to become adept at integrating these resources into therapy, students are given opportunities to reflect on the role of such practices in their own life, build knowledge about resources within their community and learn from relevant research studies.

Counselling skills

Pluralistic therapy calls for a high degree of flexibility and improvisation on the part of the practitioner, to be able to be responsive to the position of the client around what might be most helpful for them. This flexibility is achieved through building a repertoire of micro-skills, and in particular an appreciation of the ways in which different forms of words can invite the client to focus their attention on different aspects of their experience, to achieve different micro-outcomes (Hill, 2004).

Understanding the value of collaboration and dialogue

At the heart of a pluralistic approach lies a commitment to collaboration around the goals, tasks and methods of therapy, leading to episodes of dialogue. Pluralistic training includes the development of a capacity to understand what is involved in these processes, as well as strategies for facilitating their occurrence.

Adopting strengths-based orientation and values

A pluralistic perspective on therapy is part of a broader movement within the therapeutic professions to acknowledge that, while clients who seek therapy may be troubled and in crisis, they are also individuals who possess considerable strengths and personal resources (Bohart & Tallman, 1999; Wong, 2006).

Using research to inform practice

A pluralistic stance allows that there are several sources of knowledge that contribute to effective practice. Students are encouraged to reflect on their 'internal pluralism' in respect of these different sources or voices. Research knowledge is considered as a distinctive and valued source of knowledge, through being de-centred and also (potentially) derived from collective wisdom.

Commitment to lifelong learning

A pluralistic approach to therapy is not grounded in an assumption that an initial period of training can ever be sufficient. Students are encouraged to regard the pluralistic framework as a structure that will serve as a basis for lifelong learning, by specifying principles through which new knowledge can be integrated into practice. The key idea in pluralistic therapy, of being open to the ideas and practices of the client, implies that practitioners are always open to new learning.

The existence of these principles can be viewed as providing distinct points of contrast between pluralistic training and the broader field of training in integrative therapy. Both pluralistic and integrative training pursue the goal of enabling trainees to draw on a range of theories and methods. However, pluralistic training is organised around a set of clearly articulated 'metatheory', as operationalised in these principles, whereas most integrative training programmes have not developed such a framework.

Individuals who make the choice of entering training in pluralistic counselling and psychotherapy tend to do so on the basis of personal needs and values. Thompson and Cooper (2012) interviewed counsellors who were undergoing, or had recently completed, pluralistic training, and found that all of them highlighted this factor:

> 'I was never one to sort of have a one particular allegiance – I'm not, you know, like I'm not religious I might be spiritual but I'm not religious and I don't believe in singular belief systems.'

The findings of this study have important implications for the delivery of training. It is necessary, at interview and in the early part of training, to provide opportunities for students to explore relevant aspects of their values. It is also important that alternative training pathways should be available, within a city or region: not everyone possesses a pluralistic worldview, and not everyone will want to become a pluralistic therapist.

HOW PLURALISTIC TRAINING IS ORGANISED

There are two pathways that can be followed in relation to becoming a pluralistic therapist. The first option is to undertake training in a single-theory approach (such as psychodynamic or CBT) or within a different integrative tradition, and then learn about pluralism at a later stage. The second option is to complete a training that is specifically based on a pluralistic model. A number of such training programmes have been developed: in the counselling programmes at the University of East London, University of Abertay and Institute for Integrative Counselling and Psychotherapy in Dublin, and the counselling psychology courses at Glasgow Caledonian University, University of Manchester and the University of the West of England.

The Abertay training in pluralistic counselling, in which the authors are involved, comprises four cycles of learning, each lasting for one academic year of part-time study:

1. Preliminary training, mainly focusing on understanding and using counselling skills, as well as personal awareness activities, a brief introduction to pluralistic principles and selected mainstream counselling theories. This element of the programme leads to the award of a Certificate in Counselling Skills.
2. Using a pluralistic approach in work with clients. Inputs on specific pluralistic strategies such as collaborative case formulation and use of feedback tools, more detailed exploration of person-centred, psychodynamic and CBT theory and methods, coverage of professional issues, supervised practice and research awareness, and participation in personal development groups. Reflection on practice through a case report. Consolidation of conceptual learning in 'personal theory of counselling' paper.
3. Further pluralistic practice with clients. Broadening the theoretical resources and interventions available to the trainee, through sessions on existential, transactional analysis, Gestalt therapy and narrative therapy theory and practice.

Pluralistic perspectives on working with dreams, couple therapy, and working with anxiety and depression. Consolidation of pluralistic competence in a detailed case study and personal development portfolio. Completion of stages 2 and 3 leads to the award of a Postgraduate Diploma in Counselling.
4. MSc research study on a pluralistic topic, and reflexive paper.

Several strategies are employed to anchor the training in pluralistic concepts and values. Students are introduced to a pluralistic framework before they embark on in-depth exploration of 'unitary' theories and methods. This is accomplished through a two-day intensive block at the start of year 2, which weaves together theory, research and personal experience, in a way that immerses participants in a pluralistic way of thinking about human experience and interaction. Students then go on to engage with mainstream theories of therapy, where they are encouraged to make connections between what they are learning, and a broader pluralistic overview. Students are also helped to find ways that mainstream theories can contribute to pluralistic practice, by 'dismantling' these theories into elements that can be used in relation to collaborating with clients around shared understandings and alignment of goals, tasks and methods. For example, within psychodynamic theory, many students find that attachment concepts are invaluable in enabling clients to understand troubling patterns in their relationships, even in situations where the change methods that the client prefers to pursue (e.g. homework exercises) may be derived from CBT on another non-psychodynamic perspective. The message to students is that, when they learn about a mainstream unitary model such as psychodynamic psychotherapy, they should be looking for practical ways of understanding and interventions that they can see themselves incorporating into their current work with clients.

At around the mid-point of the programme, students complete an extended piece of writing on their 'personal philosophy' of counselling. In this assignment they are expected to make connections between specific theoretical ideas that are meaningful to them, and the 'metatheories' that they use in order to decide between alternative therapy theories. 'Metatheory' includes the concept of pluralism as a philosophical construct, but may also embrace a wide range of other concepts, such as democracy, sustainability, equality, feminism, scientific values, aesthetic values and spirituality. Within the assignment, students are invited to think about theory not as a 'once-and-for-all' statement of truth, but as an ongoing conversation between parts of their self, and between them, their colleagues and the field of therapy as a whole. Students are then expected to demonstrate and practice their use of theory in such contexts as reflecting on observed skills practice sessions, analysis of therapy transcripts, reflection on their personal and professional development, collaborative case formulation with clients, and writing case studies on their work.

These activities represent a set of flexible and fluid possibilities. Individual students are free to develop a theoretical 'identity' that fits them. Some students choose to focus on the task of working pluralistically from a person-centred/humanistic starting point. By contrast, other students may build their theoretical home around CBT, or around some mix of theories, or around a postmodern stance. Within the community of practice represented by the course community, this diversity makes it possible for interesting conversations to take place.

The multiple possibilities opened up by the programme are reinforced through the adoption of a collaborative, dialogical relationship between staff and participants, for example through regular 'check-in' sessions to consider the best way in which time can be used. Participants also negotiate with tutors around the focus of individual assignments.

DEVELOPING A PRACTICE-ORIENTED, CRITICAL PERSPECTIVE

In critically examining the concept of pluralism and research into change process and client preferences, students are able to recognise that there are three broad categories of therapeutic tasks that consistently emerge in work with clients: understanding and making sense of life difficulties, planning and implementing behaviour change, and resolving problematic emotions. The salience of these tasks is reinforced when students start to see clients. The implication for training is that students need to be enabled to develop competence and resourcefulness in each of these areas. Within pluralistic training, students are introduced to a range of different strategies within each area, and encouraged to develop their own personal 'toolkit'. For example, competence in being able to facilitate a conversation that generates new understanding might draw on such skills as empathic reflection, interpretation of cyclical patterns, awareness of transference/countertransference processes, psycho-education, questioning, working with imagery and metaphor, working with dreams, journal writing, and use of expressive arts techniques.

It is essential for students to be active participants in the design and implementation of their learning experience. Within the Abertay programme, students are invited at the start to write about, reflect on and share their goals for the course, and the tasks and methods that might contribute to the attainment of these goals. Students also participate in a weekly 90-minute personal and professional group, usually consisting of about eight students and a facilitator. The aim is to create opportunities for collaborative conversations around decision-making and reflective processing in relation to the work of the group. In order to orient students to this facet of the programme, the group is organised around a manual, based on McLeod and McLeod (2013), which is distributed to members.

Learning how to give and receive feedback comprises a central strand through many areas of the programme. Students learn about feedback in the context of counselling skills practice, participating in their personal and professional development group, and creating a culture of feedback in their work with clients. Technical aspects of feedback tools, such as the CORE outcome measures, are discussed in research workshops.

Research skills and awareness are integrated into the curriculum as a whole, rather than being taught as a separate module. The emphasis is on promoting an attitude of active curiosity, in which students find and read specific research studies and reviews that relate to issues that arise in their everyday practice. Early in the programme, students receive training in critical analysis and appreciation of research papers, and in ways of locating relevant research articles through online databases.

Staff talk about their own research, and provide examples of how research findings have influenced their practice. Students are expected to draw on research evidence in assignments. The aim of the MSc research dissertation is to provide an opportunity to proceed through a cycle of enquiry, resulting in a potentially publishable research article.

Examples of the kind of exercises that students might be given on the training course are: 'A client asks you to explain what counselling is, and how it can help'; 'You start a private practice and need to write something about your approach on your website'; 'At a job interview, you are challenged to justify your way of working, by a health service manager who cannot see beyond the merits of CBT'. These are scenarios that are explicitly discussed and rehearsed in pluralistic training. Being able to respond to such demands openly and non-defensively, and in a manner that matches the needs and linguistic expectations of the interlocutor, is an expression of a capacity to engage in dialogue – a key element of pluralistic competence.

THE IMPORTANCE OF ONGOING PERSONAL AND PROFESSIONAL DEVELOPMENT FOR PLURALISTIC PRACTITIONERS

Within their primary training, pluralistic practitioners are introduced to the research literature on therapist development, and in particular the studies that have examined the characteristics of 'master therapists' (Skovholt & Jennings, 2004). The intention is to convey an understanding of the idea that exceptional therapeutic work seems to be grounded in life-long learning, and enduring openness to new ideas and complexity of the human condition. The pluralistic framework for practice is portrayed as a structure within which new skills and knowledge can be assimilated. A collaborative pluralistic approach to therapy is based on the willingness of the therapist to learn from the client (Miller & Willig, 2012). The practical procedures associated with the pluralistic approach, such as eliciting and exploring client feedback, use of therapeutic metacommunication, and attention to cultural resources, mean that pluralistic therapists are routinely making new discoveries about what can be helpful for people, and are constantly on the look-out for ways to deepen their understanding of these new ideas and practices.

Initial training as a counsellor or psychotherapist can be viewed as a preparation for generic practice in front-line therapy services that offer support to individuals experiencing life crises, relationship difficulties, loss, anxiety and depression. Post-qualifying continuing professional development may lead practitioners in the direction of specialist areas of practice with specific age, gender or ethnic groups, or with complex problem areas such as psychosis, personality disorder, addictions, trauma and eating disorders. Primary training in a pluralistic way of working provides a flexible basis for this type of later specialisation (Ronnestad & Skovholt, 2013).

The use of case-based learning is particularly appropriate in pluralistic training, because a good case study or report reflects the complexity of what happens in therapy, in a manner that depicts how the work unfolds over time. Within the Abertay programme, students are taught about basic research methods in the context of involvement in group-based case study analysis (Mackrill & Iwakabe, 2013). They are encouraged to read case studies in *Clinical Case Studies*, *Pragmatic Case Studies in Psychotherapy* and other journals, and to structure their own case study assignments in accordance with the guidelines developed within these sources. A practical workshop on collaborative case formulation skills also draws on an appreciation of what is involved in attaining a coherent case analysis. Case-based learning has been found to be a powerful means for encouraging students to draw on both personal (lived experience) and formal (theory and research) sources of knowledge that are available to them, in a manner that enables them to become accustomed to bringing together multiple strands of their response to their clients.

CHALLENGES ASSOCIATED WITH PLURALISTIC TRAINING

Students and trainees undertaking training in pluralistic therapy generally find that the basic principles of the approach make sense to them and their clients, and are relatively straightforward to apply in practice. Some students have reported difficulties around finding clinical supervisors who are sympathetic to a pluralistic way of working. Other students find that some placement agencies are reluctant to allow them to use feedback tools. Engagement with pluralistic practice may present particular issues for students who have had previous training in process-based, relational therapies such as person-centred and psychodynamic, which tend not to encourage explicit conversations around the client's goals. Within a pluralistic training programme students are required to engage with a range of theoretical models, rather than developing expertise in a single approach. A 'sandwich' framework, in which study of a specific model is preceded then followed by consideration of underlying pluralistic principles, is generally effective in enabling participants to develop a sufficient level of practical knowledge in relation to each approach that is covered. Inevitably, this experience can be frustrating for students who wish to explore specific models in more depth.

SUMMARY

This chapter has highlighted the following key points:

- Training in pluralistic counselling and psychotherapy addresses core areas of professional competence: use of theory, practical skills, ability to deal with professional issues, self-awareness and making use of research to inform practice.

- Pluralistic training makes use of concepts of pluralism and dialogue to provide a coherent basis for training. The practical implications of these ideas inform all aspects of the training curriculum.
- Pluralistic training is grounded in intensive analysis and practice of generic counselling skills. In addition, specific skills associated with a pluralistic way of working with clients include the use of metacommunication, collaboration and feedback.
- A pluralistic training programme encourages students to adopt a critical and questioning approach to established 'unitary' models of theory and practice in counselling and psychotherapy.
- Initial training in pluralistic counselling is viewed as providing a basis for ongoing personal and professional development over the course of a career.

EXERCISES/POINTS FOR REFLECTION

1 To what extent are your own world-view and values, way of thinking about knowledge, and previous educational and occupational experience consistent with a pluralistic stance? What are the implications of these issues, for your choice of training?
2 What are the implications of the concept of dialogue for the type of training environment and group culture that are needed within a pluralistic training programme?
3 What are some of the learning activities that might be used to enable trainees to develop an appreciation of the therapeutic potential of cultural resources?

FURTHER READING

Boswell, J.F., Nelson, D.L., Nordberg, S.S., McAleavey, A.A., & Castonguay, L.G. (2010). Competency in integrative psychotherapy: perspectives on training and supervision. *Psychotherapy Theory, Research, Practice, Training, 47*, 3–11. A thoughtful discussion of some of the fundamental attributes of integrative practice, and how they can be actualised in training.

Brown, L.S. (2009). Cultural competence: a new way of thinking about integration in therapy. *Journal of Psychotherapy Integration, 19*, 340–353. Argues that a willingness to grapple with the reality of difference (a central tenet of pluralism) lies at the heart of therapist competence.

Gold, J. (2005). Anxiety, conflict, and resistance in learning an integrative perspective on psychotherapy. *Journal of Psychotherapy Integration, 15*, 374–383. Stimulating personal account of the sources of resistance to being open to multiple theoretical perspectives.

Marzillier, J. (2011). *The gossamer thread: my life as a psychotherapist*. London: Karnac. An accessible autobiographical account of one therapist's lifetime journey toward pluralism.

REFERENCES

Bohart, A.C., & Tallman, K. (1999). *How clients make therapy work: the process of active self-healing*. Washington, DC: American Psychological Association.

Castonguay, L.G. (2005). Training issues in psychotherapy integration: a commentary. *Journal of Psychotherapy Integration, 15*, 384–391.

Consoli, A.J., & Jester, C.M. (2005). A model for teaching psychotherapy theory through an integrative structure. *Journal of Psychotherapy Integration, 15*, 358–373.

Cooper, M., & McLeod, J. (2011). *Pluralistic counselling and psychotherapy*. London: Sage.

Hansen, J.T. (2006). Counseling theories within a postmodernist epistemology: new roles for theories in counseling practice. *Journal of Counseling and Development, 84*, 291–297.

Hill, C.E. (2004). *Helping skills: facilitating exploration, insight and action* (2nd ed.). Washington, DC: American Psychological Association.

Mackrill, T., & Iwakabe, S. (2013). Making a case for case studies in psychotherapy training: a small step towards establishing an empirical basis for psychotherapy training. *Counselling Psychology Quarterly, 26*, 250–266.

McLeod, J. (2013). *An introduction to counselling* (5th ed.). Maidenhead: Open University Press.

McLeod, J., & McLeod, J. (2013). *Personal and professional development: a practical guide for counsellors, psychotherapists and mental health practitioners*. Maidenhead: Open University Press.

Miller, E., & Willig, C. (2012). Pluralistic counselling and HIV-positive clients: the importance of shared understanding. *European Journal of Psychotherapy and Counselling, 14*, 33–46.

Ronnestad, M.H., & Skovholt, T.M. (2013). *The developing practitioner: growth and stagnation of therapists and counselors*. New York: Routledge.

Skovholt, T.M., & Jennings, L. (2004). *Master therapists: exploring expertise in therapy and counseling*. New York: Allyn & Bacon.

Stricker, G. (2010). *Psychotherapy integration*. Washington, DC: American Psychological Association.

Thompson, A., & Cooper, M. (2012). Therapists' experiences of pluralistic practice. *European Journal of Psychotherapy and Counselling, 14*, 63–75.

Ward, T., Hogan, K., & Menns, R. (2011). Perceptions of integration in counselling psychology training: a pilot study. *Counselling Psychology Review, 26*, 8–19.

Wong, Y.J. (2006). Strength-centered therapy: a social constructionist, virtues-based psychotherapy. *Psychotherapy: Theory, Research, Practice, Training, 43*, 133–146.

27
Research and Pluralistic Counselling and Psychotherapy

*Terry Hanley and
Laura Anne Winter*

THIS CHAPTER DISCUSSES

- What a pluralistic perspective to research means, and how one size does not always fit all in research as well as therapeutic practice
- The need for a pluralistic approach to research when considering counselling and psychotherapy
- How the pluralistic framework might be utilised as a research tool, and how collaboration, goals, tasks and methods can be applied within a research setting
- An agenda for research related to the pluralistic framework for counselling and psychotherapy

A PLURALISTIC PERSPECTIVE OF RESEARCH

Just as there are a multitude of therapeutic approaches from which therapists can choose, there are an ever-increasing number of research methodologies for those undertaking therapeutic research. With this in mind, the words of the philosopher Rescher (1993) prove pertinent for both activities: pluralism refers to 'the doctrine that any substantial question admits of a variety of plausible but mutually conflicting responses' (p. 79). Encapsulated within such a view is the notion that there can be numerous potentially appropriate ways to examine a particular phenomenon or topic of interest. Thus, no research methodology is automatically cast aside, or valued any more than others. This attitude towards research design is something called methodological pluralism.

This stance might be perceived as quite different to many commonplace research assessment exercises. For instance, in the UK, the National Health Service favours a hierarchy of evidence that has quantitative randomised controlled trials firmly at the top (see Figure 27.1 for a summary of this hierarchy). Therapeutic approaches meeting the required criteria (that is to say, having a number of high-quality randomised controlled trials that demonstrate the effectiveness of that approach) gain credence and are deemed evidence-based practices, which are thus more likely to be commissioned. In contrast, qualitative research or practice-based evidence research strategies may be viewed as inferior, at least when commissioning services is being considered. Such a position leads to numerous debates and arguments about whether this is always the best means of evaluating research and spending a great deal of money. It is not within the scope of the chapter to argue one way or the other on this particular issue, it is, however, put forward that pragmatic philosophy might provide one means for working *with* these different perspectives, rather than being disabled by them.

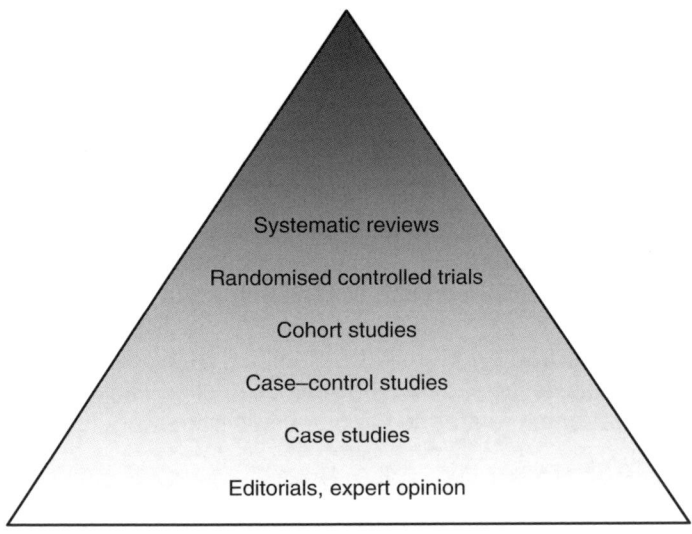

FIGURE 27.1 *Levels of evidence*

Pragmatism has its roots within the work of William James and John Dewey, two American philosophers who were writing during the early part of the twentieth century. At the heart of the position is the view that for things to work appropriately they have to be useful: James is often paraphrased as saying 'It's right because it works'; for interest, he actually stated 'What works is true and represents reality, for the individual for whom it works' (James, 1909/1978: 298). Utility is therefore greatly valued when reflecting upon multiple interpretations. If the commonplace hierarchy of evidence mentioned above is considered, one might therefore view this as a pragmatic resolution to a complex problem. True, it is a framework transferred from more medically minded sciences and can be viewed as having many flaws, but it is an approach that provides a means to making decisions. Importantly, the complexity of the task has yet to yield a fruitful workable alternative that has been mutually agreed to be strong enough to take over from the existing regime. Thus, from a pluralistic position it is important to remember that, as with therapeutic decision-making, one size does not fit all, but there are likely to be some responses that are viewed as more useful than others within particular contexts.

RESEARCHING COUNSELLING AND PSYCHOTHERAPY: IDENTIFYING THE NEED FOR PLURALISTIC METHODOLOGIES

Before delving too much further into discussions about the process of researching pluralistic counselling and psychotherapy, it is important to introduce some research methods that are commonly used. Furthermore, it is important to also consider how individuals might judge the quality of such research and to reflect upon the utility of such work.

An introduction to common research methods

Within Box 27.1, quantitative, qualitative and mixed methods approaches to research are discussed in turn. Please be mindful that these are very crude descriptions and that each approach has a wealth of literature underpinning it.

Box 27.1   Brief descriptions of research methods

Quantitative research – research in which the phenomenon of interest is summarised in numerical form (e.g. by using a questionnaire that asks participants to rate items on a scale of 1–5).

Qualitative research – research in which the phenomenon of interest is commonly summarised using the words of participants (e.g. by summarising the content of interviews or focus groups).

Mixed methods research – research that combines the use of both quantitative research methods and qualitative research methods (e.g. interviews may be utilised to gain a greater understanding of information gathered through using questionnaires).

As might be evident in the brief descriptions, each of these approaches to research comes with their associated strengths and weaknesses. If we consider quantitative research methods, these prove excellent means of summarising large amounts of information into easily digestible chunks. In contrast, these approaches can be criticised for being too simplistic and not presenting a rich enough picture of human experience. In comparison, qualitative research methods afford the opportunity to provide detailed accounts of particular events and experiences. They do not, however, provide findings that are easily generalisable to a wider population. With such challenges in mind, it is important to consider and select the most fitting tool for the research project at hand. As is described later in the chapter, the starting point for making this decision is the goal of the research, and the research questions posed.

Mixed methods research might be seen as providing the best of both worlds in research. It can provide information that is summarised into numerical form and can combine this with detailed accounts of people's experiences. However, in reality things are much more complicated. For instance, mixed methods research often involves additional complexities of considering at what point in the research, and how, different strands of information come together and are 'mixed'. Thus, commonly, a mixed methods project has the potential to become substantially larger than a project utilising one approach; first it has to look at the quantitative information, secondly at the qualitative information, and thirdly at the interaction between both the previous approaches (this is just one potential mixed methods design, there are numerous potential designs a researcher might consider). As with the realms of quantitative and qualitative research, mixed methods research now has a substantial body of literature related to its practice (see Creswell & Plano Clark, 2011).

Judging the quality of research

A major consideration, when thinking about methodological pluralism, is how to judge the quality of research, and to identify what good research looks like. Ultimately, just as the choice of methodology depends on the question posed, the answer will vary depending on the methodology adopted. Specifically, quantitative research is most appropriately considered alongside the concepts 'reliability' (i.e. is it likely that results will be more than a one-off?) and 'validity' (i.e. is it likely that something else might explain the results more effectively?), while qualitative researchers might be more interested to consider issues such as the 'trustworthiness' of the study (i.e. is enough information presented for the reader to understand how any conclusions were arrived at?). Each of these concepts requires careful consideration and has associated recommendations for good practice (see the suggestions for further reading for more information). Furthermore, it could be argued that concepts such as the trustworthiness of research represent an ethical position that pervades all research approaches and is in keeping with the foundations of the pluralistic framework (Cooper & McLeod, 2011). Thus, although the discussions and associated practices may be more commonplace in qualitative research, they may have a currency that is more far reaching (e.g. within a quantitative research project, the researchers might be transparent about why they chose the questionnaire they utilised instead of another).

Considering the utility of research

One area that may often be ignored is whether research can get neatly transferred to practice. As noted at the start of this chapter, the concept of pragmatism, and the associated emphasis upon utility, can play an important role when considering a pluralistic position. In accounting for this, a number of suggestions have been made to create more useable research outputs. A major arena for these debates has come in the guise of implementation science (e.g. see Durlak & DuPre, 2008). The implementation science movement specifically aims to promote the integration of research findings into healthcare practices and policy. It aims to redress some of the discrepancy between seemingly effective ways of working, which are demonstrated within controlled environments, and the complex reality of putting them into action in the real world. In doing so, researchers are encouraged to adopt a more systemic perspective in which any intervention is not explored without consideration of wider contextual issues. For instance, a randomised controlled trial of an intervention in a university setting may demonstrate that the particular intervention is effective when it is delivered whilst accompanied by an expensive research programme, but it may struggle to be maintained within routine daily practice that receives much less support. Such a position is likely to take account of multiple sources of research and thus embrace methodological pluralism in an integrated and coherent framework. Similarly, but potentially on a smaller scale, systematic single case study designs have developed to incorporate multiple sources of information with a view to presenting a rich account of therapeutic work (e.g. McLeod & Cooper, 2011). In much the same way to the ideas discussed within the literature around implementation science, the richer pools of information aid any associated decision-making.

Researching the pluralistic framework for counselling and psychotherapy

When researching the pluralistic framework for counselling and psychotherapy all research designs have the potential to be used fruitfully (depending on the particular needs of each research project of course). Linked to this, however, is the final point for this section, notably the need for strategic thinking. In a world where there are so many potential credible options, strategic thinking and direction around the priorities for the pluralistic framework is likely to be essential to maximise the resources available, and ultimately produce more convincing and useful outputs. It could therefore be argued that research in this area would benefit from a 'joined up' agenda to which interested participants might contribute small amounts. This is suggested in contrast to having numerous researchers working on their own individual interest areas with no wider connections or links. Such strategic, joined-up thinking within a research community would be commensurate with a more pragmatic attitude (prizing utility) and, it could be argued, would also fit with the collaborative nature of the pluralistic framework.

UTILISING THE PLURALISTIC FRAMEWORK FOR RESEARCH: ON BECOMING A PLURALISTIC RESEARCHER

The pluralistic framework has been discussed throughout this book as a means of reflecting upon the decision-making process that counsellors and psychotherapists go through within therapy. This section extends these discussions and instead reflects upon how the framework might be utilised as a research tool. In doing so, the issues of collaborative working relationships, and identifying research goals, tasks and methods, are discussed in turn.

Collaboration in research

The collaborative working relationship is central to the pluralistic framework. In therapy, much is put in place to facilitate the active involvement of, and collaboration with, clients. A similar sentiment might be considered in relation to research. Commonly, researchers are guided by hunches that are dominated by their own areas of interest. Such a position leads to the creation of much fruitful work but it has the potential to place the researcher at the top of a hierarchy in which participants/subjects in projects might be curiously observed – much as a rat's behaviour might be as they work their way out of a maze. That is to say, the researcher holds the power in the process and the participants can then be positioned in a very passive role, in which research is 'done on them'.

This power imbalance in research might be considered analogous to the power imbalances discussed in therapeutic practice (where therapy might be 'done to' a client). Again, similar to within the therapy room, this is often far from the intention of researchers; however it can be argued that the power imbalance is implicit within the structures in place. Thus, in contrast, a researcher being influenced by the more egalitarian positioning discussed in the pluralistic framework might consider adopting a similar attitude towards any research they are involved in. This attitude might translate into research practice that involves a greater degree of collaboration with research participants and stakeholders (for instance, see participatory research designs such as those discussed by Duckett, Kagan, & Sixsmith (2010) and Reason & Bradbury (2008)). The level of involvement or collaboration may vary across different research projects, from having equal collaboration through the whole project, to involving participants in some aspects of the work. Box 27.2 provides some examples of the ways in which participants and stakeholders can collaborate with researchers in the research process.

Box 27.2 Collaborative relationships in research

There are numerous points during research at which stakeholders and researchers might collaborate. 'Stakeholders' might include participants, advisory groups and co-researchers.

> **At the outset of the project**
>
> - Interested parties might form a project steering group which can be consulted with regards to project design and implementation, research ethics, etc.
> - Research designs might be arrived at collaboratively with those involved in services (service providers or service users)
> - Stakeholders and researchers might collaborate to develop materials to be used in the research, such as information sheets, consent forms and interview schedules
>
> **During the project**
>
> - Stakeholders might be involved in recruitment of participants
> - Data might be collected with co-researchers
> - Data might be analysed with co-researchers
>
> **At the end of the project**
>
> - Stakeholders and researchers might collaborate on writing publications from the research; these could be for academic or professional audiences or for the general public
> - Stakeholders and researchers might collaborate on developing and delivering presentations disseminating the research findings

Goals in research

Similar to a therapeutic encounter, in a research project there will be certain goals that are articulated at the outset. Whether collaboratively arrived at or not, the identification of goals proves vitally important for any project. These goals will be the articulation of what the research hopes and aims to achieve. These will then be further specified within the research question, which, as with the therapeutic goals, provides the focus of what is to follow. As has been hinted at earlier, the research question does not only provide a focus for the project, it also serves as a guide for determining the choice of research design to be utilised. For example, a question focusing on the effectiveness of a therapeutic approach is more likely to make use of a predominantly quantitative research design to measure specific changes, while a question focusing on the experience of being in therapy might more likely utilise predominantly qualitative research methods.

Tasks in research

Following on from the goals that are articulated by the researcher we then move on to the arena of tasks. In much a similar vein to the therapeutic discourse, it could be considered that the goals represent the desired destination of the research, whilst the tasks represent the route (or choice of routes) that the researcher will travel. One way to think about this is to consider the route as the methodological choice by the researcher. Specifically, will the project utilise a quantitative, qualitative or mixed methods research design. As indicated above, the goals of the project might provide a steer as to the most appropriate approach, with projects looking to consider effectiveness leaning towards quantitative designs and those looking to consider deeper therapeutic experiences leaning towards qualitative designs. These are, of course, by no means hard and fast rules (remember Rescher, cited above: 'a substantial question admits of a variety of plausible but mutually conflicting responses'), and ultimately any approach should be judged using criteria developed particularly for that approach.

Methods in research

Finally we come to the choice of research methods. At this stage we reach the more practical end of the research. When considering the use of the pluralistic framework as a research tool, the methods are the choices about data generation and data analysis. As in therapy, the goals and tasks will to some extent restrict the scope of potential methods you might use. For example, if your goal is to explore working-class clients' experiences of therapy when working with a middle-class therapist, and the chosen task is a qualitative design, the methods you will consider using for following that route of a qualitative methodology are unlikely to involve, for example, statistical analysis! Nevertheless there will still be considerations and choices to be made about methods. For example, if your goal is to identify the differences between client and counsellor in their perceptions of therapeutic effectiveness, and your task is a quantitative design, you might choose to utilise surveys or questionnaires, or implement an experiment for data generation.

> ### Example of a pluralistic framework as a research tool
>
> The following is an example of how the framework described above might be applied in a research project.
>
> This particular research project aims to explore the experiences of trainee therapists conducting research projects (GOAL), and the specific research question is 'How do trainee therapists experience conducting research?' There are numerous ways in which this particular research question might be addressed (i.e. numerous tasks which could be used). These include adopting a qualitative or mixed methods approach. Through discussions with a stakeholder committee comprising of trainee therapists and trainers (*collaboration*), it was agreed that the methodological approach adopted would be qualitative (*task*). A number of methods were considered, including the use of different data collection strategies (semi-structured individual interviews and focus groups for example), and the use of different data analysis strategies (grounded theory, thematic analysis or interpretive phenomenological analysis for example). It was decided that trainee therapists would be asked to talk about their experiences of conducting research in a focus group (*method – data collection*), and the data would be analysed using thematic analysis (*method – data analysis*).

For those familiar with research methods literature, this structure is likely to seem similar to traditional research descriptions (e.g. Crotty, 1998). The decision-making hierarchies presented in research literature commonly delineate between 'methodologies' (rather than tasks) and 'methods' (a term used in both instances). The contrast, however, comes at the more philosophical layer. Thus, where the pluralistic framework aligns itself to a particular view of the world, researchers more commonly have to outline this position from the outset. This more pragmatic attitude might therefore subsume many of the conversations related to philosophy and focus in upon the importance of the research question. In much the same way that this might leave therapists uneasy at times, such a position does not resonate well with all researchers.

A RESEARCH AGENDA FOR PLURALISTIC COUNSELLING AND PSYCHOTHERAPY

Within this section we aim to outline a research agenda for the pluralistic framework for counselling and psychotherapy. Six propositions are made that intend to provide some direction to the future research conducted in this area, and which proves to be in keeping with the overall perspective of the approach. These are not mutually exclusive propositions, with a number of them overlapping in various ways.

1 Research projects would benefit from a broad overarching strategy

Given the limited resources to complete research in counselling and psychotherapy, a focused approach is needed. The pluralistic framework is a relatively new approach and, as indicated above, to get the most out of the resources available (professional researchers, student researchers, etc.) a joined-up strategy would be advantageous. In doing so, more comprehensive projects might be attainable which have the potential to combine multiple streams of information (e.g. designs may include consideration of implementation science or systematic case studies). This might then have the potential for research to have a larger impact, and would contrast with lots of individual researchers examining their solitary interests.

2 Research methodologies should be tailored to the research question that is posed

Different research questions are likely to benefit from different research designs, and as discussed above, one size does not necessarily fit all. The blanket adoption or prioritisation of a single perspective of research or methodology is therefore not always helpful.

That is to say, assuming that a qualitative methodology is always the best way to conduct research does not necessarily lead to the best quality research, nor does assuming that randomised controlled trials are always the gold standard. In accounting for this, researchers should instead prioritise the use of research designs that are tailored more specifically to the questions being posed. The pluralistic framework that has been articulated throughout this book might provide a useful tool for developing an appropriate research design.

3 Where possible, stakeholders should be involved in the research process

In keeping with the collaborative nature of the pluralistic framework, researchers are encouraged to work alongside interested stakeholders in research projects, and where possible to adopt a more egalitarian relationship with those involved in or impacted by the research. This might include collaboratively working on research design, data collection and data analysis. This way of working would hopefully lead to the completion of research projects that have a tangible impact on interested others.

4 Research should be open to, and explore, multiple pathways of change

In adopting a pluralistic stance, studies should avoid being driven by particular theoretical frameworks when making sense of the information gathered. It is therefore recommended that research data are examined in an open and exploratory way with a view to gaining a rich understanding of any change being reported – possibly even putting forward multiple interpretations. Examples of research that follow these principles include work exploring helpful processes in psychological therapy (e.g. Omylinska-Thurston & Cooper, 2014) and systematic case study presentations (e.g. Ward & Hogan, 2015 – see also McLeod & Cooper, 2011 for an overview of a protocol for systematic case study work exploring pluralistic therapy).

5 The concept of trustworthiness should be used as a base for assessing the quality of all research

Research projects need to be transparent when disseminated. To provide a clear and transparent account of the decision-making processes in research, the ethically minded position of trustworthiness can prove a helpful concept. This concept is more prevalent in qualitative research; however it also has a currency within quantitative and mixed methods research.

6 Dissemination strategies should engage with multiple stakeholders

The findings from research projects should be disseminated to interested others. This may include participants, service users, therapists, service manages and the academic community more broadly. Such a strategy is important so that important research findings reach the communities that they may be able to influence, rather than remaining within academic settings only.

7 A research-informed approach to therapy should be promoted in contrast to a research-driven one

In contrast to the propositions above, this final point considers how therapists might use research in their work, rather than how they conduct it. Therapeutic practice is greatly influenced by research. In the most extreme sense, this might involve directing therapists to work in particular ways with the clients that they see, solely based on findings from randomised controlled trials, which indicate that a particular therapeutic approach has been effective with individuals with the same diagnosis. Such a one-size-fits-all approach may not always be the most helpful for the client, and other sources of information should impact upon decisions made in therapy. Therefore a research-informed approach is advocated, rather than a research-driven approach.

SUMMARY

In research, just as in therapy, one size does not fit all circumstances. The term methodological pluralism can be used to describe an approach that is accepting of the wide array of research designs on offer.

- The strengths of quantitative, qualitative and mixed methods research have been described and discussed. Here we note that the different approaches can be useful in answering different research questions.
- The concepts of *trustworthiness* and *utility* can be utilised as markers for good-quality pluralistic research. These help to ensure research is conducted and presented in an ethically minded manner and designed in collaboration with interested stakeholders.
- It is suggested that the pluralistic framework can be used as a research tool. This might be achieved by considering the aims of our research as a 'goal', the methodology adopted as the 'tasks' and the various data collection and analysis techniques as the 'methods'. Such a framework could be underpinned by the need to work collaboratively with interested stakeholders.

- A research agenda has been put forward. This recommends that researchers of pluralistic therapy should: (1) be strategic; (2) tailor the methodological approach to the specific research questions being asked; (3) involve stakeholders where appropriate; (4) be open to, and explore, multiple pathways of change; (5) utilise trustworthiness as a means of evaluating good-quality work; (6) disseminate findings to all interested stakeholders; and (7) promote research-*informed*, rather than *directed*, practice.

EXERCISES/POINTS FOR REFLECTION

Exercise 1

Take a look at a recent edition of a research journal related to the field of counselling and psychotherapy. Read through the summaries/abstracts of the papers (these are often freely available on the websites associated to the journals). Note down from these summaries what you view to be the goals, tasks and methods of the project.

Exercise 2

Using the same summary or abstract from Exercise 1, think about the following questions:

1. Who are the key stakeholders in the research?
2. At what points and how might the researchers have collaborated with them?

Exercise 3

Consider the arguments for and against the following statements:

1. Involving stakeholders in research is too much hassle.
2. There's no point in completing randomised controlled trials.
3. Research is always politically motivated.
4. Research never influences the practice of therapists.

Exercise 4

Having read through this book, what might you identify as the core research needs for the pluralistic framework for counselling and psychotherapy?

FURTHER READING

Cooper, M. (2008). *Essential research findings in counselling and psychotherapy: the facts are friendly.* London: Sage. This is an excellent introduction to the research around counselling and psychotherapy.

Fishman, D.B. (1999). *The case for pragmatic psychology.* New York: NYU Press. A research text providing a case for methodological pluralism within the applied psychology professions.

> Hanley, T., Cutts, L., Gordon, R., & Scott, A. (2013). A research informed approach to counselling psychology. Online supplementary chapter to G. Davey (Ed.), *Applied psychology*. London: BPS Wiley Blackwell. Available at http://bcs.wiley.com/he-bcs/Books?action=resource&bcsId=6483&itemId=1444331213&resourceId=29364. A chapter reflecting upon how research might be utilised by therapists in practice.
>
> Hanley, T., Lennie, C., & West, W. (2013). *Introducing counselling and psychotherapy research*. London: Sage. An introductory text focusing upon research within the counselling and psychotherapy field. This includes a rationale for conducting research from a variety of methodological approaches and outlines issues that people might encounter whilst undertaking it.
>
> McLeod, J. (2010). *Case study research in counselling and psychotherapy*. London: Sage. This book provides an overview of case study designs utilised to investigate therapy. Many of the designs discussed are pluralistic in nature and use both quantitative and qualitative methods.

REFERENCES

Cooper, M., & McLeod, J. (2011). *Pluralistic counselling and psychotherapy*. London: Sage.

Creswell, J., & Plano Clark, V. (2011). *Designing and conducting mixed methods research* (2nd ed.). London: Sage.

Crotty, M. (1998). *The foundations of social research: meaning and perspectives in the research process*. London: Sage.

Duckett, P., Kagan, C., & Sixsmith, J. (2010). Consultation and participation with children in healthy schools: choice, conflict and context. *American Journal of Community Psychology, 46*(1–2), 167–178.

Durlak, J.A., & DuPre, E.P. (2008). Implementation matters: a review of research on the influence of implementation on program outcomes and the factors affecting implementation. *American Journal of Community Psychology, 41*, 327–350.

James, W. (1978). *The meaning of truth: a sequel to pragmatism*. Cambridge, MA: Harvard University Press. (Original work published 1909.)

McLeod, J., & Cooper, M. (2011). A protocol for systematic case study research in pluralistic counselling and psychotherapy. *Counselling Psychology Review, 26*(4), 47–58.

Omylinska-Thurston, J., & Cooper, M. (2014). Helpful processes in psychological therapy for patients with primary cancers: a qualitative interview study. *Counselling and Psychotherapy Research: Linking Research with Practice, 14*(2), 84–92.

Reason, P., & Bradbury, H. (Eds.). (2008). *The Sage handbook of action research: participative inquiry and practice*. Thousand Oaks, CA: Sage.

Rescher, N. (1993). *Pluralism: against the demand for consensus*. Oxford: Clarendon Press.

Ward, T., & Hogan, K. (2015). Using client-centred psychotherapy embedded within a pluralistic integrative approach to help a client with executive dysfunction: the case of 'Judith'. *Pragmatic Case Studies in Psychotherapy, 11*(1), 1–20.

Index

absent but implicit narrative approaches 153
acceptance 141–3, 193
   as core condition 83, 101
active listening 82–3
active sharing of views 48
activity schedules 117–18
addictive behaviours 223–5
   methods 228–32
      12-step approaches 231–2
      automatic thoughts and beliefs 229–30
      family involvement 230–1
      working with ambivalence 228–9
   understandings 225–8
      client as agent 226–7
      self-reward 227–8
      stages of change model 225–6
agency 99, 226–7, 302–3
alcohol 229–30, 231–2
   see also addictive behaviours
Alcoholics Anonymous 231–2
ambivalence 187, 228–9
American Psychiatric Association (APA) 235
American Psychological Association (APA) 29, 231
Andrews, K. 50
anti-awfulising 193
anxiety
   case example 188
   challenges and recommendations 194–5
   components and process 184–7
      ambivalent features 187
      interpretation 185–6
      maladaptive responses and consequences 186
   and eating problems 237
   goals 187–9
   methods 190–4
      broad 190–1
      specific 191–4
   tasks 188–90
appointment scheduling 292–3
   patient-led approach 294–6
assertiveness skills 254
assessment 16–20
   case example 20
   collaborative 17, 18–19
   metatherapeutic issues 47–8
   models and methods 16–18

assessment *cont.*
   principles 16
   risk assessment and response 261–3
attachment, insecure 238
Australian Psychological Society (APS) 289
authentic/inauthentic being 139–40
automatic thoughts *see* negative automatic thoughts (NATs)

BACP *see* British Association for Counselling and Psychotherapy
Barlow, D.H. et al. 189
Beauchamp, T.L. and Childress, J.F. 302, 305–6
Beck, A. 108
Beck, J. 109–10
behavioural activation (BA) 215–16
behavioural experiments 118
behavioural methods 117–18
being, aspects of 137–43
beliefs
   addictive behaviours 229–30
   core 113, 117
   eating problems 240–1
   positive and negative 187
   religious 281–2
Bentham, J. 29
bereavement *see* grief and loss
Berlin, I. 300, 302
Bern Inventory of Therapeutic Goals 30
Berne, E. 95, 201
binge eating *see* eating problems
biofeedback methods 193
Bion, W. 127
black-and-white thinking 115, 238
body image 238, 239
Boelen et al. 213
Bohart, A. 289
   and Tallman, K. 69, 70, 71, 74
   and Wade, A.G. 70–1
Bordin, E.S. 70, 73, 150, 316
boundaries 288–9
   case study: patient-led appointment scheduling 294–6
   management challenges 303–4
   and purpose of therapy 289–90
   types and applications 290–6

Index

boundaries *cont.*
    contextual 292–3
    interpersonal 293–4
    professional 291–2
bracketing, process of 141
British Association for Counselling and Psychotherapy (BACP) 279, 304–5, 308–9, 310
British Psychological Society (BPS) 279, 289
British school of existential therapy 135
Buber, M. 138–9, 140
Bugental, J.F.T. 29, 82, 95, 96

cannabis 227
    see also addictive behaviours
case formulation 20–3, 24
case-based learning 333–4
Castonguay, L. 327
cathartic methods 242
CBT *see* cognitive behavioural approaches
chair work 103–4, 217–19
change
    foundations of 190–1
    stages model 225–6
child and adolescent mental health services (CAMHS) 45
client agency 99, 226–7, 302–3
client contributions to therapy 69–72
client preferences 19
client problems
    assessment 18–19
    converting into purpose 31–2
client strengths and resources 19, 68–9
    anxiety-related goals and tasks 190
    case examples 69, 72–3, 74, 76
    CBT 110
    challenges 76
    evidence base 69–72
    policies and training implications 75
    practice implications 72–5
    value of 76–7
client-directed therapy 269
client/life factors 69–70
cognitive behavioural approaches (CBT)
    alignment with pluralistic principles 109–10
    anxiety 185, 191–4
    common factors model 163
    foundations 108
    grief 213
    integrative perspectives 109
    methods 114–19
        behavioural 117–18
        'downward arrow' technique 116
        evaluating underlying cognitions 116–17
        identifying 'thinking errors' 115–16
        'mindfulness' 118–19
        monitoring NATs 114–15

cognitive behavioural approaches (CBT) *cont.*
    suicide potential/self-injury 267
    understandings 111–13
        developmental model of problems 112–13
        information processing model 111
        interconnectedness of thoughts, emotions, physical responses and behaviours 112
        learning theory for behaviours 111–12
collaboration
    assessment 17, 18–19
    case formulation: time line map 21–2
    CBT 109
    difference and diversity 281–3
    harm reduction 263–5
    interpersonal relationships 201–2, 204–5
    research 342–3
    style 18
    training 329
    and transparency 124–5
collective integration 160
common factors model 163–4
Complicated Grief Therapy (CGT) 214
conflict
    in relationships 199, 201
    splits 104
    therapist and client goals 34–5
congruence 101
constructive growth 98
content direction and process direction, compared 101
contextual boundaries 292–3
conversation tools 153–4
Cooper, M. 49, 81, 134–5, 136, 137, 140, 141
    et al. 45
    and Joseph, S. 198
    and McLeod, J. 1–2, 29, 35, 42–3, 57, 73, 75, 81, 97, 101, 124, 136, 149, 178, 224, 251, 254, 276, 289, 300, 315, 317, 318, 321, 322, 327, 340
    Omylinska-Thurston, J. and 248–9
    Papayianni, F. and 46
    Thompson, A. and 330
core beliefs 113, 117
core conditions 101
core counselling methods 80–1
    active listening 82–3
    asking questions 85
    establishing goals 81–2
    expressing acceptance and care 83
    helping client re-decide 89
    helping client re-evaluate 88–9
    helping client self-understanding 87–8
    here-and-now focus 86–7
    minimal encouragers 83–4
    reflecting, paraphrasing and summarising 84–5
    symbols and metaphors 85–6
Coulter, A. and Collins, A. 43

Counselling Goals System (CoGs) 33
counselling skills 328–9
countertransference/transference 130–1
couples therapy *see* interpersonal relationships
creative artefacts in narrative approaches 153
crisis/'keep safe' plan 268–9
critical philosophy 328
cultural discourses and practices 328
cultural resources 178, 254
    in training 328
culturally adapted therapy 159–60

De Leo, D. et al. 260
'de-identification' 193
decision-making
    ethical 305–11
    and professional boundaries 291–2
    shared *see* metatherapeutic communication
depression/happiness
    alternative theoretical perspectives 174–6
    case examples 175–6, 177, 179–80
    in contemporary society 173–4
    shared understanding 175–6
    therapeutic challenges 180–1
    therapeutic strategies and methods 176–7, 178–80
        everyday resources 178
        life planning and positive future-orientation 178–9
        restorative emotional experiences 179–80
        self-undermining cognitions 178
description
    ethical decision-making 307, 308
    phenomenological practice 141
developmental model of difficulties 112–13
dialogue
    imaginal 217–19
    metatherapeutic communication/shared decision-making 49
    narrative approaches 149, 152
    in training 329
dichotomous/black-and-white thinking 115, 238
Diercks, M. 124
difference and diversity
    case examples 277–8, 280–2, 283–4
    definition and types 275–6
    implications in therapeutic practice 281–4
        goals, tasks and methods 283–4
        therapeutic relationship and collaboration 281–3
    importance and impact in therapeutic practice 278–81
    individual and group 278
    pluralistic framework 276–8
directed journaling 214–15
documents and letters in narrative approaches 153
Doran, G.T. 31
'downward arrow' technique 116

drama triangle 201
Dual Process Model (DPM) 213, 215
Duncan, B. 69, 71, 72
    et al. 44, 45, 50, 72, 76, 99, 289
    and Miller, S.D. 17, 161
    see also Partners for Change Outcome Management System (PCOMS)
dyad working 204–8

eating problems 235–6
    counsellor attributes 239–40
    tasks and methods 240–3
        alternatives to food 242
        beliefs and attitudes 240–1
        interpersonal relationships 243
        learning 'normal' eating skills 241
        letting go and healing old wounds 242
        making sense of the problem 240
        self-care and self-soothing 241–2
    understandings 236–9
        emotional and psychological factors 237–8
        family factors 239
        psychobiological and genetic factors 236–7
        sociological factors 239
eclecticism 159
    see also integrative/eclectic approaches
Eells, T.D. 20
Egan, G. 82–3
Ellis, A. 108
emotion-focused therapy (EFT) 162
empathy 84, 101
    interpersonal relationship therapy 205
    motivational interviewing 228
Empirically Supported Relationship (ESR) Task Force 190
empty chair method 103–4, 217–19
ethics 300–1
    of assessment 16–17
    case example 303–4
    challenges 301–5
        boundary management 303–4
        therapeutic alliances 302–3
        therapist self-care 304–5
        training 302
    codes/frameworks 289–90, 304–5, 308–9, 310
    decision-making model (case examples) 305–11
    difference and diversity 279
event story *see under* grief and loss
evidence base 4–5
    client strengths and resources 69–72
    evidence-based practice 329
    metatherapeutic communication/shared decision-making 44–5
    see also research
existential approaches 134–5
    anxiety model 185
    integrative perspectives 135–6

existential approaches *cont.*
  interpersonal relationships 199
  methods 140–3
    acceptance of freedom and limitations of being 141–3
    finding values, meaning and purpose 143
    I-Thou stance 139, 140
    phenomenological working 140–1
  pluralistic principles, commonalities and differences 136
  understandings 137–40
    aspects of being 137–40
    primacy of experience 137
experience
  phenomenological working 140–1
  primacy of 137
exposure methods 192
external vs internal threat 185–6
externalising the problem 151–2

Fairburn, C.G. et al. 237, 239
family
  factors in eating problems 239
  involvement
    addictive behaviours 230–1
    decision-making 291–2
  therapy and community work 147–8
feedback
  CBT 110
  concept of 37
  strength-based approach 74
  supervision 319–20
  see also Partners for Change Outcome Management System (PCOMS)
feminist therapy 160
focusing 102–3
Frank, J. 164
Frankl, V.E. 135, 138
freedom and limitations of being 137, 138, 141–3
Freud, S. 122–3, 128
future-orientation 138, 178–9

Gendlin, E. 102–3
Goal Form 33
goals
  articulation/goal-oriented approaches 28–30
    philosophical and theoretical underpinnings 28–9
    research 29–30
  assessment 18–19
  establishing 81–2, 117–18
  linking to tasks and methods 36, 110
  in practice 30–4
    case example 33–4
    converting problem into purpose 31–2
    creating achievable goals 31

goals, in practice *cont.*
    intrinsic values and goals 30–1
    managing multiple goals 32
    measures 32–3
    starting the conversation 30
  practice challenges 34–6
    client struggle to articulate goals 35
    client stuckness 35
    conflict between therapist and client goals 34–5
    'perverse' goals 35–6
  research 343
  see also specific problems and approaches
Gottman, J.M. 201
graded exposure 118
grief and loss 211
  back story 216–19
    imaginal dialogues 217–19
    legacy work 219
  case examples 216, 218–19
  processing event story 212–13
    behavioural activation 215–16
    directed journaling 214–15
    restorative retelling 213–14
  and quest for meaning 212
Grosse Holtforth, M. and Grawe, K. 30

happiness *see* depression/happiness
healing old wounds 242
health conditions, long-term 247–9
  case examples 249, 250, 253
  methods and interventions 252–4
    assertiveness skills 254
    cultural resources 254
    reading 253
    stress management techniques 254
    talking 252–3
    writing 253
  practice challenges 249–50
  tasks 251–2
  therapeutic relationship 252
  typical 251
  therapist issues and self-awareness 255
The Health Foundation 43, 44, 45, 50
here-and-now focus 86–7
Herman, J.L. 242
humanistic approaches
  alignment with pluralistic principles 97–8
  historical development 95–6
  integrative and pluralistic perspectives 96–7
  methods 99–104
    chair techniques 103–4
    focusing 102–3
    individualised formulation 102
    non-directive working 100–1
    therapeutic relationship and core conditions 101

humanistic approaches *cont.*
  understandings 98–9
    constructive growth 98
    unique person perspective 98–9
Hunter, C. et al. 17

I-Thou stance 139, 140
imagery methods 193
imaginal dialogues 217–19
'implicitness', notion of 153
inauthentic/authentic being 139–40
individual clients
  interpersonal relationships 200, 202–3
  metatheories and 165–6
  tailored/personalised interventions 50–1, 102, 109, 224, 226, 278
information processing model 111
information sources in assessment 17–18
insecure attachment 238
integrative/eclectic approaches
  alignment with pluralistic principles 160–1
  case examples 162–3, 166
  concepts and methods 161–6
    'common factors' 163–4
    'markers' 162
    metatheories and individual cases 165–6
    problem-oriented practice 164–5
    self-practice 161–2
  historical development 158–60
  types 159–60
intentionality, concept of 301
interconnectedness (thoughts/emotions/physical responses/behaviours) 112
interpersonal boundaries 293–4
interpersonal relationships 198–9
  beyond couples 207–8
  case example 205–7
  collaborative working 201–2, 204–5
  dyad working 204–8
  eating problems 243
  goals 206–7
  individual client working 202–3
    noticing 202–3
    self-care 203
    specific techniques 203
  sex therapy 207
  understandings 199–201
    existentialism 199
    individual psychology 200
    relationship dynamics 201
    social constructionism 200
interpretation
  psychodynamic approaches 127–8
  of threat 185–6

James, W. 338

Kant, I. 29
Karpman, S.B. 201
'keep safe'/crisis plan 268–9
Kleinplatz, P.J. 207

Lambert, M. 56, 69
  and Shimokawa, K. 56
learning
  and change *see* integrative/eclectic approaches
  'normal' eating skills 241
  skills and application 194
  theory 111–12
  therapists
    lifelong 329–30
    and supervision 317–19, 322
legacy work 219
Leichsenring, F. and Salzer, S. 185, 189
Lent, R. et al. 101
letters and documents in narrative approaches 153
letting go 242
life goals 32
life planning 178–9
listening, active 82–3
long-term health conditions *see* health conditions, long-term
loss *see* grief and loss

MacCormack, T. et al. 252
McLeod, J. 148, 300
  and McLeod, J. 250, 253, 332
  see also Cooper, M.
McPherson, S. et al. 180–1
Makoul, G. and Clayman, M. 43, 45, 49–50
maladaptive responses to threat 186
'markers' 162
meaning-oriented therapies/methods 135, 143, 191, 305
  grief 212
  psychodynamic approaches 125, 126, 128–9
measures
  conversation tools 153–4
  goals 32–3
  metatherapeutic communication 50
  see also Partners for Change Outcome Management System (PCOMS)
metacommunication 34, 37, 101
metaphors and symbols 85–6
metatheories and individual cases 165–6
metatherapeutic communication/shared decision-making
  CBT 110
  critical reflections 51–2
  definitions 42–4
  dimensions 46–7
  evidence base 44–5
  need for 44

metatherapeutic communication/shared
    decision-making *cont.*
  in practice 47–51
    at start of therapy 47–8
    describing options 49–50
    inviting active sharing of views 48
    measures 50
    as ongoing event 48
    participating in dialogue 49
    tailoring to client needs 50–1
    uncertainty as predictor 49
    whole service approach 51
Miller, W.R. and Rollnick, S. 228
Milton, J. 123
mindfulness 118–19, 193
minimal encouragers 83–4
Minnesota Model 231
moral principles and values in decision-making 309
motivational interviewing 228–9
multiple goals 32
multiple perspectives
  assessment 17–19
  ethical decision-making 310
  pathways of change 346
  psychodynamic approaches 128–9

narrative approaches 147–9
  case examples 151–2, 154
  pluralistic elements, commonalities and
    differences 149–51
  suicide potential/self-injury 268
  understandings and methods 151–5
    absent but implicit 153
    conversation tools 153–4
    dialogue 152
    documents, letters, songs and creative
      artefacts 153
    externalising the problem 151–2
    re-authoring 152
    unique outcomes 152–3
    witnessing and reflecting 154
National Institute for Health and Care Excellence
    (NICE) 108
negative automatic thoughts (NATs) 113
  addictive behaviours 229–30
  modifying 178
  monitoring 114–15
negative capability 126–7
non-directive working 100–1
non-judgemental approach 83
non-verbal strategies 82–3
Norcross, J.C. 29, 96
  et al. 226
noticing 202–3

'obesogenic' environment 239
'object relations' 123

Omylinska-Thurston, J. and Cooper, M. 248–9
O'Neill, P. 16–17
open dialogue therapy 149
open-ended questions 85
outcome evaluation
  ethical decision-making 311
  see also measures; Partners for Change Outcome
    Management System (PCOMS)
Outcome Rating Scale (ORS) 58–9, 60–2, 64

Papayianni, F. and Cooper, M. 46
paradoxical methods 194
paraphrasing, reflecting and summarising 84–5
'parent-adult-child' model 201
Partners for Change Outcome Management System
    (PCOMS) 55–6
  case example 62–3
  clinical process 59–62
  elements 58–9
  limitations 63–4
  and pluralistic approach 57–8
  value 64–5
Patient Expectations (PEX) scale 19
patient-led appointment scheduling 294–6
Pennebaker, J. 253
perfectionism 236, 238
Perls, F. 95, 96
person-centred therapy (PCT) 96, 97, 98, 99, 101
  anxiety model 185
  motivational interviewing 228–9
personal and professional development 333–4
personalised/tailored interventions 50–1, 102, 109,
    224, 226, 278
'perverse' goals 35–6
phenomenological working 140–1
physiological control of anxiety 193
placebo effects 71
pluralistic approach 4–5
  challenges and future directions 23
  development of 1–3
  pillars and principles 3–4
  research evidence 4–5
potentiality model 98
problem-oriented integration/practice 159, 164–5
process direction and content direction,
    compared 101
process and outcome measures *see* measures;
    Partners for Change Outcome Management
    System (PCOMS)
Prochaska, J.O.
  and DiClemente, C.C. 225, 226
  et al. 71
professional issues
  boundaries 291–2
  development 333–4
  see also ethics; supervision; training
Project MATCH 224

PSYCHLOPS 33
psychodynamic approaches
    alignment with pluralism 124–6
        collaboration and transparency 124–5
        meanings 125, 126
        thinking and practice 125–6
    anxiety model 185
    historical development 122–3
    integrative perspectives 124
    methods 129–31
        resistance 129–30
        transference/countertransference 130–1
    schools 123
    understandings 126–9
        interpretation 127–8
        multiple perspectives 128–9
        negative capability/uncertainty 126–7

qualitative and quantitative methodologies 339–40
questing, concept of 305
questions
    asking 85
    Socratic questioning 110, 163, 305

re-authoring 152
re-decision 89
re-evaluation 88–9
reading 253
referrals 35
reflecting
    paraphrasing and summarising 84–5
    witnessing and 154
reflective practice 34
relationships
    being as with-others 138–9
    supervision 315–16
    see also interpersonal relationships; therapeutic relationship
relaxation 193, 254
religious beliefs 281–2
    see also difference and diversity
Rennie, D. 34, 42–3, 44, 48, 101
Rescher, N. 3, 337
research 337–9
    agenda 345–7
        appropriate methodologies 345–6
        dissemination to stakeholders 347
        multiple pathways of change 346
        research-informed vs research-driven approaches 347
        stakeholder involvement 346
        strategic thinking 345
        trustworthiness 346
    collaboration in 342–3
    example of pluralistic framework 344
    goals, tasks and methods 343–5
    humanistic approach 99

research cont.
    methodologies 339–41
        approaches 339–40
        judgement of quality 340
        strategic thinking 341
        utility 341
    skills training 332–3
    see also evidence base
resistance 129–30
resources see client strengths and resources; cultural resources
restorative emotional experiences 179–80
restorative retelling 213–14
review of ethical decision-making 308–9
reward 227–8, 237
risk assessment and response 261–3
Rogers, C. 73, 83, 84, 95, 96, 98, 100, 101, 109, 137, 185
role play 118
Rynearson, E.K. and Salloum, A. 214

Salkovskis, P. 185, 194
Sartre, J.-P. 137, 199
Schön, D.A. 34
self-awareness, therapist 181, 255
self-care 203, 241–2
    therapist 304–5
self-harm see suicide potential/self-injury
self-healing capacity 71
self-help groups 254
self-practice and integrative approach 161–2
self-responsibility 269
self-reward 227–8, 237
self-soothing 241–2
self-support 269
self-undermining cognitions see negative automatic thoughts (NATs)
self-understanding 87–8
Session Rating Scale (SRS) 59, 61, 64
sex therapy 207
sexuality 284
    see also difference and diversity
shared decision-making see metatherapeutic communication/shared decision-making
shared understanding 175–6
SMART goals 31
SMARTER goals 117–18
smoking
    motivational interviewing 228–9
    see also addictive behaviours
SMS text reminders 292–3
social constructionism 200
social justice perspective 276–7
Socratic questioning 110, 163, 305
Socratic teacher role 226
solution-focused therapy 31–2, 135–6, 203, 226–7, 240–1

'solving the moment' 205, 206
songs and creative artefacts in narrative approaches 153
Spicer, J. 231
stages of change model 225–6
Stiles, W.B. and Wolfe, B.E. 190
strength-based approach
  supervision 319
  training 329
  see also client strengths and resources
stress management techniques 254
Stroebe, M. and Schut, H. 213, 215
suicide potential/self-injury 259–60
  case example 261–2, 263–5, 266
  definitions 260
  practice challenges 260–6
    client 'position' 265–6
    harm reduction 263–5
    risk assessment 261–2
    risk response 262–3
  therapeutic approaches 266–9
    CBT 267
    client-directed 269
    crisis/'keep safe' plan 268–9
    narrative 268
    self-support/self-responsibility 269
summarising, reflecting, paraphrasing and 84–5
supervision 314–15
  case example 318, 320
  competency and training 322
  feedback 319–20
  personalised goals, tasks and methods 316–19
  in practice 320–2
  relationship 315–16
  strength-based approach 319
Supervision Personalisation Forms (SPF/SPF-A) 316–17
Swift, J.K. et al. 4, 44, 45
Swinburn, B. et al. 239
symbols and metaphors 85–6
systemic sculpts 203

tailored/personalised interventions 50–1, 102, 109, 224, 226, 278
tasks and methods 36–7
  agreement on 37–8
  case example 37–8
  linking goals to 36, 110
  research 343–5
  theory 36
  see also specific problems and approaches
therapeutic process, assessment as 17
therapeutic relationship
  client contribution 70–1, 73–4
  and core conditions 101
  difference and diversity 281–3
  ethical decision-making 309, 310

therapeutic relationship cont.
  long-term health conditions 252
  narrative therapy 150
therapists
  and client goals 34–5
  self-awareness 181, 255
  self-care 304–5
  see also professional issues; supervision; training
Therapy Personalisation Form (TPF) 19
'thinking errors' 115–16
Thompson, A. and Cooper, M. 330
thought and feelings record 114–15, 117
threat, interpretation of 185–6
time/timing
  case formulation map 21–2
  metatherapeutic communication 46, 47
  therapeutic relationship 252
touch, appropriate 294
tragic dimension of being 139
training
  challenges 302, 334
  objectives and elements 326–7
  on-going personal and professional development 333–4
  organisation 330–2
  practice-oriented, critical perspective 332–3
  principles 327–30
    collaboration and dialogue 329
    counselling skills 328–9
    critical philosophy 328
    diversity of cultural discourses and practices 328
    evidence-based practice 329
    lifelong learning 329–30
    personal and cultural resources 328
    strength-based orientation and values 329
  research skills 332–3
  supervision 322
transactional analysis model 201
transference/countertransference 130–1
transparency 124–5
truth 126, 128
12-step approaches 231–2
two-chair work 104

uncertainty
  metatherapeutic communication/shared decision-making 49
  psychodynamic approaches 126–7
unconditional positive regard 73
underlying cognitions, evaluation of 116–17
unique outcomes 152–3
unique person perspective 98–9

van Deurzen, E. 139
VandenBos, G.R. 231

vicious cycles 112, 117, 237
Vos et al. 143

Ward, T. et al. 327
White, M. 153
   and Epston, D. 73, 148, 153
whole service approach 51
Wile, D. 205, 206
witnessing 154

Wolfe, B.E. 185
   Stiles, W.B. and 190
Woody, S.R. and Ollendick, T.H. 194–5
working alliance *see* therapeutic
   relationship
writing 253
   directed journaling 214–15

Yalom, I.D. 139, 253